YOUNG PEOPLE AND WORK

Young People and Work

Edited by

ROBIN PRICE
Queensland University of Technology, Australia

PAULA MCDONALD
Queensland University of Technology, Australia

JANIS BAILEY
Griffith University, Australia

and
BARBARA PINI
Curtin University of Technology, Australia

Routledge
Taylor & Francis Group

LONDON AND NEW YORK

First published 2011 by Ashgate Publishing

2 Park Square, Milton Park, Abingdon, Oxon OX14 4RN
711 Third Avenue, New York, NY 10017, USA

Routledge is an imprint of the Taylor & Francis Group, an informa business

First issued in paperback 2016

British Library Cataloguing in Publication Data
Young people at work in the developed world.
 1. Youth–Employment–Developed countries. 2. Age and
 employment–Developed countries. 3. High school students–
 Employment–Developed countries. 4. Young adults–
 Developed countries–Attitudes.
 I. Price, Robin.
 331.3'4'091722-dc22

Library of Congress Cataloging-in-Publication Data

Young people and work / by Robin Price ... [et al.].
  p. cm.
 Includes bibliographical references and index.
 ISBN 978-1-4094-2236-5 (hardback : alk. paper)
 1. Youth–Employment. I. Price, Robin, 1960-
 HD6270.Y65 2011
 331.3'4–dc23

2011023636

ISBN 978-1-4094-2236-5 (hbk)
ISBN 978-1-138-26118-1 (pbk)

Contents

List of Figures

List of Tables

Notes on Contributors

Danaë Anderson

Completing an MPhil at Auckland University of Technology's Business School, where she is also lecturing in employment relations. She previously completed a BA and BCom Honours at the University of Auckland. Her current research focuses on the working lives and experiences of New Zealand children, with particular focus on age, wage and health and safety concerns. Her other research interests concern the political economy of gender and work, migrant workers and superannuation.

John Baffoe-Bonnie

Professor of Economics at Pennsylvania State University, Brandywine Campus. His research interests have been in the areas of labor economics, applied macroeconomics and development economics. In the area of labor economics, Dr Baffoe-Bonnie's research has focused on labor market segmentation, efficiency wage models, transfer programs, wage differentials among different demographics, and full-time/part-time issues, while topics on macroeconomics and development economics deal with issues of inter-temporal consumption behavior in both developed and developing countries, and the dynamic effects of government policies. His research has been published in refereed journals. He is the co-editor of *Contemporary Economic Issues in Developing Countries* (Greenwood – Praeger Publishers, 2003).

Janis Bailey

Associate Professor in the Department of Employment Relations and Human Resources, Griffith University, Gold Coast, Australia. Her recent publications include articles on school-aged workers published in the *Journal of Industrial Relations, Australian Bulletin of Labour, Industrial Relations Journal*, and *Work, Employment and Society*, and articles on the intersection of labour and environmental history published in *Labour History*. In 2007 she co-authored commissioned reports on the effects of Australia's Work Choices legislation on low-paid women workers. She is currently carrying out on projects on comparative retail union strategy, gender equity in universities and campaigns for better wages in the social and community services sector. She has previously worked as a union industrial officer and for state government.

Sampson Lee Blair

Associate Professor of Sociology at the State University of New York. After completing his BS and MS degrees at Virginia Tech, where he specialized in family and child development, he obtained his PhD in family sociology at The Pennsylvania State University. He has published in a variety of family, child development, demography, and mainstream sociology journals. His research has dealt with a variety of family issues, such as marital quality, the division of household labor, and mate selection, but his primary interests are with child and adolescent development. Over the years, he has served on the editorial boards of *The Journal of Family Issues*, *Marriage and Family Review*, and *Social Justice Research*. He has served as the chair of the Children and Youth Section of the American Sociological Association, and also served twice as the senior editor of *Sociological Inquiry*. Most recently, he served as a Fulbright Scholar at Xavier University (Ateneo de Cagayan), in the Philippines, where he conducted research on parental involvement and children's educational performance.

Helena Carvalho

Sociologist and Assistant Professor at ISCTE-University Institute of Lisbon. She administrates the Department of Social Research Methods at ISCTE-University Institute of Lisbon. She coordinates a postgraduate in Data Analysis in Social Sciences. She is an expert in methodological issues and data analysis. She is a senior researcher at the Center for the Research and Study of Sociology (CIES-ISCTE-IUL). Her area of research is focused inside the quantitative and multivariate methods for categorical variables, mainly methods of interdependence and dependence via optimal scaling (School of Leiden). She has been participating in several research projects, developing her skills of data analysis. She has published several books and several articles in Portugal and abroad.

Linda Esders

Completed a Master of Business (Research) in the School of Management in the QUT Business School at Queensland University of Technology. Her thesis investigated how different actors within the union movement constructed the problem of declining youth trade union membership. Linda is an experienced primary school teacher with a long history of trade union involvement and is currently working as an organizer for the Queensland Teachers' Union.

Lonnie Golden

Professor in Economics and Labor Studies and Employment Relations, Penn State University, Abington College. Lonnie's research focuses on working hours, work scheduling, well being consequences, FLSA overtime law, overwork, daily time use, work-life balance and students' work hours. He is co-editor of *Working Time: International Trends, Theory and Policy* and of *Nonstandard Work: The Nature and Challenge of Changing Employment Arrangements*. His research has appeared in journals such as *Industrial Relations, Monthly Labor Review, Journal of Business Ethics, Cambridge Journal of Economics, Journal of Family and Economic Issues, Journal of Socio-Economics* and *American Journal of Economics and Sociology*. He is an affiliate of the Economic Policy Institute and Sloan Work and Family Research Network.

Zeenobiyah Hannif

Lecturer in the School of Management at the University of Technology Sydney, Australia. Her doctoral thesis was completed through the University of Newcastle in 2007 and examined the quality of work life in the Australian call centre industry. Her recent research activity has centred on precarious employment, and human resources management in multinational corporations and call centres.

Ryan Lamare

Lecturer in Human Resource Management at the Manchester Business School and a Visiting Research Fellow at Auckland University of Technology. His research interests include the political and organizing activities of trade unions, HRM practices at multinational companies, health and safety of migrant workers, and workplace alternative dispute resolution. He received his PhD from Cornell University's School of Industrial and Labor Relations in 2008, and worked previously as a Research Scholar at the University of Limerick.

Felicity Lamm

Associate Professor of Employment Relations at the Auckland University of Technology's Business and Law School. She has an extensive research background and has written a number of books and journal articles over the past 20 years. She has also completed major research reports for New Zealand and overseas public and private sector organizations in areas such as occupational health and safety, employment relations and the small business sector. Dr Lamm is also co-editor of the *New Zealand Journal of Employment Relations* and is on the editorial board of the *Journal of Industrial Relations*.

Paula McDonald

Paula McDonald is an Associate Professor in the Business School at the Queensland University of Technology in Brisbane, Australia. Her research focuses on the social context of work within the broader discipline of employment relations, including a focus on early work experiences, workplace discrimination and harassment and flexible work arrangements. She published the co-authored book *Women and Representation in Local Government: International case studies* (with Barbara Pini) with Routledge in 2011 and her forthcoming co-authored book *Men's Wage and Family Work* (with Emma Jeanes) will be published with Routledge in 2012. Journal articles have appeared in *Work, Employment & Society, Gender Work & Organization, International Journal of Management Reviews, Psychology of Women Quarterly* and *British Journal of Management.*

Christopher D. O'Connor

Assistant Professor of Criminal Justice at the University of Wisconsin, Superior. His research and teaching interests are in policing, risk, crime, and young people. His current research examines how young people navigate school and work in the energy 'boomtown' of Fort McMurray, Alberta, Canada.

Luísa Oliveira

Professor at ISCTE-University Institute of Lisbon, administrator of ISCTE Foundation, coordinating the life long learning ISCTE Foundation Program and senior researcher at the Centre for the Research and Study of Sociology in ISCTE-University Institute of Lisbon, where she co-coordinates the research area of Work, Organizations and Professions. She is an expert in sociology of labour, employment and innovation. Her research projects combine these areas, in order to the study of education and qualification of the labour force, employment policies and their impact in the labour market regulation and youth employment in the European Union, the social construction of professions and the impact of innovation in development. She has been director of the Portuguese Observatory of Youth Employment and has published several articles and books in Portugal and abroad.

Damian Oliver

Researcher at the National Centre for Vocational Education Research and an Adjunct Researcher at the Centre for Work + Life, both in Adelaide, Australia. Damian's primary research interests involve young people's involvement in employment relations, training and education. He has researched young people's attitudes to work, labour market transitions, and intersections between the education system and the labour market. In 2008–2009, he spent a year as a visiting researcher at the University of Duisburg-Essen, Germany. Damian has an honours degree in industrial relations and a doctorate from Griffith University.

Jonas Olofsson

Jonas Olofsson is Senior Lecturer in working life science at Kristianstad University, Sweden and has extensively researched vocational education and labour market policy in Sweden. During later years his main focus has been on the problems facing youth inside and outside the education system, in Sweden as well as in other Nordic countries. He is part of a larger research group based at the universities in Lund and Umeå, researching the complex relationship between labour market institutions and educational change. Jonas Olofsson has been in charge of several research projects on young people's labour market establishment and municipal programs aiming to support transitions and counteract social exclusion and has been funded by the Swedish Council for Working Life and Social Research and the Nordic Council of Ministers.

Wendy Patton

Executive Dean, Faculty of Education at Queensland University of Technology, Brisbane, Australia. She has taught and researched in the areas of career development and counselling for many years. She has co-authored and co-edited a number of books, and is currently Series Editor of the Career Development Series with Sense Publishers. She has published widely with more than 100 refereed journal articles and book chapters. She serves on a number of national and international journal editorial boards.

Barbara Pini

Barbara Pini is a Professor in the Curtin Business School, Curtin University. She has an extensive publication record with a large body of work focused on gender relations in rural areas. Her co-authored book *Gender and Rurality* (with Lia Bryant) was published by Routledge in 2011 while an earlier book *Masculinities and Management in Agricultural Organisations Worldwide* was published by Ashgate in 2009.

Robin Price

Senior Lecturer in Management in the QUT Business School, Brisbane, Australia. Robin has worked in retail management positions, learning and development roles in the private and public sector and as an academic. Her PhD investigated labour usage strategies in the retail industry. Robin was awarded an ARC post-doctoral fellowship to research young people's experiences of work in 2007. Her research centres on young workers, service sector employment relations and the interplay between employment relations and regulatory structures.

Steven Roberts

Lecturer in lifelong and work-related learning, at the School of Education, University of Southampton, UK. He undertook his first degree in Industrial Relations, Human Resource Management and Social Policy at Kent Business School, University of Kent, before completing an Economic and Social Research Council sponsored MA in Social Research Methods and subsequent PhD in Social Policy at the School of Social Policy, Sociology and Social Research at the University of Kent. He is a regular contributor to the international *Journal of Youth Studies,* and his primary research interests include young people's experiences of the labour market, the role the retail sector might play in skills development, and the implications of policies aimed at widening and increasing participation in higher education.

Tobias Samuelsson

Social Anthropologist and has a PhD in Child Studies from Linköping University in Sweden. He presently works as an Assistant Professor in the department of Thematic Studies – Child Studies at Linköping University. He has done extensive research on children and work in Sweden and in 2008 he published the book *Children's Work in Sweden. A Part of Childhood, a Path to Adulthood* (Linköping: Linköping University).

Erica Smith

Professor of Education at the University of Ballarat. Prior to entering academia she had careers as a personnel manager in the retail industry, as a community worker and as a further education teacher. Her major areas of research are the interface of work and education for young people, training policy, apprenticeships and the work of further education teachers. She is President of the Australian Vocational Education and Training Research Association and Co-Chair of the international research network Innovative Approaches to Apprenticeships (INAP).

Andrew Stewart

The John Bray Professor of Law at the University of Adelaide, a consultant to the national law firm Piper Alderman, and President of the Australian Labour Law Association. One of Australia's leading experts in employment law and industrial relations, he has played a prominent role in explaining the effect of workplace reforms, and analysing their implications for businesses, workers and unions. He also helped advise the Australian government on the drafting and structure of its Fair Work legislation. Andrew's many publications include Creighton and Stewart's *Labour Law* and *Stewart's Guide to Employment Law*.

Natalie van der Waarden

Business law lecturer at Murdoch University. She teaches workplace law, occupational health and safety, and employee relations. Natalie authors a text for business students on employment law, and is currently researching comparative regulation of child employment. Natalie is immediate Past President of the Industrial Relations Society of Western Australia and a convener for the Western Australian Chapter of the Australian Labour Law Association.

Luísa Veloso

Sociologist and a senior researcher at Centre for the Research and Study of Sociology in ISCTE-University Institute of Lisbon (where she co-coordinates the research area of Work, Organizations and Professions) and at the Institute of Sociology, Faculty of Arts – University of Porto. Besides research, she has a career (1990–2008) as a professor at the University of Porto. She has a PhD in Sociology and is involved in various research projects at the national and international level as researcher, coordinator and consultant. Her main research domains are employment, work and labour market dynamics, education and training. She has published several articles and books in Portugal and abroad. She is also involved in several activities interrelating research and cultural activities with, namely, the Portuguese Filmmuseum and the Serralves Foundation, Museum of Contemporary Art.

Margaret Vickers

Author of several studies of part-time student employment, youth in transition, VET in schools, and reforms to senior secondary schooling. For 30 years she has been involved in research and policy development work on these topics. She began her working life as a high school teacher, and her career includes senior appointments in the Australian Public Service and the Paris-based OECD, where she participated in country reviews focusing on young people's transitions from school to work and further study. She completed her Doctoral studies at Harvard University and is currently a Professor of Education at the University of Western Sydney.

Eskil Wadensjö

Professor of Labour Economics at the Swedish Institute for Social Research at Stockholm University since 1980. He received a PhD in economics at Lund University in 1972 on a study of economic aspects on immigration. His main research interests are the economics of international migration, labour market policy and social security. Current research topics are the economics of international migration, temporary employment agencies and economic aspects of pension reform. He is director of SULCIS (Stockholm University Linnaeus Center for Integration Studies), a large ten-year research program founded by the Swedish Research Council.

A Majority Experience: Young People's Encounters with the Labour Market

Robin Price, Paula McDonald, Janis Bailey and Barbara Pini

Young people are frequently the focus of study in social science. Education, employment, leisure, criminality and family life are all spheres within which the different experiences of young people have been examined (Pollock 2008). A still relatively small, but expanding strand of this broader scholarship addressing youth-related issues is a body of theoretical and empirical literature which focuses on young people's participation in work. This growing interest in young people's employment has followed a significant shift in many western societies. Younger and much larger numbers of young people, still engaged in full-time education, are entering the formal labour market. Indeed, in many countries, employment is a majority experience for children (Hobbs and McKechnie 1997), and for young people in general. While in such work there has been a tendency to blur definitional lines, here we adopt the term 'young people' which incorporates the definitions of 'children' as those under 18 years and 'youth' as those under 24 (UN n.d.).

This book compiles a series of empirical studies on young people and paid employment. In the context of increasing youth labour market participation rates and the 'normalization' of young people in part-time work (Lavalette 2005), an empirical focus was thought critical to increasing the visibility of youth employment (McKechnie and Hobbs 1999). Mizen, Pole and Bolton (2001), for example, described children's work as invisible or hidden, on the basis that working children are often associated with developing countries in the global south or as an historical phenomenon that was phased out as a result of labour regulation, technological developments and the widespread adoption of compulsory education. The material covered examines employment concerns for school and university students as well as young people not engaged in full-time education, moving beyond questions of youth transitions from education to work (Hall and Coffey 2007), and the effects of employment on educational outcomes (Marsh 1991, Greenberger and Steinberg 1986), which have been the major focus of published work. Rather, the book takes a more holistic approach, examining the patterns and characteristics of young people's work from a variety of perspectives and in different national contexts. It takes account of the intersections between young people's work and non-work lives; the broader economic context of youth employment; the relationships between young workers and employers and unions; and the impact of relevant regulatory frameworks. Several chapters also give young people 'voice', through data generated from young people themselves about their jobs and the social context in which they work. Finally, the book includes chapters from different disciplinary perspectives and utilizes quantitative and qualitative approaches.

Below, we firstly introduce the field of youth employment via a brief summary of the literature where we highlight salient themes including patterns of participation, structural changes in society which have had an impact on these participatory shifts, and the vulnerability of young people in employment. Each of the three sections of the book explores a key aspect of young people's employment: their experience of work, intersections between work and education, and the impact of other actors and institutions. While these divisions are somewhat arbitrary, in that many of the authors transverse multiple terrains in their chapters, they nevertheless provide a structure for examining the complexities of youth employment. In introducing the chapters, we signal their contribution to broadening and strengthening knowledge about the opportunities and constraints that young people face during their formative experiences in the formal economy. In the final section of the chapter we canvass critical avenues of future research in the field.

Summary of Key Themes in the Literature

A ubiquitous theme running through the literature addressing patterns of young people's participation in employment is a concern with the increasing numbers of ever-younger children taking part in paid work. Consistent evidence supports this substantial change in the constitution of the broader labour market, prompting fears about the social effect of this phenomenon and the extent to which it accentuates labour's commodity status (Vosko 2000). Data from Britain, Ireland, The Netherlands, Canada and Australia, for example, show that between a third and a half of secondary school children are engaged in paid work at any one time, and around three quarters of school students will have worked for some time before completing school (Mizen, Bolton and Pole 1999, Canny 2002, Smith and Wilson 2002, OECD 2006, ABS 2007). University student working is also extensive in developed countries globally (see Oliver, this volume). Comparative Organisation for Economic Co-operation and Development (OECD) (2006) figures show The Netherlands has the highest proportion of 15–19 year olds (some of whom are tertiary students) both working and studying (44.4 per cent), followed by Australia (36.5 per cent), the United Kingdom (UK) and Canada (around 28 per cent) and the United States (US) (21 per cent). This compares to an OECD participation average amongst young people in this age group of 16.5 per cent (OECD 2006).

It is worth noting however that despite increasing numbers of young people working, *overall* labour force participation rates of young workers have changed little. Rather, there has been a significant shift from a predominantly full-time workforce to a part-time one, driven principally by an increasing participation in schooling. Indeed, school participation rates for 17 year olds have risen markedly in many countries in recent decades (for example, ABS 2004). There also appears to be a strong association between age and employment intensity which is reflected in increasing involvement in formal jobs as children get older (Smith and Green 2001). Alongside statistics identifying who participates in work has also been research documenting where young people work. In general, very young workers' jobs tend to be manual in nature, most typically casual, low paid and generally considered as unskilled. UK data for example, reveals that more than half of 15–19 year olds are employed as elementary and intermediate clerical, sales and services workers, almost all of these in the retail industry, with smaller but still significant numbers employed in the hospitality sector (Lucas and Keegan 2007: 573).

Some limited literature on youth participation patterns also documents the ways in which modalities of difference may mediate a young person's involvement in paid work. Studies, for example, have generally found that males are more likely to work than females (Greenberger and Steinberg 1986, Usalcas and Bowlby 2006). This gender participation gap may be attributed to the nature of the service work available in the labour market as well as the higher involvement of females in informal work, caring for children or the elderly. British and Australian studies have also found evidence that the chances of having employment are unevenly distributed by socio-economic status where a lack of social and familial capital may *reduce* very young workers' chances of obtaining a job (Dustman et al. 1996, Mizen et al. 1999, Unions SA 2005). In a similar way, Morrow (1994: 141) refers to '"enterprising" children', doubly advantaged by their socio-economic family background and the social capital they gain from readier access to paid work compared to their more socially disadvantaged peers. Despite this increasingly detailed picture of participation rates in various countries and sectors of the labour market, there remain some important limitations in our knowledge of the labour market profile of young people and particularly very young workers. In most cases, labour force statistics fail to include individuals below 15 years of age (see Samuelsson, this volume). Similarly, data on young workers and their injuries are often inaccurately captured in official statistics (WHO 1995, 2009).

The significant shifts in the patterns of young people's employment summarized above have evolved in response to a range of labour market, social and cultural phenomena. A major structural change in the labour market for example has been a shift from manufacturing to service sector employment. This has been accompanied by the creation of a relative abundance of casual jobs in retail and services, the growth of deregulated trading hours, the low cost of youth labour, increased consumerism and changes in government policies (Standing 1997, Campbell 2000, Haque 2002, Langer 2005, Lloyd 2008, Sargeant 2009). Relevant to young workers in particular is the replacement of collective agency in employment contexts and a recognition of structural constraints based on social location (gender, class, rurality), with an individualistic ethos and 'enterprise culture' (Reiter and Craig 2005, Hearn and Knowles 2006: 233, Harris, Wyn and Younes 2007). At the same time, employers often view child workers as self-interested and lacking in discipline, communication skills and an appropriate 'work ethic', (for example, Konstam 2007, Smith and Patton 2009, Price, Bailey,

McDonald and Pini 2011), and themselves as the victims of children's lack of acceptable work habits.

As the above literature indicates, the contemporary work environment is one in which the terms of labour have eroded various aspects of employment safety, security and remuneration (Standing 2002), and in which youth are rendered vulnerable. Young people have less experience in employment relationships and less capacity to bargain with employers, relative to their adult counterparts, based on endemic disparities in power (Denniss 2005). They tend not to take advantage of legal rights, including the right to union representation and they are unaware of other rights such as procedural fairness in dismissal (Allegretto and Chase 2005). Indeed, the empirical literature paints a somewhat gloomy picture in terms of the wide range of detriments young people suffer at work. These include: non-payment for certain work, particularly attending meetings and training; underpayment; not receiving meal breaks; working illegally long shifts and/or late hours; pressure to work overtime; lack of supervision; discrimination on the basis of gender, age and ethnicity; bullying, sexual harassment and assault (Caritas 2003, Job Watch 2004, Unions SA 2005). A specific body of literature has also detailed the occupational health and safety concerns of young people including high rates of workplace injury (Bohle and Quinlan 2000, Mourell and Allan 2005).

The literature on the working conditions of young people has not just documented the illegal underpayment of youth, but also systemic and institutionalized forms of underpayment via the provision of youth wages lower than the adult minimum, or (more rarely) no minimum wages for youth. Lucas and Keegan (2007) detailed the British case where minimum wages are 62 per cent of the adult wage for 16 and 17 year olds, and 82 per cent for 18–21 year olds although many British employers pay 18 year olds the adult rate (see also Lucas 1997). The New Zealand situation has been similarly documented by Caritas (2003) who explained that New Zealand labour law recognizes 18 year olds as adults for the purposes of minimum pay and sets a flat rate for all those under 18 years of age at 80 per cent of the adult rate. The existence and extent of a youth/adult differential in wages remains a contentious topic, not least because low-cost youth labour underpins the profitability of many enterprises (Campbell and Chalmers 2008). Orthodox labour economists link low wage levels (including those of young workers) to lower levels of skills and productivity, thus 'normalizing' the existence of youth wages (Miles 2000 cited in Lucas and Keegan 2007). In contrast, institutional economists argue that demand and supply factors interact to result in labour market segmentation, whereby young people, much like women, are over-represented in the 'low paid' category (Lucas and Langlois 2000) because the labour market is as much *socially* as *economically* constructed, with skills being *undervalued* rather than non-existent. The institutionalization of youth wages is thus another central element of young workers' vulnerability.

A somewhat more positive picture of youth employment is evident in research suggesting that despite their vulnerability, young people enjoy many of the social aspects of work. Research has shown for example that young people actively evaluate their work and their workplaces, and can articulate good and bad aspects of both (McKechnie and Hobbs 2001: 14). An Australian study of young fast food workers found low satisfaction with employers' industrial relations and work organization strategies, resulting from cost minimization approaches, but higher degrees of satisfaction with human resource management and social relations at the workplace (Allan, Bamber and Timo 2005). Similarly, US teenagers viewed their low-paid coffee shop jobs as sociable and empowering, allowing them to express their creativity and individuality (Besen 2006). Hence, the 'story' of youth employment is more complex than a simple narrative of exploitation of all young people by all employers.

Part I: Experiences of Work

Notwithstanding the relatively smaller employment literature which focuses on young people compared to adults, a number of consistent themes are beginning to emerge around young people's experiences of employment and some of these themes are taken up in Part I of the book. Chapter 1 by Tobias Samuelsson for example, directly addresses the invisibility of children's work through the adoption of a child-centred perspective on children's work in Sweden. Giving 'active voice' (Wyn and Dwyer 2000) to the young people in his study, he explores the way children see the connections between their activities and 'real work', demonstrating that working children, despite being excluded from many national labour market surveys and frequently employed outside the formal economy, are certainly not anomalous. Samuelsson draws upon ethnographic data of children's work in two communities in Sweden examining questions such as how children define work, where and when children work and what they do, and the types of payments and incentives they receive. By using the children's own perspectives as the starting point he opens up to scrutiny some of the orthodoxies of industrial relations research including, for example, what constitutes 'work' and the 'labour market'. At the same time he reports that children themselves are sometimes reluctant to define what they do as 'real' work or themselves as 'real' workers, thus inadvertently reproducing the widespread belief that in the developing world, childhood and employment are mutually exclusive.

Continuing the theme of young people's experiences of work, Chapter 2 by Christopher D. O'Connor examines via interview data, the multiplicity of life experiences that shape young people's understandings of work in a boomtown environment in Canada. This is a context which he notes has been little investigated in terms of young people's experiences and perceptions of work, yet as Pini, Price and McDonald (2010) found in youth research focused on the current Australian resource boom, local specificities are critical to understanding one's relationship to the workplace. O'Connor's research demonstrates that young people's work in this particular town provided on the one hand, unique opportunities while on the other exposed them to context-specific risks. Such a focus highlights the call for employment researchers to pay more attention to how the quality and experiences of work for young people can vary according to different local contexts. The geography and anthropology literature has argued for the importance of connectivities between youth transitions and place or locality (Hall, Coffey and Lashua 2009), and offers important insights from which more nuanced insights about place can be made. Of course, experiences of employment are different not just in varying local contexts, but are also marked by the effects of systematic social inequalities. This is demonstrated by O'Connor as he reports on the gender differences in how youth, in the very masculine space of Fort McMurray, navigate employment, with young women demonstrating a much higher level of reflexivity and critique about issues such as structural constraints.

In Chapter 3, Danaë Anderson, Ryan Lamare and Zeenobiyah Hannif explore the particularly stark susceptibilities of young student migrant workers. This is a sub-group of the larger category of migrant workers, who in general, work longer and more unsociable hours than non-migrant full-time workers (Quinlan and Mayhew 2001, Loh and Richardson 2004), but who have been relatively neglected in prior research which typically focuses on the educational experiences of international students. The vulnerability of young migrant workers is emphasized by the fact that the authors report none of the respondents in the research were members of a union and had either limited or incorrect knowledge about their employment rights and obligations. Meanwhile migrant youth report low wages and poor conditions of employment including significant health and safety concerns. What is highlighted therefore is that in the context of globalization, employment policy and regulation is intricately connected to policy and regulatory debates in areas of international education and immigration.

Chapter 4 by Steven Roberts also examines a group of workers in a particular social location – young men who work in front-line retail sector jobs. Drawing on previous work on men and masculinities, he addresses the interaction of service work and masculine identity in the UK, illustrating the ways in which young men negotiate the scripts of service work and young masculinities. Roberts' work is particularly notable on two specific counts. Firstly, he focuses on non-student employees. This is important as it is student employees who have traditionally been afforded the most attention in the literature. Focusing on this population also introduces a classed dimension to understandings of young men's masculine identity work in the service sector because employment in low level retail work is likely to be very different according to whether one is simultaneously participating in university studies. A second key contribution of Roberts' chapter is that he demonstrates both shifts and continuities in how working-class men construct their identities in relation to work generally and retail work in particular. The picture painted by the data is that the connections between gendered subjectivities and the nature of work are changing, and in potentially unexpected and contested ways.

Chapter 5, the final chapter in Part I by Danaë Anderson, Zeenobiyah Hannif and Felicity Lamm explores, in a New Zealand context, a well-documented and apparently universal phenomenon when considering young people's employment and that is the poorer health and safety conditions that are frequently experienced by this group. Their study reveals a lack of transparency in documenting workplace injuries, an over-reliance on single-method survey-based experimental approaches and low adherence to legislative requirements by employers. It also raises a number of definitional, methodological and legal challenges associated with the goal of improving the health and safety of young workers more generally, including a lack of data on children aged under 15 years, the under-reporting of accidents and injuries, a decline in union density and poor employment practices. The chapter therefore empirically demonstrates the lack of adherence to health and safety standards that is associated with young people's employment and which is highlighted as a particular aspect of vulnerability in the literature.

Part II: Intersections between Work and Education

Part II of the book takes up the issue of the intersection between work and education. The principal tool for many studies which explore the work–education nexus has been a focus on the origins, journeys and destinations associated with these transitional pathways (Pollock 2008). As we have documented earlier, one widely espoused claim is that engaging in paid work has a number of potential short- and long-term benefits for young people such as increasing knowledge of employment relations and easing the transition into full-time employment (Vickers, Lamb and Hinkley 2003). However, there are numerous concerns about the potential downsides to simultaneously undertaking paid work and full-time education. Studies internationally have attempted to identify the maximum number of hours where employment has a negative impact on educational outcomes. Indeed, as Margaret Vickers points out in Chapter 6, this literature reveals a conundrum in that on the one hand, moderate to long hours of student part-time employment have *negative* impacts on academic outcomes, while on the other hand student employment appears to have *positive* effects on the likelihood of being employed after leaving school.

Drawing on studies from the US, UK and Australia and contrasting a number of relevant theoretical perspectives, Vickers suggests that below a certain threshold, working has negligible effects on educational outcomes, but as the number of hours worked increases above this threshold, the likelihood of gaining low grades and/or dropping out increases, with some groups of students seemingly immune to this effect. Vickers' chapter, through an analysis of Australian students' views, goes on to report on the problems young people encounter as they attempt to balance the competing demands of study and work and explores institutional changes in *school-level* policies and practices that might facilitate balance. Her study reveals that students report greater difficulties in balancing work and study when they are working longer hours, but that they also report a significant degree of pressure from employers to work longer hours than is their preference.

The effect of employment on educational outcomes is pursued further by Lonnie Golden and John Baffoe-Bonnie in Chapter 7 in the context of American college students. Using American time use survey data, they examine the relationship between time spent in employment and time spent in education for college students. The results from their study show that students' time spent on work had a direct linear effect; that is, time spent working directly reduced time spent on educational activities. Their findings indicate that the negative effect of work on educational engagement began to take effect after as few as five hours work a week. These findings have important implications for regulators in an environment where social support for students is diminishing and young people need to work to finance their educational pursuits.

In Chapter 8, Sampson Lee Blair also addresses the effects of youth employment, but here the focus is on adolescents' future work aspirations. He demonstrates a strong positive relationship, for both male and female students, between a preference for a greater number of working hours and valuing the intrinsic rewards associated with work. His study also reveals that while employment during the adolescent years is the dominant experience of American youth, work appeared to have a deleterious effect on the aspirations of adolescent females, but not for males. That is, when teenage girls were employed, they appeared to have less desire for extrinsic rewards, influence in the workplace, leisure time and job security. Blair ascribes this as possibly resulting from the types of part-time work in which adolescent girls engage, supporting Beck's (1992) assertion that the 'equalisation of prerequisites' in education and law have not extended to the spheres of employment and domestic labour. Clearly, however, further exploration is necessary to determine the precise effects of employment on the occupational aspirations of young women.

In Chapter 9, Luísa Oliveira, Helena Carvalho and Luísa Veloso explore how young people in the European Union (EU) transition between education and part-time work to full-time employment. In this analysis, the structural effects of the different welfare state regimes are considered, as well as economic and sectoral changes in employment. The authors argue that the rise of temporary or precarious work across EU countries has made transitioning to full-time jobs more difficult for young people although the effects differ across countries. Their research shows that in countries where there has been rapid growth in precarious employment, it is young people who predominately bear the brunt of this in that fewer full-time jobs are available, making transitioning from education to full-time jobs significantly harder. Oliveira, Carvalho and Veloso consequently advocate a role for the state in minimizing the negative effects of precarious employment on young people.

Part III: The Other Actors

Young people's vulnerability in employment is frequently framed as related to broader structural and regulatory mechanisms and actors, including unions, employers and policy makers. These themes are developed in Part III of the book. The rights of children in employment are generally enshrined in legislation that derives from the conventions of the International Labour Organisation (ILO). Clearly, concerns in this area are strongest in the developing world, and so the volume of literature on child labour in non- or newly industrialized countries is substantial (Woodhead 1999, Besen-Cassino 2008, Butler 2009). Recently, however, the subject of children's work has received research attention in industrialized economies (TUC 1997, 2001, McKechnie and Hobbs 1999, Newman 1999, 2000, Mourell and Allan 2005, Riley 2007). This work emphasizes the role of the state in protecting children as a particular class of workers who are vulnerable due to their age and inexperience. Andrew Stewart and Natalie Van der Waarden, in Chapter 10, explain the regulatory approaches to child employment in Britain and Australia, commenting on the appropriateness of a modern statement of rights for young workers in the context of discussion of various sources of regulation in the two countries. Some of the failings of present frameworks are highlighted, and a set of principles are put forward to guide the design of child employment regulation which the authors argue will promote a better *understanding* in the community of what is required when engaging a child to perform work, and, in turn, achieve a better level of *compliance* with those requirements.

Employers are also key actors when it comes to considering young people and work. However, analysis of their roles has generally only been considered with respect to two features: employers' needs for employability skills in young workers and how the education system can facilitate the attainment of such skills (Canny 2002, Smith and Green 2001, Smith and Comyn 2004, Smith and Patton 2007); and how employers' patterns of labour usage and recruitment choices affect young people's capacity to transition between school and employment, or unemployment (Maguire and Maguire 2007). In contrast to this focus in previous work, Erica Smith and Wendy Patton in Chapter 11 examine why Australian employers choose to employ student labour and the strategies they use to manage and retain a young, sometimes transient, workforce. Using interviews conducted with managers and young people in a discount retail company and a multi-national fast food chain, they find that senior managers' understanding of young people's needs was not always matched by branch managers, who were often young people themselves, and who faced daily operational realities.

Chapter 12 by Jonas Olofsson and Eskil Wadensjö contrasts employment conditions for youth across the five Nordic countries, seeking to understand how equitable these conditions are and what structural factors might account for any differences. This chapter takes an interesting approach by comparing countries with, on the surface, seemingly similar labour market institutions and socio-economic conditions, but they find that 'small differences' add up. When combined, differences in education systems (including vocational training), welfare arrangements and labour market programs lead to contrasting 'fairness outcomes' for young people.

While overall union density has been decreasing since the 1970s in most Anglophone countries, even larger falls in youth density have occurred (Bryson et al. 2005). If however the vulnerability of young workers is at issue, which is clear from research, then unions can play a key protective role – that is, if young workers join them. Damian Oliver in Chapter 13 presents a comparative study of Germany and Australia that examines the impact of university students' experiences of union membership on their intention to join a union after graduation, and then looks at the specific effects of the duration, intensity and quality of that employment. Oliver finds that the effects are small, but that there is some effect at the margins. Students who have been in low quality student employment, for example, are more likely to wish to join a union in graduate employment. Oliver offers a number of strategies to unions in each country based on his findings. Chapter 14 by Lin Esders, Janis Bailey and Paula McDonald takes a somewhat different approach to the problem of union density by asking, in an Australian context, how the union movement itself attributes the steep decline in youth membership rates. The approach and findings emphasize union agency and the urgent need to engage with youth in a new social, cultural and economic environment in order to make the recruitment of young workers a central plank of union renewal.

Future Research Directions

The empirical work detailed in this book contributes to knowledge on a range of themes evident in the broader youth-focused employment relations literature. There are however, numerous important questions still to be asked on the subject and we canvass here several important trajectories for future research.

Over the past decades there have been repeated calls in the literature for greater attention to be paid to the question of young people and work (for example Maguire and Maguire 1997, McKechnie, Lavalette and Hobbs 2000). This is a contention with which we would agree but with the caveat that it is not just a question of 'what' but 'how' which is of significance in relation to research on employment and youth. The existing 'youth and industrial relations' literature focuses on young workers' rights and responsibilities, and on the structural and material conditions of young people's work and their vulnerability from a somewhat static standpoint that treats young workers as objects of control. In contrast, and from a sociological perspective, there are few studies of tacit and explicit norms around power and hierarchy in the workplace, and issues of voice, with respect to young workers (see Mizen et al. 2001 and Stokes and Wyn 2007 for exceptions). There are also few studies of young people and work that focus on young people as subjects (see Liebel 2004 and Besen-Cassino 2008 for exceptions). We thus have little understanding of how young people construct their identities as workers and, importantly, how they experience their first jobs; that is, how they 'learn to labour' in a critical employment relations sense.

Despite a lacuna in labour market knowledge which is 'child-centred', a rich and dynamic methodological literature exists on research with children which could be usefully engaged by employment scholars to give young people voice in social research about work (for example Grover 2008). Utilizing approaches which position children as active rather than passive research participants would significantly add to the production of more relevant knowledge by transferring meaning with integrity to an academic field with fewer researcher imposed restraints (Leyshon 2001, Claveirole 2004). Such approaches also open up to interrogation some of the normative definitions and constructs in industrial relations which have largely been produced and reproduced without reference to children's own work-related experiences and perspectives.

In affording children greater voice and power in the production of knowledge about work, researchers will require greater reflexivity to questions of difference and diversity. Too often 'youth' has been homogenized in labour market research yet, as contributors to this book have demonstrated, young people's relationship to the labour market is shaped by their social location including for example their gender, ethnicity, class status and geography. This has been starkly demonstrated over recent years in our own country of Australia where the 'resource-boom' generated by the demand from Asia for mineral resources has provided opportunities for some youth to gain relatively high wages for unskilled labour, but such work has been largely the preserve of males and of non-Indigenous Australians (Pini, McDonald and Mayes 2011). Attending to the heterogeneity of youth in research on work would not only enrich knowledge about employment relations, but also ensure that such knowledge was informing broader theoretical debates about fractured subjectivities, identity categories, systemic disadvantage and social exclusion in a globalized and postmodern world (see MacDonald et al. 2005).

The sociological literature has argued how societal shifts have transformed and fractured youth's social structure and their passage through the lifecourse (Wyn and Wright 1997, Brannen and Nilsen 2002). For example, there is no longer a clear timetable to govern young people's navigation through life's pathways (Furlong and Cartmel 1997), and status passages, such as leaving home, marriage, parenthood and entry into the labour market are considered to be no longer linear, but reversible, blended, synchronic or deferred (Du Bois-Reymond 1998, Skrede 1999, Nilan, Julian and Germov 2007). It is in this broader socio-cultural context that the contributors to this book explore a range of contemporary subjects relevant to young people and work. Nevertheless, there is a greater need for research which attends to differences amongst youth, particularly those which may be reflected in occupational segmentation of the labour market. A case in point is gendered occupational segregation which may commence very early (ABS 2007), highlighting a need to avoid obscuring the nuances and diversity of young people's experiences of work and to understand the way the prism of difference may be reflected.

Finally, while a number of chapters in this book address a relative lack of empirical work that is conducted cross-nationally, few studies have investigated employment phenomena as they affect adolescents and young adults in countries which are culturally dissimilar to Western, industrialized ones and even fewer have employed cross-cultural methods of analysis. This Western-centrism has, unsurprisingly, also been identified in reviews of other disciplines and areas of interest (for example Pitt-Catsouphes and Christensen 2004; Suzuki 2004). In contrast to single-country studies, cross-cultural comparisons of young people's employment offer the opportunity to address not only region-specific problems, but may also better illuminate the political, economic and cultural variables that differentially impact on labour market actors including young workers, employers, parents and policy-makers. Such research also challenges assumptions which may be country and culture bound (Pitt-Catsouphes and Christensen 2004). Given that most empirical work on youth at work ignores the employment relations environment surrounding youth labour, such a focus would also contribute to knowledge of multi-scalar perspectives, including those at individual, structural and institutional levels.

References

Allan, C., Bamber, G. and Timo, N. 2005. McJobs, student attitudes to work and employment relations in the fast food industry. *Journal of Hospitality and Tourism Management*, 12(1), 1–11.

Allegretto, A. and Chase, T. 2005. *Inquiry into Workplace Relations Amendment 'Work Choices' Bill 2005*. Submission to Senate Employment, Workplace Relations and Education References Committee. Brisbane: Young Workers Advisory Service.

Australian Bureau of Statistics (ABS) 2004. *Schools*, Catalogue No. 4221.0, Canberra: ABS.

Australian Bureau of Statistics (ABS) 2007. *Child Employment, Australia*, Catalogue No. 6211.0, ABS: Canberra.

Beck, U. 1992. *Risk Society. Towards a New Modernity*. London: Sage.

Besen, Y. 2006. Exploitation or fun? The lived experience of teenage employment in suburban America. *Journal of Contemporary Ethnography*, 35(3), 319–40.

Besen-Cassino, Y. 2008. The study of youth labor: The shift toward a subject-centred approach. *Sociology Compass*, 2(1), 352–65.

Bohle, P. and Quinlan, M. 2000. *Managing Occupational Health and Safety*. South Yarra, Australia: MacMillan.

Brannen, J. and Nilsen, A. 2002. Young people's time perspectives: From youth to adulthood. *Sociology*, 36(3), 513–37.

Bryson, A., Gomez, R., Gunderson, M. and Meltz, N. 2005. Youth-adult differences in the demand for unionization: Are American, British and Canadian Workers all that different? *Journal of Labor Research*, 26(1), 155–67.

Butler, U. 2009. Freedom, revolt and 'citizenship': Three pillars of identity for youngsters living on the streets of Rio De Janeiro. *Childhood*, 16(1), 11–29.

Campbell, I. 2000. The spreading net: Age and gender in the process of casualisation in Australia. *JAPE*, 45, 68–98.

Campbell, I. and Chalmers, J. 2008. Job quality and part-time work in the retail industry: An Australian case study. *The International Journal of Human Resource Management*, 19(3), 487–500.

Canny, A. 2002. Flexible labour: The growth of student employment in the UK. *Journal of Education and Work*, 15(3), 277–301.

Caritas Aotearoa New Zealand. 2003. *Protecting Children at Work: Children's Work Survey*. Wellington, NZ: Caritas, Available from: http://www.caritas.org. nz/dox/Domestic%20Advocacy/Caritas%20childrens%20work%20survey. pdf [accessed 12 January 2008].

Claveirole, A. 2004. Listening to young voices: Challenges of research with adolescent mental health service users. *Journal of Psychiatric and Mental Health Nursing*, 11, 253–260.

Denniss, R. 2005. Young people's attitudes to workplace bargaining. *JAPE*, 5, 145–155.

Du Bois-Reymond, M. 1998. 'I don't want to commit myself yet': Young people's life concepts. *Journal of Youth Studies*, 1(1), 63–79.

Dustmann, C., Micklewright, J., Rahah, N. and Smith, S. 1996. Earning and learning: Educational policy and the growth of part-time work by full-time pupils, *Fiscal Studies*, 17(1), 79–103.

Furlong, A. and Cartmel, F. 1997. *Young People and Social Change: Individualization and Risk in Late Modernity*. Buckingham: Open University Press.

Greenberger, E. and Steinberg, L. 1986. *When Teenagers Work: The Psychological and Social Costs of Adolescent Employment*. New York: Basic Books.

Grover, S. 2008. Why won't they listen to us? On giving power and voice to children participating in social research. *Childhood*, 11(1), 81–93.

Hall, T. and Coffey, A. 2007. Learning selves and citizenship: Gender and youth transitions. *Journal of Social Policy*, 36(2), 279–96.

Hall, T., Coffey, A. and Lashua, B. 2009. Steps and stages: Rethinking transitions in youth and place. *Journal of Youth Studies*, 12(5), 547–61.

Haque, R. 2002. Migrants in the UK: A descriptive analysis of their characteristics and labour market performance, based on the Labour Force Survey. London: Refugee Council.

Harris, A., Wyn, J. and Younes, S. 2007. Young people and citizenship: An everyday perspective, *Youth Studies Australia*, 26(2), 19–27.

Hearn, M. and Knowles, K. 2006. The National Narrative of Work in *Rethinking Work, Time, Space and Discourse*, edited by M. Hearn and G. Michelson. Melbourne: Cambridge University Press, 215–38.

Hobbs, S. and McKechnie, J. 1997. *Child Employment in Britain*. London: The Stationary Office.

Job Watch 2004. *Fast Food Industry: A Research Study of the Experiences and Problems of Young Workers.* Researched and written by Vera Smiljanic, Melbourne: Job Watch.

Konstam, V. 2007. *Emerging and Young Adulthood: Multiple Perspectives, Diverse Narratives.* New York: Springer.

Langer, B. 2005. Consuming anomie: Children and global commercial culture. *Childhood*, 12(2), 259–71.

Lavalette, M. 2005. 'In defence of childhood': Against the neo-liberal assault on social life, in *Studies in Modern Childhood: Society, Agency, Culture*, edited by J. Qvortrup. Houndmills: Palgrave Macmillan, 147–66.

Leyshon, M. 2001. On being 'in the field': Practice, progress and problems in research with young people in rural areas. *Journal of Rural Studies*, 18(2), 179–91.

Liebel, M. 2004. *Cross Cultural Perspectives on Working Children.* London: Zed Books.

Lloyd, C. 2008. Australian capitalism since 1992. *Journal of Australian Political Economy*, 61, 30–55.

Loh, K. and Richardson, S. 2004. Foreign-born workers: Trends in fatal occupational injuries. *Monthly Labor Review*, 127(6), 42–53.

Lucas, R. 1997. Youth, gender and part-time work – Students in the labour process. *Work, Employment & Society*, 11(4), 595–614.

Lucas, R. and Keegan, S. 2007. Young workers and the National Minimum Wage, *Equal Opportunities International*, 24(6), 573–89.

Lucas, R. and Langlois, M. 2000. *The National Minimum Wage and the Employment of Young People.* The Centre for Hospitality Employment Research (CHER), Manchester Metropolitan University.

MacDonald, T., Shildrick, T., Webster, C. and Simpson, D. 2005. Growing up in Poor Neighbourhoods: The significance of class and place in the extended transitions of 'socially excluded' young adults. *Sociology*, 39(5), 873–91.

Maguire, M. and Maguire, S. 1997. Young people and the labour market, in *Youth, The 'Underclass' and Social Exclusion*, edited by R. MacDonald. London: Routledge, 26–38.

Maguire, M. and Maguire, S. 2007. Young people and the labour market, in *Youth, the 'Underclass' and Social Exclusion*, edited by R. MacDonald. London: Routledge, 26–38.

Marsh, W. 1991. Employment during high school: Character building or subversion of academic goals? *Sociology of Education*, 64(3), 172–89.

McKechnie, J. and Hobbs, S. 1999. Child labour: The view from the north. *Childhood*, 6(1), 89–100.

McKechnie, J. and Hobbs, S. 2001. Work and education: Are they compatible for children and adolescents? in *Hidden Hands: International perspectives on children's work and labour*, edited by P. Mizen, C. Pole and A. Bolton. London: Sage, 9–23.

McKechnie, J., Lavalette, M and Hobbs, S. 2000. Child employment research in Britain. *Work, Employment and Society*, 14(3), 573–80.

Mizen, P., Bolton, A. and Pole, C. 1999. School age workers: The paid employment of children in Britain. *Work, Employment and Society*, 13(3), 423–38.

Mizen, P., Pole, C. and Bolton, A. (eds) 2001. *Hidden Hands: International perspectives on children's work and labour*. London: Routledge Falmer.

Morrow, V. 1994. Responsible children? Aspects of children's work and employment outside school in contemporary UK, in *Children's Childhoods: Observed and Experienced* edited by B. Mayall. London: Falmer Press, 128–43.

Mourell, M. and Allan, C. 2005. *The Statutory Regulation of Child Labour in Queensland*. Paper presented at 19th AIRAANZ conference, Reworking Work, 9–11 February, University of Sydney: Sydney.

Nilan, P., Julian, R. and Germov, J. 2007. *Australian Youth. Social and Cultural Issues*. Frenchs Forest, Australia: Pearson Education Australia.

Newman, K. 1999. *No Shame in My Game: The Working Poor in the Inner City*. New York: Vintage and Russell Sage Foundation.

OECD 2006. *Education at a Glance 2006: OECD Indicators*. OECD Publishing. doi: 10.1787/eag-2006-en

Pini, B., Price, R. and McDonald, P. 2010. Teachers and the emotional dimensions of class in resource affected rural Australia. *British Journal of Sociology of Education*, 31(1), 17–30.

Pini, B. McDonald, P. and Mayes, R. 2011. Class contestations and the Australian resource boom: The emergence of the 'cashed-up bogan'. *Sociology*, in press.

Pitt-Catsouphes, M. and Christensen, K. 2004. Unmasking the taken for granted. *Community, Work and Family*, 7(2), 123–42.

Price, R., Bailey, J., McDonald, P. and Pini, B. 2011. Employers and child workers: An institutional approach. *Industrial Relations Journal*, 42(3), 220–235.

Pollock, G. 2008. Youth transitions: Debates over the social context of becoming an adult. *Sociology Compass*, 2(2), 467–84.

Quinlan, M. and Mayhew, C. 2001. *Evidence Versus Ideology: Lifting the Blindfold on OHS in Precarious Employment*. Working paper. Sydney: University of New South Wales.

Reiter, H. and Craig, G. 2005. Youth in the labour market: Citizenship or exclusion?, in *Young People in Europe: Labour markets and citizenship*, edited by H. Bradley and J. van Hoof. Bristol: The Policy Press, 15–39.

Riley, J. 2007. Employing minors in New South Wales: The Industrial Relations (Child Employment) Act 2006 (NSW). *Australian Journal of Labour Law*, 20(3), 295–301.

Sargeant, M. 2009. *Health and Safety of Vulnerable Workers in a Changing World of Work*. Working Paper. Rome: Adapt.

Skrede, K. 1999. The dream and the virtue, in *Responsibility and Resistance. Gender and Education in Late Modernity*, edited by G. Birkelund, A. Broch-Due and A. Nilsen. Bergen: University of Bergen Press, 281–309.

Smith, E. and Green, A. 2001. *School Students' Learning from their Paid and Unpaid Work*, Adelaide: NCVER.

Smith, E. and Wilson, L. 2002. The new child labour? The part-time student workforce in Australia. *Australian Bulletin of Labour*, 28(2), 120–37.

Smith, E. and Comyn, P. 2004. The role of employers in the development of employability skills in novice workers, *Research in Post-Compulsory Education*, 9(3), 319–36.

Smith, E. and Patton, W. 2007. *A Serendipitous Synchronisation of Interests: Employers and Student Working*. Paper presented at 10th Annual Australian Vocational Education and Training Research Association (AVETRA) Conference, Evolution, Revolution or Status Quo? VET in new contexts, 11–13 April 2007 Melbourne, Australia.

Smith, E. and Patton, W. 2009. School students and part-time work: Workplace problems and challenges. *Youth Studies Australia*, 28(3), 4–14.

Standing, G. 1997. Globalization, labour flexibility and insecurity: The era of market regulation. *European Journal of Industrial Relations*, 3(1), 7–37.

Standing, G. 2002. *Beyond Paternalism: Basic Security as Equality*. New York: Verso.

Stokes, H. and Wyn, J. (2007) Constructing identities and making careers: Young people's perspectives on work and learning, *International Journal of Lifelong Education*, 26(5), 495–511.

Suzuki, A. 2004. Review of the gender research in cross-cultural psychology Since 1990: conceptual definitions and methodology. *Japanese Journal of Psychology*, 75(2), 160–72.

Trades Union Congress. 1997. *Working Classes: A TUC Report on School Age Labour in England and Wales*. London: TUC Publications.

Trades Union Congress 2001. *One in Ten School Kids Play Truant to Work*. Press release Thursday 29 March 2001, Available from http://www.tuc.org.uk/em_research/tuc-2973-f0.cfm [accessed: 20 January 2010].

Unions SA 2005. *Dirt Cheap and Disposable: A Report about the Exploitation of Young Workers in South Australia*. Available at http://www.actu.asn.au/data/files/general/dirt_cheap.pdf [accessed: 20 October 2007].

United Nations (UN) n.d. *Youth and the United Nations*. Available at: http://www.un.org/esa/socdev/unyin/qanda.htm [accessed: 16 April 2011].

Usalcas, J. and Bowlby, G. 2006. *Students in the Labour Market, Education Matters: Insights on Education, Learning and Training in Canada*. Statistics Canada Catalogue No. 81-004-XIE.

Vickers, M., Lamb, S. and Hinkley, J. 2003. *Student Workers in High School and Beyond*, Longitudinal Surveys of Australian Youth Research Report No. 30. Melbourne: ACER.

Vosko, L. 2000. Temporary Work: The Gendered Rise of a Precarious Employment Relationship. University of Toronto Press: Toronto.

Woodhead, M. 1999. Combatting child labour: Listen to what the children say. *Childhood*, 6(1), 24–49.

World Health Organisation (WHO) 1995. *Global Strategy on Occupational Health for All*. Geneva.

World Health Organisation (WHO) 2009. *Work Injuries in Children and Young People*, Fact Sheet 4.7. Available at: http://www.euro.who.int/data/assets/pdf_file/ [accessed: 12 July 2011].

Wyn, J. and Dwyer, P. 2000. New patterns of youth transition in education. *International Social Science Journal*, 52(164), 147–59.

Wyn, J. and Wright, R. 1997. *Rethinking Youth*. London: Sage Publications.

PART I
Experiences of Work

Chapter 1

Making Money, Helping Out, Growing Up: Working Children in Sweden

Tobias Samuelsson

In Sweden 100,000–120,000 children in the age range 7–14 years sell 'Christmas magazines' every year, and consequently participate in a business with an annual turnover of between 200 and 250 million Swedish crowns (1 USD = 6–7 Swedish crowns) (Roxvall 2006, Schmidt and Olsson 2004, Tonström 2009, Åkerberg 2003). Similarly, in the spring of 2009 more than 100,000 Swedish school children in the age group 9–12, collected 49.5 million crowns by selling May-flowers, small artificial flowers, for the philanthropical organization Majblommans Riksförbund (www.majblomman.se). These two examples demonstrate the widespread use of child labour in contemporary western nations. This labour occurs not only outside the home but also in the home. Despite this, it is often assumed that working children are associated with developing countries in the global south or an historical phenomenon that disappeared as a result of labour regulations, technological development and the introduction of widespread schooling. As a result, children's work is described as hidden and/or as invisible (Mizen, Pole and Bolton 2001).

De Coninck-Smith, Sandin and Schrumpf (1997: 9) have claimed that the perception that children do not work in industrialized nations occurs because of 'empirical ignorance'. Indeed, an illustration of the fact that even official reporting tends to neglect child labour is the monthly labour force survey undertaken by Statistics Sweden. The aim of these surveys is primarily to identify how many individuals in the total population are working. However, in pursuing this objective, the surveys also define what is to be understood as work and who is to be understood as a worker. To be counted in these surveys, an individual has to be employed and needs to be between 16 and 64. This necessarily excludes the many children who are indeed working but are not formally employed and/or who are under the age of 16. Thus, just as Dahl (1984: 129) has critiqued studies of work for being 'male centred' and 'market driven' so too could the Swedish labour force surveys be critiqued for their narrow focus on paid employment and their age restrictions. Overall, the often informal productive activities children undertake in and outside the home are not categorized as work, nor are the entities which often remunerate children for their labour (for example parents) seen as employers. The type of exclusionary focus of the Swedish labour force surveys has, of course, been mirrored in much of the broader scholarship on industrial relations which, as different scholars have shown, has typically been devoted to paid work and employment in industrial environments (de Coninck-Smith et al. 1997, Hengst and Zeiher 2000). This is not, however, reflective of children's work and has contributed to the belief that working children are part of Sweden's past rather than present or what de Coninck-Smith et al. (1997: 10) refer to as a sort of 'cultural blindness' in terms of the question of children's work in society.

This chapter addresses the continued invisibility of children's work in the literature by drawing on data from a Swedish study which utilizes a child-centred perspective. The aim is to give emphasis to how children themselves view their world rather than impose definitions and perspectives of the world upon them. In this respect I seek to circumvent (rather than merely replicate) preconceived ideas of children's relation to work embedded in the normative definitions of what constitutes 'work' and 'the labour market' which have been central to rendering children's work invisible. The broad definition of work adopted in the chapter opens up to scrutiny both formal and informal paid activities that might not traditionally be considered part of the mainstream labour market, or be constructed as employment. As well as exploring the diversity of children's views about what encapsulates 'work' I also detail the types of work children undertake and their incentives for engaging in work. While some of the children included school and spare time activities in their definitions of work I have enumerated upon these responses in detail elsewhere (Samuelsson 2008) and consequently focus in this chapter on their experiences of work where payment in cash or in kind is involved. Before turning to these issues, however, I first provide a brief overview of the study's methodology.

Methodology

This ethnographic study took place in two different communities in Sweden, in Ekköping, between 2004 and 2005, and in Vikåsa between 2005 and 2006. Ekköping is a rural community in southern Sweden, approximately 45 minutes by car from the closest major city. Vikåsa is an urban community close to one of Sweden's largest cities. I chose these two communities because they appear to be average Swedish communities. The inhabitants represent a mix of living situations; some people live in houses, others in flats. The situation might be rather different in urban and rural communities as well as in sparsely populated areas, and all this might affect the children's childhoods. The point of using two communities was not to make quantitative large-scale comparisons between them.

In total, 100 children participated in the study. Sixty-six of them were from Ekköping and 34 from Vikåsa. The children were in grades 4–9. This means that the participants overall ranged in age from 9–10 years up to 15–16 years. In Ekköping, 35 boys and 31 girls took part in the study while in Vikåsa, 13 boys and 21 girls participated. By including boys and girls of different ages from two different communities, I hoped to obtain breadth and variety in the material and thereby to be able to account for some of the childhood variety in the study. However, the chapter will demonstrate when it comes to children's work the variations between these two communities was not significant.

While the involvement of both males and females allowed me to consider gender differences I did not explore social class or ethnicity. Categories such as social class and ethnicity are, as Morrow (1994: 130) suggests, 'adult categories that children may have difficulty "fitting" themselves into'. Given this, I did not ask the children to define themselves along ethnic or class lines, nor did I gather any information on their parent's ethnicity or their socio-economic background. There is, thus, no basis in the material I collected for drawing conclusions related to such factors. Still, these factors might, as Morrow (1996) points out, very well have certain effects on what activities children take part in both in and outside the home and on the accounts the children give of themselves.

The fieldwork involved a variety of methods including group interviews, written essays, drawing and questionnaires as well as participant observation. Different methods suit different fields and different research participants better than others and, by using a variety of methods, the chance increases that individual research participants will feel they are able to express themselves in the way they prefer. A combination of materials can thereby better capture the wealth of the children's experiences (Christensen 2004, Eder and Fingerson 2003).

Interviews, essays and questionnaires were undertaken during school hours. The children in grades 6–9 were interviewed in groups of 2–5. I equipped the groups of children, whom I was to interview, with disposable cameras and asked them to photograph what they themselves saw as work and to photograph themselves while working. After one week, I collected the cameras and then brought the developed pictures to the interview session to use as stimuli material. The children in grades 4 and 5 were not interviewed and they did not take photos. Instead, they wrote short essays on the topic 'my work is' and drew pictures of themselves doing their work. All 100 children completed questionnaires. These, along with other methods were complemented by participant observation of a small number of children at work. This provided a vast amount of source material but the focus here is on data derived from the questionnaires and interviews.

Children's Definitions of Work

In order to ensure that the children's own definition of work was brought to the fore I commenced the questionnaire with the open ended question 'According to you, what is work?' The accounts provided by the children demonstrated great variety in understandings of the nature of work as they described both formal and informal, and paid and unpaid activities. For some children there was an expressed connection between the categories work and money or payment. For these children work was spatially defined as for example, occurring in an office, an advertising agency or in a child care centre. Some children mentioned that work is a place where adults work. Other connections were made to certain occupations such as being a carpenter, a fire fighter and nurse. Work was, many asserted, a 'job'.

Not all children confined their sense of work to activities and spaces outside the home. For quite a few, work also encompassed the domestic realm. For example, one Vikåsa girl in the fifth grade, stated that work is to 'work with the house' while an Ekköping boy in the eighth grade, claimed that work is when you 'work with something at home'. These students, along with others incorporated a range of domestic activities in their descriptions of work such as doing the dishes and other forms of housework as well as baby-sitting, chopping wood, painting houses and feeding animals.

What is notable, when inspecting the children's accounts overall, is that a significant number of children distinguished between, or even graded different forms of work. Indicative was the comment from Dan, a Vikåsa boy in the eighth grade, who suggested that work in the domestic space is 'a kind of work'. In an echo of this perspective, Kajsa, a Vikåsa girl also in the eighth grade, referred to work in this domain as 'more like helping'. A sixth grade female counterpart from Vikåsa provided a similar response positing that activities undertaken at home, such as doing the dishes, cooking and cleaning, constitute 'another kind of work'. The construction of work in these terms could be interpreted in different ways. Given that most children mentioned several different chores that they carry out in their everyday life it may be, for example, that there is an understanding that domestic labour is just one type of work which occurs alongside other forms of labour. Conversely, the descriptor of domestic labour as 'another kind of work' could imply that there is a perception that there is a single legitimate mode of work and a number of divergent or subsidiary forms of work. This latter interpretation is potentially more likely as numerous children conflated 'real' work with something that was a daily occurrence, paid, full-time and undertaken outside the home environment. Dominant therefore was a sense that 'real' work is associated with the formal labour market and familial or domestic work is 'other'.

In defining work, participants also drew distinctions between the work done by adults and children. Dan and Tor, two Vikåsa boys in the eighth grade, argued that there are some obvious differences between the work of children and adults. Adults, they argued, are better paid, undertake harder jobs, do them every day for several years, and they are often dependent on the money they make for their survival (cf. Mayall 2002, Näsman and von Gerber 2003). Children, they suggested, work a bit now and then, maybe once a week, have choice about whether to work because they do not need money to pay the bills; their parents do that. Other children mentioned similar differences. Moreover, the children often defined their own work as 'helping'.

The Places and Activities of Children's Work

To further trace the children's relationship with work the questionnaire asked 'Where do you work?' In response, only nine of the 100 children mentioned places that would be traditionally considered part of the formal labour market where people have gainful employment. They included 'my father's job'; 'taking care of invoices at an accounting office'; 'cleaning a day-care centre, it is a job'; 'in a restaurant'; 'in my father's barber shop answering the phone'; 'helping my dad in his company'; 'at home in my mother's block of flats' and in 'Estonia [where relatives of this boy have a farm]'. These answers were all given by boys and girls in the seventh, eighth and ninth grades and indicate that children in these age groups possibly have a somewhat stronger connection to the formal labour market. Again, there were no great differences in the responses of children across the two different communities. The remaining and far greater proportion of responses to the question of 'Where do you work?' demonstrated that the majority of children have a very weak connection to the formal labour market.

Instead of the formal labour market, the children involved in the study worked at places such as sport clubs (for example selling lottery tickets to raise money for their team), and at schools, (for example, selling May-flowers in the spring and Christmas cards to raise money for school-trips). Children in the study also work in their own homes where they assist with chores, do the laundry, do the dishes, cook, shovel snow and help out with renovating the house. Finally, many children mentioned selling Christmas magazines during a couple of weeks in the autumn.

Some children were less specific about the places where they work. Instead of places, these answers contained statements such as: 'Not a real job, takes care of bunnies and washing machine', 'It is not really work but I walk the neighbour's dog' and 'Sometimes at weekends with pony horse riding'. Ingenhorst (2001: 145) argues, in a study from Germany, that 'Child labour represents a broad range of activities, intensities and forms, which is very difficult to put into clearly defined categories'. This was the case here as well. The examples above indicate that the children have a weak connection to the formal labour market. However, more importantly, the children's statements illustrate that they are somewhat unsure as to whether their activity really is work or what constitutes work. Although the children use a wide definition of work in general, they still do not appear to be completely certain that their own activities can be legitimately defined as work. This is particularly true when it comes to activities they take part in around the house and at home.

The data revealed that labour regulations are important in shaping children's ideas about their capacity to be involved in employment. The Swedish labour law regulates the kind of work and the volume of work children may undertake. However, as Sjöberg (2007) argues, the legislation does not completely prevent people in the age range 13–18, or even younger children, from working. From a legal point of view, quite a few of the children in the current study are permitted to participate in the formal labour market, although under some restrictions. The children in the study however, understand the situation differently. According to their interpretations, labour regulations are a major factor inhibiting their participation in the labour market. Many of the children did not seem to recognize that it is even possible for them to have a job. For example, Fredrik, an Ekköping boy in the sixth grade, argued that it is forbidden for children to have summer jobs before the age of 16. Similarly, Dan, a Vikåsa boy in the eighth grade, explained that he had refrained from applying for a summer job as a dishwasher in a restaurant due to the legal regulations. According to Dan, a person at his age is not legally allowed to work in such a place due to safety regulations. Thus, Fredrik, Dan and the other children who expressed similar views did not recognize that they can be employees according to the law. This then affected their approach to the formal labour market and their perception of their own productive activities as something else than work, or as 'non-work'.

When Do Children Work?

As is the general trend across Sweden and Europe, most of the work in which children are involved is temporary (Mizen et al. 2001, Pole 2007, Söderlind and Engwall 2008). Their work is largely concentrated on long weekends and during extended breaks from school. It was during these times that some children reported spending a couple of days helping out at different workplaces. This was the case for Leo, an Ekköping boy in the sixth grade who explained that, 'last summer I helped my dad at his work. And then I got 50 crowns per day', 'he [Leo's father] is the janitor at the hospital'. In other cases several children mentioned that during holidays relatives provided them with employment on the periphery of the formal labour market or outside of it. Tor, for example, a Vikåsa boy in the eighth grade, stated, 'I help my granddad with stuff so I get some money'. Another example is Ola, an Ekköping boy in the eighth grade, who 'usually hangs out with a guy [a farmer] that my granddad knows in [name of a town in Sweden] and help them a little like this', 'to drive the tractor', 'carry fire-wood' and usually 'I get, you know, money and so at Christmas and things like that'. In a further illustration, Peggy, an Ekköping girl in the eighth grade explained that it was during non-schooling periods that '[I] usually clean the stairs in my parents' set of flats and then I get some money for this'.

In Sweden, the summer vacation is the longest period away from school for children and spans from June to August. This might subsequently be considered the most suitable time of year for work. Having a summer job could demonstrate one's connection to the part of the labour market with formal, paid, gainful employment. In the questionnaire, I asked the children 'Did you have a job for which you earned money last summer?' Out of the 100 children, 60 answered 'No' and 26 'Yes' while 15 children did not answer the question (one person answered both Yes and No and is counted as both). The frequency with which students held summer jobs turned out, somewhat surprisingly, to be slightly higher in the lower age groups, but in general it was around 20 to 30 per cent across the age groups. As interviews were not undertaken with the younger cohort it is not possible to know where this group had been working, but interviews with the children in grades 6–9, included mention of places such as 'a café', 'an apple farm in Estonia', 'a restaurant', 'a golf-club' and 'selling strawberries outside a supermarket'. The many 'No' answers further illustrate a weak connection to the part of the labour market with formal, paid, gainful employment.

Payment and Children's Work

Notably, only eight children out of 100, four in each community, stated that they were never remunerated for their work. It therefore appears that the majority of children live their everyday life in a monetary system outside the formal labour market. The children mentioned household chores, such as cleaning and vacuuming, doing the dishes, emptying the dishwasher and taking out the garbage as activities that could generate money. Outdoor activities, such as running errands and doing the grocery shopping, doing garden work, shovelling snow, washing the car, throwing firewood into the boiler room and taking the dog for a walk, were also mentioned as activities that they could be paid for. However, the level and the form of payment for children's work varied. For example, one Vikåsa girl in the fourth grade wrote in her questionnaire that, 'I take care of a rabbit and have one myself and that I do not get money. When I looked after the rabbit for two months I received a cup and a bracelet [from her parents]'. Similarly, Emil, an Ekköping boy in the sixth grade, explained:

> [I] also baby-sit. Once I baby-sat almost a whole week, my little sister, because they [his parents] had to leave in the morning every day. And you know, do some work. And then, after a week or so, I got a movie because I had been so good.

Hence, payment for a job well-done can be made in cups, bracelets and movies. Other children claimed they received candy or new jeans as salary for various work activities they had undertaken. Receiving an allowance is also an often connected or integral part of the more or less formalized system of reciprocity that can be found in both Ekköping and Vikåsa. Sixty out of the 100 children stated that they receive a monthly allowance and fifteen indicated that they receive a weekly one. Allowance is sometimes depicted as a gift or as part of a parental pedagogical or socialization project, where parents are trying to teach their children the value of saving or handling their own money (Hungerland et al. 2007, Näsman and von Gerber 2003). Nevertheless, more than 50 per cent of the Ekköping and Vikåsa children who stated that they receive either a monthly or weekly allowance, also reported in their questionnaire that they have to meet some kind of demand or produce some kind of service to receive their allowance. This could be smaller chores, like in the case of Mona, a Vikåsa girl in the eighth grade, who stated,

'I have to clean my room once a month to get my monthly allowance'. Other children, however, mentioned that they had to meet more obligations to receive their allowance such as washing up, cleaning, running errands, grocery shopping, picking up younger siblings from school and caring for younger siblings.

To organize the children's work, some families use a system with a schedule stating who in the family is required to undertake different domestic tasks on a daily basis. In many cases, completing these activities gives children money, and some children told me that they had a price list in their family, which stated how much the children could receive for undertaking different household tasks. Ada, an Ekköping girl in the sixth grade, explained that her mother had created such a system during the summer. Next to every chore on the list, she had written what the children would receive if they completed different tasks. Ada explained that 'For example if we mowed the lawn, we got 3 crowns and if we trimmed the hedges we got 5 crowns'. The list contained ten chores and they were all in the domestic arena. Similarly, different Vikåsa children explained that their mothers offered them 25–50 crowns to do the dishes, 100 to clean the apartment and 100 to take in one of the family's horses. Notable is that these children explained that they would never do these chores if their parents did not offer them money, underlining that this is not just any chore or favour completed by the children to please their parents but a paid service that the children can choose to do or not.

Incentives for Children to Work

A further issue addressed in the questionnaire was that of incentives for working. The children were asked 'Why do you have a job in addition to going to school?' and were invited to consider both paid and unpaid work. They were then presented with five alternatives. These were (a) I need money for my daily expenses (pocket money); (b) I save money for something special; (c) The work is relaxation from school/I think it is fun to work (d) I want to support myself and; (e) other (where they could add any other incentives they may have for working).

The children could, if they wished, mark several alternatives. Some of the children used this possibility, underlining that children have mixed motives for working. The trend was very similar in the two communities. Alternative three, where work is characterized as relaxation from school and/or as something fun, was marked 16 times in the children's questionnaires and it is also a factor which has been commonly found to be a motivating force for children's work in other research (Hungerland et al. 2007, Mizen et al. 2001). Nevertheless, a far more common reason to work seemed to be for money. Money for daily expenses was marked 21 times, saving money 37 times and supporting themselves was marked five times. All these answers emphasize that money is a critical enticement to work for children. Seventeen children used the open-ended alternative and gave their own explanation for why they work. Money was one of three dominant themes in these responses. However, there were also children who stated that they work to help out or to give something back to their parents. Finally, there were children who stated that they work because they are required to do so.

While parents may demand children work, it is also possible that work can have liberating potential in a child's life. Ulrik, an Ekköping boy in the seventh grade described being involved in a large range of work activities for which he is paid in kind with additional and more expensive gifts at Christmas and at his birthday. Ulrik and his family reside in the countryside about half an hour by car from the main community of Ekköping. They live on a farm beside Ulrik's grandparents. Ulrik's parents work away from home, but his grandparents work on the farm area by the houses. Ulrik explained that when he works on the farm, he begins at half past six each morning. Ulrik also assists his grandfather in a floor heating company. For Ulrik working with his grandparents was far more attractive than being at home because he could choose his favourite work activities. In contrast, at home he might be told to do work he does not like. Ulrik's claim that being at home may result in him being 'told to do' things indicates something important about children's everyday life. The phrase, to be 'told to', encapsulates, as James and James (2004) argue, the authority parents and adults generally have over their own child and over children as a social category. Parents and adults, in general, influence children's everyday life by making different decisions and by imposing these decisions on their children. Ulrik prefers being able to choose for himself. Working away from home gives him such opportunities, so Ulrik chooses, if possible, to work at his grandparents. Hence, work does not need to be a demanding chore. Work away from home makes possible independence and autonomy.

Various scholars argue that a desire for independence can be an important motivation for work (for example, Leonard 2004, Mizen et al. 2001). In particular, work provides children with their own money, which they can use for private consumption without adult interference (Leonard 2003, Näsman and von Gerber 2003). The relationship between work and independence was evident in comments from Ralf, a Vikåsa boy in the ninth grade, who asserted that involvement in domestic work '… show[s] that you can take the responsibility and can clean, and then you get to stay out longer and you get a larger monthly allowance and stuff like that'. Involvement in domestic work is thus not just about monetary reward but also about engendering greater autonomy.

Some scholars studying working children argue that children are 'Working to be someone' (Hungerland et al. 2007). Through work, they argue, children can acquire knowledge and experience they cannot obtain via formal school education. In different work settings they can both meet people and see parts of society they may not necessarily encounter. In a work situation they might also have to take on more responsibility than what they would normally do. This may foster the children's growth, in their own eyes and in the eyes of others and help prepare them for the future. Although the children in Ekköping and Vikåsa, as I have described elsewhere (Samuelsson 2008), were very future oriented in their choice of spare time activities and in regard to their school activities, the Ekköping and Vikåsa children never explicitly expressed this kind of motivation in regard to paid work.

Despite this, a connection to the future could be traced in the children's description of their paid work. Children's work is often seen by parents, teachers, and law and policymakers as a challenge to the children's school education, taking up valuable study time and wearing the children out so they do not have the energy to study (de Coninck-Smith et al. 1997, Leonard 2003, Mayall 2002). The children did not recognize this dilemma. Conversely, they argued that work undertaken in their spare time can enhance their formal school education. Lena and Frida, two Vikåsa girls in the sixth grade, arguing that through work, selling different items and counting money, they practised their mathematics. Lena for example, asserted that 'it's not enough to just run around [trying to sell something], you have to think about how to proceed'. Thus, when working the children get to practice skills learned in school, this can, by proxy, help them prepare better for work life after school.

Conclusion

This chapter commenced with an explanation of the widespread and popular belief in Sweden that working children belong to a distant past or at least exist only in developing countries. While this pervasive perspective is afforded support by official labour force surveys, the data presented in this chapter challenge this assumption. Utilizing a child-centred perspective which concentrated on giving voice to children's own accounts about work has widened the definition of work and thereby demonstrated the meaning of work in which Swedish children are currently engaged.

Some scholars argue that modern childhood is taking place on 'islands' spread out in society (for example, Qvortrup 1994, Zeiher 2003). These islands are the modern institutions created for children, such as school, pre-school and so on, where children spend their days while their parents and other adults are away working and taking part in society (Zeiher 2003). From a societal perspective, it might appear as if children live their everyday life on islands completely isolated from the labour market and the work that takes place in society. However, when we look at the children's definitions of work and their descriptions of their participation in work, this picture changes somewhat. As I have shown, the children do participate in different work activities in the Ekköping and Vikåsa communities. Nevertheless, the distinctions made by the study respondents regarding their own work convey, as has been suggested by Mayall (2002: 69), the impression that the children 'regard themselves as separated out from the world of serious, responsible work ...'. The children were often reluctant to see the connection between their activities and real work. Scholars have argued that children are not fully recognized as social and cultural agents by society when it comes to questions regarding the labour market and that there is a general reluctance to acknowledge children's participation in the traditional, formal labour market (de Coninck-Smith et al. 1997). It is also notable that children share at least some of this reluctance. Instead of portraying their activities as real work and themselves as workers they categorized both their work activities and themselves in less auspicious terms, thereby contributing to the invisibility of children's work.

It is unclear whether children's work will decrease or increase in the future. Some scholars have argued that the modern capitalist economy has entered a new phase, a phase in which manual labour has lost its importance to symbolic activities (for example, Qvortrup 2001, Reich 1992). The economy, it is argued, has moved from 'producing use values to producing exchange values, and from simple to extended production' (Qvortrup 2001: 96). One consequence of this high-technological, post-industrial production system is a reduced need for unskilled manual labour. This may create the impression that the division between the work skilled adults undertake and children's work will increase and strengthen further. However, there are also other consequences of the composition of the labour force in general and of working life in particular. Beck (2007) argues that due to economic changes people in the countries of Europe will have to use a variety of economic strategies to try to make a living in the near future. Using Brazil as an example, Beck (2007) shows how people survive the new economic climate by combining different temporary forms of paid and unpaid, formal and informal work. This, Beck (2007) argues, will soon be the case, if it is not already, in the heartland of Europe too.

Thus, this societal change has two facets. On the one hand, the post-industrial changes in the modern capitalistic system demand highly skilled symbolic analysts. On the other hand, many new forms of work will have to be created to support the many who are not symbolic analysts. These forms of work, which will be found in the expanding service sector, will include many jobs that do not require a high level of vocational or academic training or specific skills (Nic Ghiolla Phádraig 2007). When it comes to time and place, the forms of employment will change and labour patterns will be broken. Flexible work and short-term project employment are expanding (Beck 2007, Strandell 2007) and the distinction between work and non-work activities as well as work and non-work sites is becoming blurred (Strandell 2007).

If these scholars' predictions are correct, in the near future production will predominantly take place outside the formal labour market with paid jobs. This may have consequences for children's work. In a discussion of the economy and production system in, what he calls, the 'Third Wave' of our society, Futurologist Toffler (1980/1990) predicts that much of the work in society will take place within the domestic arena and that the demand for children's work will increase when production returns to the home setting. Toffler (1980/1990: 220) further asserts that 'Certain forms of work ... might be specifically designed for youngsters and even integrated with their education'. Castells (2000) posited similar claims in *Network Society* arguing that paid work among children is increasing, not just in developing countries, but all over the world. Thus, in the industrialized economies of late modernity, working children are no anomaly. Rather, as Nic Ghiolla Phádraig (2007: 213) states 'children's work can be situated in the contemporary phase of capitalism as regards labour market segmentation and the extent to which goods and services have been commoditised'. As the present study has demonstrated, children in both Ekköping and Vikåsa participate in various forms of work in many parts of the societal arena. Given the outlined trend above, in a coming post-industrial work order, children might, for better or worse, participate in the world of work to an even greater extent.

References

Åkerberg, N. 2003. Barnarbete som affärsidé. _Dagens Industri_ [Online, 23 April] Available at: http://www.ad.se/nyad/arkiv/artikelarkiv_ny.php [accessed: 17 May 2004].

Beck, U. 2007. _The Brave New World of Work_. Cambridge: Polity Press.

Castells, M. 2000. _The Information Age: Economy, Society and Culture. Vol. 3, End of Millennium_. Oxford: Blackwell.

Christensen, P. 2004. Children's participation in ethnographic research: Issues of power and representation. _Children and Society_, 18(2), 165–76.

Dahl, G. 1984. Det nyttiga barnet, in _Barn i tid och rum_, edited by K. Aronsson, M. Cederblad, G. Dahl, L. Olsson and B. Sandin. Malmö: Liber förlag, 128–47.

de Coninck-Smith, N., Sandin, B. and Schrumpf, E. 1997. Introduction, in _Industrious Children: Work and Childhood in the Nordic Countries 1850–1990_, edited by N. de Coninck-Smith, B. Sandin and E. Schrumpf. Odense: Odense University Press, 7–16.

Eder, D. and Fingerson, L. 2003. Interviewing children and adolescents, in _Inside Interviewing. New Lenses, New Concerns_, edited by J. A. Holstein and J. F. Gubrium. London: SAGE Publications, 33–53.

Hengst, H. and Zeiher, H. 2000. Unter legitimationsdruck. Das arbeitsverbot im kindheitsprojekt der moderne, in _Die Arbeit der Kinder. Kindheitskonzept und Arbeitsteilung zwischen den Generationen_ edited by H. Hengst and H. Zeiher. Weinheim: Juventa, 7–20.

Hungerland, B., Liebel, M., Milne, B. and Wihstutz, A. (eds). 2007. _Working to Be Someone: Child Focused Research and Practice with Working Children_. London: Jessica Kingsley _Publishers_.

Ingenhorst, H. 2001. Child labour in the Federal Republic of Germany, in _Hidden Hands. International Perspectives on Children's Work and Labour_, edited by P. Mizen, C. Pole and A. Bolton, London: Routledge Falmer, 139–48.

James, A. and James, A. L. 2004. _Constructing Childhood. Theory, Policy and Social Practice_. Basingstoke: Palgrave MacMillan.

Leonard, M. 2003. Children's Attitudes to Parents', Teachers' and Employers' Perceptions of Term-Time Employment. _Children and Society_, 17(5), 349–60.

Leonard, M. 2004. Children's views on children's right to work. Reflections from Belfast. *Childhood*, 11(1), 45–61.

Mayall, B. 2002. *Towards a Sociology for Childhood. Thinking from Children's Lives.* Buckingham: Open University Press.

Mizen, P., Pole, C. and Bolton, A. (eds). 2001. *Hidden Hands. International Perspectives on Children's Work and Labour.* London: Routledge Falmer.

Morrow, V. 1994. Responsible children? Aspects of children's work and employment outside school in contemporary UK, in *Children's Childhoods: Observed and Experienced*, edited by B. Mayall. London: Falmer Press, 128–43.

Morrow, V. 1996. Rethinking childhood dependency: Children's contributions to the domestic economy. *The Sociological Review*, 44(1), 58–77.

Nic Ghiolla Phádraig, M. 2007. Working children and the descholarisation of childhood, in *Childhood, Generational Order and the Welfare State: Exploring Children's Social and Economic Welfare. Volume 1 of COST A19: Children's Welfare*, edited by H. Wintersberger, L. Alanen, T. Olk and J. Qvortrup. Odense: University Press of Southern Denmark, 201–23.

Näsman, E. and von Gerber, C. 2003. *Från Spargris till Kontokort. Barndomens Ekonomiska Spiraltrappa.* Linköping: ITUF, Linköpings Universitet.

Pole, C. 2007. Vocabularies, motives and meanings – School-age workers in Britain: Towards a synthesis? in *Working to Be Someone: Child Focused Research and Practice with Working Children*, edited by B. Hungerland, M. Liebel, B. Milne and A. Wihstutz. London: Jessica Kingsley *Publishers*, 151–60.

Qvortrup, J. 1994. Childhood matters. An introduction, in *Childhood Matters. Social Theory, Practice and Politics*, edited by J. Qvortrup, M. Bardy, G. Sgritta, and H. Wintersberger. Brookfield VT: Avebury, 1–23.

Qvortrup, J. 2001. school-work, paid work and the changing obligations of childhood, in *Hidden Hands. International Perspectives on Children's Work and Labour*, edited by P. Mizen, C. Pole and A. Bolton. London: Routledge Falmer, 91–107.

Reich, R. B. 1992. *The Work of Nations: Preparing Ourselves for 21st Century Capitalism.* New York: Vintage Books.

Roxvall, A. 2006. Jultidningar guldgruva för små entreprenörer. *Svenska Dagbladet Näringsliv*, 23 October, 27.

Samuelsson, T. 2008. *Children's Work in Sweden. A Part of Childhood, a Path to Adulthood.* (Diss.). Linköping: Linköpings universitet.

Schmidt, L and Olsson, L. 2004. Jultidningsförsäljning – en lönsam historia. *Svensk bokhandel*, (21), 31.

Sjöberg, M. 2007. Protection, hindrance or possibility? Child labour legislation 1975–2000, in *Children's Work in Everyday Life*, edited by K. Engwall and I. Söderlind. Stockholm: Institute for Futures Studies, 117–31.

Strandell, H. 2007. New childhood space and the question of difference, in *Flexible Childhood? Exploring Children's Welfare in Time and Space Volume 2 of COST*

A19: Children's Welfare, edited by H. Zeiher, D. Devine, A. T. Kjørholt and H. Strandell. Odense: University Press of Southern Denmark, 49–68.

Söderlind, I. and Engwall, K. (eds). 2008. *Barndom och Arbete*. Umeå: Boréa förlag.

Toffler, A. 1980/1990. *The Third Wave*. New York: Bantam Books.

Tonström, E. 2009. Barn ger förlag miljoner i julklapp. *Svenska Dagbladet* [Online, 11 November] Available at: http://www.svd.se/nyheter/inrikes/barn-ger-forlag-miljoner-i-julklapp_3781583.svd [accessed: 22 December 2010].

www.majblomman.se. 2010. Majblommans Riksförbund.

Zeiher, H. 2003. Shaping daily life in urban environments, in *Children in the City. Home, Neighbourhood and Community*, edited by P. Christensen, and M. O'Brien. London: Routledge Falmer, 66–81.

Chapter 2
Young People Experiencing Work in a Boomtown Labour Market

Christopher D. O'Connor

Recent decades have been characterized by significant changes within labour markets in the developed world. For example, labour markets are increasingly typified by uncertainty, unemployment and a replacement of full-time work (for example well-paid, highly skilled and life-long employment) with casual employment (for example contract and part-time work) (Beck 2000). These changes have had a significant impact on the lives of young people, and in particular, their school-to-work transitions (Furlong and Cartmel 1997, Lowe and Krahn 1999). For example, young people navigating contemporary times are the group most likely to experience, or be at risk of, underemployment or unemployment (Loughlin and Barling 1999, Lowe and Krahn 1999). Also, the labour market places demands on young people to be educated and highly skilled, thus increasing the number of years they spend in school (Furlong and Cartmel 1997).

In examinations of how young people navigate contemporary labour markets, much of the research has focused on contexts where young people are economically marginalized (for example areas with high unemployment). This has meant that young people navigating economically prosperous contexts has largely gone unexamined. In addition, few researchers have attempted to examine aspects of the school-to-work transition from the perspective of the young people experiencing this transition. This chapter adds to the literature on young people and work by examining how young people themselves understand their experiences navigating a rapidly changing and economically prosperous city.

Young People Navigating Contemporary Labour Markets

Much of the research conducted on young people's experiences with changing labour markets in contemporary times has been situated within larger debates concerning the opening up of opportunities for young people to direct their own life courses. Some youth researchers have argued that the opening up of choices has meant young people do indeed have greater agency in shaping their life courses in contemporary times compared with previous decades (for example, Arnett 2004). Alternatively, others suggest that despite the apparent opening up of choices, young people's life courses are still heavily guided by traditional social structures (for example, Andres and Adamuti-Trache 2008). While there is not space to discuss the intricacies of these larger debates here, I want to briefly expand on how the concept of 'choice' has been integral to our understandings of young people navigating contemporary labour markets.

Furlong and Cartmel (1997) have been particularly influential in helping to clarify how 'choices' impact upon young people in contemporary times. Drawing on data primarily from the United Kingdom, they argue that present times can be characterized by the *appearance* of greater choice to navigate one's own life course, but in actuality people's lives remain highly structured (for example by gender and class). Furlong and Cartmel (1997: 5) refer to this as the 'epistemological fallacy of late modernity' in that the social changes being experienced (for example in the labour market) distract from underlying structural forces that limit choice and help to shape individual action. For young people this has meant that changes in the institutions of education and work have helped promote the idea that they have greater choices in contemporary times when it comes to their schooling and work. For example, the availability of schooling and training options has increased and there are increasingly more and more types of jobs to choose from due to the rapid expansion of technology. However, while this might be true on a superficial level, Furlong and Cartmel (1997) suggest that upon closer examination these changes in work and education have only helped to obscure structuring effects.

Therefore, when examining the concept of choice in contemporary times, of key importance to consider are the available resources people have to make choices (Brannen and Nilsen 2005). That is, not all young people have the same resources when it comes to choosing a career direction (Hodkinson and Sparkes 1997). For example, Bynner (2005), examining young people's transitions in Britain, found that those who had more resources were more likely to be able to take advantage of the 'choices' that have opened up as a result of changes in the institutions of education and work in recent decades. Thus, young people with more resources were able to utilize these resources to obtain education and training, and thus better employment than those with fewer resources.

Risks then are by no means evenly distributed amongst people (Furlong and Cartmel 1997, Lehmann 2004). Adding to Furlong and Cartmel's (1997) argument that structures of inequality still exist, Mythen (2005) argues that while the changing nature of employment (for example increased unemployment and part-time work) has the *potential* to affect everyone, in *actuality* the most vulnerable to these types of risks can be determined by their class positions. People who have traditionally been more vulnerable to the inequalities inherent in the labour market are still the most vulnerable (for example the lower classes). Therefore, while there might be a growing perception on a subjective level that risks are shared by everyone, when looked at more closely it does not appear that risks affect everyone equally. It would seem that the opening up of choice and opportunity in contemporary times has not created choice and opportunity for everyone. Starting at a point of advantage helps individuals keep that advantage.

More specifically, it is argued that young people seem to be especially susceptible to the risks of a changing labour market in comparison to adults. For example, as already mentioned, young people as a group are highly likely to experience underemployment or unemployment (Loughlin and Barling 1999, Lowe and Krahn 1999). Given this, it is important to look at the quality of the work in which young people participate. The research that does exist on this topic suggests that young people's work experiences often includes low pay, low skill, poor working conditions and limited choices in terms of type of employment (Loughlin and Barling 1999, Lowe and Krahn 1999). Further, Mortimer, Harley, and Staff (2002) found that poor quality part-time work can have negative impacts on young people's mental health. Others have found that young people's inexperienced position within the labour market make them more vulnerable to workplace dangers and exploitation. For example, Breslin et al. (2007) found that young people perceived the injuries they obtained at work to be 'part of the job' and that they had little power to change their situations. In summary, it appears that the ability of young people to 'choose' within the world of work in contemporary times is tempered by a variety of structural forces which leave them vulnerable in the labour market.

Methodology

Given that youth researchers have tended to focus on contexts of marginalization and deprivation, the literature on young people's experiences with contemporary labour markets has little to say about how young people experience work within a boomtown context. And yet, local contexts play an important role in shaping young people's current and future 'selves' (Hodkinson and Sparkes 1997). This chapter then addresses the question 'how do young people experience a booming labour market?' In order to answer this question I draw on in-depth interviews conducted between October 2008 and August 2009, primarily with high school students and some interviews with (adult) key informants to provide additional context. These interviews were part of larger research project that also examined the school-to-work transitions of post-secondary students and young workers in a prosperous economic environment.

Research Setting: The 'Boomtown' of Fort McMurray, Alberta, Canada

Over the last several years, the city of Fort McMurray has increasingly generated much interest both nationally and internationally. Fort McMurray, located in the regional Municipality of Wood Buffalo in northern Alberta, Canada, is the hub for oilsands activity in the region. Canada's oilsands are estimated to contain close to 180 billion barrels of oil which places Canada second only to Saudi Arabia in terms of world supply (Canadian Centre for Energy Information 2006). With a growing worldwide demand for oil, in part due to emerging industrial economies in India and China, the market price of oil has increased to a level (US$75 and higher) where the costly extraction of oil from oilsands is profitable. This has placed Fort McMurray at the forefront of what is likely to be the world's last great oil boom.

The rapid development of the oilsands in recent years has meant dramatic changes for Fort McMurray. Three factors are relevant to my study of young workers. First, Fort McMurray's population has grown from 30,000 people in the late 1990s to over 75,000 people by 2007 (Government of Alberta 2008). Second, economic investment in the development of the oilsands in recent years has also been dramatic. For example, to date there has been approximately C$20 billion invested in completed oilsands projects (National Energy Board 2010). Finally, while the increased pace of oil production during the 2000s produced economic benefits in Fort McMurray, as well as for Alberta, Canada, and other countries, it also raised a variety of social concerns for the city. For example, there were severe labour shortages in a variety of industries which led to an increasing number of people migrating both permanently and temporarily from within Canada and internationally to fill this demand for labour in the city (Flakstad 2006, Hiller 2009). Labour shortages also raised concerns about young people possibly dropping out of school for lucrative jobs in the oilsands industry (Harding 2006). Fort McMurray then, presented an opportunity to examine young people's work experiences within a city that was rapidly changing and had a booming economy centred around a single industry (that is, the extraction of oil/energy).

Recruiting Participants

With the goal of obtaining a diverse set of participants, high school students were recruited with the assistance of high school staff who identified Grade 12 students – those in their last year of secondary schooling before obtaining a diploma – with a variety of different social backgrounds and characteristics (for example gender, race/ethnicity and class). Once Grade 12 students were identified, I met with them individually, in small groups, and gave brief presentations in classrooms to explain my research project and to ask if they would like to participate. Specific individuals (key informants) within Fort McMurray were also contacted and asked to participate and/or to forward my information to anyone they thought might be interested in participating in my research project. The goal was to make contact with individuals who would represent a wide range of key informants in the community.

Research Sample Characteristics

Of the 30 interviews conducted with high school students, 18 were with young men and 12 were with young women. The average age of the participants was approximately 18 (ranging from age 15 to 19). Fifteen young people were white, five were black, two were Asian, and eight were Aboriginal. However, within these overly broad categories there were a range of countries and ethnicities represented including Lebanese, Vietnamese, French, British, Polynesian and Ukrainian as well as individuals claiming multiple racial/ethnic identities. Given that the goal of this research project was to garner young people's understandings and that key informants were providing only contextual understandings, the social characteristics of the 23 key informants that I interviewed were not collected. However, this included one interview with a human resources manager, one interview with a municipal government employee, one interview with a health professional, two interviews with law enforcement officers, three interviews with community leaders, five interviews with those working for a youth organization, and ten interviews with people working in the field of education.

Interviewing Participants

This chapter draws on in-depth qualitative interviews primarily with young people and is supplemented where relevant by interviews with (adult) key informants familiar with Fort McMurray. Conducting in-depth interviews with participants provided me with rich data about people's lives (Mason 1996). More specifically, in-depth interviewing allowed me to access how people made sense of their local contexts and how they understood their experiences (Siedman 1991).

Utilizing the school-to-work transition as a focal point, interviews with young people were designed to examine the multiplicity of life experiences and contextual factors that shaped young people's school-to-work transition understandings (for example working in a boomtown). Interviews were dynamic and contained open-ended questions leading in various directions. All of the high school student interviews were conducted face-to-face at local high schools and lasted an average of 45 minutes. In addition, key informants were asked to discuss the city of Fort McMurray and the particular risks, problems and advantages young people encountered growing up and living in a boomtown environment. Interviews with key informants lasted an average of 40 minutes with 11 of these interviews taking place over the phone and the remaining 12 being conducted face-to-face. All participants in this study were assured confidentiality and thus, are referred to only by a pseudonym.

Analytical Strategy

Interviews were digitally recorded (with the exception of two key informants who preferred not to be recorded) and subsequently transcribed. After transcription, I analysed the interviews with the assistance of the data analysis program HyperRESEARCH. HyperRESEARCH allowed me to assign codes to relevant themes (or blocks of quotes) in the interview transcripts. Initially, I read each transcript and grouped quotes under an appropriate (broad) code. I then reread each code to ensure coding was accurate. Second, I analysed the quotes within each broad code for themes and assigned more specific codes/groupings. As this was undertaken, I made comments and notes regarding the data and its possible relevance to theory and the broader literature. Third, I reread the themes and made additional comments and clarifications choosing illustrative quotes to represent the themes that emerged from the interviews. As Creswell (2003) notes, the analysis of qualitative data is a continuous process of thinking and rethinking about (or analyzing and reanalyzing) data, theory and questions/answers that emerge out of the data.

Experiencing Work in a Booming Labour Market

At the time I conducted my research, Fort McMurray offered young people a somewhat unique work context in comparison to other non-boomtown cities given that the city was relatively isolated, employment was plentiful, and incomes were high. In what follows I examine high school students' (subsequently referred to as the *high schoolers*) understandings of working in the booming labour market of Fort McMurray.

Most of the high schoolers I spoke with worked part-time while attending their final year of high school or had worked part-time in the past. Given the labour shortage in Fort McMurray, part-time jobs were abundant and most high schoolers worked in some sort of service type employment (for example at a grocery store or restaurant). High schoolers appeared to play a pivotal role in ensuring the city was able to function by taking jobs that could not easily be filled by adult workers given the higher wages and greater job opportunities offered by oilsands-related employment. Given the labour shortage, high schoolers were paid generously for their part-time work. The average hourly wage for high schoolers was C$13.50 which amounted to an average weekly income of approximately C$280. When this is compared to Alberta's minimum wage of C$8.40, and given that most minimum wage earners in Alberta are between the ages of 15 and 19 (Alberta Employment and Immigration 2008), high schoolers in Fort McMurray received a substantial amount of money for their part-time work.

High schoolers' current work experiences in Fort McMurray were often described in positive terms. Part-time work in Fort McMurray appeared to become an extension of high schoolers' high school social lives in that the labour shortage meant that workplaces were mostly staffed by people around the same age as themselves. For example, after being asked how he liked working at his part-time restaurant job, Kirk (an 18 year old Aboriginal male) stated:

> Oh it's so fun ... Everybody there, it's like a big family ... Like everybody gets along and then if there's one person out of the group that has a problem, there's not that big of an issue where ... you're afraid to talk to people ... You can talk to anyone there and ... they'll help you out.

Further, Kami (an 18 year old white female) stated that, 'I've met some of my lifelong friends at that job' while David (a 17 year old white male) emphasized that 'seventy-five per cent of the people I know [at work] are my good friends'. Within this context of high wages and positive work environments, there seemed to be little disincentive to work.

Balancing High School and Work

There is little consensus in the literature as to the impact that working part-time whilst in high school has on young people. Some authors suggest that if young people work too many hours a week – typically defined as working more than 20 hours – it can have negative outcomes (for example drug use, participation in minor crimes) (Frone 1999, Warren and Cataldi 2006). Other researchers suggest that part-time work generates positive outcomes for young people (for example by providing job experience), particularly for those who have difficulties with schooling (Entwisle, Alexander and Steffel Olson 2000). For example, Lee and Staff (2007) found that young people who have few plans to attend post-secondary school might see more value in cultivating their work experiences rather than finishing their high school diplomas. Additionally, Staff and Mortimer (2007) found that part-time work in high school encouraged young people to pursue further education post-high school and that part-time work provided them with the skills to manage/balance attending post-secondary school and working part-time.

On the basis of these studies, it is difficult definitively to suggest an optimum number of part-time working hours for high school students, although the key informants I spoke with in Fort McMurray believed that young people were often working too much. The high schoolers I spoke with worked on average 20 hours a week at their jobs while attending their final year of high school which is approximately the Canadian average (Loughlin and Barling 1999). Loughlin and Barling (1999) suggest that rather than focus on the *quantity* of young people's part-time work, it might be more informative to focus on its *quality*. That is, how do young people experience work? Below I further examine how high schoolers perceived the quality of their part-time jobs and how this was linked to their ability to manage/balance both high school and work in a boomtown.

As already discussed, high schoolers generally held favourable views of their workplaces. These favourable views were often linked to the flexibility that many of the high schoolers seemed to be afforded at their jobs. For example, high schoolers often had flexibility in scheduling shifts and time to finish homework during downtimes at work. For example, Garry (an 18 year old Aboriginal male) remained at a job that provided him with considerably less pay than his friends in part because of the flexibility the job offered as well as the work environment. As Garry stated: 'I mean my friends get paid more than I do … But for the amount of work I actually do … it's a good job … The hours are really flexible … they really schedule me around my school'. In a city that was short on labour, high schoolers appeared to have certain advantages when it came to their part-time work.

Interestingly, when high schoolers were directly asked if they had difficulty balancing their part-time jobs and high school commitments, the responses differed substantially between young men and women. The young men, despite often working long hours, stated that they did not have difficulty balancing their work and school commitments. For example, when asked if he found that work interfered with his ability to do well in school, Abir (a 15 year old black male) stated: 'No I can manage because I don't like work that many hours [he worked 20 hours a week] that I don't have any time [for school]'. Additionally, CJ (a 16 year old white male) commented: 'I have the highest mark in my English class and I have eighties in art too'. Overall, the young men tended to emphasize their ability to easily manage their busy schedules.

Alternatively, the young women stated that they often found it difficult to manage both school and work commitments. For example, Mortisha (a 16 year old Aboriginal female) reflected: 'Yeah it's pretty hard. Like it's a late night … And then you get home and it's like four hours of homework and then by one o'clock you're like dead and then you got to get up at five-forty'. Similarly, Karen (an 18 year old white female) explained: 'But like then with the working, it was hard to find time for school, dance, work, friends'.

Given that there is little evidence to suggest that young men in this study possessed greater skills at managing time than young women, this disjuncture in understandings between young men and women suggests that women possessed, or at least articulated, a greater thoughtfulness when it came to discussing school-work balance. For example, while young men often simply stated that they could manage both school and part-time work easily, young women often showed a more considered understanding:

> It's just figuring it all out with homework, and job, and it's stressful when you're working … People work out at site [the oilsands] for … 12 days straight and get two days off, it's unbelievable. And I go to school, like nine o'clock in the morning, come home at three, go to work at four until ten and that's my life, right? I might have an hour in between to do homework, and I can barely do that for four days straight … And here the people out at site are doing that 12 days straight … Like for me, it's hard to balance. (Kami, 18 year old white female)

Kami was able to articulate cogently both her own difficulties in managing a busy boomtown life as well as the difficulties experienced by oilsands workers in the city. This level of thoughtfulness was not something that was apparent in the young men's understandings.

Despite the gendered differences in levels of thoughtfulness, young men and women both ultimately placed responsibility on themselves for any ill-effects caused by having a busy work-school schedule. For example, despite having stated that she had difficulty balancing school and work, when Mortisha was asked whether she thought her part-time job interfered with her grades she stated: 'Um, no it's just me slacking a bit'. Similarly, David when asked whether he found it hard to balance school and work, answered: 'No not really ... I'm going to be honest, I'm lazy'. Individual agency was often prominent in high schoolers' responses over that of structural constraint.

Young people articulating that they are responsible for directing their own life courses is a common finding in the literature (for example, Brannen and Nilsen 2005, Furlong and Cartmel 1997). However, the understandings of the high schoolers I spoke with appeared to be gendered. That is, young women recognized structural constraints and at the same time took responsibility for their own actions whereas young men took responsibility for their actions but did not acknowledge possible structural constraints. As several authors have noted gendered practices unfold differently within particular contexts (Connell 1993, Paechter 2003, Thorne 1993). The boomtown context of Fort McMurray was no exception.

Job Choice and Risk in a Boomtown

What the high schoolers in Fort McMurray had in common with most other non-boomtown youth their age was that they tended to work in service type employment that required few skills. Generally, most young people in developed countries tend to encounter very little choice in terms of employment options (Loughlin and Barling 1999, Lowe and Krahn 1999). However, Fort McMurray high schoolers differed from most young people in that they had a wide variety of jobs to choose from for their part-time work even though this was limited to, or structured by, service type employment. In a city where high school students were in high demand to fill jobs, if high schoolers were not treated with respect, not provided with flexibility and/or did not like their work environment, they could easily move to another job.

While high schoolers discussed their *current* part-time jobs in mainly positive terms, their framings of their employment histories showed movement through a succession of different job and illustrated several negative experiences. For example, Ian (an 18 year old white male) ultimately left his grocery store job in part because he felt he was being taken advantage of:

> They think they can take advantage of younger people ... I think that they think that they can boss you around more, and get you to do all the dirty work ... Like the produce manager would always get the young kids to do the crappy jobs ... And I think if I messed up, they'd give you a lot of shit and if one of the older people messed up it's just like a mistake.

Similarly, Kami (an 18 year old white female) left her restaurant job after only three months:

> They were crazy. They expected a lot out of me, from a Grade 9, just starting high school ... I wanted to quit for the longest time and when I would talk to my managers about it they would just say 'well you can't quit until you get

somebody else to replace you' ... Like they just kept putting me on the schedule
and I mean you tell them, you can't work right and they just didn't listen so
finally I had to move on ... It was ridiculous.

For Kami, the combination of a lack of flexibility in scheduling shifts, the high
demands of the job, the expectation that she could only quit if she found her own
replacement, and the poor management of the restaurant (generally by people not
much older than herself) left Kami with little choice but to quit her job.

Therefore, while the abundance of options in Fort McMurray for part-time work
allowed high schoolers to move to jobs with more desirable working conditions,
high schoolers (as well as key informants) suggested that some businesses in Fort
McMurray had responded to the labour shortage by attempting to take advantage
of young people's inexperience. Further, some businesses provided little in terms
of helping high schoolers to gain skills from their jobs. As Jack (a 19 year old
Aboriginal male) explained about his grocery store job:

Like on my first day of work, they showed me what everything was and how
to do some things and then my supervisor was like 'okay, we're going to go so
you can just close up by yourself'. And I was like 'alright', so I just like kind
of stood around and just cleaned things and just made it seem like I was doing
something, go on breaks, and I don't know, it was funny ... [It was like] 'alright,
we're going, the new guy, just leave him to do all the work or something. Have
like the day off, cause he doesn't really know what's going on'.

This seems like a counterproductive business strategy in light of the high turnover
rates of workers in the city and the fact that high schoolers were more likely to stay
at jobs that were more accommodating to their needs.

The inadequate job training provided to high schoolers also raises concerns
about the risks that high schoolers were exposed to at their part-time jobs. While
the high schoolers I spoke with did experience several on-the-job risks, the
prevalence of job opportunities in Fort McMurray also offered them a certain level
of protection against these risks in that they could easily move to another less risky
job. For example, David (a 17 year old white male) stated:

I went from [one workplace] which was smoking, but you could still work there,
right? And I told him [the owner], I said I'm sorry but I'm going to have to
quit. I can't be around this smoke anymore. I thought I could but I can't. So I
went on to [another workplace] which paid me less ... [because] I like the work
environment.

Similarly, Jack left his restaurant job because of the harsh work environment:

Their fans, they didn't work that good. And when the inspectors came in, they
said that the fans need to be replaced, so [the restaurant] closed for a week or

something because it was so smoky in there sometimes. Like when they made burgers ... the smoke would burn your eyes in the middle of the rush, so you can't really just go wash out your eyes or go get air because it's super busy.

The choice to leave risky employment is not always afforded most young people in service type employment (Lowe and Krahn 1999).

The availability of job choices in Fort McMurray also raises concerns that high schoolers simply avoided workplace conflicts by moving to another job rather than acquiring skills to resolve these conflicts. For example:

> In Grade 10 I got a job at [workplace name] because my sister worked there and she got me a job and then my best friend wanted me to come work with him. So I quit there and went over to [another workplace]. I left there because me and my friend had issues, so I stopped working with him ... So I left there and then I went over to [another workplace] ... I did that, and then I quit there because I did what I was supposed to, I went on my break and I told the person at the counter, but they said I never told anybody. I didn't bother arguing with people, I just wanted to get fired anyways cause I didn't like that job. It was really boring ... Then after that, like the same day I got fired from there I went over and applied at [another workplace], and I was a cashier there. (John Doe, 18 year old white male)

If high schoolers do not learn the skills to resolve workplace conflicts, this could potentially have serious repercussions on their future work experiences especially within a non-boomtown context (for instance if high schoolers moved to a non-boomtown city or if the availability of job options diminished in Fort McMurray).

Concerns over young people being exposed to 'unrealistic' work environments growing up in Fort McMurray and the potential repercussions of this (for example young people acquiring a poor work ethic) were highlighted by many of the key informants. However, while key informants expressed concerns that young people might be acquiring a poor work ethic, they overlooked young people's ability to exercise agency (that is, leave risky jobs) within a boomtown labour market. High schoolers moving from job to job, rather than being viewed as only negative (for example not learning to effectively deal with workplace conflict), could also be interpreted positively as high schoolers avoiding risky workplaces and protesting poor treatment by employers. It appears that part of high schoolers' job transience can be attributed to some employers in Fort McMurray failing to adjust to boomtown realities where the sheer number of jobs puts employers at a slight disadvantage.

Gender and Service Jobs

In recent decades, traditionally 'masculine' manufacturing jobs have declined substantially in number while traditionally 'feminine' service type jobs have expanded in developed economies. This has meant that men entering the workforce must now find ways to navigate what has traditionally been considered a feminine domain (Brandth and Haugen 2005, Mac an Ghaill and Haywood 2007). While traditionally masculine jobs were abundant for post-high school graduates in Fort McMurray, it was mostly service type jobs that tended to be available for the high schoolers. How young men and women spoke about their part-time jobs clearly reflected gendered understandings.

For the young men, interacting with customers (which is considered a traditionally feminine quality) for their part-time jobs was often described as challenging. For example, when Ted (a 17 year old white male) was asked about some of the bad things about his job he replied: 'It's like really people orientated ... I don't know if you know this, but in this town, it's really fast pace ... And some things take time. Like to look up [customer orders], it takes time. So people around here don't realize that, right?' Similarly, Kirk, the 18 year old Aboriginal male whose comments were discussed earlier in the chapter, stated: 'I'm not too good with like people, like complaining about food ... We already tried that and it didn't turn out too well'.

While the young men downplayed the 'feminine' aspects of their part-time work and described these as negative, they at the same time emphasized stereotypically masculine qualities when describing the good aspects of their jobs. For example, David emphasized the 'great pay' and the ability to take on new responsibilities at work while Ian suggested that he had found a way to make money without really doing much work: 'It was really slack, like there wasn't much to be done ... I was getting paid to just kind of go hang out at [the grocery store]'. It appears that the young men attempted to construct a masculine self within what is considered a stereotypically feminine domain. Similarly, McDowell (2002) found that young men in service jobs often placed importance on traditionally masculine qualities when describing their work.

Alternatively, young women often considered interacting with customers a positive aspect of their jobs. For example, when Natalie (a 17 year old white female) was asked to describe some of the good things about her retail job she stated: 'I liked talking to people'. Similarly, Cate (an 18 year old white female) stated 'I like it ... I get to interact with the public'. The young women I spoke with described building relationships with people as a positive experience. For example, Kami stated:

> You build up so many relationships. You meet people and it's just ironic kind of how, with everyone coming in [to the city], like you know how busy it is in town, you meet so many people that like, when you hear of your friend talking about so and so, you can make a connection to them through work.

Further, even though Karen, the 18 year old white female whose comments were discussed earlier in the chapter, had bad experiences with customers, she considered it a learning experience:

I've had bad experiences where I'm like in a bad mood so I don't care about the customers but then, like that doesn't help the situation at all ... Like that I've learnt, like you really have to like put that, whatever's going on with you outside and just like focus on the customer and what they need because they're like actually paying for your paycheque.

It appears as though young women embraced the 'feminine' qualities of their service jobs and utilized these to help construct a feminine self.

Conclusions

Examining the high schoolers' accounts has illuminated how young people experience work in the booming labour market of Fort McMurray. It seems that having ties to this context affords young people certain advantages over most young people in developed countries. For example, unlike most young people (Loughlin and Barling 1999, Lowe and Krahn 1999), young people with ties to Fort McMurray had job choice and were provided generous incomes. However, while the job choice that had opened up in Fort McMurray on account of the labour shortage provided many unique opportunities to young people that isolated them from certain risks (for instance unemployment, low incomes), it at the same time exposed them to other risks (such as, risky work environments, long work days, making large amounts of money). High schoolers' employment in Fort McMurray also lacked quality in that their jobs provided them with few tangible skills and little training. In addition, one particularly interesting finding is the apparent heightened awareness exhibited by young women when it came to describing their work experiences in Fort McMurray. This may be partly explained by young women having to navigate a 'masculine' city with an emphasis on 'masculine' jobs (that is, jobs in the trades). It is possible that young women's almost 'outsider' status in the city has enhanced their awareness.

Given these findings, it is important that youth researchers pay more attention to different local contexts. Overly general statements concerning 'choice' and the 'epistemological fallacy of late modernity' require more nuance and need to pay more attention to local labour market conditions where young people's work understandings and experiences coalesce. This chapter has only illustrated the context of the boomtown of Fort McMurray but there are many diverse contexts that need to be more fully explored and compared to economically prosperous environments. For example, the immediate places that come to mind are the cities of Hamilton and Windsor, Ontario, Canada where the collapse of manufacturing in the region has led to a sharp decline in jobs. A comparison of young people's understandings in different contexts would provide additional insights into how the local context intersects with young people's understandings of, and experiences with, work.

In summary, the findings from this chapter illustrate that while high schoolers in a boomtown environment share some similar work experiences to their non-boomtown counterparts, there are also many unique aspects. While there were benefits for high schoolers, there were also risks. In one of the few articles to examine young people in a boomtown environment, Freudenburg (1984) found that in comparison to adults, young people bore many of the negative consequences of boomtown living. Therefore, boomtowns must be extra vigilant in ensuring that prosperity is not created at the expense of young people's education and/or from their inexperience in the labour market.

Acknowledgements

I would like to thank Gillian Ranson, Harvey Krahn, Tom Langford, and Amy Egan for helpful suggestions throughout this research project. I would also like to thank the participants for taking the time to speak with me. This research project was also made possible through a Doctoral Fellowship provided by the Social Sciences and Humanities Research Council of Canada and through funding support from the University of Calgary.

References

Alberta Employment and Immigration 2008. *Alberta Minimum Wage Profile: April 2007–March 2008* [Online]. Available at: http://employment.alberta.ca/documents/LMI/ LMI-WSI_ minwageprofile.pdf [accessed: 24 March 2009].

Andres, L. and Adamuti-Trache, M. 2008. Life-course transitions, social class, and gender: A 15 year perspective of the lived lives of Canadian young adults. *Journal of Youth Studies*, 11(2), 115–45.

Arnett, J. 2004. *Emerging Adulthood: The Winding Road From the Late Teens Through the Twenties*. New York: Oxford University Press.

Beck, U. 2000. *The Brave New World of Work*. Cambridge: Polity Press.

Brandth, B. and Haugen, M. S. 2005. Doing rural masculinity: From logging to outfield tourism. *Journal of Gender Studies*, 14(1), 13–22.

Brannen, J. and Nilsen, A. 2005. Individualisation, choice and structure: A discussion of current trends in sociological analysis. *The Sociological Review*, 53(3), 412–28.

Breslin, F. C., Polzer, J., MacEachen, E., Morrongiello, B., and Shannon, H. 2007. Workplace injury or 'part of the job'?: Towards a gendered understanding of injuries and complaints among young workers. *Social Science & Medicine*, 64(4), 782–93.

Bynner, J. 2005. Rethinking the youth phase of the life-course: The case of emerging adulthood? *Journal of Youth Studies*, 8(4), 367–84.

Canadian Centre for Energy Information 2006. *Canada's Oilsands*. Calgary: Canadian Centre for Energy Information.

Connell, R. 1993. The big picture: Masculinities in recent world history. *Theory and Society*, 22(5), 597–623.

Creswell, J. 2003. *Research Design: Qualitative, Quantitative, and Mixed Methods Approaches*. Thousand Oaks: Sage.

Entwisle, D., Alexander, K. and Steffel Olson, L. 2000. Early work histories of urban youth. *American Sociological Review*, 65(2), 279–97.

Flakstad, N. 2006. Black earth boom. *Canadian Consulting Engineering*, 47(1), 28–37.

Freudenburg, W. 1984. Boomtown's youth: The differential impacts of rapid community growth on adolescents and adults. *American Sociological Review*, 49(5), 697–705.

Frone, M. 1999. Developmental consequences of youth employment, in *Young Workers: Varieties of Experience*, edited by J. Barling and E. K. Kelloway. Washington: American Psychological Association, 89–128.

Furlong, A. and Cartmel, F. 1997. *Young People and Social Change: Individualization and Risk in Late Modernity*. Philadelphia: Open University Press.

Government of Alberta 2008. *Fort McMurray–Alberta: Labour Market Information* [Online]. Available at: http://www.woodbuffalo.net/linksFACTSPop.html [accessed: 30 January 2008].

Harding, K. 2006. Alberta's boom enticing students to drop out. *The Globe and Mail*, 25 September, A1 and A7.

Hiller, H. 2009. *Second Promised Land: Migration to Alberta and the Transformation of Canadian Society*. Montreal: McGill-Queen's University Press.

Hodkinson, P. and Sparkes, A. C. 1997. Careership: A sociological theory of career decision making. *British Journal of Sociology of Education*, 18(1), 29–44.

Lee, J. and Staff, J. 2007. When work matters: The varying impact of work intensity on high school dropout. *Sociology of Education*, 80(2), 158–78.

Lehmann, W. 2004. 'For some reason, I get a little scared': Structure, agency, and risk in school-work transitions. *Journal of Youth Studies*, 7(4), 379–96.

Loughlin, C. and Barling, J. 1999. The nature of youth employment, in *Young Workers:Varieties of Experience*, edited by J. Barling and E. K. Kelloway. Washington: American Psychological Association, 17–36.

Lowe, G. and Krahn, H. 1999. Reconceptualizing youth unemployment, in *Young Workers: Varieties of Experience*, edited by J. Barling and E. K. Kelloway. Washington: American Psychological Association, 201–34.

Mac an Ghaill, M. and Haywood, C. 2007. *Gender, Culture and Society: Contemporary Femininities and Masculinities*. New York: Palgrave MacMillan.

Mason, J. 1996. *Qualitative Researching*. Thousand Oaks: Sage Publications.

McDowell, L. 2002. Transitions to work: Masculine identities, youth inequality and labour market change. *Gender, Place and Culture*, 9(1), 39–59.

Mortimer, J., Harley, C., and Staff, J. 2002. The quality of work and youth mental health. *Work and Occupations*, 29(2), 166–97.

Mythen, G. 2005. Employment, individualization and insecurity: Rethinking the risk society perspective. *The Sociological Review*, 53(1), 129–49.

National Energy Board 2010. *Canada's Oil Sands: Opportunities and Challenges to 2015* [Online]. Available at: http://www.neb.gc.ca/clf-nsi/rnrgynfmtn/nrgyrprt/lsnd/ pprtntsndchllngs20152004/qapprtntsndchllngs20152004-eng.html [accessed: 26 May 2010].

Paechter, C. 2003. Masculinities and femininities as communities of practice. *Women's Studies International Forum*, 26(1), 69–77.

Seidman, I. 1991. *Interviewing as Qualitative Research: A Guide for Researchers in Education and the Social Sciences*. New York: Teachers College Press.

Staff, J. and Mortimer, J. 2007. Educational and work strategies from adolescence to early adulthood: Consequences for educational attainment. *Social Forces*, 85(3), 1169–94.

Thorne, B. 1993. *Gender Play – Girls and Boys in School*. New Jersey: Rutgers University Press.

Warren, J. and Cataldi, E. 2006. A historical perspective on high school students' paid employment and its association with high school dropout. *Sociological Forum*, 21(1), 113–43.

Chapter 3

The Working Experiences of Student Migrants in Australia and New Zealand

Danaë Anderson, Ryan Lamare and Zeenobiyah Hannif

Indicative of developments worldwide and consistent with Organisation for Economic Co-operation and Development (OECD) trends (2009), precarious employment has become increasingly commonplace (TUC Commission on Vulnerable Employment 2008, Brosnan and Walsh 1998, Nossar, Johnstone and Quinlan 2003, Quinlan and Mayhew 2001). Migrant workers are over-represented in such employment (see Australian Bureau of Statistics 2010a, 2010b, Statistics New Zealand 2010), and the growing concern surrounding these workers is reflected in the increasing volume of literature on the subject (see Benach and Muntaner 2007, Bohle et al. 2004, Dörre, Kraemer and Speidel 2006, Department of Trade and Industry 2006).

While there is extensive research addressing migrant workers, international students have scarcely made an appearance in labour-studies literature and the student migrant is typically not characterized as emblematic of a vulnerable worker (ILO 2010, Pollert and Charlwood 2009). However, in deregulated labour markets, with jobs characterized by low wages, insecurity and unclear employment relations legislation (Haque 2002, Sargeant 2009, May et al. 2006, Standing 1997), potential for exposure to unsafe and illegal work practices for this group may be multiplied.

This chapter redefines and broadens the definition of *vulnerable worker* to argue that migrant students might rightfully be included in this group because they are frequently compelled to accept extremely poor conditions of employment. Discussion begins with the background of student migration in an Australian and New Zealand context, followed by an examination of the definitional issues inherent in researching vulnerable work. Finally, the initial findings of an exploratory study will be presented, along with discussion of potential implications for the labour market.

Student Migration to Australia and New Zealand

Financial, cultural, and educational exchange in a 'shrinking world' (Infometrics NRB and Skinnerstrategic 2008: 12) has meant nearly three million tertiary students worldwide pursue opportunities in formal education outside their own countries

(Binning 2010). In an era of knowledge as a commodity to be traded (Kritz 2006), export education industries are of paramount importance to Australia and New Zealand, ranking fourth and fifth in exports respectively (Yuile 2010, Stevens 2010). The Institute of International Education's (2008, cited in Austrade 2010) data on international student mobility notes Australia ranks fifth for the number of international students, and is the third most popular English-speaking destination behind the United States (US) and the United Kingdom (UK). In the 2009–2010 year student migrants in Australia numbered 585,000 (or 3.9 per cent of the total labour force). Export education contributes an even greater share of GDP in New Zealand than Australia – 1.13 per cent compared to 1.06 per cent (Crawford 2009), numbering 73,000 or 2.13 per cent of total labour force (Infometrics, NRB and Skinnerstrategic 2008, Australian Government Department of Immigration and Citizenship 2010b, Statistics NZ 2010). In addition to geographic proximity, Australia and New Zealand are widely perceived to be 'safe countries that provide a studious environment' (Mazzoral et al. 2001).

Legislation governing migration and conditions of work for migrant students are similar in Australia and New Zealand, due in part to the Closer Economic Relations (CER) Agreement legislating greater policy alignment between the countries (Ministry of Foreign Affairs and Trade 1983). Consequently, both countries share similar migrant entry categories: primarily for professional migrants, business entry, educational purposes or seasonal work (see Benson-Rea, Haworth and Rawlinson 1998, Australian Government Department of Immigration and Citizenship 2010b). In both countries student migrants are limited by their visa conditions to working a maximum of 20 hours per week during the academic year. This caveat assumes that students will have alternative means of financial support and that work in the host country will be an additional means of income.

With the internationalization of education (Kritz 2006, Edwards and Edwards 2001), student migration can be considered part of a global movement of people and is often argued to be the precursor of highly skilled migration (Skeldon 1992). Further, educational migration is seen as a legitimate response to skill shortages and an ageing workforce, and offers economic benefits (Bexley et al. 2007, Chen and Madamba 2000, Department of Labour 2006, Glover et al. 2001). The positive impact of work may be experienced in terms of practical experience, socialization, improved language skills and the opportunity for improved 'life chances'. For the host country, migration can address skills shortages, provide financial investment and enhance diversity. However, the relationship between the Australian and New Zealand export education industries is a balancing act between competition and cooperation; where students will often choose between studying in Australia or New Zealand as opposed to Europe or the US. Nevertheless, Australia's economy and labour market are much larger and in 'economic terms it is a more attractive destination for immigrants, legal or illicit' (Talcott 2000: 5).

While immigration policies of both countries aim to 'attract and retain international students' (Merwood 2007: 6), the path to permanent residency has become increasingly restricted, where entry categories and requirements are more limited than previously. Nonetheless, while visa limitations regulate those who work legally, anecdotal and documented evidence from both countries points to illegal work trends, primarily through the violation of hours' restrictions.

The Student Migrant Worker: Definitions and Contradictions

While little is known about the working experiences of student migrant workers, they are nonetheless emblematic of internal and external diaspora of labour and the increased interdependence between countries in terms of the exchange of labour (Cerny, Menz and Soederberg 2005). There is evidence, however, that the fragmentation of employment relationships and the declining rate of trade union membership and collective action has eroded worker protection, particularly for vulnerable workers. Low pay, lack of representation or bargaining power, and precarious working conditions (Funkhouser 2008, Pollert and Charlwood 2009, TUC Commission on Vulnerable Employment 2008) typify the areas of employment where migrant workers are concentrated. Precarious employment is defined by Cranford, Vosko and Zukewich (2003: 3) as 'all forms of employment that involve atypical contracts, limited social benefits and statutory entitlements, job insecurity, low earnings, poor working conditions and high risks of ill health'. Research shows that the employment of migrant labour is widespread in industries where non-standard, precarious employment is the norm (see Dyer, McDowell and Batnitzky 2008, Goldring, Berenstein and Bernhard 2009, OECD 2009). Other causes of vulnerability include an individual's sectoral occupation (such as retail and service), the absence of human resources departments and non-unionism (Department of Trade and Industry 2006: 6). In addition, as student migrants are primarily young they tend to have less power in the employment relationship and are more likely to tolerate flexibility and unpredictability in their working lives (Cellier, Eyrolle and Bertrand 1995, Ehrlich et al. 2004). The International Labour Organisation (ILO) (2009b) estimates the informal sector accounts for the majority of all jobs available to young people, cognisant that wages in the informal sector are lower than the formal economy and protection and benefits are minimal. Hence, for many student migrants, the potential for poor working conditions and/ or exploitation is multiplied by the dual factors of migration and youth (Smith and Wilson 2002, Anderson 2008).

While there is an acknowledgement by some of the actual or potential vulnerability of migrant student workers, they may also be seen to experience some relative privilege in terms of education and opportunity. As student migrants have access to not-inconsiderable amounts of investment to fund their studies and lifestyle, questions also arise as to the extent to which their working characteristics are typical of migrants as a whole? While quantitative research suggests generally poor labour market outcomes for migrants (Bauder 2006, Bennett 1993, Garson 1999), little is known about whether student migrants conform to these generalizations, particularly in Australia and New Zealand. Rather, the extant

literature tends to focus on quantifying the proportion of students employed
and related financial imperatives (Bexley et al. 2007), and the effect of their
employment on academic results and wellbeing (Manthei and Gilmore 2005,
Merwood 2007, Riggert et al. 2006, Zimmer-Gembeck and Mortimer 2006).

While there is a general perception that many of the students coming to
Australia and New Zealand to study are wealthy, this is often not the case. Some
may have their families financially supporting them, but the support may be seen as
an investment, to be 'paid back' in the future. Many will be the first in their family
to attend a tertiary institution and so may have considerable familial expectations
in addition to financial pressures. Butcher and McGrath (2004) state many need
to accept low standard accommodation and to work to support themselves, where
'Stories of incredible sacrifice by family to fund a son or (more rarely) a daughter
were much more the norm than conspicuous consumption by affluent students'
(Rodan 2009: 3). Although financial requirements for student migration are around
AUD$18,000 per year in Australia and NZ$10,000 per year or NZ$1,000 for each
month of stay in New Zealand, evidence of funds is not regulated, so available
data may not accurately represent evidence of actual means of financial support
(Australian Government Department of Immigration and Citizenship 2010a,
Immigration New Zealand 2010).

Methods

During earlier research (Anderson 2010b, Naidu 2011), while not explicitly
seeking to focus on student migrant workers, concerning issues regarding this
group were identified. There are inherent difficulties associated with researching
migrant labour, such as problems locating research participants who are willing to
be forthcoming about their experiences for fear of illegal work being revealed and
language or cultural differences which affect comprehension. Further, definitional
inconsistencies are inherent in attempting to gather data of this kind (Marginson et
al. 2005, Boocock et al. 2010, Benach and Muntaner 2007).

During the exploratory research, 74 surveys were collected, followed by ten
semi-structured interviews which explored the survey themes in greater detail.
Survey questions were designed to explore typical working experiences, focusing
on types of work, wages, hours worked, working conditions, health and safety
and union membership. The interviews reflected multiple 'realities', while
acknowledging differences between individuals (Patton 2002). Transcripts and
notes were then analysed for common themes relating to international students'
working experiences (Miles and Huberman 2003). The small sample size is not
intended to be generalizable, although patterns were found that were consistent
with other research findings (Sargeant and Tucker 2009, Neill et al. 2004, McLaren
et al. 2004). While the research presented in this chapter presents exploratory New
Zealand findings, they are compared to existing Australian research by Nyland and

colleagues (2008) who conducted interviews with 200 higher education students across nine Australian universities.

Survey respondents were all university students, while interviewees were derived from students attending universities and private training institutes. The gender breakdown was 43.2 per cent female and 58.6 per cent male. Ethnicity was varied, with Asians reflecting the majority of the sample (85.1 per cent). Of that group, 27 identified as Chinese, 37 as Indian, and the remainder as Malaysian, Japanese and Vietnamese. Eleven of the participants were European, including Russian (4), German (2) and French (2). Africans numbered three. All were aged between 18 and 25 years, consistent with our definition of 'youth' and the dominant age group for migration for tertiary education (Kritz 2006, International Labour Office 2009).

Research Findings and Discussion

Survey findings indicate workers on overseas student visas provide a supplementary source of labour. That is not to say all student migrants are inherently vulnerable, rather that the characteristics of the work they engage in may make them so. Indicators of vulnerability were identified, namely working hours in excess of visa conditions, rates of pay below legal minima, and insecurity of work, either through a lack of protection or the type of work performed.

Types of Work

While the work engaged in was varied, over half the workers (42 or 56.8 per cent) were concentrated in the hospitality and service sectors, while a small but significant number were employed in the agriculture sector (12 or 16.2 per cent). Typical of vulnerable workers, they were engaged in peripheral positions within the agriculture, construction and service sectors (see Table 3.1). Such work has been found to be associated with poor and/or illegal working conditions (Shelley 2007, Pai 2008, Minto 2009). Interviews indicated many new student migrants quickly obtain jobs through 'word of mouth' within their ethnic communities, assuming positions in low-skilled manual labour. Often positions are organized through networks soon after arrival and migrant students are commonly pressured to take jobs not wanted by local workers. This reflects the 'redistribution' of work in local economies due to the willingness of migrant workers to work in substandard conditions and for lower wages.

Table 3.1   Types of work

Job category	Types of work
Manual labour	labourer, tiling, maintenance for a hire firm, light labouring, bulldozer operator, house painter
Agriculture/ horticulture	tomato packing, hothouse work, agricultural production, stable hand, milking cows, strawberry picking, fruit picking
Administration	receptionist, office administration, data entry
Retail	gift shop, clothing, checkout operator, fast food, cashier
Hospitality	bar waitress, bartender, pub work, translator, receptionist, delivery driver, dishwasher, waiting tables
Other	cleaning, paper round, factory work, housecleaning, computer repairs, car groomer, busboy, shelf stacker

Wages

Survey respondents were asked how much they were paid, and 28 out of 74 (37.8 per cent) respondents had been paid below the statutory minima in New Zealand (at the time, NZ$12.50 per hour). This is a sizeable proportion, meaning almost four in ten workers were being paid illegally and many were also paid 'cash in the hand'. An example was a Chinese female student, 18 years of age who was enrolled at university and working at a discount store: 'I couldn't find anything. I know the (minimum) wage is more than $10 [$12.50] but [I] am lucky to work. Most of my friends can't find anything – so $7.00 is ok'.

Particularly low pay rates were widespread in agriculture and horticulture, where almost all workers (21 out of 23 or 91.3 per cent) were paid illegally (75 per cent of all workers reported illegal pay rates). This finding is consistent with Ross and Rasmussen's (2009: 96) contention that 'migrant workers are found working in horticulture "under the table" for as little as $6 an hour (less than half the statutory wage)'. The finding is also consistent with Nyland et al.'s (2008) Australian research, which reported low and illegal pay rates. In this study, 58.1 per cent of students surveyed were paid below AUD$15 an hour, with 33.9 per cent receiving less than AUD$10 an hour, and where the federal rate was AUD$13.74 (The Australian Fair Pay Commission 2008: 21).

This undercutting of statutory minima is particularly concerning in the current recessionary climate although it is obvious that Australian and New Zealand labour markets rely on migrants: both the legal and illegal variety (see Bauder 2006, Department of Labour 2009). As well as illegal pay rates, there are implications for tax revenue and national medical insurance schemes: Medicare in Australia and Accident Compensation Corporation (ACC) in New Zealand. Of note is that in both studies more than a third of respondents had been paid less than the minimum wage, suggesting that this practice is widespread rather than an isolated incident for student migrant workers.

Hours of Work

While the majority of respondents worked between 15–20 hours per week (42 or 56.8 per cent), the second largest proportion indicated that they worked over 20 hours (28 or 37.8 per cent). Of that group, eight admitted to working full-time (40 hours or more), in clear violation of visa conditions. Of particular concern were those who were 'on call' and working on a casual basis, leading to precarious conditions and reduced protection in the labour market (28 or 37.8 per cent). Such conditions are not illegal, but in the current economic climate, with a lack of jobs *in general,* the employment environment for migrant workers appears to have worsened (Wu, Sheehan and Guo 2010, ILO 2010). Often migrants work longer and more unsociable hours than many non-migrant, full-time workers in standard employment (Loh and Richardson 2004, Quinlan and Mayhew 2001). Students may also work in excess of their visa conditions due to financial imperatives such as repayment of educational loans, as well as finding the cost of living in the host country higher than anticipated, compelling them to take jobs 'off the books' with no employment relations protection. Examples of these responses were the following:

> It's expensive to live … more than they said. So sometimes I miss class, for
> extra money. I don't like it [the job], but I need to work. (Chinese male training
> institute student, 22 years, liquor store manager without a manager's license)

> It's [the job] not so bad. Too much travel – but they pay for that. Sometimes
> it is hard to fit in study, but I need a job. They want me more hours [than I am
> allowed]. And they are not nice to me. Boring? Yes, but I have a job. (Korean
> male university student, 24 years, horticultural worker)

> Good to earn some money, but late nights, long hours. It is hard to get home [at
> that time]. And I can't get time off when I need, only when he wants. There is no
> minimum working hours – makes it difficult when there is no work. (Malaysian
> female student, 20 years, waitress)

These findings are consistent with previous research suggesting many migrants work far in excess of stipulated hours (for example, Boocock et al. 2010, Chen and Madamba 2000, Green et al. 2007). Results should however be framed within McInnis and Hartley's (2002) research indicating international students are often unwilling to admit to working more than 20 hours per week because in Australia and New Zealand, this can lead to the mandatory withdrawal of visas. Hence, speculatively, these findings about excess working hours and substandard working conditions are likely to be conservatively reported.

Indications are that long hours compromise the student's attendance and performance at their tertiary institution. The adverse effects of working while studying were highlighted by McDonald et al. (2007) in Australia, while research by Neill et al. (2004: 136) identifies 15 hours of work as a point beyond which 'there may be a detrimental effect on academic performance'. Furthermore, health and safety implications of this work are signposted as being poor. This theme is discussed in the following section.

Health and Safety

Growing evidence indicates migrant workers are frequently exposed to hazardous work conditions, and have higher rates of injury and illness compared to non-migrant workers in standard employment (Sergeant and Tucker 2009, McKay et al. 2006). In addition, workers employed in informal work arrangements also have an above-average level of injury and illness, and report higher levels of work-related stress compared with workers employed in more formal working arrangements within the primary labour market (Quinlan and Mayhew 2001, Virtanen et al. 2005). As a result, there is acknowledged difficulty in accurately measuring the wellbeing of all migrant workers as government databases rarely capture the working experiences, occupational injury, fatalities and compensation claims of precariously-employed workers (Boocock et al. 2010).

Student migrants were asked whether they felt safe in their workplaces, and why this was or was not the case. Of the 74 surveys, five chose not to respond, while 46 (62.2 per cent) answered they did feel safe. However, a number answered with qualifiers such as 'But I get left alone at night', 'Drunk men make me feel nervous', or 'I know some of what I do is not my job and I shouldn't [be performing the tasks], but that's ok'. The remainder (23 or 31.1 per cent) answered they felt unsafe in the course of their work and had experienced unsafe work practices:

> Often I don't feel safe ... Late nights and by myself. I worry ... hope they [the customers] are not shoplifting. My English is not good to tell them no. (Chinese female training institute student, 19 years, retail worker in a gift shop)

> I got the job from a guy I met here, he knew the family. Everyone is Indian, they know we work hard. The job is bad, but I have a loan, and if I stay I need [work] experience'. They [the owners] are not friendly – if you ask for anything they let you go. So I just do my job. (Indian female university student, 19 years, dishwasher at an Indian restaurant)

> Language difficulties you know. Sometimes it hard to understand what they [bosses] are saying. Cleaning job is so hard, and it makes a lot of physical problems. (Vietnamese male student, 24 years, cleaner in a hotel)

Around 10 per cent of the sample also mentioned having an accident at work. For example:

I have been injured, mainly cuts and grazes. I did fall badly once but I kept working. [If you are] absent you know, they don't like you, see you are [sic] lazy, maybe not keep you working. (Vietnamese male student, 22 years, manufacturing worker in a factory)

Such workplace disparities have very real implications not only for health and safety, but also wider labour market outcomes, domestically and internationally. Poor working conditions signal an inability of vulnerable workers to enforce contract or statutory rights. The commodification of workers occurs where local workers' wages are cut because migrant workers lack legal work rights and will accept worse conditions.

A Role for Unions?

McDonald et al. (2007) note that student workers are vulnerable to employer exploitation because of their limited work skills, high unemployment and underemployment, and poor knowledge of their rights. At the interviewing stage participants were asked about their knowledge of employment rights and obligations. All ten respondents had limited or incorrect knowledge; while some had been threatened that if they questioned their pay rates and working hours that they would be reported to immigration. No respondents belonged to a union. Grünell and van het Kaar (2003) argue that immigrants are more likely to work in low-skilled jobs in the services sector and in smaller firms in the retail and construction sectors, consequently magnifying the disadvantage associated with low levels of unionization. When work is illegal, it becomes even more difficult for workers to organize for better conditions and for unions there is a conflict in their role. That is, where race is seen as a political issue and a primary union goal is to protect local jobs, often at the expense of migrant workers, this contradiction may mitigate against union involvement in organizing in the secondary labour market, where migrants are known to congregate and poor and dangerous work practices proliferate.

Conclusions

The increasing movement of people for work and educational opportunities to Australia and New Zealand is indicative of global trends. Historically, there has been considerable interest in the poor working conditions experienced by migrant workers, arising against the backdrop of broader debates surrounding precarious work and definitions of worker vulnerability. Nevertheless, little concern has been raised regarding the working lives and experience of *student* migrants. Rather, research to date has primarily concentrated on either the working experiences of migrants or the educational experiences of international students, rather than examining the working experiences of international students who are an important sector of the migrant workforce.

While these trends may be considered typical of the impact of the increasing migrant workforce (see Dyer, McDowell and Batnitzky 2003, Loh and Richardson 2004, Bennett 1993) they signal a negative impact for the student migrants, where participation in undocumented, precarious work has implications for the worker's ability to remain in the country and pursue career opportunities post-study. Many student migrants undertake courses with the hope of entering gainful employment and/or permanent residency in their host countries (see Anderson and Naidu 2009, Department of Labour 2006, Glover et al. 2001, Nyland et al. 2008). Almost a quarter of international students choose to study in Australia with the aim of becoming permanent residents (Harrison 2010). Indeed, by 2007, two thirds of skilled migrants were former international students rather than offshore recruitments; a 'two-step migration' (Hawthorne 2010). However a 2010 policy change dictates that international students who apply for residency must have gained relevant work experience in Australia (Koleth 2010); the same requirement as for New Zealand (Immigration New Zealand 2010). Further, the Department of Labour's 2008 report indicated that 73 per cent of students surveyed did not transition to work or residence, and most had left New Zealand within five years of getting their first student visas. A counter argument would be that they are able to pursue work opportunities overseas. The longer term gain for many of these migrants, however, is questionable at best.

The apparent lack of interest from policymakers and enforcement agencies in protecting this vulnerable group is often supported by a choice argument: that is, student migrants choose to come here so *their* situation is of *their* own making. Anderson (2008: 2) suggests a dominant paradigm is that of 'good' and 'bad' migrants, dividing these workers into either the hard-working foreigner necessary for the economy, or a thief of jobs and opportunity. Nonetheless, student migrants may be representative of both groups; that is, 'good' in that they bring diversity, potential labour and internal investment, yet 'bad' when 'taking' jobs from residents, while accepting (in some cases, drastically) lower wages and conditions.

In summary, the exploratory research findings revealed here show that international students' working experiences are typical of migrant workers as they are often located in contingent and precarious employment, working long hours in unsafe conditions for low wages. Additionally, student migrants may experience workplace marginalization on multiple levels, where the working conditions they routinely labour under add little to their prospects of securing permanent residency or work relating to their studies. While these working conditions may be illegal, little government impetus for monitoring or enforcement is evident, and to date unions in both countries have not taken a leading role in protecting these workers. While this research has an Australasian focus, these findings have a wide-ranging impact on harnessing the benefits of migration to build high-performance workforces, but also for the student migrant workers whose working lives are dominated by substandard working conditions with little opportunity for progression.

References

Anderson, B. 2008. Illegal immigrant: Victim or villain? Working Paper 64. Oxford: ESRC Centre on Migration, Policy and Society, University of Oxford.

Anderson, B. 2010a. Migration, immigration controls and the fashioning of precarious workers. *Work, Employment and Society*, 24(2), 300–19.

Anderson, D. 2010b. *Safe Enough? The Working Experiences of New Zealand Children.* MPhil Thesis. Auckland: Auckland University of Technology.

Anderson, D. and Naidu, K. 2009. *The Land of Milk and Honey? The Contemporary Working Lives of Contingent Youth Labour in New Zealand.* Paper presented at 90 Years of the ILO Conference. Auckland: New Zealand Work and Labour Market Institute.

Austrade 2010. *Education and Training.* Available at: http://www.austrade.gov.au/Home/Education-and-Training/default.aspx [accessed: 12 July 2010].

Australian Bureau of Statistics 2010a. *Labour Force, Australia, July 2010.* Catalogue 6202.0, Canberra, Australian Bureau of Statistics.

Australian Bureau of Statistics 2010b. *Employee Earnings, Benefits and Trade Union Membership Australia.* Catalogue 6310.0, Canberra: Australian Bureau of Statistics

Australian Government Department of Immigration and Citizenship 2010a. *Student Visa Living Costs and Evidence of Funds.* Available at: http://www.immi.gov.au/students/_pdf/student- living- costs.pdf [accessed: 22 July 2010].

Australian Government Department of Immigration and Citizenship 2010b. *Migration categories.* Available at: http://www.immi.gov.au/living-in-australia/choose-australia/regional-life/visas.htm [accessed: 22 July 2010].

Bauder, H. 2006. *Labor Movement: How Migration Regulates Labor Markets.* Oxford: Oxford University Press.

Benach, J. and Muntaner, C. 2007. Precarious employment and health: Developing a research agenda. *Journal of Epidemiology and Community Health*, 61(4), 276–7.

Bennett, S. 1993. Inequalities in risk factors and cardiovascular mortality among Australia's immigrants. *Australian Journal of Public Health*, 17(3), 25–6.

Benson-Rea, M., Haworth, N. and Rawlinson, S. 1998. *The Integration of Highly Skilled Migrants into the Labour Market: Implications for New Zealand Business.* Wellington: New Zealand Immigration Service.

Bexley, E., Devlin, M., James, R. and Marginson, S. 2007. *Australian University Student Finances 2006.* Centre for the Study of Higher Education, University of Melbourne, Australian Vice Chancellors Committee.

Binning, E. 2010. *Focus on Students, Not Dollars, Sector Told.* New Zealand Herald, Available at: http://www.nzherald.co.nz/business/news/article.cfm?c_id = 3andobjectid = 10663973 [accessed: 4 August 2010].

Bohle, P., Quinlan, M., Kennedy, D. and Williamson, A. 2004. Working hours, work-life conflict and health in precarious and 'permanent' employment. *Rev. Saude Publica*, 38 (Supl.), 19–25.

Boocock, M., Hannif, Z., Jamieson, S., Kjaer, T., Lamare, R., Lamm, F., Markey, R., Martin, C., McDonnell, N., Rasmussen, E., Schweder, P., Shulruf, B. and Wagstaffe, M. 2010. *Methodological Issues Related to Researching OHS of Migrant Workers: A Cross-National Comparison.* Paper presented at Work Employment and Society Conference, Brighton: British Sociological Association.

Brosnan, P. and Walsh, P. 1998. Employment security in Australia and New Zealand. *Labour & Industry*, 8(3), 23–42.

Butcher, A. and McGrath, T. 2004. International students in New Zealand: Needs and responses. *International Education Journal*, 5(4), 540–56.

Cellier, J., Eyrolle, H. and Bertrand, A. 1995. Effect of age and level of work experience on occurrence of accidents. *Perceptual and Motor Skills*, 80(3), 931–40.

Cerny, P., Menz, G. and Soederberg, S. 2005. Different roads to globalization: Neoliberalism, the competition state, and politics, in *A More Open World, Internalizing Globalization: The Rise of Neoliberalism and the Erosion of National Models of Capitalism*, edited by S. Soederberg, G. Menz and P. G. Cerny. Hampshire and New York: Palgrave, 1–30.

Chen, R. and Madamba, M. 2000. *Migrant Labour: An Annotated Bibliography.* International Migration Paper No. 33. Available at: http://www.ilo.org/public/english/protection/migrant/download/imp/imp33.pdf [accessed: 12 December 2009].

Cranford, C., Vosko, L. and Zukewich, N. 2003. The gender of precarious employment in Canada. *Industrial Relations*, 58(3), 454–71.

Crawford, R. 2009. *Universities Key to Building Export Education Industry.* Universities New Zealand. Available at: http://www.nzvcc.ac.nz/node/364 [accessed: 12 August 2009].

Department of Labour 2006. *People on the Move: A Study of Migrant Movement Patterns to and from New Zealand.* Wellington, Department of Labour.

Department of Labour 2009. *Migration Trends and Outlook 2008/09.* Available at: http://dol.govt.nz/publications/research/migration-outlook-200809/mto-0809-fig47-large.asp [accessed: 22 July 2010)].

Department of Trade and Industry 2006. *Success at Work: Protecting Vulnerable Workers, Supporting Good Employers. A Policy Statement for This Parliament.* London: Department of Trade and Industry.

Dörre, K., Kraemer, K. and Speidel, F. 2006. *The Increasing Precariousness of the Employment Society: Driving Force for a New Right-Wing Populism?* Paper presented at the 15th Conference of Europeanists, Chicago.

Dyer, S., McDowell, L. and Batnitzky, A. 2008. Emotional labour/body work: The caring labours of migrants in the UK's National Health Service. *Geoforum*, 39(6), 2030–38.

Edwards, R. and Edwards, J. 2001. Internationalization of education: A business perspective. *Australian Journal of Education*, 45(1), 76–89.

Ehrlich, P., McClellan, W., Hemkamp, J., Islam, S. and Ducatman, A. 2004. Understanding work-related injuries in children: A perspective in West Virginia: Using the state-managed workers' compensation system. *Journal of Paediatric Surgery*, 39(5), 768–72.

Funkhouser, E. 2008. Do immigrants have lower unionization propensities than natives? *Industrial Relations*, 32(2), 248–61.

Garson, J. 1999. Where do illegal migrants work? *OECD Observer* No. 219.

Glover, S., Gott, C., Loizillon, A., Portes, J., Proce, R., Spencer, S., Srinivasan, V. and Willis, C. 2001. *Migration: An Economic and Social Analysis, RDS Occasional Paper 67*. London: Home Office.

Goldring, L., Berenstein, C. and Bernhard, J. 2009. Institutionalizing precarious migratory status in Canada. *Citizenship Studies*, 13(3), 239–65.

Green, A., Owen, D. and Jones, P. 2007. *The Economic Impact of Migrant Workers in the West Midlands*. Coventry: West Midlands Regional Observatory.

Grünell, M. and van het Kaar, R. 2003. *Migration and Industrial Relations*. Available at: www.eiro.eurofound.eu.int/2003/03/word/at0212203s.doc [accessed: 21 August 2006].

Harrison, D. 2010. Residency lures foreign students, *Sydney Morning Herald*, February 15 2010.

Haque, R. 2002. *Migrants in the UK: A Descriptive Analysis of their Characteristics and Labour Market Performance, Based on the Labour Force Survey*. London: Refugee Council.

Hawthorne, L. 2010. How valuable is 'two-step migration'? Labor market outcomes for international student migrants to Australia. *Asian and Pacific Migration Journal*, 19(1), 5–37.

Immigration New Zealand 2010. *Requirements for Studying in New Zealand*. Available at: http://www.immigration.govt.nz/migrant/stream/study/canistudyinnewzealand/whatisrequired/ [accessed: 12 January 2011].

Infometrics, NRB, and Skinnerstrategic 2008. *The Economic Impact of Export Education*. Wellington: Education New Zealand and Ministry of Education.

International Labour Office. 2009. *Module 4: Key indicators of youth labour markets: Concepts, definitions and tabulations*. Available at http://www.ilo.org/wcmsp5/groups/public/ed_emp/documents/instructionalmaterial/wcms_140860.pdf [accessed: 11 January 2011].

International Labour Organisation/International Institute for Labour Studies 2010. *World of Work Report 2010: From One Crisis to the Next?* Geneva: International Labour Organisation.

Koleth, E. 2010. *Overseas Students: Immigration Policy Changes 1997–May 2010: Background Note*. Parliament of Australia, Department of Parliamentary Services. Available at: http://www.aph.gov.au/library/pubs/BN/sp/OverseasStudents.pdf [accessed: 11 January 2011].

Kritz, M. 2006. *Globalisation and Internationalisation of Tertiary Education*. Paper presented at the International Symposium on International Migration and Development, Turin.

Loh, K. and Richardson, S. 2004. Foreign-born workers: Trends in fatal occupational injuries. *Monthly Labor Review*, 127(6), 42–53.

Manthei, R. and Gilmore, A. 2005. The effect of paid employment on university students' lives. *Education and Training*, 47(2/3), 202–15.

Marginson, S., Deumert, A., Nyland, C., Ramia, G. and Sawir, E. 2005. *The Social and Economic Security of International Students in Australia: A Study of 202 Student Cases Summary Report*. Paper presented at the annual conference of the Australian Association for Research in Education, Melbourne.

May, J., Wills, J., Kavita, D., Yara, E., Herbert, J. and McIlwaine, C. 2006. *The British State and London's Migrant Division of Labour*. London: Queen Mary University of London.

Mazzoral, T., Soutar, G., Smith, A. M. and Foster, C. 2001. *Perceptions, Information and Choice, Understanding how Chinese Students Select a Country for Overseas Study*. A. M. G. Smith and C. Foster. Australian Education International, Department of Education, Training and Youth Affairs, Canberra.

McDonald, P., Bailey, J., Oliver, D. and Pini, B. 2007. Compounding vulnerability? Young workers' employment concerns and the anticipated impact of the WorkChoices Act. *Australian Bulletin of Labour*, 33(1), 60–89.

McInnis, C. and Hartley, R. 2002. *Managing Study and Work, The Impact of Full-Time Study and Paid Work on the Undergraduate Experience in Australian Universities*. Canberra: Evaluations and Investigations Programme, Department of Science, Education and Training.

McKay, S., Craw, M. and Chopra, D. 2006. *Migrant Workers in England and Wales: An Assessment of Migrant Worker Health and Safety Risks*. London: Health and Safety Executive.

McLaren, E., Firkin, P., Spoonley, P., Dupuis, A., de Bruin, A. and Inkson, K. 2004. *At the Margins: Contingency, Precariousness and Non-Standard Work. Research Report 2004/1*, Albany/Palmerston North: Labour Market Dynamics Research Programme, Massey University.

Merwood, P. 2007. *International Students: Studying and Staying on in New Zealand*. Wellington: Department of Labour.

Miles, B. and Huberman, A. 2003. *Qualitative Data Analysis: An Expanded Sourcebook* (3rd ed.). Thousand Oaks: Sage.

Ministry of Foreign Affairs and Trade 1983. *Australia and New Zealand Closer Economic Relations*. Wellington, Ministry of Foreign Affairs and Trade.

Minto, J. 2009. Migrant Workers: *A Unionists Position. Unite Union*. Available at: http://www.unite.org.nz/node/595 [accessed: 12 December 2009].

Naidu, K. 2011. *Employers' Use of Professional Contractors: Supplement or Substitute?* MCom Thesis. Auckland: University of Auckland (publication forthcoming).

Neill, N., Mulholland, G., Ross, V. and Leckey, J. 2004. The influence of part-time work on student placement. *Journal of Further and Higher Education*, 28(2), 123–37.

Nossar, I., Johnstone, R. and Quinlan, M. 2003. *Regulating Supply-chains to Address the Occupational Health and Safety Problems Associated with Precarious Employment: The Case of Home-based Clothing Workers in Australia, Working Paper 21*. National Research Centre for OSH Regulation. Available at: http://ohs.anu.edu.au/publications/pdf/wp%2021%20-%20 Nossar,%20Johnstone%20and%20Quinlan.pdf [accessed: 12 July 2010].

Nyland, C., Forbes-Mewett, H., Marginson, S., Ramia, G., Sewer, E. and Smith, S. 2008. *International Student-Workers in Australia: A New Vulnerable Workforce. Centre for the Study of Higher Education*. Available at: http://www. cshe.unimelb.edu.au/people/staff_pages/Marginson/IntStuandWorkFeb2008. pdf [accessed: 12 July 2010].

OECD 2009. *The Future of International Migration to OECD Countries*. Paris, OECD.

Pai, H. 2008. Migrants: Britain's hidden labour army. *Socialist Review*. Available at: http://www.socialistreview.org.uk/article.php?articlenumber = 10389 [accessed: 26 August 2010].

Patton, M. 2002. *Qualitative Evaluation and Research Methods* (2nd ed.). California: Sage.

Pollert, A. and Charlwood, A. 2009. The vulnerable worker in Britain and problems at work. *Work, Employment and Society*, 23(2), 343–62.

Quinlan, M. and Mayhew, C. 2001. *Evidence Versus Ideology: Lifting the Blindfold on OHS in Precarious Employment*, Working Paper. Sydney: University of New South Wales.

Riggert, S., Boyle, M., Petrosko, J., Ash, D. and Rude-Parkins, C. 2006. Student Employment and Higher Education: Empiricism and Contradiction. *Review of Educational Research*, 76(1), 63–92.

Rodan, P. 2009. The international student as student, migrant and victim. *Australian Universities Review*, 51(2), 27–31.

Ross, C. and Rasmussen, E. 2009. Chronicle: June–September 2009. *New Zealand Journal of Employment Relations*, 34(3), 92–101.

Sargeant, M. 2009. *Health and Safety of Vulnerable Workers in a Changing World of Work*. Working Paper. Rome: Adapt.

Sargeant, M. and Tucker, T. 2009. Layers of vulnerability in occupational health and safety for migrant workers: Case studies from Canada and the United Kingdom. *Policy and Practice in Occupational Health and Safety*, 7(2), 51–73.

Shelley, T. 2007. *Exploited: Migrant Labour in the New Global Economy*. London: Zed.

Skeldon, R. 1992. International migration within and from the East and Southeast Asian Region: a review essay. I, 1(1), 19–63.

Smith, E. and Wilson, L. 2002. The new child labour? The part-time student workforce in Australia. *Australian Bureau of Labour*, 28(2), 120–137.

Standing, G. 1997. Globalization, labour flexibility and insecurity: The era of market regulation. *European Journal of Industrial Relations*, 3(1), 7–37.

Statistics NZ 2010. *Household Labour Force Survey Estimated Working-age Population: June 2010 Quarter*. Available at: http://stats.govt. nz/browse_for_stats/work_income_and_spending/employment_and_ unemployment/HouseholdLabourForceSurveyEstimatedWorkAgePopulation_ MRJune10quarter.aspx [accessed: 24 July 2010].

Stevens, R. 2010. *An Important, Lucrative Industry Comes of Age*. Available at: http://www.nzherald.co.nz/tertiaryeducation/news/article.cfm?c_id = 341andobjectid = 10622027 [accessed: 11 January 2011].

Talcott, G. 2000. *The Context and Risk of Organised Illegal Immigration to New Zealand: An Exploration in Policy Relevant Research*, Working Paper 15/00. Wellington: Centre for Strategic Studies, Victoria University of Wellington.

The Australian Fair Pay Commission 2008. *Wage-Setting Decision and Reasons for Decision July 2008*. Canberra: The Commonwealth of Australia, 20–21.

TUC Commission on Vulnerable Employment 2008. *Hard Work, Hidden Lives: The Full Report of the Commission on Vulnerable Employment*. London: Trades Union Congress.

Virtanen M., Kivimaki M., Joensuu M., Virtanen, P., Elovainio, M., and Vahtera, J. 2005. Temporary employment and health: A review. *International Journal of Epidemiology*, 34(3), 610–22.

Wu, B., Sheehan, J. and Guo, L. 2010. *Briefing Series – Issue 62: Economic Recession, Employment and Working Conditions of Chinese Migrant Workers in the UK*. Nottingham, China Policy Institute, the University of Nottingham.

Yuile, P. 2010. *Austrade, Address to Australian Technology Network of Universities*. Available at: http://www.atn.edubb.au/atnconference/2010/Yuile_Marketing_ Australian_internationaleducation.pdf [accessed: 12 July 2010].

Zimmer-Gembeck, M. J. and Mortimer, J. T. 2006. Adolescent work, vocational development, and education. *Review of Educational Research*, 76(4), 537–66.

Chapter 4

Men at Work? Emerging Nuances in Young Masculinities in the United Kingdom's Retail Sector

Steven Roberts

The emergence of the service sector as a key driver of the economy in many industrialized nations and the concomitant collapse of youth labour markets has meant that much youth policy in the last three decades has been aimed at the democratization of the education system. As a result, increasing participation rates of young people remaining in vocational education and an attendant 'massification' of higher education have been primary policy aims internationally (Teichler 1998). This move into post–compulsory education is often supplemented by part-time jobs in retail, bars and restaurants. However, such young people are, more often than not, just 'passing through', on their way to their perceived graduate destinations (Osterman 2001, Huddleston 2011). Yet, a proportion of young people attempt to enter the labour market on a more permanent basis. Increasingly, many of the employment opportunities on offer to such young people are predominantly low-level, often insecure jobs in the service sector that attract low-level salaries.

Internationally, researchers have afforded considerable attention to considering questions mobilizing around young people and service sector employment. They have for example considered, the precariousness of this type of work (for example Inui et al. 2006), the implications of this type of work for moving into adulthood (Arnett 2000), along with the broader social consequences of the increased number of youth employed in service roles (for example MacDonald 2009). There have, however, been two key limitations in the literature. Firstly, non-students have often been overlooked, or had their views compounded with those of students (for example Warhurst and Nickson 2007, Maguire 2010), in spite of what might seem very different motivations for work. Indeed, the group has been recently described as a missing middle of youth research (Roberts 2011a). Secondly, there has been little attention given to the specific experiences of young men in service employment. As Nickson and Korczynski (2009: 298) have argued, while there is research on young men's attitudes to taking up low level service sector employment (for example Furlong and Cartmel 2004, Nixon 2009), there has been little focus on young men's actual experience of this work.

This chapter addresses these gaps in the literature by drawing on qualitative interviews with 24 young men based in the county of Kent, in the South East of

England. The experiences of these respondents have much to tell us, because, as MacDonald (2009: 167) has recently noted, due to young people's 'status as harbinger of the future, the nature of the younger generation's engagement in "new" forms of employment has relevance beyond the sphere of youth studies'.

After contextualizing the study within the appropriate literature, the chapter briefly discusses the research methods and context. The substantive focus of the chapter is then addressed: the interaction of service work and masculine identity. As service sector jobs are often considered to be at odds with traditional modes of masculinity, the chapter details how this interaction plays out in the retail work place and problematizes the understanding that men have an inherent disregard for service work. After establishing that men can and do take up this kind of work in substantial numbers, the chapter moves on to illustrate some of the ways in which these young men negotiate the scripts of service work and young masculinities. Ultimately the data here provide a nuanced account that reveals a set of attitudes that reflect both continuity and change in the ways in which masculine identities are played out in the contemporary economy.

Men, Masculinities and Service Work

Connell's contribution to theorizing gender, over many years, has been critical in developing awareness of the existence of a range of different masculinities as opposed to a singular form of masculinity (for example Connell 1987, 1995, 2000, Carrigan, Connell and Lee 1985). Indeed, Connell suggests that there are 'different ways of enacting manhood, different ways of learning to be a man, different conceptions of the self ...' (Connell 2000: 10). These different modes of being a man are relational and are situated in a hierarchy of dominance. At the summit of this hierarchy is 'hegemonic masculinity': that which is most respected, desired or dominant in society. In industrialized societies, this is largely associated with men who are successful economically, heterosexual, and 'racially superior' (i.e. white). This form of masculinity is characterized by disembodied rationality and expertise – the kind of attributes that lead to professional and managerial positions of power in the labour market. Contrasted to this, there is a range of subordinate masculinities (and femininities) which are inferior on the basis of ethnicity, sexuality or class position. Traditional working-class masculinities, for example, are often exemplified by a polar opposite – embodiment. Strength, physical prowess and sweating to get the job done, are all characteristics that typify such masculinities. Linked to this, oppositional or 'protest' masculinities, associated with spectacular, macho, resistant, laddish behaviour, can also be constructed. Despite recent critiques regarding the hierarchical nature and the historical situatedness of Connell's conceptualization (for example Anderson 2005, 2009, Wetherall and Edley 1999), this understanding nonetheless provides an essential starting point for this chapter.

The context of the data presented here is the transformation of paid work in industrialized economies, from being largely dominated by manufacturing and heavy industry up until the late 1970s, to becoming dominated by service sector employment. Alongside equal rights legislation, increased educational access and the subsequent academic success of young women, such radical change has been argued to destabilize earlier notions of *working-class* masculinity. The changes in work, of course, were fundamentally changes to working-class work.

Previous notions of working-class masculinity relied heavily on the male breadwinner model of the family, which was based on a fairly strict gendered division of labour. For men, then, work was a primary location for constructing a masculine identity (Connell 1995) and 'the main orientation point, in reference to which all the other pursuits could be planned and ordered' (Bauman 1998: 17).

In this model, employment tended to require men to demonstrate characteristics of physical toughness and solidarity against employers and managers. Such a 'macho masculinity' was often replicated by boys during their school days, imitating the 'hardness' of their fathers' work based habits (for example Willis 1977). This resistance was, in a way, a complicit means of readying oneself for the 'shit jobs' that young working-class men would face upon finishing their compulsory education (Coffield, Borrill and Marshall 1986).

Organizations still remain intrinsically gendered (Acker 1990), and service work in particular exhibits a substantial degree of vertical and horizontal gender segregation (Adkins 1995, Du Gay 1996, Pettinger 2005). Indeed, Tolich and Briar (1999) suggest that this may be the central feature of work in contemporary economies. However the congruence of manliness with the demands of new and pervasive service sector employment, such as care, docility and deference (McDowell 2003, 2009) is a question that has captured the attention of many researchers.

In contemporary interactive service jobs, employees are required to perform 'emotional labour' (Hochschild 1983). They are required to manage their emotions and present themselves in a way congruent with the organization's expectations, whilst also inducing an emotional state in those they are serving. This is a clear antithesis to the behaviours often associated with normative working-class and/or protest masculinity (Connell, 1995), and is often argued to be make service work unattractive to young men (see Leidner 1993, Bourgois 1995, McDowell 2003, 2009, and Nixon 2009). This represents a significant historical shift. For example, where the 'privatised' workers found in the Affluent Worker studies by Goldthorpe et al. (1968) were found to not enjoy their work, it did however allow them to enact 'appropriate' masculinities through manual labour, endurance, productivity and wages sufficient to support a family. Yet, nowadays, '[t]he mundane reality of the new economy is that the service-sector jobs that the young men and women can realistically obtain ... are routine, subservient, low-paid and often insecure' (Gunter and Watt 2009: 527).

A growing amount of research focuses on working-class men's experiences of confronting this dilemma. Within this research, there is an almost universal recognition that women are disproportionately located in low-level positions and that they have to provide the majority of the required emotional labour (Henson and Rogers 2001, Cross and Bagilhole 2002, Lupton 2006, Tolich and Briar 1999). This situation is severely problematic. Women are at once often expected to produce a sexualized identity as part of the job (Adkins 1995), or 'do' their gender appropriately, yet are not rewarded for this as it is presumed to be natural. A failure to comply with this 'naturalised labour of identity' (Adkins and Lury 1997: 604) can result in sanction or reprimands. Men, conversely, are able to use their identity as an occupational resource, thus the performance of emotion work can be rewarded or seen as a skill (Adkins and Lury 1997, McDowell 2003). Furthermore, by being restricted to these types of roles, women miss out on the chance to develop their skills in other areas (Tolich and Briar 1999), whereas men have been shown to benefit from a minority status in a variety of female-dominated occupations (Simpson 2004).

While some researchers have argued that men reject any notion of involvement in service work even if they are unemployed (for example Lindsay and McQuaid 2004, Nixon 2006, 2009), other researchers have suggested that men will engage in this work but adopt strategies to ensure their masculine identities are not compromised (for example Simpson 2004, Cross and Bagilhole 2002, Lupton 2006). These strategies can be differentiated by class. Nixon (2009) explains that middle-class men often possess the requisite skills and qualifications that would facilitate employment in relatively high level service roles that might provide potential routes for progression into higher status managerial roles. However, 'the low-skilled feminized service work accessible to poorly educated working-class men offers few such masculine compensations' (Nixon 2009: 309). This is largely due to the fact that embodied masculinity, that is, physically working hard and 'grafting', has been the particular form of labour that working-class men have used to provide a positive and respectable discursive position in relation to women and middle-class men (McDowell 2003, Nixon 2009). As a result, men in the service sector tend to occupy more obviously masculine roles in areas such as warehousing, distribution, transportation and protective services, or show a preference for 'shelf stacking' over jobs that necessitate customer interaction. These preferences allow for autonomy and discretion, important elements of working-class masculinities (Beynon 1973, Milkman 1997).

The respondents in this study add to this perspective on what it is to be a young man in the twenty first century. With several years of (often consistent) labour market experience in the service sector, they clearly do not find such work too abhorrent to undertake. Consequently, their experiences allow us to analyse the notion that contemporary work attitudes are affected by the dominant, traditional version of masculinity that is associated with young men in both leisure arenas and in the domestic sphere (McDowell 2003). The accounts here reveal a somewhat more nuanced reality.

Methods and Context

The retail sector accounts for more than 11 per cent of the United Kingdom's (UK) workforce, just under 3 million people. More than half of the retail workforce is based in lower-level sales and customer service related roles, with another 18 per cent classified as elementary or administrative roles. In terms of the distribution of part-time and full-time work, retail has the highest proportion of part-time workers within the UK economy, more than double the UK average of 25 per cent (Skillsmart 2010).

Retail figures even more prominently in the employment of 18–24 year olds. Almost one in four workers in this age group are employed in the combined fields of Retail, Wholesale and Motor trade, nearly 2.5 times as many as the nearest other fields of 'Manufacturing' and 'Hotels and Restaurants' (see Figure 4.1). Over representation of young people in general in this industry section is common internationally. However, its position as the biggest employer of 18–24 year olds in the UK marks it out as being slightly different from both the USA and Australia, where industry sections made up of other service jobs in restaurants, cafés and various hospitality based services are the dominant employers of this age group (see respectively Maloney 2010, O'Brien 2006).

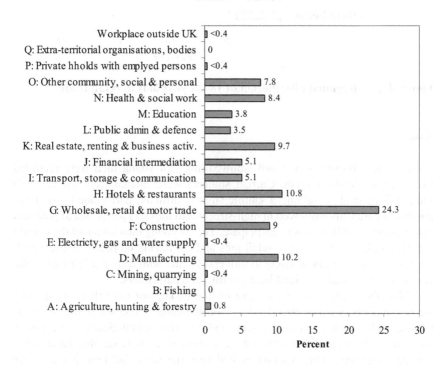

Figure 4.1   All 18–24 age group, industry distribution

72

Young People and Work

Retail has a major presence across the UK and in every region (Skillsmart, 2010), making it pervasive in a very real sense. However, Figure 4.2 demonstrates the significance of retail for young people in the South East of England. The South East is the only region in England where young men outnumber young women in retail jobs.

Figure 4.2   Regional distribution of 18–24 year olds in retail trade

Sample

Using store-approved access and 'snowballing', 24 young men were recruited to participate in the project. Current students were filtered from the research sample. This made obtaining a sample slightly difficult, partly due to the large numbers of students employed in high-street retail jobs and partly due to potential respondents' unwillingness to participate. The 24 young men who met the criteria (i.e. (i) employed in low-level retail jobs and (ii) having no prior experience of/ no immediate intention of going to university), and who fully participated in the research, were equally divided between full- and part-timers.

Using the occupation of the head of household, just over three quarters of the respondents could be described as working-class in relation to the Registrar General's classification of occupations, and they were all ethnically white. Given the relative homogeneity of the ethnic composition in Kent, this latter point was not surprising. One respondent had kept the same full-time job for over two years since leaving school. However, the work histories of the sample were largely characterized by several sideways movements between low-level jobs. The respondents were individually interviewed using a biographical approach to discuss their lives to date. This allowed for past experiences, present circumstances and future aspirations in the realms of education and work, among other themes, to be discussed at length. With one exception, the interviews lasted between 40 minutes and 2.5 hours, averaging about an hour in duration.

Men at Work: Change and Continuity in Contemporary Youth Masculinities

Despite assertions that service work, subsequent customer interaction and the attendant need to show deference make entry level jobs in the service sector unpalatable, 'many working class men find themselves in such jobs' (Lupton 2006: 117). For young men, this is even more the case. In light of this, in terms of their experiences of work, a key issue to consider is whether front-line service sector jobs are 'incongruent with manliness' (Leidner 1993: 199). Given that such a high proportion of young men work in the retail industry in sales or elementary service-based positions in the UK, at first glance we might assume one of two things: either that masculinity does not necessarily pose a threat to taking up this kind of employment, or that the men in these jobs are there because they have no other choice and are consequently performing them under duress.

In contrast to the latter assertion the data reveal that service work is not necessarily an anathema to young men. In fact, when asked about the elements of the job they most enjoyed respondents were emphatic that it is customer interaction which was central to their employment satisfaction. They commented:

> If you have a nice customer and you can have a good chat you sell them what you want ... I enjoy that and I enjoy talking to people. Like, we got some regulars and I'll have a chat with them. I enjoy that bit, the banter if they remember who you are. (Adam)

> I like having conversations with the customers and everything. I find it quite easy to just get a flowing conversation going, especially with older ladies as well, they laugh at anything. So it is quite easy to get a conversation flowing. (Carl)

At the same time as they accentuated the pleasures of customer interactions, many of the young men expressed their preference to be busy, to be physically doing something. Folding a table of jumpers, or 'working the stock' were tasks they talked about enjoying, with customers coming and 'making a mess' of the display often being a source of frustration. They also often emphasized their dislike of working on the tills:

> I find them [tills] really boring and I much rather do stock cos I feel like I'm
> actually doing something ... if I work department for four hours, after two hours
> you can actually see what you have done. (James)

> I didn't really wanna work on tills, just cos I preferred working on the floor ...
> there's just more to do, yeah, than standing on a till all day. There is *actually*
> more to do. (Respondent's emphasis in italics.) (Tim)

In part, this would appear to lend support to the idea that such young men, in
protection of their masculinity, reject the servitude required in the job. They are
aware of the intangibility of the emotional work of the till and dismiss it as not
'doing something'. As with the literature outlined above, these comments seem
to reflect masculine preferences to be physically active and involved in labour
which is visible, and so likely to be recognized and rewarded. Two respondents
enumerated on this theme when asked whether they prefer not to interact with
customers at the till. They replied:

> No, you *can interact* with customers on the floor. You *can help* the customers
> on the floor. Cos if you are on the checkout and they ask you where something
> is or they ask you for your advice on something you can't leave your post and
> go and help them out, whereas on the floor you can show them where the thing
> is you can talk to them about what they're doing ... (Respondent's emphasis in
> italics.) (Tim)

> Well, with tills you have got to socialize with customers who you are only like
> having five second conversations with. That's like 'hi, how are you?' and that's
> it, and it's kinda, like, pointless conversations just to make the packing not seem
> so slow. But when you're out stacking you can have, like, proper conversations
> with customers on the shop-floor and you can proper stand there for 5 minutes
> making them feel comfortable shopping in the stores. It's, like, you feel the
> conversation is worth it. (Carl)

The above quotations highlight two key themes that resonated across the sample.
Firstly, young men in the research were very positive about customer service
situations and constructed interaction as an important aspect of their work.
Furthermore, they embraced protracted interactions positively. Secondly, and
importantly, however, the type of interaction they privileged was on 'the floor'
rather than at 'the till'. This spatial differentiation is manifest in the fact that the
floor allows more physical and verbal freedom for the young men to not only assist
customers but demonstrate their knowledge and expertise.

This research is thus consistent with work that has shown the ways in which
men have re-constituted their jobs to pursue apparently more masculine activities
(Leidner 1993, Lupton 2006, Simpson 2004), That is to say, these attitudes operate
as a source of distancing themselves from the routine emotional labour of the till

point. Indeed, it became abundantly clear that the rushed nature of interaction, the scripted dialogue, and the heavy surveillance of such dialogue at the till point was what most frustrated the young men. This was not genuine service; instead this was part of their job they had to complete under almost Tayloristic conditions. As with Beynon's (1973) discussion of factory workers, this source of frustration was derived from a lack of autonomy alongside enhanced monotony. In essence, the till point is comparable to mechanical production lines. Furthermore, it *prevents* a service encounter. The rejection of till work, therefore, can be seen as reflective of this lack of autonomy and enhanced monotony, and the ways in which these issues are exacerbated by the need to engage in the 'lip service' emotional labour involved in quickly meeting and greeting customers.

In a study of McDonalds, Leidner (1993: 199) identified a number of work requirements which could be viewed as 'incongruent with manliness' such as an ingratiating manner, taking orders and holding one's tongue. For respondents in this study, negative interaction in which they were belittled, undermined or berated was, of course, a source of immense frustration. Yet, in these circumstances, these young men *did* 'hold their tongue' and retained an ingratiating manner:

> ... as soon as it happens you just deal with it in your own way. And deal with it in a responsible and respectful manner. (Tim)

> If there is no customers then there's no job. It's obvious that you can't just shout at people or turn your back on them. It's not nice when they have a go, but when you think about it only a few of them are complete tossers. (Pat)

Whilst the young men did not feel the need to make excuses about the nature of their work, they defended themselves fairly articulately, and quite vehemently, when the idea that their work made them subordinate or lesser in relation to typically conceived working-class embodied masculinity was put to them. Moreover, in defending their own position they subverted traditional masculinity and ascribed it a lesser status in a hierarchy of dominance:

> I mean, I think there are arseholes that think that you've gotta be a labourer to feel like a man. But I mean, I don't, like, spend eight hours at work and then check my shorts to see if I still got a cock. I know I'm a man, I don't need to drink beer and, er, treat women bad. (Christian)

> Like everyone is gonna be a labourer? I know plenty of lads who labour and get laid off all the time, or don't have any work for ages. How fucking manly is that? (Johnny)

This could be seen as being indicative of typical working-class masculinity. However, it should be recognized that these comments were made in relation to a potential attack on their identity. Instead of withdrawing their positive comments about service interaction, they disparaged the undesirable elements of masculinity that 'other men' might have perceived to be appropriate behaviour. As per Johnny's comments, rather than continuing to imbue manual labour with the social superiority of masculinity and suggesting emotional labour was antithetical to a masculine subject position (Nixon 2009), it was having a job at all, and, moreover, the permanence of such work that instilled a sense of masculinity. This latter point is consistent with much research into work and identity (for example Cross and Bagilhole 2002, McDowell 2003). Indeed, the quotes here resonate with MacDonald's (2008: 240) work, which uncovered 'an insistent valuing of work as a source not just of income but of self and family respect: old-fashioned, 'respectable' working-class views about the importance of working for a living.

Whilst the young men were quick to defend themselves against the idea that their jobs made them less manly, at times they mentioned the lack of status accorded to retail workers more widely. Such reflections emphasized that gender is not the only social category that informs how retail work is experienced. Indeed, classed based differences between men (and between women) clearly informed not just daily interactions amongst retail staff but practices and beliefs relating to future employment retail prospects. This was most frequently the case when the respondents talked about the perceptions of university students who were often, but not always, fellow retail workers. Pat and Jez's recollections of being negatively evaluated as lacking in worth and value by middle-class male colleagues are illustrative of this:

> It was quite obvious, especially in my first job, the staff who were students thought they were better than us. Or that, you know, they expected to be my manager one day or something. They'd make it known that they'd got bigger plans than working in a shop. (Pat)

> I think for uni students they actually judge people who work full-time in a shop. They still judge you and think you are not capable of things. And there's a lot of [students] in retail! (Jez)

These comments are indicative of a key point made earlier in the chapter; the experiences outlined here are largely those of working-class men's trajectories. The experiences and motivations of the pre-dominantly middle-class student-worker population are likely to be quite distinct to that of the young man trying to establish an independent life using retail as a career to facilitate this (Roberts 2011b). Indeed, this is something that the young men in this sample not only recognized, but, recognized as being a potential barrier to their own ambitions if the student worker did intend to 'be their manager one day':

> It's hard [promotion]. You get manager designates, which are these weird people that are like half-managers, they have just been hired or brought in as managers, from another business or straight out of university. (Mike)

I know there are definitely some students, or like, some people that have now left uni who work in retail. Some of them are in full-time positions too! I have been kicking around in retail since I was 16, and I'm not full-time. (Pat)

Mike, Pat and their counterparts' negotiation of retail work is clearly marked by their class identities. While women no doubt continue to experience discrimination in the retail sector and predominate in low paid and low status positions (Mason and Osborne 2008) the young men's narratives reveal that class also informs opportunities in retail work whether it be in terms of access to full time work or promotion.

Re-labelling and Re-focusing

Despite the negative status they felt they were ascribed by virtue of their employment in retail, the respondents did not really seem ashamed of their jobs. Yet, under closer scrutiny many of them went out of their way to qualify that they had a particular role in the retail process which allowed them to distance themselves from the lack of status afforded to a standard retail assistant. For example, despite all their roles being dominated by activities typically associated with retail sales assistants, Billy described himself first as a 'bike mechanic', Simon explained he was an 'in-store visual merchandiser', and Mike was clear in detailing that he was as an 'audio fitter'. Furthermore, many others depicted a retail employment status hierarchy where some employers were ascribed lower social status, whilst others were truly positions of aspiration:

I've been trying to get a job in *Cult* for a long time, and it's a very niche person that gets a job there. It's an affinity with the product and the atmosphere ... everyone wants to work where they want to work. Not where they don't want to work. So the whole working somewhere where you don't like, like a supermarket – the money is good but do I really wanna work there? No. I'd just feel that a little bit of my identity has been taken away ... I could see it wearing on me quite a lot cos it's just day in day out, drudgery. (Adam)

No, I wouldn't [work in *Primark*] ... it's all about the brand for me. I wanted to go to *USC* because it was a clothes fashion brand, whereas like *Qube* was fashion shoes, and was a really cool place to work [when I worked there]. (Jez)

This type of re-labelling or re-focusing of job titles and primary responsibilities follows the trend set by men in a number of other typically feminine occupations. For example, to enhance their status of their role and to avoid the stigma of being de-masculinized by their job, men have been found to refer to themselves as 'information technologists' instead of librarians (Lupton 2006), or to emphasize the organizational aspects of male nursing over and above the caring involved (Cross and Bagilhole 2002).

In the case of these respondents, this understanding was also partly bound up with the specificity of the product being sold and its associations with the employees' out-of-work identity – something that also appeared to contribute to a greater acceptance of the nature of retail work. While not an exclusive sentiment, the respondents largely felt that their jobs were a means to an end. However, given a choice, their preference was to work in a store and with a product that bore some relationship with their interests outside of work. Consequently, for Adam it was important to wear the 'right clothes', to be recognized for doing so and to be able to immediately recognize the clothes brands that his friends and others were wearing on nights out. Billy, the bike mechanic, discussed at length the relationship between his job and his primary interest of 'riding' (semi-extreme BMX riding through urban centres) and enhancing and modifying his bike. For Dave, working in a sports shop was a natural extension of his love for football, which he regularly played and attended as an observer. Among the respondents who were not employed in their retailer of choice, many spoke of their desire to work in music and film chain *HMV*, claiming it was an ideal and obviously desirable employment destination because 'everyone loves music and films' (Danny).

Simultaneously, the relationship between outside interests and the nature of the retailer can be seen to be reciprocal. Damian, for example, claimed he knew nothing about camping or hiking before he joined the outdoor pursuits store. Working there had given him a taste for the products and he had become a camping enthusiast *because* of his employment. This was equally the case for Pat, who had also generated an increasing interest in and awareness of fashion as a result of working for a medium level fashion retailer.

In all these circumstances the organization utilizes and manages more than aesthetic (Warhurst and Nickson 2007) and emotional (Hochschild 1983) aspects of labour in the service encounter. As Gibson (2004: 176) eloquently identifies, given their increasing spending on toiletries and clothing in particular, 'men are avid consumers'. Indeed, it is the fact that consumption has become such a key component of newly emerging masculine identities (for example Nixon 1996, Galilee 2002) that ensures that the product-enthusiast employee is complicit in becoming part of the commodity on offer.

Conclusion

Rather than being simply a case of working-class men avoiding, despising, disparaging and rejecting front line service roles in retail work, as has often been depicted in research about masculinities to date, a more nuanced picture begins to emerge from the voices heard in this chapter. The attitudes and experiences of contemporary young men, it seems, portray both continuity and change in the ways masculinity is negotiated, enacted and accepted.

An important starting point is taking note of just how many men, particularly young men, actually work in retail and related service based industries. The Eurostat Labour Force Survey (LFS) data at the outset of the chapter illustrates powerfully that despite much research indicating that unemployed men could not bring themselves to engage in such employment (Nixon 2009, Furlong and Cartmel 2004) a significant number of men do just that. In fact, young men make up an almost equal proportion of such positions relative to their female counterparts. Of the relatively large number of young men working in the front-line retail sector jobs in the UK, these can largely be divided into two classed groups. There are those who are passing through – students working to help supplement their university fees and/or life style – and there are others who are in search of a more permanent engagement with the labour market. The latter group remain highly under-researched.

In this chapter, contrary to the findings of much research in the field of masculinity and work, evidence of considerable enjoyment in customer service/ interaction work emerged. The respondents appear to have few problems reconciling their position in a service-based job and their masculinity. This is not without qualification, however. Enjoyment of their jobs was, perhaps obviously, contingent on pleasant service interactions. The 'few tossers' – customers who are condescending or unduly demanding – were clearly still a source of frustration. Furthermore, there is an apparent spatial divide to consider. The young men talked about their protracted service encounters on the sales floor as being the moments of service they enjoyed the most. In contrast, the quick exchanges at the till point were not deemed to be anywhere near as satisfying. The respondents made sense of this dislike for this element of the job by consistently referring to the monotony of the task, its lack of discretion and the fact it was a position subject to increased surveillance. Such an attitude could lead to an active avoidance of till work at the expense of the female counterparts, though this was not explicitly conveyed by the respondents.

An important point to consider here, however, when considering till point interactions is that many retail entry level jobs require till work from all employees in low-level positions. The divide is far less sharp in high street retail per se, than it is in major supermarkets for example (Tolich and Briar 1999). Another important consideration is that as customer service grows in importance across the economy, long standing divisions between front and back of house worker activity have become increasingly blurred. Consequently, 'the ability to handle customers becomes a key skill for increasing numbers of workers in the service economy' (Nixon 2009: 306).

A distinct impression derived from this research was that the decline of typically masculine jobs in manufacturing, heavy industry and so forth do not continue to be nostalgically wished for by all contemporary young men, despite the attention often given to such feeling (for example Nayak 2006). Again, however, this needs to be carefully qualified. This study addresses a specific group – young males *in* retail work – in just one locality, so further locally based studies are needed as a direct point of comparison. The LFS data provided earlier illustrates the fairly proportionate spread of retail work and relatively even distribution of young retail workers around the UK regions, yet locality can have a huge impact. It could, for example, explain some of the variation between the respondents in this study and the kind of results reported by McDowell (2003), MacDonald and Marsh (2005) and Nayak (2006). Given that these studies were largely based in areas with a rich industrial heritage, the move to a service economy could have had particularly profound affects: it might be that locality is incredibly important in shaping transitions and identities in a way that was not obviously evident in the localities used in the present study. Nayak (2006: 818), for example, paints a vivid picture of the way a traditional form of masculinity is embedded within the 'landscapes of power' in the North East of England, resulting in young men turning to alternative means to ensure that a 'local, white masculine identity is being preserved, recuperated and ultimately refashioned'. Though not static, the nature of men's jobs in the South East has arguably not changed as much as the North East. Pockets of mining communities in the Kent coalfields, manufacturing and various dockyards across the county were part of a far more varied local labour market in comparison to the industrial heartlands of the North East, where working-class 'manly' jobs had been ubiquitous for many decades. In addition to post-industrial developments in various regions, the divide between rural and urban locations is also worthy of attention. The present research was conducted in highly urbanized centres, but research in rural localities has found a stronger adherence to physicality and its relationship to masculinity (for example Campbell 2006, Hogan and Pursell 2008).

In any case, these apparent changes in attitude, such as openness to and enjoyment of service encounters, form only one part of the story. The young men here also simultaneously exhibited elements associated with typically working-class masculinity as they negotiated their identities. This was clear in the ways in which they defended themselves against accusations that they might be considered 'less masculine' than other men by virtue of their occupation, and perhaps more so by their active decisions to reconstitute their job titles or re-emphasize more traditionally masculine parts of their job. Even these responses, however, need to be recognized as being suitably nuanced. Whilst the crucial driver of masculine identity was paid employment regardless of the content of the work, much as it has been for men over the years (for example Connell 1995, Bauman 1998), the respondents did not retract their positive statements about service interaction. Instead, they feminized a lack of employment security and disparaged excessive drinking and poor treatment of women as fundamentally flawed strategies for feeling masculine.

In many ways these attitudes over spill into the limits we can read into the re-labelling processes invoked in relation to their job titles. There can be little question that the respondents often and, somewhat obviously at times, reconstituted their job titles into a more 'gender appropriate' form. Yet, while some authors, such Henson and Rogers (2001) and Cross and Bagilhole (2002) have shown how such strategies are often simultaneously combined with active efforts at rejecting the notion that the role has compromised one's own 'maleness', this was not apparent in this research. The present study also sits at odds with the evidence provided by McDowell (2003). While McDowell also posits that a singular view of 'laddish' masculinity is a flawed class stereotype and that the ways that white young men 'do' masculinity varies across time and space, she ends by suggesting that a 'continued dominance of a version of traditional sexist, masculinity … that affect workplace participation and attitudes towards women and family life' remains prevalent (2003: 226). However, contrary to her assessment that 'new forms of masculinity are more in tune with the dominant attributes of a service based economy … [and] … have yet to find any expression' (2003: 226), in line with McCormack and Anderson (2010), to some extent contemporary young men appear to be exhibiting an attenuated, 'softened' version of masculinity.

Lastly, the narratives provided here have clear consequences in relation to the meaning of work and the place of work in (young) people's lives more generally. Ultimately, whilst the fragmentation of and changes to work in contemporary capitalism are argued to be at odds with the construction of coherent and continuing self identity (Sennett 1998, Bauman 2005), the narratives here illustrate an active negotiation of personal (masculine) identity through and *because* of certain types of work. This finding sits well with Cote's (2009) assessment that agency should be taken more seriously in contemporary perspectives on identity and Strangleman's (2007) contention that writers seeking to support the 'end of work' thesis (Rifkin 2003) need to include in-depth qualitative research in a bid to better unpick the complex ways in which meaning and identity are formed.

References

Acker, J. 1990. Hierarchies, jobs, bodies: A theory of gendered organisations. *Gender and Society*, 4(2), 139–58.

Adkins, L. 1995. *Gendered Work: Sexuality, Family and the Labour Market.* Buckingham: Open University Press.

Adkins, L. and Lury, C. 1997. The labour of identity: Performing identities, performing economies. *Economy and Society*, 28(4), 598–614.

Anderson, E. 2005. Orthodox and inclusive masculinity. *Sociological Perspectives*, 48(3), 337–55.

Anderson, E. 2009. *Inclusive Masculinity.* London: Routledge.

Arnett, J. J. 2000. Emerging adulthood: A theory of development from the late teens through the twenties. *American Psychologist*, 55(5), 469–80.

Bauman, Z. 1998. *Work, Consumerism and the New Poor.* Buckingham: Open University Press.

Bauman, Z. 2005. *Liquid Life.* Cambridge: Polity Press.

Beynon, H. 1973. *Working for Ford*. Harmondsworth: Penguin.

Bourgois, P. 1995. *In Search of Respect: Selling Crack in el Barrio*. Cambridge: Cambridge University Press.

Campbell, H. (ed.) 2006. *Country Boys: Masculinity and Rural Life*. Penn State Press.

Carrigan, T., Connell, B. and Lee, J. 1985. Toward a new sociology of masculinity. *Theory and Society*, 14(5), 551–604.

Coffield, R., Borrill, C. and Marshall, S. 1986. *Growing Up at the Margins: Young Adults in the North East*. Milton Keynes: Open University Press.

Connell, R. W. 1987. *Gender and Power*. Stanford, CA: Stanford University.

Connell, R. W. 1995. *Masculinities*. Cambridge: Polity Press.

Connell, R. W. 2000. *The Men and the Boys*. Cambridge: Polity Press.

Cote, J. 2009. Youth-identity studies: History, controversies and future directions, in *Handbook of Youth and Young Adulthood*, edited by A. Furlong. Abingdon: Routledge, 375–83.

Cross, S and Bagilhole, B. 2002. Girls' jobs for the boys? Men, masculinity and non-traditional occupations. *Gender, Work and Organization*, 9(2), 204–26.

Du Gay, P. 1996. *Consumption and Identity at Work*, London: Sage Publications.

Furlong, A. and Cartmel, F. 2004. *Vulnerable Young Men in Fragile Labour Markets: Employment, Unemployment and the Search for Long-Term Security*. York: Joseph Rowntree Foundation.

Galilee, J. 2002. Class consumption: Understanding middle-class young men and their fashion choices. *Men and Masculinities*, 5(1), 32–52.

Gibson, A. C. 2004. Queer looks, male gazes, taut torsos and designer labels: Contemporary cinema, consumption and masculinity, in *The Trouble With Men: Masculinities in European and Hollywood Cinema*, edited by B. Powrie, A. Davies and B. Babington. London: Wallflower Press, 176–86.

Goldthorpe, J. H., Lockwood, D., Bechhofer, F. and Platt, J. 1968. *The Affluent Worker: Industrial Attitudes and Behaviour*. Cambridge: Cambridge University Press.

Gunter, A. and Watt, P. 2009. Grafting, going to college and working on road: Youth transitions and cultures in an East London neighbourhood. *Journal of Youth Studies*, 12(5), 515–29.

Henson, K. D. and Rogers, J. K. 2001. 'Why Marcia you've changed!' Male clerical temporary workers doing masculinity in a feminized occupation. *Gender and Society*, 15(2), 218–38.

Hochschild, A. R. 1983. *The Managed Heart: Commercialization of Human Feeling*. Berkeley, CA: University of California Press.

Hogan, M. P. and Pursell, T. 2008. The 'Real Alaskan': Nostalgia and rural masculinity in the 'last frontier'. *Men and Masculinities*, 11(1), 63–85.

Huddleston, P. (2011) 'It's alright for Saturdays, but not for ever': The employment of part-time student staff within the retail sector. Just passing through, in *Retail Work*, edited by I. Grugulis and O. Bozkurt. London: Palgrave, 109–27.

Inui, A., Furlong, A., Sato, K., Sano, M., Hirastuka, M., Fukit, H. and Miyamoto, M. 2006. *Young People Living in Precarious Situations: Freeter, NEET and Unemployed in Japan and the UK*. Tokyo: Kadensha

Leidner, R. 1993. *Fast Food, Fast Talk: Service Work and the Routinizations of Everyday Life*. Berkeley and Los Angeles: University of California Press.

Lindsay, C and McQuaid R. 2004. Avoiding the McJobs: Unemployed jobseekers attitudes to service work. *Work, Employment and Society*, 18(2), 297–319.

Lupton, R. 2006. Explaining men's entry into female-concentrated occupations: Issues of masculinity and social class. *Gender, Work and Organization*, 13(2), 108–28.

MacDonald, R. 2008. Disconnected youth? Social exclusion, the underclass and economic marginality. *Social Work and Society*, 6(2), 236–48.

MacDonald, R. 2009. Precarious work: Risk, choice and poverty traps, in *Handbook of Youth and Young Adulthood*, edited by A. Furlong. Abingdon: Routledge, 167–75.

MacDonald, R. and Marsh, J. 2005. *Disconnected Youth? Growing Up in Britain's Poor Neighbourhoods*. Basingstoke: Palgrave Macmillan.

Maguire, S. 2010. 'I just want a job' – What do we really know about young people in jobs without training? *Journal of Youth Studies*, 13(3), 317–33.

Maloney, C. 2010, *Understanding the Economy: Unemployment Among Young Workers*, A report by the US Congress Joint Economic Committee.

Mason, G. and Osborne, M. 2008. Business strategies, work organisation and low pay in United Kingdom retailing, in *Low Wage Work in the United Kingdom*, edited by C. Lloyd, G. Mason, and K. Mayhew. New York: Russell Sage Foundation, 131–68.

McCormack, M. and Anderson, E. 2010. It's just not acceptable anymore?: The erosion of homophobia and the softening of masculinity in an English state school. *Sociology*, 44(5), 843–59.

McDowell, L. 2003. *Redundant Masculinities? Employment Change and White Working Class Youth*. London: Blackwell.

McDowell, L. 2009. New masculinities and femininities: Gender division in the new economy, in *Handbook of Youth and Young Adulthood*, edited by A. Furlong. Abingdon: Routledge, 58–65.

Milkman, R. 1997. *Farewell to the Factory: Auto Workers in the Late Twentieth Century*. Berkeley: University of California Press.

Nayak, A. 2006. Displaced masculinities: Chavs, youth and class in the post-industrial city. *Sociology*, 40(5), 813–31.

Nickson, D. and Korczynski, M. 2009. Editorial: Aesthetic labour, emotional labour and masculinity. *Gender, Work and Organization*, 16(3), 291–99.

Nixon, D. 2006. 'I just like working with my hands': Employment aspirations and the meaning of work for low-skilled unemployed men in Britain's service economy. *Journal of Education and Work*, 19(2), 201–17.

Nixon, D. 2009. 'I can't put a smiley face on': Working-class masculinity, emotional labour and service work in the 'New Economy'. *Gender, Work and Organization*, 16(3), 300–22.

Nixon, S. 1996. *Hard Looks*. London: UCL Press.

O'Brien, M. 2006. *The Youth Labour Market in Australia – Implications from Work Choices Legislation.* Working Paper 06–08, Department of Economics, University of Wollongong.

Osterman, P. 2001. Employers in the low-wage/low-skill labor market, in *Low Wage Workers and the New Economy*, edited by R. Kazis and M. S. Miller. Washington: Urban Institute Press, 67–87.

Pettinger, L. 2005. Representing shop work: A dual ethnography. *Qualitative Research*, 5(3), 347–64.

Rifkin, J. 2003. *The End of Work*. New York: Penguin.

Roberts, S. 2011a. Beyond NEET and tidy pathways: Considering the missing middle of youth transition studies. *Journal of Youth Studies*, 14(1), 21–39.

Roberts, S. 2011b. 'The lost boys': An overlooked detail in retail?, in *Retail Work*, edited by I. Grugulis and O. Bozkurt. London: Palgrave, 128–48.

Sennett, R. 1998. *The Corrosion of Character: The Consequences of Work in the New Capitalism*. London: W.W Norton.

Simpson, R. 2004. Masculinity at work: The experiences of men in female dominated occupations. *Work, Employment and Society*, 18(2), 349–68.

Skillsmart. 2010. *Skills Priorities for the Retail Sector in the UK and its Four Nations*. London: Skillsmart Retail.

Strangleman, T. 2007. The nostalgia for permanence at work? The end of work and its commentators. *Sociological Review*, 55(1), 81–103.

Teichler, U. 1998. Massification: A challenge for institutions of higher education. *Tertiary Education and Management*, 4(1), 17–27.

Tolich, M and Briar, C. 1999. Just checking it out: Exploring the significance of informal gender divisions amongst American supermarket employees. *Gender, Work and Organisations*, 6(3), 129–32.

Warhurst, C. and Nickson, D. 2007. Employee experience of aesthetic labour in retail and hospitality. *Work, Employment and Society*, 21(1), 103–20.

Wetherell, M. and Edley, N. 1999. Negotiating hegemonic masculinity: Imaginary positions and psycho-discursive practices. *Feminism and Psychology*, 9(3), 335–56.

Willis, P. 1977. *Learning to Labour: Why Working Class Kids Get Working Class Jobs*. Saxon House: Farnborough.

PART II
Intersections between Work and Education

Chapter 5

The Good, the Bad and the Ugly: The Health and Safety of Young Workers

Danaë Anderson, Zeenobiyah Hannif and Felicity Lamm

By the mid-1990s child and youth labour was pronounced by both the International Labour Organisation (ILO) and United Nations Children's Fund (UNICEF) to be one of the dominant issues of our time (UNICEF 1997, ILO 1998, 1999, 2006). Meanwhile, the World Health Organisation (WHO) has identified young employees as a high-risk group of workers (WHO 1995, 2009). Nevertheless, child and youth labour continues to be characterized by precarious, hazardous and unregulated conditions in some countries and sectors (Roggero et al. 2007, Nokov 2000, Lilley et al. 2004).

Although significant regional variations in work practices exist, there are commonalities in terms of the type of work children and youth engage in, and the inherent work-related hazards they face. In the past two decades particularly, young workers entering the labour market have been faced with a rising level of non-standard, precarious, poorly paid employment and emerging new risks within the milieu of an increasingly flexible labour market (Mizen, Pole and Bolton 1999, Mills 2004, Taylor-Gooby 2004, cited in Tranter 2009). Youth employment is also characterized by a lack of distinction between paid and unpaid work; which in turn is cited as one of the possible reasons why there is still weak legal protection for workers under 16 years of age and a reticence to ratify United Nations' (UN) conventions on child and young workers (Anderson et al. 2008). Further, there is a growing trend for young workers to be located in the informal economy working under illegal employment conditions, including non-compliance with health and safety regulations (ILO 2006).

Well documented within this broader literature are the negative occupational health and safety (OHS) outcomes associated with precarious, hazardous employment in which health and safety is a low priority and where there is an absence of trade union representation (Quinlan, Mayhew and Bohle 2001, Quinlan, Bohle and Lamm 2010). Unlike previous generations of workers, reduced trade union membership has left many young workers vulnerable and isolated. Given the undesirable employment situations many young workers find themselves in, it is not surprising that they are over-represented in the occupational injury and fatality statistics (Vocaturo et al. 2007, Accident Compensation Corporation 2009, Alsop et al. 2000). Although New Zealand has a long history of protective employment legislation and was one of the first signatories to the original United

Nations Human Rights Convention, New Zealand does not entirely conform to the principles and provisions of the United Nations Convention on the Rights of Children and related ILO Conventions on occupational health and safety. In particular, there is no universal prescribed minimum age for young workers as per ILO Convention 138 (ILO 1973), or restrictions on the numbers of hours worked (Parkinson 2001, Department of Labour 2009). In addition, the level of legal protection in employment for young workers varies considerably in New Zealand and is based entirely on the age of the worker – that is, adult workers are afforded protection while children and youth are frequently omitted (Boyden, Ling and Myers 1998).

The purpose of this chapter is to draw attention to knowledge that has been accumulated in a small body of work on the OHS of young workers, with a particular focus on recent initiatives designed to address the health and safety of young workers in New Zealand, and to present selected results from a recent study conducted there. Consistent with ILO definitions (ILO/IPEC-SIMPOC 2007) and New Zealand legislation, children are defined here as those aged under 18 years of age while youth are classified as those aged between 18–25 years of age. Our research shows that many of these young workers are to some extent 'invisible' and are largely unrecorded in the official injury and compensation records which in turn present a number of empirical and practical issues. We suggest that one of the reasons for this is that these workers are more likely to fall outside the conventional state apparatus designed to protect workers and assist injured or ill adults. Further complicating this picture is that young peoples' employers are frequently a family member. First however, we address the literature on the vulnerability of youth to OHS risks compared to other employed cohorts.

Are Youth More Vulnerable to OHS Risks?

The link between injuries suffered by young workers and interconnected social, economic, legal and political factors, has been muted. Rather, the emphasis has typically been on blaming and/or changing the behaviour of the individual young worker (see Quinlan et al. 2010 for a more in-depth discussion). In response to these short-comings, there have been recent attempts to provide a coherent framework around the experiences of vulnerable workers, including young workers. In the WHO (2007) report *Employment Conditions and Health Inequalities* a number of factors were highlighted explaining the disparities in working conditions among vulnerable workers. These include employment status, conditions of recruitment, sector of employment or occupation, employment in the informal sector, lack of freedom of association and collective bargaining rights, as well as discrimination and xenophobia in the workplace. The outcome of this report was the emergence of a theoretical model presented as two interrelated frameworks by the WHO's Employment Conditions Knowledge Network (EMCONET) in 2007. The model was later used by Sargeant and Tucker (2009) as the basis of their 'Layers of

Vulnerability' model (see Table 5.1) which aimed to map the complex web of factors that impacted on the health and safety of vulnerable workers.

Table 5.1   Layers of vulnerability

Layer 1 – The Prevailing Political, Social and Economic factors: The macro conditions in which young workers are employed; access to, and strength of, collective representation; access to, and strength of regulatory protection; social inclusion/ exclusion; living on employer's premises; urban/rural location; role of unions/civil society groups, e.g. Church and community groups.
Layer 2 – Employment factors: For example, employment status and whether employment status is tied to legal protection, level of wages and conditions, the enforcement of regulations.
Layer 3 – Individual worker factors: Reasons for working, such as socio-economic conditions; the education, language and skill levels of the young worker; the availability and access to decent work.

Source: Derived from Sargeant and Tucker (2009: 53)

The model aims to provide a better understanding of the origins and consequences of different employment relationships and to link these to key political and economic variables, working conditions, and health inequalities of vulnerable workers, including youth labour. More importantly, it shows 'the interaction between key employment conditions, social mechanisms, and health inequality outcomes in multilevel contexts' (WHO 2007: 15) In particular, EMCONET (WHO 2007: 14) argue that the way inequalities in health are understood and approached by any society is a political issue. Moreover, they state that inequalities in health derived from employment are closely linked to other kinds of social exclusion including poverty, living conditions, political participation and education. Thus, '… through regulating employment relations, main political actors can redistribute resources affecting social stratification, but also have an impact on the life experiences of different social groups including opportunities for well-being, exposure to hazards leading to disease, and access to health care' (WHO 2007: 14).

It is argued that if young workers are exposed to a high level of occupational risk, have poor working conditions and pay, and are employed precariously they could be viewed as 'vulnerable' (see Sargeant and Tucker 2009). At a fundamental level, young workers face considerable occupational risks regardless of their place of work as they are not only susceptible to the same dangers faced by adult workers, but also they are more seriously affected because they differ from adults in their anatomical, physiological and psychological characteristics (Alsop et al. 2000, Windau and Meyer 2005, IPEC 2008). Further, evidence suggests that young workers are more susceptible to injuries than adult workers due to their physical and emotional immaturity, their lack of work experience and their limited awareness of existing or potential risks (Ehrlich et al. 2004: 786). This is borne out by European statistics indicating that 18–24 year olds are 50 per cent more likely to be injured in the workplace compared to more experienced workers (Breslin et al. 2003, Breslin and Smith 2005, European Agency for Safety and Health at Work 2006). In addition, the Australian National Health Survey showed that in the period between 2004–2005 the age group most likely to sustain an injury was workers aged between 0–14 years of age (Australian Bureau of Statistics 2006), consistent with the Accident Compensation Corporation (2009) figures showing that health and safety outcomes for young workers are worse compared to adult workers. This can also be attributed to young workers being employed in prevalently poor and/or hazardous working conditions and the lack of supervision in the workplace (Quinlan et al. 2010).

Research undertaken by the non-government organization Caritas (2003) is a good illustration of the link between hazardous working conditions, poor pay and vulnerability. It is also one of the few Antipodean studies on the health, safety and welfare of children not based entirely on hospital injury surveillance data but instead on surveying nearly 5000 New Zealand children in 2003. The subsequent report highlighted a number of concerns (Caritas 2003: 11). Firstly, the majority of children work for very low wages and yet a significant number of children had to work to financially support their families. Secondly, there was a disturbingly high incidence of children working under dangerous and/or illegal working conditions. For example, there was evidence that children were working in age-restricted employment including working with heavy machinery, in environments where alcohol was being consumed by adults, and in child care. Many children were also working unsupervised, most concerningly younger children aged 11–12 who were more likely to work without adult supervision than older age groups. There were also incidences of children under the age of 16 working between 10pm and 1am. Finally, the findings of the Caritas study indicated that working children were indeed at risk as many of the respondents reported injuries, including broken bones and burns.

The sector where vulnerable young workers are predominantly located and which has the highest rates of youth injury and illness is the farming sector. Findings from the International Programme on the Elimination of Child Labour Agency's (IPEC) survey of 26 developed and developing countries indicated that a high proportion of children and youth surveyed were injured or fell ill at work (39 per cent), with agriculture accounting for 70 per cent of all working injuries. This may be due to the large number of young workers in the agricultural sector (nearly ten times higher than the number of child and youth labourers in other sectors (ILO 2006, cited in Murray and Hurst 2009), and the continued dominance of the agricultural industry in developing and developed countries. This industry is considered particularly hazardous due to 'farm machinery, unsafe transportation, pesticides, caustics and other chemicals in use, physically demanding work, poor sanitation, and other risks' (Manheimer 2006: 360).

In a similar study undertaken in New South Wales (NSW), Australia, nearly 11,000 children aged between 12–15 years of age were surveyed (NSW Commission for Children and Young People 2005). Findings indicate Australian children are exposed to a number of hazards in their work and they sustain a significant number of workplace injuries. Forty per cent of children sustained some type of work-related injury, with almost 20 per cent receiving injuries serious enough to need treatment. The types of jobs with the highest risks of injury were agricultural and horticultural work, labouring, food preparation and delivery work (NSW Commission for Children and Young People 2005, Forastieri 2002). Further, while such workers may primarily work in areas of 'low risk' such as the service and hospitality sectors, these jobs may have significant stressors in terms of conditions of work, hours worked and location of work (Lo and Lamm 2005).

The service sector is another sector in which young workers predominate (Pugh 2007, Black 1995, Department of Labour 2009b). In international research studying injury surveillance data gathered by 91 emergency departments, Hendricks and Layne (1999) attempted to examine the burn-related injuries sustained by teenagers 15–17 years of age working in restaurants in North America. They estimated that 108,060 injuries were sustained by teens on the job; 63 per cent of those injuries occurred solely in fast-food establishments, representing 26 per cent of all teen occupational injuries. Teens working in restaurants and fast food establishments sustained 71 per cent of all burns. Among the total injuries identified, the authors found an overall injury rate for adolescents 15–17 years working in restaurants was '1.7 times higher than the rate for all other industries' (Hendricks and Layne 1999: 1148). This indicates an exponentially high injury rate for youth in a low-wage industry.

However, while there has been a tendency to link vulnerability, age, and level of occupational injury and illness, Tranter (2009) argues that this is not necessarily accurate. In her study of OHS experiences of young, part-time fast food workers in the United Kingdom and Canada, she maintained that the controlling independent variables, namely work experience and age, do not significantly contribute to any of the OHS outcomes regarding injury or ill health (injuries, occupational violence and psychological wellbeing). Instead, she argues, it is more useful to consider multiple risk factors when evaluating OHS outcomes of young workers. Nevertheless, she acknowledges that sampling of age and work experience has been limited, so the ability to find significant linkages was constrained, and exposure to a greater number of hazards increased the odds of injury. Moreover, a single-industry analysis decreases the ability for the findings to be generalized to other workplaces where youth may congregate.

Occupational Health and Safety and Young Workers in New Zealand

The situation regarding the OHS of young workers in New Zealand is not quite as pessimistic as it first appears as there have been a number of global, national and industry level OHS initiatives that may lessen the rates of injury and illness among young workers. At the global level, several ILO Conventions stress the importance of legislation as a protective mechanism for organizing OHS for young workers. In particular, the Occupational Safety and Health Convention, 1981 (No. 155), the Occupational Health Services Convention, 1985 (No. 161) and more recently, ILO Convention 182 on the Elimination of the Worst Forms of Child Labour refer to the need for worker representation underpinned by effective OHS policies and regulatory agencies to be extended to all workplaces. The extent to which these Conventions have been ratified by the signatory countries, however, is variable. Convention 155 (ILO 1981) was ratified by New Zealand in 2007, but New Zealand has not yet ratified Convention 161 (ILO 1985), and only 29 countries in the UN have to date done so.

There have also been national campaigns aimed at highlighting the lack of protection for young workers, often prompted by the UN directives. For example, submissions by non-governmental organizations to the recent United Nations' Periodic Review on New Zealand were especially critical of the employment laws covering child and young workers and note that 'children have a general lack of awareness about their employment rights and whether or not their employers are complying' (Ministry of Youth Development 2009: 8). Research identifies that young workers are rarely given information on employment legislation and therefore are often unaware of their rights, responsibilities or workers' compensation procedures (NSW Commission for Children and Young People 2005, Chauby et al. 2007, Pugh 2007). In response to these and other criticisms regarding the inequitable treatment of young workers and the lack of information, New Zealand's Department of Labour has begun to provide comprehensive web-based information on relevant employment legislation and a summary of the key employment rights and obligations for young workers. However, such sources presuppose awareness of its availability and young workers' capacity to access this information (Pugh 2007, Anderson 2010).

At the industry level, trade apprenticeship training has historically included safety and health. However, apprenticeship schemes in New Zealand have been weakened by successive governments in the past two decades (Higgins 2002). The situation is further complicated by reforms to the apprenticeship scheme and the insertion of a framework of generic unit standards linked to competency-based learning. Successive New Zealand governments have been looking to employers to provide the apprenticeship training, which has been particularly difficult for small business employers as most lack resources and expertise (Rasmussen 2009). In response to the declining number of apprenticeships and the inconsistent quality of training, an increasing number of industry training associations, such as New Zealand's Engineering, Food and Manufacturing Industry Training Organisation (ITO) (see http://www.competenz.org.nz/) now act as the employer and *ipso facto*, have responsibility for the health and safety of the apprentice.

Historically, trade unions have also traditionally provided OHS protection and training for young workers, as seen in the Sweating Commissions of the 1890's. However, lack of union membership in general, and more specifically among young workers, means that the union's reach is limited (in New Zealand membership rates are 17.9 per cent (Employment Relations Service 2009)), impacting collective bargaining rights and negotiating working conditions. More recently, there have been renewed attempts to increase membership rates and collective bargaining among young workers. The creation of the New Zealand trade union UNITE with its emphasis on industry sectors with a high prevalence of young workers, such as hospitality and services sectors, is one such initiative. However, the problem for trade unions remains how to engage the majority of young workers who are unaware of their rights as well as the role of unions. Further, for a group widely acknowledged as vulnerable and on the periphery of the labour market, there is little discussion about how rights and power in the workforce are acquired and controlled (Nokov 2000, Cole 1991).

Difficulties Tracking Occupational Health and Safety Information

As the above literature attests, there is some evidence that young workers experience poorer health and safety outcomes compared to the general population. However, identifying the true extent of work-related injuries and illness among young workers is problematic for a number of reasons. First, researching the OHS of young workers is complicated by the lack of consensus on the definition of youth. For example, the United Nations Convention on the Rights of the Child defines a child as: 'every human being below the age of 18 years unless under the law applicable to the child, majority is attained earlier' (UN 1989: 6). This definition is also adopted by the ILO. The ILO does not have an explicit focus on adolescents as a category but does focus on the adolescent age group (10–19 years) in relation to the categories of child labour and youth employment, and follows the UN definition of youth as the age group between 15–24 years. Australian and New Zealand legislation is consistent with these definitions; children are aged up to 18 while youth are categorized as those up to the age of 25.

Second, there is a lack of reliable data, including injury surveillance data, on the working conditions and safety and health of employed young people (Ashagrie 1998, Bequele and Myers 1995, Robotham 2003, Cigno and Rosati 2005, Lieten and White 2001). More importantly, although information is available regarding adult workers, there is no statistical collection of injury data on workers under 15 years of age in most Organisation for Economic Co-operation and Development (OECD) countries. Further, evidence suggests widespread under-reporting of injuries and, consequently, the under-reporting of accident compensation claims. This is particularly the case in the informal labour market where injuries may be attributed to non-work accidents as a way of avoiding increased insurance premiums for the employer (National Occupational Health and Safety Advisory Commission 2005, Quinlan et al. 2010). Further, there is often little or no information on the circumstances surrounding the accident. Therefore, extant data should be treated with caution; indeed, the actual number of work-related injuries for youth is likely to be much higher than 'official' statistics would suggest. Most government departments responsible for collecting such information acknowledge the issues around data reliability and validity, particularly where 'work-relatedness' is not necessarily clear cut, for example youth fatalities on family farms (Commission for Occupational Safety and Health 2005).

A third problem with identifying the true extent of injury and illness amongst young workers is that the research methods used, especially quantitative research methods, often fail to capture the nuances that permeate youth work, for example, youth working in family-owned or managed businesses (Caspi et al. 1998, Ehrlich et al. 2004, Gasson et al. 2003, Barry and Reddy 2005). That is, the application of orthodox single-method, survey-based, experimental, randomized, controlled research designs are also unlikely to capture sufficient, legitimate data on the topic, particularly if young workers are located in the small business sector. Fourth, the little research undertaken on the OHS of young workers often focuses on industry sectors while overlooking other differences, such as physiological differences within the young worker population and variations in work experiences and health and safety outcomes of different age groups. Nonetheless, there are a few studies which acknowledge that different cohorts of young workers may have a variety of working experiences according to their age, experience and type of work (Lavalette 1994, Black 1995, Blanchflower and Freeman 2000, Fassa et al. 2000, Godfrey 2003, Barwick 2006).

We now turn to the presentation of selected results from a study which addressed the OHS and working experiences of young workers in New Zealand.

Methods

The study applied a triangulated methodological approach in which multiple data collection methods were used. The primary methods of data collection were interviews with policymakers, employee and employer groups, government departments, non-government organizations and young people themselves. A survey of 250 young adults (25 years and under) with 159 usable responses was collected during 2009. In order to capture the working experiences of a wide range of young workers, an ethnically diverse sample was targeted. A university environment in urban New Zealand was ideal to 'capture' this cohort due to the quantity and variety of young students. These students were invited to complete an anonymous survey, the only identifiers being gender, age and ethnicity.

There were a total of 54 male and 105 female participants (n = 159). This gender breakdown was consistent with the gender profile of university students overall (Ministry of Education 2009). Unlike previous studies (in particular Caritas 2007, 2003), no survey respondents had been in paid employment before the age of ten, while the majority of respondents began paid work around 15 years of age.

Results

Respondents were asked to list all the jobs they had had until the age of 18 and the responses have been grouped into sectors together with a description of the types of work undertaken. The range and types of jobs performed by the respondents were similar to those documented in other studies of children's work in industrialized countries. Most positions were located in the service and agriculture sectors, but there was significant variety around the level of pay and working conditions. Respondents often held multiple jobs, typically straddling different work categories, skill levels and workplaces, as outlined in Table 5.2.

Table 5.2   Types of work

Job category	Types of work
Manual labour	house painter, labourer, tiling, golf course maintenance, maintenance for a hire firm, light labouring, bulldozer operator
Agriculture/ horticulture	tomato packing, hothouse work, vet assistant, agricultural production, stable hand, milking cows, strawberry picking, zoo, tree maintenance
Administration	receptionist, office administration, advertising accounts, data entry
Retail	gift shop, video shop, Lotto, clothing, electronics, checkout operator, fast food, travel bookings, cashier
Food	bakers apprentice, waitress, butchers assistant, barista, cook, kitchen hand
Instruction/ children	swimming instructor, dance tutor, babysitting, sports referee, coach, English teacher, camp counsellor, sailing instructor, day care centre
Hospitality	bar waitress, bartender, pub work, movie guide events company, delivery driver
Health and beauty	dental assistant, lab assistant, caregiver, make up artist, hairdresser, beautician, AVON representative
Other	family business (resort, race car production), engineering apprentice, cleaning, paper round, factory work, housecleaning, computer repairs, car groomer, busboy, shelf stacker, milk delivery

The survey asked respondents whether they felt unsafe in their workplaces. While the majority of respondents answering this question (n = 155) answered no (84.5 per cent or 131 respondents), 24 of the respondents (or 15.5 per cent) answered they had felt unsafe. Examples of unsafe working conditions recounted included experiences of unsafe work environments, such as heavy lifting, the use of dangerous equipment and lack of personal protective equipment, as well as being exposed to physical workplace hazards. Respondents noted that: 'Some jobs I had to do I knew weren't safe'. The survey also highlighted issues around physical safety of young workers, including being left in sole charge with little or no training or supervision, and being asked to undertake illegal and/or underage work, for example 'I worked in a very dodgy bar and was often left on my own *and* I was really very young at the time'. A recurring comment from the respondents was the fact that they had to work late and then attempt to get home safely using public transport. Respondents also commented on the high level of non-compliance and lack of enforcement of regulations controlling the hours of work and the number of breaks to which young workers are entitled. There were also examples given of insufficient protection against drunk and/or abusive customers, particularly by those workers employed in the hospitality industry. Harassment by fellow workers and customers was particularly prevalent for women, as some of the responses illustrate: 'He [boss] slapped my ass and swore every five minutes' and 'I was targeted by a manager and verbally abused'.

Respondents were asked whether they had had an accident while working, and over a fifth (n = 34) answered yes. They were then asked to detail their employer's response to their accident. In particular they were asked to use a scale that ranged from total compliance to non-compliance (and which also contained a description to illustrate what each term meant) in order to judge the level of the employer's compliance with the Health and Safety in Employment Act (1992) requirements to report and record work-related incidents, injuries, and illnesses. Based on the three-tiered compliance scale, the responses were categorized according to three levels. The category 'total compliance occurred when the employer recorded the accident and ensured the appropriate medical treatment and compensation. Of the 34 respondents who identified as having had an accident only four (12 per cent) indicated their accident had been recorded and/or treated appropriately. In the category 'partial compliance', (23 or 68 per cent), which was the most common response, the injured worker was taken to the local doctor, but neither the Accident Compensation Corporation nor the Department of Labour were notified of the injury. As these regulatory agencies were not notified the injuries remained unrecorded and as a result, medical bills and accident compensation could not be claimed by the worker. Most concerning were instances where respondents stated they had encountered 'non-compliance', where employers (seven in total or 20 per cent) deliberately chose not to comply with the regulations pertaining to the reporting and investigation of workplace injuries. Workers were actively discouraged from reporting or claiming for an injury and those that received medical treatment had paid for it themselves.

Overall, a low level of compliance was evident, with most employers being partially-compliant or non-compliant and a minimum of employers demonstrating total compliance with legislation concerning reporting mechanisms. The data also indicate that young workers are generally able to obtain medical treatment, but are very rarely compensated for their injury. The level of non-reporting was high (88 per cent) and this provides strong support for the contention that injury surveillance statistics on young people are incomplete and unreliable as indicated by Quinlan et al. (2010) and Ehrlich et al. (2005). The lack of reliable and complete data sets is argued to have significant detrimental ramifications for well-informed public policy on young workers.

For almost a quarter of respondents, their first working experience was working for family or friends of the family (24.5 per cent or 40 people). Those who had worked for family members were overall more likely to record positive experiences, perceptions of fairness and safety, and higher pay, and were generally happier in their employment. In general, the respondents and interviewees were employed in positions that could be seen as peripheral in the labour market (Atkinson 1984), and as a result, felt that they were unable to exert leverage on the conditions they were offered. The extent of injury and lack of reporting are indicative of a broader reduction in '… the state's role in labour relations as well as the legal protections offered to workers individually and collectively' (Buchanan and Nicholls 2003: 2). While trade unions potentially provide a mechanism for seeking redress, over 97 per cent (155 out of 159) of respondents were not members of a trade union while working. Decades of research shows that effective and strong inspectorates and trade unions are essential ingredients for achieving employer compliance with employment law, including occupational health and safety regulations (Walters 2006, Lamm 2010).

In summary, this study signposts a number of worrying aspects of youth employment, and in particular the health and safety of young workers. Non-compliance by employers with basic employment, OHS and workers' compensation law highlighted in this and other studies continues to undermine the wellbeing of young workers. The power imbalance inherent in young people's working relationships constrains their ability to effect and improve their working conditions. International research also indicates similar findings, regardless of country and industry (Cole 1991, Black 1995, Barling and Kelloway 1999, European Agency for Safety and Health at Work 2006, Australian Bureau of Statistics 2006, Caritas 2003, Pugh, 2007).

Conclusion

The OHS of young workers is more complex than simply calculating how many young people die or are injured (see Layne et al. 1994, Lilley et al. 2004, ABS 2006), although accurate statistics in this regard would be a useful starting point. Ascertaining how best to protect young workers is complicated by definitional issues (that is, what is a 'young worker'?), plagued by inadequate and contradictory legislation and exacerbated by industry characteristics and employment practices within the workplace. In this chapter, we have highlighted the issues surrounding this contentious topic. In particular, there is growing evidence to show that this group of workers are to some extent vulnerable in that they are frequently exposed to hazardous conditions for low pay and are concentrated in industries where precarious employment is prevalent, such as agriculture, manufacturing and service. Moreover, young workers are often considered as 'invisible' as they are rarely recorded in the official injury and compensation records. In addition, they are more likely to fall outside the conventional state apparatus designed to assist injured workers. Working arrangements and the health and safety of young workers are further complicated by the fact that their employer is frequently a family member.

While the issues are perennial, the solutions addressing the level of injuries and illness among young workers are still evolving and need to respond to the changing working environment in which there is an increase in precarious, non-standard working arrangements and where there has been a decline in collective bargaining and trade union membership and density. International conventions concerning the treatment and welfare of child and young workers that emanate from the UN and other international organizations provide a useful platform for OHS and employment relations reforms. The challenge for politicians, public servants and industry representatives, however, is to translate these conventions into effective and transparent protective measures that can be applied to a myriad of different workplaces. However, for this to occur there needs to be a shift in the way in which we view the nature of work and the way we treat young workers.

References

Accident Compensation Corporation 2009. ACC Injury Statistics 2008/2009, Section 3.1. All Work-Related Claims. Available at: http://www.acc.co.nz/ PRD_EXT_CSMP/groups/externalip/documents/reports_results/wpc088563. pdf [accessed: 13 July 2010].

Alsop, J., Gifford, J., Langley, J., Beg, D. and Firth, H. 2000. Occupational injury in a cohort of young adults. *Journal of Occupational Health and Safety – Australia and New Zealand*, 16(2), 107–16.

Anderson, D. 2010. Safe Enough? The Working Experiences of New Zealand Children. MPhil Thesis. Auckland University of Technology.

Anderson, D., Lamm, F, Shuttleworth, P., McMorland, J. and Rasmussen, E. 2008. Child Labour: What is Happening in New Zealand? 2008 Labour Employment and Work Conference, Wellington.

Ashagrie, K. 1998. Statistics on Child Labor and Hazardous Child Labor in Brief. Geneva: ILO.

Atkinson, J. 1984, August, Manpower Strategies for Flexible Organisations. Personnel Management, 16(8), 28–31.

Australian Bureau of Statistics 2006. Injury in Australia: A Snapshot: 2004–05, Catalogue No. 4825.0.55.001, Canberra: Australian Bureau of Statistics

Barling, J., and Kelloway, E. K. (eds) 1999. *Young Workers: Varieties of Experience*. Washington: American Psychological Association.

Barry, C. and Reddy, S. 2005. International Trade and Labor Standards: Draft 1.60. Available at: http://organizations.lawschool.cornell.edu/ilj/symposium/papers/just_linkage.pdf [accessed: 8 August, 2008].

Barwick, H. 2006. *Youth Work Today: A review of the issues and challenges.* Wellington: Ministry of Youth Development.

Bequele, A. and Myers, W. E. 1995. *First Things First in Child Labour: Eliminating work detrimental to children.* Geneva: ILO.

Blanchflower, D. G and. Freeman, R. B. 2000. The declining economic status of young workers in OECD countries, in *Youth Employment and Joblessness in Advanced Countries,* edited by D. G. Blanchflower and R. B. Freeman. Chicago: University of Chicago Press and NBER, 19–56.

Black, M. 1995. *In the Twilight Zone: Child Workers in the Hotel, Tourism and Catering Industry.* Geneva: ILO.

Boyden, J., Ling, B and Myers, W. 1998. *What Works for Working Children.* RaddaBarnen and UNICEF: Stockholm.

Breslin, C., Koehoorn, M., Smith, P., Manno, M. 2003. Age related differences in work injuries and permanent impairment: A comparison of workers' compensation claims among adolescents, young adults, and adults. *Journal of Occupational Environmental Medicine,* 60(9), 1–6.

Breslin, C., and Smith, P. 2005. Age-related differences in work injuries: A multivariate, population-based study. *American Journal of Industrial Medicine,* 48(1), 50–56.

Buchanan, P., and Nicholls, K. (2003). *Labour Politics in Small Open Democracies: Australia, Chile, Ireland, New Zealand and Uruguay.* Hampshire; New York: Palgrave MacMillan.

Caritas, 2003. *Protecting Children at Work: Children's Work Survey.* Thorndon: Caritas.

Caspi, A., Moffitt, B., Wright, B. and Silva, P. 1998. Early failure in the labour market: child and adolescent predictors of unemployment in the transition to adulthood. *American Sociological Review,* 63(3), 424–51.

Chauby, J., Perisic, M., Perrault, N., Laryea-Adji, G. and Khan, N. 2007. *Child Labour, Education and Policy Options.* Working Paper. New York: United Nations Children's Fund.

Cigno, A., and Rosati, F. C. 2005. *The Economics of Child Labour.* Oxford: Oxford University Press.

Cole, P. 1991. *Children at Work: Peril or Promise?* Albany, New York: AFL-CIO.

Commission for Occupational Safety and Health 2005. *General duty of care in Commission for Occupational Safety and Health. 2005. General Duty of Care in Western Australian Workplaces.* Available at: http://www.commerce.wa.gov.au/worksafe/PDF/Guidance_notes/general_duty_of_care.pdf [accessed: 24 August, 2010].

Cryer, P. and Fleming, C. 1987. A review of work-related fatal injuries in New Zealand 1975–84: Numbers, rates and trends. 100, 1–6.

Department of Innovation, Industry, Science and Research. 2010. *Services Sector Fact Sheet*. Available at: http://www.innovation.gov.au/Section/AboutDIISR/ FactSheets/Pages/ ServicesSectorFactSheet.aspx [accessed: 12 October 2010].

Department of Labour 2009. *Youth in the New Zealand Labour Market: National Monitoring Series*. Wellington: Department of Labour.

Ehrlich, P. F., McClellan, W. T., Hemkamp, J. C., Islam, S. S. and Ducatman, A. M. 2004. Understanding work-related injuries in children: A perspective in West Virginia using the state-managed workers' compensation system. *Journal of Paediatric Surgery*, 39(5), 768–72.

Employment Relations Service 2009. *Union Membership Return Report*. Wellington, Department of Labour.

European Agency for Safety and Health at Work 2006. *Too Many Young People are Getting Hurt at Work*. Available at: http://osha.europa.eu/press_room [accessed: 13 January 2011].

Fassa, A., Facchini, L. A., Dall'Agnol, M. M., and Christiania, D. 2000. Child labor and health: Problems and perspectives. *International Journal of Occupational and Environmental Health*, 6(1), 55–62.

Forastieri, V. 2002. *Children at Work: Health and Safety Risks*. Geneva: ILO.

Gasson, R., Gasson, J., Linley, T. and Powell-Chalmers, J. 2003. *Young People and Work*. Dunedin: Dunedin College of Education.

Godfrey, M. 2003. *Youth Employment Policy in Developing and Transition Countries: Prevention as Well as Cure*. Social Protection Discussion Paper Series No. 0320. World Bank: Washington.

Hendricks, K. and Layne, L. 1999. Adolescent occupational injuries in fast food restaurants: An examination of the problem from a national perspective. *The Journal of Occupational and Environmental Medicine*, 41(2), 1146–53

Higgins, J. 2002. Young people and transitions policies in New Zealand. *Social Policy Journal New Zealand*, 18, 44–61.

International Labour Organisation (ILO) 2006. *The End of Child Labour: Within Reach*. Geneva: International Labour Organisation.

International Labour Organisation (ILO) 1999. *ILO Convention 182: The Worst Forms of Child Labour Convention*.

International Labour Organisation (ILO) 1998. *Conference Report VI (I) Child Labour: Targeting the Intolerable*. Geneva: ILO.

International Labour Organisation (ILO) 1985. *Convention 161: Occupational Health Services Convention*.

International Labour Organisation (ILO) 1981. *ILO Convention 155: Occupational Health and Safety Convention*.

International Labour Organisation (ILO) 1973. *ILO Convention 138: Minimum Age Convention*.

ILO/IPEC-SIMPOC 2007. *Towards an Internationally Accepted Statistical Definition of Child Labour: Children's Activities and their Definitions*. Geneva: ILO.

International Programme on the Elimination of Child Labour (IPEC) 2008. *Hazardous Child Labour.* Available at: http://www.ilo.org/ipec/facts/ Hazardouschildlabour/index.htm [accessed: 12 July 2010].

Lamm, F. 2010. Participative and productive employment relations: The role of health and safety committees and worker representation, in *Employment Relationships: Workers, Unions and Employers in New Zealand* (2nd ed.), edited by E. Rasmussen. Auckland University Press, Auckland, 168–84.

Layne, L., Castillo, D., Stout, N. and Cutlip, P. 1994. Adolescent occupational injuries requiring hospital emergency department treatment: a nationally representative sample. *American Journal of Public Health*, 84(4), 657–60.

Lavalette, M. 1994. *Child Employment in the Capitalist Labour Market.* England: Avebury.

Lieten, G. and White, B. 2001. *Child Labour Policy Options.* Amsterdam: Aksant Academic Publishers.

Lilley, R., Feyer, A., Langley, J. and Wren, J. 2004. The New Zealand child work-related fatal injury study: 1985–1998. *The New Zealand Medical Journal*, 117(1194), 891. Available at: http://www.nzma.org.nz/journal/117-1194/891/ [accessed: 6 October 2009].

Lo, K., and Lamm, F. 2005. Occupational stress in the hospitality industry – An employment relations perspective. *New Zealand Journal of Employment Relations*, 30(1), 23–47.

Manheimer, A. (ed). 2006. *Child Labor and Sweatshops.* San Diego: Greenhaven Press.

Ministry of Education 2009. *International Student Enrolments in New Zealand: 2002–2008.* Wellington: Ministry of Education.

Ministry of Youth Development 2009. *3rd and 4th Periodic Report: United Nations Convention on the Rights of the Child.* Available at: http://www.myd. govt.nz/documents/working-with-young-people/uncroc/uncroc-in-nz-3rd-and-4th-periodic-report-full-doc.pdf [accessed: 4 November 2010].

Mizen, P., Bolton A. and Pole C. 1999. School age workers: The paid employment of children in Britain. *Work, Employment and Society*, 13(3), 423–38.

Murray, U. and Hurst, P. 2009. *Mainstreaming Responses for Improvement of the Employment Conditions of the Girl Child in Agriculture.* Paper presented at the FAO- IFAD-ILO workshop on gaps, trends and current research in gender dimensions of agricultural and rural employment: differentiated pathways out of poverty. Rome.

National Occupational Health and Safety Advisory Commission. 2005. *Surveillance of Occupational Disease and Injury in New Zealand.* Report to the Minister of Labour. Wellington: NOHSAC.

Nokov, J. 2000. Historicizing the figure of the child in legal discourse: The battle over the regulation of child labour. *The American Journal of Legal History*, 44(4), 369–494.

NSW Commission for Children and Young People 2005. *Children at Work.* NSW: NSW Commission for Children and Young People.

Parkinson, P. 2001. *The Child Labour Problem in Australia.* Defence for the Children International- Australia. Available at: http//www.dciau.org/html/ parksinson.html [accessed: 12 October 2010].

Pugh, J. 2007. *Health and Safety Knowledge of Young Workers: A Study of School-aged, Part-time Workers in the Taranaki Region.* Wellington: Department of Labour.

Quinlan, M., Mayhew, C. and Bohle, P. 2001. The Global expansion of precarious employment, work disorganization, and consequences for occupational health: A Review of recent research. *International Journal of Health Services*, 31(2), 335–414.

Quinlan, M., Bohle, P. and Lamm, F. 2010. *Managing Occupational Health and Safety: A Multidisciplinary Approach.* Sydney: Macmillan.

Rasmussen, E. 2009. *Employment Relations in New Zealand (2nd ed.).* Auckland: Pearson.

Robotham, G. 2003. *Discussion Paper: The Lost Time Injury Frequency Rate.* Available at: http://www.ohschange.com.au/articles/The_Lost_Time_Injury_ Frequency_Rate/The_Lost_Time_Injury_Frequency_Rate.html-   [accessed: 12 October 2010].

Roggero, P., Mangiaterra, V., Bustreo, F. and Rosati, F. 2007. *The Health Impact of Child Labor in Developing Countries: Evidence from Cross-Country Data.* American Journal of Public Health, 50(4), 271–6.

Sargeant, M. and Tucker, E. 2009. Layers of vulnerability in OHS for migrant workers: Case studies from Canada and the UK. *Policy and Practice in Health and Safety*, 7(2), 51–73.

Tranter, M. 2009. *Occupational Health and Safety of Young Part-time Workers in the United Kingdom and Canada.* Thesis submitted for DPhil, University of New South Wales, Australia.

UNICEF 1997. *The State of the World's Children.* Oxford: Oxford University Press.

United Nations. 1989. *United Nations Convention on the Rights of the Child (UNCROC).* New York: United Nations.

Vocaturo, E., Kunseler, E., Slovakova, G., Ruut, J., Cavoura, O. and Otorepec, P. 2007. *Work Injuries in Children and Young People.* Bonn: European Environment and Health Information System.

Walters, D. 2006. One step forward, two steps back: Worker representation and health and safety in the United Kingdom. *International Journal of Health Services*, 36(1), 87–111.

Windau, J. and Meyer, S. 2005. Occupational injuries among young workers. *Monthly Labor Review*, 128(10), 11–23.

World Health Organisation (WHO). 1995. *Global strategy on occupational health for all.* Geneva.

World Health Organisation (WHO). 2007. *Employment Conditions and Health Inequalities, Employment Conditions Knowledge Network (EMCONET).* Final Report, Commission on Social Determinants of Health (CSDH).

World Health Organisation (WHO). 2009. *Work Injuries in Children and Young People, Fact Sheet 4.7*. Available at: http://www.euro.who.int/data/assets/pdf_ file/ [accessed: 12 July 2011].

Chapter 6

Juggling School and Work and Making the Most of Both

Margaret Vickers

Young people who work during high school are undertaking a complex balancing act. How much work should they do? How can they balance the demands of homework and exams over and against the pressures of their part-time jobs? Will they be better off because they have gained work experience, or will their academic results suffer, leading them to miss out on future educational opportunities?

The literature reviewed in this chapter summarizes results from quantitative studies over the past 20 years that have examined the implications of combining study and work during the high school years in the United States (US), the United Kingdom (UK) and Australia. In summary, this literature reveals a conundrum: it appears on the one hand that moderate to long hours of student part-time employment have *negative* impacts on academic outcomes, yet on the other hand student employment appears to have *positive* effects on the likelihood of being employed after leaving school. As discussed below, the scale of the phenomenon is substantial: statistics suggest that in Australia, the US and the UK, approximately one half of all senior-level students are working. With such high rates of student participation in part-time employment, the phenomenon deserves careful analysis to ascertain its impacts on young people. There is a clear need to develop and implement policies that will support young people who are attempting to balance the competing demands of study and work.

As indicated below, numerous studies suggest that part-time employment diminishes academic achievement and reduces the likelihood of high school completion. Based on this, some might argue that policies should be introduced to curb the levels of student employment at the high school level. However, recent changes in global labour market dynamics mean it is unlikely that countries with high levels of student employment will see a decline in this phenomenon. Labour market deregulation, extended working hours (especially in the retail sector), and increased casualization means that relatively high levels of student part-time employment are likely to be sustained in the US, UK and Australia (Buddelmeyer and Wooden 2007). Assuming that a substantial proportion of high school students will continue to work part-time, it falls to parents, educators and young people themselves to ascertain what needs to be done to make the best of this situation. The aim of this chapter, therefore, is to discuss issues that have largely been neglected in previous research, specifically:

1. What problems do young people encounter as they attempt to balance the competing demands of study and work?
2. What institutional changes in *school-level* policies and practices might help young people balance the demands of study and work? and
3. What might employers do to help young people deal with these competing demands?

Preliminary findings from the first phase of a new Australian study of students' views about the problems of balancing the demands of study and part-time work are reported. The chapter concludes with an overview of some Australian initiatives that are making it possible for students to make the most of their part-time work and still do well at school.

The Scale of Student Employment

Teenage employment data provided by the Organisation for Economic Co-operation and Development (OECD) and subsequently analysed by the US Bureau of Labor Statistics (US BLS 2008) provide useful cross-national comparisons. These data cover both part-time and full-time employment of 15–19 year olds, including those who are in school, in post-secondary study, or in the workforce and not studying. The data clearly indicate that levels of teenage employment vary substantially across the OECD member countries. In general the English-speaking countries tend to have the highest levels of teenage employment, but participation in part-time employment is also quite high in the Netherlands and the Scandinavian countries (US BLS 2008). In Germany, Austria and Switzerland, teenage employment falls between 32 and 45 per cent, as a result of the 'dual system' of apprenticeships. The dual system provides highly regulated forms of student employment linked to workplace training. Elsewhere in Europe teenage labour force participation rates are relatively low; for example in France, Italy and Portugal it lies between 10 and 15 per cent. In Japan (also an OECD member) the level of teenage employment is 16 per cent. These levels contrast sharply with the higher participation rates reported in the US, Canada, the UK, New Zealand and Australia. As the US Bureau of Labour Statistics (2008) reported, the overall level of teenage labour force participation was 40 per cent in the US, 53.5 per cent in the UK and 59 per cent in Australia.

Cross-national comparisons regarding high school students' levels of participation in part-time work are more difficult to obtain, and the data are not always comparable across countries. Using the large national data base *Longitudinal Survey of Australian Youth* (LSAY) as the basis of her report to the 2009 House of Representatives Committee on Combining School and Work (HoR SCET), Anlezark (2009) reported that the proportions of high school students who are employed increases as they move into the senior years. Using the LSAY-2003 sample, she found that the proportion of high school males working rose from 39 per cent to 52 per cent between Year 9 and Year 12, while the proportion of females working rose from 45 per cent to 62 per cent over the same period. Data from the UK provided by Payne (2003) refer only to students in the twelfth and thirteenth years of secondary education. Based on analyses of the UK *Youth Cohort Study*, she reported that 45 per cent of Year 12 students and 59 per cent of Year 13 students were in a job at the time of the survey. Using data from the *Minnesota Youth Development Survey*, Mortimer (2003) reported that the workforce participation of boys rose from 40 per cent to 58 per cent between Year 9 and Year 12, while the workforce participation of girls rose from 63 per cent to 70 per cent over the same period. Based on substantial data from the *Monitoring the Future* survey, Staff and Schulenberg (2010) reported similar figures: namely, that the proportion of US students who work rises from 40 per cent in Year 10 to 75 per cent in Year 12. To summarize: it appears that by the time students are in their final year of secondary school, whether they are in the US, the UK or in Australia, more than half of them are working.

Part-time Student Work and Future Employment Success

Participation in part-time work during high school facilitates successful labour market entry and reduces the risk of unemployment. Studies by both labour market economists and educational researchers have consistently found that part-time student employment increases the likelihood that a young person will be employed rather than unemployed after high school. Indications that student work has positive effects on post-school employment have consistently been reported by Australian researchers. Employing the large national data base known as LSAY (Longitudinal Surveys of Australian Youth) three substantial studies have been carried out independently by different groups of researchers covering four separate student cohorts over a fourteen-year period. In addition, analyses of the more recent LSAY-2003 data have been conducted by Anlezark and were presented as evidence before the 2009 Australian House of Representatives Standing Committee (HoR SCET 2009) on combining school and work. The LSAY studies are discussed below. Each of them came to similar conclusions about the benefits of part-time employment in relation to future labour market success.

The evidence presented by Anlezark, to the House of Representatives 2009 inquiry (HoR SCET 2009) analysed data from LSAY-03 a national sample of 10,370 young people who were aged 15.7 years in 2003. She found that, among those who did not engage in full-time post-secondary study, the probability of being employed rather than unemployed two years after completing high school was substantially greater for students who had been employed part-time during Year 12. In a study published in 2006, Marks used LSAY-98, a national survey of 13,613 students who were initially surveyed in Year 9 in 1998; and in an earlier study, Vickers, Lamb and Hinkley (2003) used LSAY-95, a similar national survey of students who were in Year 9 in 1995. Both these studies found that employment during high school increased the likelihood of being employed in the post-school period. Marks's study suggested that this benefit persisted over time, since those who had been part-time student workers continued to show better labour-market attachment four years after completing high school. Vickers et al. (2003) found the positive effects of student employment were substantial, boosting the odds being employed full-time (rather than unemployed) by 46 percent, and boosting the odds of gaining an apprenticeship by 65 percent. Using a related survey – the Youth in Transition longitudinal series – Robinson (1999) gained similar results for students whose birth year was 1975 (these young people would mostly have been in Year 9 in 1989). Using a relatively small sample, Smith and Green (2001) conducted a longitudinal study that distinguished itself from the above through the use of student and employer interviews as well as student surveys. This allowed them to explore the nature of students' experiences at work; analyses of the interview texts suggested that young people's experiences at work contributed in important ways to developing their employability skills for their future.

There is also a substantial body of American literature which suggests that part-time student employment during high school contributes to future labour market success. Staff and Mortimer (2007) noted that 80 per cent of higher education students in the US are in the workforce and that most of these find it necessary to work in order to remain in college. Using a longitudinal sample survey, they found that students who developed the capacity to balance study and part-time work while at high school benefited during their college years. For students of lower socio-economic status, the capacity to combine study and work was especially beneficial. Marsh and Kleitman (2002, 2005) mainly focused on reporting the negative effects on academic outcomes of part-time student employment, but they also found that student workers were less likely than those who had never worked during high school to be unemployed in the post-school period. Similar findings regarding the effects of part-time student employment on labour market success have also been reported in other studies (Mortimer 2003, Carr, Wright and Brody 1996, Ruhm 1995, Stern and Nakata 1989).

There appears to be a dearth of longitudinal studies in the UK regarding the connection between high school employment and future labour market success. Much of the published research from the UK focuses on the impact of participation in part-time employment on school achievement (Payne 2003, McVicar and McKee 2002). These studies did not examine labour market outcomes during the post-secondary years. However, recent studies by McKechnie et al. (2010) and Howieson, McKechnie and Semple (2006) suggest that young people as well as their employers and parents find that participation in paid employment leads to greater independence and confidence, an awareness of the need for higher qualifications, and development of appropriate work-related skills and attitudes.

Part-time Student Employment and Educational Outcomes

A large body of research has focused on asking whether part-time student work enhances or detracts from *educational* outcomes. The findings from these studies are not always consistent. In part, this lack of consistency may result from methodological problems, such as the use of small local surveys rather than large, national longitudinal surveys, or from certain difficulties in variable specification. Participation in part-time work – the prime explanatory variable – is itself difficult to define. Different groups of individuals may *begin working* at different grade levels, and the overall *duration* of their work may also vary, in that some will stop working before the end-of-year exams. *Work intensity* also varies, with some students working less than ten hours per week, while others work 15 hours, 20 hours or well over 20 hours per week. In addition, *work intensity* may not be consistent over time. Australian studies suggest that these methodological choices do make a difference to the research findings.

For example, Robinson (1999) and Marks et al. (2000) sought to establish whether Australian students who participated in part-time work were more likely to drop out than those who did not. Both these studies used work intensity in Year 11 as a predictor, and both found working had no effect on the likelihood of completing school. A subsequent analysis by Vickers et al. (2003) used work intensity in Year 9 and produced contrasting results to those of Robinson. This suggests that while participation in part-time work at the Year 11 level may not have a measurable effect, students who worked long hours in Year 9 are more likely to drop out than those who work short hours or do not work at all. Vickers et al. (2003) argued that the contradictions between these studies relates to the fact that student workers in Year 11 represent a selected group that differ from the Year 9 group. Until recently in Australia, the end of Year 10 was a major exit point for early leavers, since many students entered the apprenticeship system after Year 10. Thus, the Year 11 group were survivors: they had educational intentions that involved graduating from high school and continuing on to tertiary study. By Year 11 they had already stayed on beyond the point at which many others had left.

Three essentially different arguments regarding the educational consequences of participation in part-time work emerge from the literature. First, *threshold theory* suggests that the negative effects of working only apply to students who work long hours (Staff and Schulenberg 2010, Payne 2003, Stern and Nakata 1989, D'Amico 1984). These studies suggest that there is a threshold below which student employment has no effect on academic outcomes, and above which negative consequences emerge. Using data from the UK *Youth Cohort Study,* Payne (2003) found that students in Years 12 and 13 studying for their A or A/S levels were able to work 15 hours per week without negative consequences, but for those who worked 16 hours or more there was a steady deterioration in the results students obtained. Staff and Schulenberg (2010) defined 'intensive' employment in terms of 20 hours per week, finding that more successful students limited their hours of work to below 20. Staff and Schulenberg (2010) also found that the *type* of work students engage in has an impact in addition to its intensity; that is, work that is heavy and dirty and involves late-night hours has a more negative impact on students than 'light' work conducted during regular hours. Stern and Nakata (1989) and D'Amico (1984) also supported the argument for a threshold, but set the number of 'safe' hours at a lower level – that is, 14 hours per week – for tenth year students. In Australia, where the average number of hours worked by teenagers tends to be lower than in the US, Vickers et al. (2003) found that students who worked more than 5 hours per week in Year 9 were more likely to drop out than those who worked 5 hours or less, and that the negative effects of working on dropping out were positive and linear after 5 hours. However, Vickers et al. (2003) also found that this threshold effect did not apply to all students, suggesting that time allocation may not be the only factor involved. In a model that separated males and females, substantial negative effects of working were found for males, but there were no significant effects for females even if they worked quite long hours. Further investigation is needed to ascertain whether this difference results from girls mostly being employed in 'light' work during regular hours while boys are doing physically demanding work on late-night schedules, or whether girls have better time-management strategies than boys.

The second group of proposals which attempt to explain the educational consequences of participation in part-time work could broadly be referred to as *zero-sum theories*. According to these theories, the hours allocated to part-time employment compete with the hours allocated to schoolwork. It is argued that participation in part-time work detracts from scholarly commitments, interferes with continuity in education, and lowers the quality of school performance (Marsh 1991, Steinberg and Dornbush 1991). Among zero-sum theories, two positions have been articulated. The simplest of these proposes that the *time allocated* to work, in itself causes the problem. In support of the time allocation argument, there is some indication that participation in part-time work might reduce the number of hours students spend on homework (Marsh 1991, D'Amico 1994). However, this argument is questioned by researchers who have found that the time spent doing a part-time job tends to crowd out teenage leisure activities rather than compete with study (Mortimer 2003).

A more nuanced version of the zero-sum approach proposes that while time counts, the critical variable may be *commitment,* rather than time per se (Marsh 1992). Studies by Marsh and Kleitman (2002, 2005), Schoenhals, Tienda and Schneider (1998) and D'Amico (1984) and are consistent with this theory. Using NELS–88 data and controlling for demographic background factors, Schoenhals et al. (1998) found that the number of hours students spend watching television falls substantially as the number of hours they work per week increases. They also found that participation in part-time work does not reduce the number of hours students spend on homework. In an earlier study, D'Amico (1984) also noted that students who work have less time for non-academic activities at school, again suggesting that students may compensate for the hours they lose at work by reducing leisure activities.

Marsh and Kleitman (2005, 2002) make a clear case against the simple time allocation argument. If time itself is the problem, then anything that detracts from scholarly activity should have negative effects, and this should also apply to engagement in extra-curricular school activities (ESAs). However, they found that the allocation of substantial amounts of time to ESAs has predominantly *positive* effects on Year 12 and post-secondary outcomes. At the same time, they found that part-time employment during the school year has predominantly negative effects. Juxtaposing these two findings, they argue that while ESAs increase identification with and commitment to school, work undermines identification and commitment; long hours of work have substantial negative effects. This suggests that there is no *inevitable* link between participation in part-time work and reduced commitment to school. As Marsh noted in his 1992 study, for the small group of student workers who saved their earnings to pay for future education, working during the school year seemed to have positive effects. Taken together, these findings suggest that students who are committed to doing well at school may actually be able to balance the demands of study and work.

A third argument focuses on *selectivity effects*, which proposes that those who work long hours may be a self-selected group who differ in various ways from those who work short hours. They may, for example, be less committed to school in the first place, or have different reasons for working during high school when compared with students who work shorter hours. Some young people choose not to work, and some choose to work short hours only. For example, most studies find that while girls are more likely to be employed than boys, in general, boys tend to work longer hours than girls (Keithly and Deseran 1995, Vickers et al. 2003, Marsh 1991, D'Amico 1984). In the US, black students are less likely to work than white students (D'Amico 1984, Keithly and Deseran 1995). In Australia, high school students from language backgrounds other than English are less likely to work than students from English-speaking families (Robinson 1999, Vickers et al. 2003). Students who work long hours are not a random selection of the broader student population; they have distinctly different profiles. Therefore, one cannot view hours of work as an 'experimental intervention' applied to a sample of students who are otherwise similar to those who did not experience this 'intervention'. It is more likely that the impact of working on educational outcomes results from *interactions* between the effects of part-time employment and pre-existing characteristics of the student worker.

The question is: does participation in part-time work lead to poorer educational outcomes by itself, or are its effects mediated by other factors, such as student background characteristics, dispositions towards scholarly activity, and plans for the future? Several studies have examined this question. Schoenhals et al. (1998) used national (NELS–88) data, while Entwisle, Alexander and Steffel-Olsen (2000) used the *Beginning School Survey* to examine early school performance and teenage work experiences (ages 13–18) for Baltimore youth. The study by

Schoenhals et al. (1998) began by examining the characteristics of students who worked during Year 10 compared with those who were not working. They found that boys were more likely to work than girls, and that the decision to participate in part-time work did not differ substantially by educational ability, as measured by a Year 8 test-score composite. A further analysis indicated that those who worked *long hours* did differ in educational ability from those who worked short hours: students with low test scores worked far more hours per week than students with high test scores. Students were also compared on a school-detachment index, which comprised Year 8 students' self-reports of being unprepared for class, skipping or being late for class, and engaging in deviant activities at school. These analyses indicated that, on average, students who worked the longest hours in Year 10 had also scored higher on the school-detachment measure two years before, in Year 8. They concluded that those who elected to work most intensively in high school were already detached from school *before* they engaged with the workplace.

Schoenhals et al. (1998) then analysed the relationship between hours worked in Year 10 and academic results. As expected, a linear negative association between hours of work and results was established, with significant effects for all participation in part-time work above 10 hours per week and increasing magnitudes as the hours worked increased. Inclusion of controls typical of prior studies (sex, race, parental education and family income) weakened but did not eliminate the negative association between hours currently worked and results. However, when additional control variables that included school detachment, Year 8 test score, absences, type of school and type of curriculum were included in the model, the effects of participation on part-time work on school results were substantially reduced and all but one were no longer statistically significant. Addressing this same issue in their study of Baltimore students, Entwisle et al. (2000) found that many students who subsequently chose to work long hours were already poor performers at age 8, and showed low levels of commitment to school and erratic attendance patterns *before* they started to work part-time.

Both studies conclude that students who work differ from those who do not, and among student workers, those who work long hours have further distinguishing characteristics. Schoenhals et al. (1998) argued that the negative educational effects previously attributed to student employment are spurious, since they are largely driven by pre-existing differences between workers and non-workers and between those who work short hours rather than long hours. More recent studies by Lee and Staff (2007) and Staff, Schulenberg and Bachman (2010) add further support for the selectivity effects argument. Lee and Staff (2007) argued that the relationship between the intensity of part-time employment and dropping out is spurious and can largely be attributed to pre-existing differences in socio-economic background, school performance, aspirations, and orientations toward work and school.

The Entwisle et al. (2000) study supported the selectivity effects argument, but also placed a strong emphasis on the positive effects of part-time student work on post-school employment. They wrote, 'we suspect that the predominant causal process linking youth work to poor school performance is that poorly performing students lose interest in school and are more willing to spend long hours on the job' (Entwisle et al. 2000: 292). At the sametime, Entwisle et al. (1998) emphasize that youth work produces human capital, since it enables young people to accumulate experience and skills that have value in the labour market. For male students who were poor academic performers, and especially for those from families of low socio-economic status, their research found that employment during high school (at ages 13–14) considerably improved young people's prospects of gaining a semi-skilled job later on.

To summarize: overall, the literature on student participation in part-time employment suggests that below a certain threshold, working has negligible effects on educational outcomes. As the number of hours worked increases above this threshold, the likelihood of gaining low grades and/or dropping out increases. However, some groups of students seem to be relatively immune to this effect and are able to work relatively long hours without negative consequences. In general, it seems that students who are more committed to academic success are better able to balance the demands of study and work.

Helping Young People Achieve a Balance between the Demands of Study and Work

In Australia, the UK and the US, a large proportion of young people now divide their time between student and worker roles from early adolescence. The literature reviewed above overwhelmingly suggests that participation in part-time work facilitates labour market entry, even though it may diminish academic outcomes. It seems reasonable, then, to propose that young people who envision their futures in terms of a successful transition directly from school to work may choose to invest more energy in their part-time jobs than in their studies.

Approximately 38 per cent of Australia's school leavers enter full-time or part-time employment directly, without enrolling in further study (ABS 2003). Many of these young people come from backgrounds of social exclusion and economic hardship, and thus need to gain a secure foothold in the labour market in order to support themselves and their families. Many of them live in remote–rural or poor–urban regions where job opportunities are scarce. Since having a job during high school significantly increases the chances of being employed later on, new policies and programs that help these young people to balance study and work are urgently needed (Vickers et al. 2003). In addition, for the 42 per cent of young Australians who graduate from school and enter full-time study at a university, a technical and further education college, or another institution (ABS 2003), an employment track record also matters. Most of them, and especially those from low-income backgrounds, will need to work part-time during their tertiary studies.

Preliminary Results from the Staying On Study

In 2009, the author and her colleagues initiated a new study of student participation in part-time employment. This study is part of a larger project, titled *Staying On at School*, (subsequently referred to as the 'Staying On' study) funded by the Australian Research Council and the New South Wales Department of Education and Training (NSW DET). The study is being conducted by the University of Western Sydney in collaboration with Charles Sturt University. The design of the *Staying On* study is longitudinal, entailing survey-based research, individual student interviews and school case studies. Students participating in Wave 1 were in Years 7, 8 and 9 in 2009, and by the end of Wave 3, in 2011, these students will be in Years 9, 10 and 11. The study is being conducted in nine schools drawn from three regions of NSW. All the schools serve communities of low socio-economic status. Two of the nine schools are in major rural towns, four are in small rural or coastal centres and three are in Sydney's multicultural western suburbs. The initial sample size was 1,966 students, with 670 Year 9 students completing the survey in 2009. This chapter provides a preliminary analysis of a small fraction of the data from Wave 1 of the study. Since the employment participation questions were only administered to students at the Year 9 level, these data relate only to that sub-sample. Insignificant numbers of students in Years 7 and 8 were in paid employment during Wave 1 since they were mostly below the legal working age. However, as the study moves through Waves 2 and 3, data on employment patterns will be collected from the entire sample.

The *Staying On* study covers the usual variables associated with studies of student employment research; that is, demographic background variables including socio-economic status, ethnicity, gender and location. Measures of academic self concept, engagement with school and academic motivation are also included. Students are being asked how many hours per week they were employed (work intensity), where they worked (occupation and type of work) and why they were working. What distinguishes this study from much of the research conducted hitherto is the inclusion of survey questions designed to ascertain how well they think they are managing the competing demands of study and work, and whether they would prefer to work more hours or fewer hours. Interviews will also be conducted with student workers to explore what kinds of practices they think might make it easier for them to establish a balance between study and work. Such practices might include, for example, part-time school schedules, greater school timetable flexibility, restrictions on the rights of employers to make young employees work very late hours, or training in negotiating employment schedules that help them balance competing demands.

Preliminary results from the *Staying On* survey indicated that of the 670 Year 9 students who completed the questionnaire, 133 were in part-time employment, representing 19.9 percent of the Year 9 sample. This is lower than current national estimates derived from LSAY data. Using LSAY, Anlezark stated in the Australian House of Representatives Standing Committee report (2009) that 39 percent of

Year 9 students had part-time jobs. However the lower proportion found in the *Staying On* research is consistent with the difficulties faced by students in the geographical locations where this research is being conducted. These are rural and urban locations which are characterized by low socio-economic status and high unemployment levels; they are locations in which teenagers may be competing with adults for low-skill jobs such as super-market cashier, shelf filler or fast food kitchen hand. Thus, the levels of employment of high school students are likely to be lower in these locations than those achieved in a national sample such as LSAY.

Consistent with data from LSAY, the *Staying On* survey found that the most common form of employment for Year 9 students was serving in a fast food café, or working as a waiter or kitchen hand (41 per cent). This was followed by working in a supermarket or other retail store (17 per cent). Consistent with the young ages of these student workers, several were working as referees for sporting events (9 per cent). The remaining 33 per cent were distributed across a range of occupations – domestic, trade, farming, gardening and so on. The average work intensity was 9.35 hours per week. Two thirds of the students worked less than 10 hours per week, and only one third worked more than 10 hours per week. However, among the students who were working in fast food, half of them were employed for *more than 10 hours* per week. The average work intensity in fast food was 13.20 hours per week. Analyses of the average work intensities for different occupations showed that for the Year 9 students in this survey, mean work intensity in fast food was significantly higher than the mean work intensity for all other occupations ($t = 4.017$, $p < 0.000$).

This brings us to a question that is implied but rarely discussed explicitly in most studies. It is often suggested that students who work are choosing to abandon their academic goals and that their motivation to succeed in school is diminished as work intensity increases. An alternative possibility is that many young workers are being pressured by their employers to work long hours, and that if they had a choice, they would reduce their working hours in order to pay more attention to their studies. Preliminary results from the *Staying On* survey support this proposition. Two questions included in the survey were question A: 'My employer asks me to work more hours than I want to' and question B: 'I find it difficult to balance the demands of work and study'. Responses were recorded using a Likert scale, from 1 (completely disagree) to 5 (completely agree). Table 6.1 presents the mean responses to these two questions, in relation to the number of hours worked.

Table 6.1   Mean responses to questions A and B, in relation to hours worked

Hours worked	1–5 Hours	6–10 hours	11–15 hours	16–20 hours	20+ hours	*r*	*p*
Q A	1.70	2.15	2.38	2.88	4.75	0.409	< 0.000
Q B	2.09	2.27	2.76	2.82	4.25	0.304	< 0.001

It is clear from Table 6.1 that there is a significant correlation between work intensity (the number of hours worked) and positive answers to both questions A and B. For question A, the results indicate that, in comparison with students who work short hours, those who work long hours are substantially more likely to say they feel pressured to work longer hours than they want to. Taking the example of the fast-food sector, half of the 53 students in this sector worked 10 hours per week or less, and three quarters of these were happy with the number of hours worked. However, among those who worked 16 hours per week or more, only one in three were happy. Two thirds of this high-intensity group felt they were being asked to work longer hours than they wanted to. The results for question B are similar. These results indicate that students who work longer hours are substantially more likely to find it difficult to balance the demands of work and study, compared with those who work shorter hours. The correlation between work intensity and having difficulty balancing work and study is 0.304, with a significance level of $p < 0.001$.

As already noted, these analyses provide a small indication of the directions emerging from the first wave of the *Staying On* study. This study will provide longitudinal data measuring a range of background demographic variables as well as measures of academic engagement and motivation, beginning before young people entered the workforce, and continuing on until they have entered the senior secondary phase. In future analyses, therefore, it will be possible to analyse the consequences of participation in part-time employment while taking account of pre-existing differences among students who self-select to enter the workforce. The quantitative longitudinal analyses carried out through the *Staying On* project will be complemented by interview data which will allow us to explore how students think about juggling school and work, and what strategies they are adopting as they attempt to balance the two.

Conclusion: Policies and Practices for Supporting Student Workers

Statistics presented at the beginning of this chapter indicate that by the time students are in their final years of secondary education, whether they are in the US, the UK or in Australia, more than half of them are working part-time. A consistent finding across the literature on student employment is that it appears to have a *positive* effect on the likelihood of being employed rather than unemployed after leaving school. This is important for those who leave school to enter the workforce, as well as for those who enter higher education, since for most university students part-time work provides an important income stream. It appears that for most young people, part-time employment is now a taken-for-granted part of the high school experience. Given the immediate and longer-term benefits of part-time work, it is unlikely that young people will 'give it up'. And given the low cost of youth labour for employers, their incentives for recruiting and employing high school students are also clear.

The literature reviewed suggests that working may have a negligible effect on educational outcomes provided the number of hours worked remains below a certain threshold. It also appears that some groups of students are able to work relatively long hours without significant negative effects. That is, there are young people who participate in part-time employment who nevertheless complete high school, gain excellent grades, and often proceed to post-secondary education. Selectivity effects provide a possible explanation for this, since students who are more committed to academic success seem less vulnerable to the educational detriments of paid employment (Schoenhals et al. 2000, Entwisle et al. 2000). However, some of the most substantial quantitative studies in this field suggest that participation in part-time employment erodes academic commitments and diminishes educational outcomes (Marsh and Kleitman 2002, 2005, Vickers et al. 2003). Preliminary data reported here, drawn from the *Staying On* study, indicates that students who are working long hours tend to report more difficulty in balancing study and work compared with those who work short hours, and they are also more likely to say that their employers are pressuring them to work more hours than they want to. A possibility that demands further attention is that there is an interaction between selectivity and threshold effects: that is, it may be that students who are less engaged from the outset are more willing to accept long working hours than those who have higher levels of engagement and academic motivation.

During 2009, the House of Representatives Standing Committee on Education and Training conducted an inquiry into the nature of student part-time employment, and published a final report titled *Adolescent Overload*. In her forward to this report, the Committee Chair, Sharon Bird, noted that:

> [T]he nature of part-time work for school students has changed significantly
> ... Student workers can be susceptible to exploitative working conditions ...
> The vulnerability of students in the workplace highlights the need for adequate
> protections and a shared community responsibility by parents, employers and
> schools to ensure they are protected against working excessively long, and often
> very late or early, hours. (HoR SCET 2009: vii)

The concept of a shared, inter-generational community responsibility for young people who work is introduced and discussed in the report. The report also provides descriptions of programs through which schools, unions and employers are seeking to help young people combine study and work. For example, the NSW Teachers Federation has developed a resource for the four stakeholder groups: students, teachers, parents and employers. The students@work website provides a sub-site providing 'how-to' guidelines for each group (see http://www.students@work. org.au). The sub-site for students, for example, includes links such as 'looking for a job', 'applying for a job', 'accepting a job offer', 'staying safe at work' and 'bullying, discrimination and harassment'. The employer sub-site includes a link on 'being a model employer of students' and emphasizes the importance of helping students understand their entitlements. Employers are encouraged to ask students to notify them about conflicting demands, such as examinations. A time-management tool built into the website helps students to plan their time and communicate with their parents, peers, teachers and employers.

Schools around Australia are adopting a range of innovations to help students combine study and work effectively. These are especially important for young people from communities of lower socio-economic status. For example, the South Australian Department of Education and Children's Services has established a flexible approach to support extended completion of high school. A substantial number of South Australian high schools provide Year 11 and 12 programs on a half-time basis. For example, the Mount Gambier School, and other proactive part-time schools in South Australia, emphasize individual case management, where teachers broker in- and out-of-school learning and act as advocates for their students in relation to employers (HoR SCET 2009: 107). In New South Wales, there are a number of senior colleges where a more work-friendly timetable has been instituted. For example, at the Illawarra College in Port Kembla, the school runs on a four-day week, and support for individual work and learning plans is built into the system (HoR SCET 2009: 108).

Across Australia, the state education systems have developed vocational education and training programs through which students are able to gain credit for out-of-school employment. These programs provide the potential for recognition of alternative Year 12 qualifications, accreditation for skills developed at work and opportunities for a second chance education.

It is clear that in the US, UK and Australia, high levels of student participation in part-time employment are with us to stay. The dangers and difficulties this presents are evident. It is important to provide conditions that encourage all young people to complete high school, regardless of whether they plan to go on with post-secondary study or enter the workforce. However, extended trading hours in the retail sector and the very long hours of operation of fast-food outlets mean that high school students are working longer hours and later hours than ever before, so the challenges involved are becoming more intense. Some employers have set a positive example by inviting students to let them know about assignment deadlines and exams, and establish rosters that allow students to fulfil their scholarly responsibilities (HoR SCET 2009).

The policies and practices the current situation demands will have an impact on all stakeholders. In Australia, there is a need for more consistent employment regulation for youth that sets standards to protect them from workplace hazards and from unreasonable expectations related to very early and very late hours. While some schools have taken a lead, there are many schools and many teachers who need to adopt a more flexible approach to timetabling and a more inclusive approach to the recognition of learning that occurs outside of school. Young people themselves need to remain committed to their studies and to developing their time management skills. Finally, research is needed to identify and evaluate practices that allow all stakeholder groups to support an effective work-study balance for young people.

References

Australian Bureau of Statistics (ABS). 2003. *Australian Social Trends.* Canberra: ABS

Buddelmeyer, H. and Wooden, M. 2007. *Transitions from Casual Employment in Australia.* Melbourne: Melbourne Institute Working Paper, University of Melbourne.

Carr, R. V., Wright, J. D. and Brody, C. J. 1996. Effects of high school work experience a decade later: Evidence from the national longitudinal study. *Sociology of Education*, 69(1), 66–81.

D'Amico, R. 1984. Does employment during high school impair academic progress? *Sociology of Education*, 57(3), 152–64.

Entwisle, D., Alexander, K. and Steffel-Olsen, L. 1998. Early work histories of urban youth. *American Sociological Review*, 65(2), 279–97.

House of Representatives Standing Committee on Education and Training (HoR SCET). 2009. *Adolescent Overload: Report of the Inquiry into Combining School and Work.* Canberra: Commonwealth of Australia.

Howieson, C., McKechnie, J. and Semple, S. 2006. *The Nature and Implications of the Part-time Employment of Secondary School Pupils.* Glasgow: Scottish Executive Social Research. Available at: http://www.scotland.gov.uk/Resource/Doc/154159/00 [accessed: 27 September 2010].

Keithly, D. and Deseran, F. 1995. Households, local labor markets, and youth labour force participation. *Youth and Society*, 26(4), 463–92.

Lee, J. and Staff, J. 2007. When work matters: The varying impact of work intensity on high school dropout. *Sociology of Education*, 80(1), 158–78.

Marks, G. 2006. *The Transition to Full-time Work of Young People Who Do Not Go to University.* LSAY Research Report No. 49. Melbourne: Australian Council for Educational Research (ACER).

Marks, G., Fleming, N, Long, M. and McMillan, J. 2000. *Patterns of Participation in Year 12 and Higher Education in Australia: Trends and Issues.* LSAY Research Report No. 17. Melbourne: ACER.

Marsh, H. 1991. Employment during high school: Character building or a subversion of academic goal? *Sociology of Education*, 64(3), 172–89.

Marsh, H. 1992. Extracurricular activities: Beneficial extension of the traditional curriculum of a subversion of academic goals? *Journal of Educational Psychology*, 84(4), 533–62.

Marsh, H. and Kleitman, S. 2002. Extracurricular school activities: The good, the bad, and the non-linear. *Harvard Education Review*, 72(4), 464–502.

Marsh, H. and Kleitman, S. 2005. Consequences of employment during high school: Character building, subversion of academic goals, or a threshold? *American Education Research Journal*, 42(2), 331–69.

McKechnie, J., Hobbs, S., Simpson, A., Anderson, S., Howieson, C. and Semple, S. 2010. School students' part-time work: Understanding what they do. *Journal of Education and Work*, 23(2), 161–75.

McVicar, D. and McKee, B. 2002. Part-time work during post-compulsory education and examination performance: Help or hindrance? *Scottish Journal of Political Economy*, 49(4), 393–406.

Mortimer, J. 2003. *Working and Growing Up in America*. Cambridge, MA: Harvard University Press.

Payne, J. 2003. The impact of part-time jobs in Years 12 and 13 on qualification achievement. *British Education Research Journal*, 29(4), 599–611.

Robinson, L. 1999. *The Effects of Part-time Work on School Students*. LSAY Research Report No. 9. Melbourne: ACER.

Ruhm, C. 1995. The extent and consequences of high school employment. *Journal of Labour Research*, 16(3), 293–303.

Schoenhals, M., Tienda, M. and Schneider, B. 1998. The educational and personal consequences of adolescent employment. *Social Forces*, 77(2), 723–62.

Smith, E. and Green, A. 2001. *School Students' Learning from their Paid and Unpaid Work*. Adelaide: National Centre for Vocational Education Research (NCVER).

Staff, J. and Mortimer, J. 2007. Educational and work strategies from adolescence to early adulthood: Consequences for educational attainment. *Social Forces*, 85(3), 1169–94.

Staff, J. and Schulenberg, J. E. 2010. Millennials and the world of work: Experiences in paid work during adolescence. *Journal of Business Psychology*, 25(2), 247–55.

Staff, J., Schulenberg, J. E. and Bachman, J. G. 2010. Adolescent work intensity, school performance and academic engagement. *Sociology of Education*, 83(3), 183–200.

Steinberg, L and Dornbusch, S. 1991. Negative correlates of part-time employment during adolescence: Replication and elaboration. *Developmental Psychology*, 27(2), 304–13.

Stern, D. and Nakata, Y. 1989. Characteristics of high school students' paid jobs, and employment experience after graduation, in *Adolescence and Work: Influences of Social Structure, Labor Markets, and Culture*, edited by D. Stern and D. Eichorn. Hillsdale, NJ: Erlbaum, 189–233.

United States Bureau of Labour Statistics (US BLS). 2008. *Labor Force Participation Rates for Two Categories of Youths, 2008*. Available at: http://www.bls.gov/fls/chartbook [accessed: 4 October 2010].

Vickers, M., Lamb, S. and Hinkley, J. 2003. *Student Workers in High School and Beyond: The Effects of Part-time Employment on Participation in Education, Training and Work*. LSAY Research Report No. 30. Melbourne: ACER.

Chapter 7

Work-study Conflict or Facilitation? Time Use Tradeoffs among Employed Students

Lonnie Golden and John Baffoe-Bonnie

Does paid employment during high school and college displace the time students spend in educational activities? Most enrolled college students in the United States (US) now work in paid jobs, almost half of whom work 25 or more hours per week (US Department of Education 2010). An economics-based approach to students' time allocation suggests that students consider the tradeoffs involved with work versus study time in terms of current income and future earnings capacity, as well as their health consequences. There may be some complementarities, not just substitutability, between work and education time, regarding educational outcomes. Thus, it is an empirical question whether paid work time displaces time devoted toward education. This research applies the pooled 2003–2005 American Time Use Survey (ATUS) data, among those aged 16–24 (n = 1,314, including 1,121 full-time) college and high school students, to observe the association between time spent in paid work and in educational activities. It investigates two central questions:

1. Are paid work hours of students inversely associated with time spent doing homework or research and/or attending class?
2. If so, at what threshold point of paid work hours are hours of students' schooling time displaced? Are there are nonlinearities in that such displacement is stronger at longer hours of paid work than at shorter hours?

The conclusion explores implications of the results for policies, such as extending existing youth employment regulatory protections, to increase the time youth might devote toward educational purposes.

Previous Literature

As in many other countries, in the US a surprisingly high proportion of youth are attempting to combine both paid work and schooling activities. There is evidence that both rates of employment and average hours of work have been rising over time, at least among college students, through the mid-2000s (see Figure 7.1).

Percent

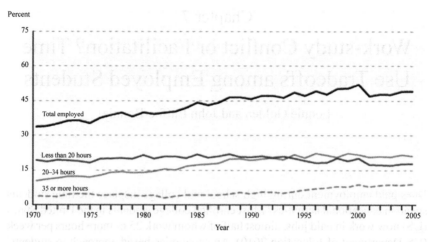

Figure 7.1   Percentage of 16–24 year old full-time college students who were employed, by hours worked per week: October 1970 through October 2005

Note: College includes both two- and four-year institutions. College students were classified as full-time if they were taking at least 12 hours of classes (or at least 9 hours of graduate classes) during an average school week and were classified as part-time if they were taking fewer hours.

Source: US Department of Commerce, Census Bureau, Current Population Survey (CPS), October Supplement, 1970–2009.

While rising in most countries, the levels appear to be slightly higher in the US than in most of Europe, particularly in non-Anglo countries (see for example Häkkinen 2006, Moreau and Leathwood 2006). In the US, during 2003–2004, about 26 per cent of teens aged 15–19 worked more than 20 hours per week at paid or unpaid work (Porterfield and Winkler 2007). Nearly 80 per cent of undergraduates work for pay while in college (*Student Aid News* 2006, Riggert et al. 2006). Estimates in the US are that about 30 per cent of full-time students work over 20 hours a week while attending college, with 70 per cent of their part-time students working over 20 hours each week (NCES 2005; Heiselt and Bergerson 2007). Students' working hours are uniformly distributed across the spectrum, with similar proportions reporting that they work full-time (over 35) hours as those who work 15 or fewer hours. Among those students in two-year community colleges, students work an average of 32 hours per week, while for the nation's 16–17 year old high school students, over 40 per cent hold jobs during the school year. About 25 per cent of them work 20 hours or more per week.

Perhaps not coincidentally, about 62 per cent of teens who work spend less than 5 hours per week on homework and less than 18 per cent spend more than 10 hours per week. The number doing short hours of homework has risen, and the number doing long hours has shrunk, since a similar mid-1970s time diary survey. The prime motivation of students to work in paid jobs is largely attributed to the cost of higher education and other relevant expenses outpacing household real income gains, parental transfers and government subsidies (Oettinger 2006, Kalenkoski and Pabilonia 2010). Full-time students who work 25 hours or more a week often do so because they cannot afford to go to college if they work any less. Neither federal financial aid for higher education nor state subsidies has been keeping up with increasing college tuition costs. About 84 per cent said they were primarily working to meet college expenses. Students from low income families often find themselves working long hours to finance their way through college. Some research finds that students from low-income families are more likely to work than wealthy students to pay for tuition, fees or living expenses, rather than to earn spending money or to gain job experience (Lerman 2000). Others find that among high school students, employment rates and weekly hours are higher among those with relatively higher family income levels, where the primary reason for teens working is to purchase and maintain a car (Hannah and Baum 2001). How much do youth enrolled in school tend to work and why does it matter? This chapter will review previous attempts to study this question, develop a theoretical foundation to frame a student's time use allocation dilemma, empirically test with conventional regression methods for the association between time spent working and time spent in educational type activities, and briefly discuss the implications of the findings in the light of the literature and public policy options.

Most previous studies use cross-sectional data to evaluate specified outcomes in relation to either the amount or the nature of student employment. Surprisingly few theoretical models have been developed to explain the relationship between employment and student outcomes and, strikingly, many inconsistencies are found (Riggert et al. 2006).The literature tends to focus on the empirical connection between paid work hours and indicators of students' academic performance and achievement (for example, grade point average (GPA), dropout/retention rates, exam scores, attendance records and the like). Other literature explores the connection of paid work hours to the amount of time spent in educational and studying activities – a key input into academic outcomes for students. It is well recognized that time use is subject to a zero sum assumption or at least substitutability. Generally speaking, previous research tends to find that when paid hours exceed some threshold level, typically somewhere between 15 and 25 hours per week, various indicators of students' academic performance become lower.

Employment can be a dual edged sword. For academic performance, there are some potential complementarities and positive spillovers from work to schooling. There are potential long-term positives of youth employment for future earnings capacity in the labour market, not only additional current earnings (Ehrenberg and Sherman 1987, Ruhm 1997, Häkkinen 2006). Thus, on the one hand, work provides both income and a higher income trajectory which funds both current consumption needs and investment in one's future human capital, including experience and soft skills development (Rich 1996, Ruhm 1997). Work also tends to promote incentives for improved time management and personal efficiency in one's use of time. Performing paid work while at college may sustain one's enrolment and minimize subsequent debt. Students often extol the benefits of working, which are not only monetary but include the development of skills, greater understanding of the world of business and an increase in confidence, all of which can be advantageous to their studies, both at the present time and in the future (US BLS 2005). Youth development outcomes are positive, provided that work hours are moderate and in higher quality jobs (Staff and Schulenberg 2010). For example, with moderate hours per week, students from low income families experiencing high work intensity actually exhibited improved school engagement and schoolwork performance (Lerman 2000).

On the other hand, many studies have found that an increase in studying time indeed boosts student achievement. Thus, to the extent work time crowds out class time or studying time, work may come at the expense of performance in school and knowledge gained. Additional hours of studying are often found to be a fairly reliable predictor of a higher GPA. Often, however, the findings regarding the effects of time spent studying are not unequivocal. For example, when controlling for a student's ACT score (that is, ability), time spent studying has a significant effect on their semester GPA, but not when controlling for an indicator of the student's achievement striving or motivation (Nonis and Hudson 2006, Kalenkoski and Pabilonia 2010). There are adverse effects of employment on study time in the form of missed lectures, and students' perceptions are that coursework grades are lower than they would have been had they not been working (Curtis and Shani 2002). Students recognize that working full-time may not only compromise their academic progress, but may also limit their ability to engage in other extracurricular activities such as civic learning and community service. The consequences in no small part depend on the nature of students' occupations, the number of hours of commitment, and summertime versus school year work. While many students are working at levels that are likely to negatively impact their academic achievement and the quality of their education, they often simply cannot afford to cut back their work hours.

A preponderance of evidence shows several negative associations between the employment commitment of students toward paid work with their current and future academic performance or achievement. This includes the tendency to drop out, graduate later or fail to become an honours student (for example, Lillydahl 1990, Steinberg 1996, Bailey and Mallier 1999, Lerman 2000, Rau and Durand 2000, Hannah and Baum 2002, Curtis and Najah 2002, Stinebrickner and Stinebrickner 2004, Hawkins et al. 2005, US BLS 2005, Singh, Chang and Dika 2007). Most studies find that the number of paid hours of work matters more than whether a student is employed or not (for a differing view, see Kalenkoski and Pabilonia 2010). Generally speaking, working in a full-time job is far more likely to lead to negative effects than part-time hours (Orszag, Orszag and Whitmore 2001). Any adverse effects are likely to occur either directly, by reduced time and energy for class time, time studying alone or with peers and assignment work, or indirectly via its effect on sleep time and other physiologically restorative activities (Rothstein 2007). As many as 42 per cent of students reported that working full-time hours has hurt their grades, limited their class schedule and limited their class choice. Working hours, at least among high school students, may not necessarily translate into negative school-related performance outcomes provided that usual weekly hours are relatively short (US–BLS 2005). Longer work hours, however, often do translate into relatively lower grade point averages (Ehrenberg and Sherman 1987, Crawford, Johnson and Summers 1997, Dundes and Marx 2006–07). Ten additional hours of work per week reduced math test performance scores (Tyler 2003). Even part-time jobs were associated with reduced math and science achievement or course-taking (Singh and Ozturk 2000). The effects on math proficiency vary across countries, but the general pattern is that weekly hours beyond 19 have negative consequences (Post and Pong 2009). Working during high school had negative effects on 15 of 23 Year 12 and post-secondary outcomes such as achievement, coursework selection, educational and occupational aspirations and college attendance (Marsh and Kleitman 2005). A 20 hour per week job reduced GPA by 0.22 grade points on average and a one standard deviation reduction in SAT score (Oettinger 2006). For every extra hour of work per week, GPA decreased by 0.16 (Stinebrickner and Stinebrickner 2004). High school employment during the school year was inversely associated with grades if the hours were more than modest (Oettinger 1999). This association between self-reported grades and amount of work time holds when including a wide range of controls, such as family background, students' educational aspirations and school engagement (Singh, Chang and Dika 2007). In addition, paid work demands and job activities reduced course effort, and thus indirectly led to lower GPA scores (Svanum and Bigatti 2006). Moreover, students working 15 or fewer hours were found to be much less likely than students working longer hours to report that work limited their class choices or class schedules, the number of classes they could take, or access to the library (NCES 1998).

Nevertheless, students working a limited number of work hours per week seem to actually outperform both students working 20 or more hours as well as those not working at all, in terms of better grades, test scores and/or the likelihood of going to college (Singh, Mido and Dika 2007). Students working 10–19 hours per week performed better in college, particularly if their GPA fell in the 2.0–2.9 range (Dundes and Marx 2006). Although there are quite strong negative effects of high school students' work hours on academic credits taken (larger than the impact of current or recent employment on students' GPA), these are in large part attributed to a 'fixed person effect' (Svanum and Bigatti 2006). That is, striving students, with high 'unobserved motivation' (or low preference for leisure time) may take on both heavier course loads and more hours of employment as well (Oettinger 2006, Rothstein 2007). Considering the confounding effects of selectivity or endogeneity is important also because students who work more may be doing so as a strategy that arises from having poor grades or low interest in school, or low aspirations for career. Furthermore, teens who work long hours could be less academically inclined to begin with. The students most likely to have a job working 20 hours or more are those with low GPAs and no aspirations for the future. For example, when controlling for the endogeneity of the work hours and dropout decisions of high school students, the negative effect on GPA of current and recent past employment is markedly diminished (Rothstein 2007). Nevertheless, the effects of hours worked are primarily negative and consistent across demographics, initial ability levels and different types of jobs. In sum, the bulk of research evidence continues to support the 'inverted U' (Stern et al. 1995, Mortimer and Johnson 1998), but often with qualifications.

Thus, isolating precise effects of work hours on student performance, and the intermediate step of schooling and studying time, has been challenging and generalizations have thus been elusive. This is at least partly because the effects on school behaviour and grade performance may be moderated and mediated by the student's family environment (Roisman 2002). For example, in a UK sample of college students, of whom 81 per cent held at least one job during term time (for an average 14 hours per week), work hours reduced time for study, social activities and recreation (Manthei and Gilmore 2005). Teens who work long hours not only have lower school performance, but also diminished engagement in school, increased psychological distress, higher drug and alcohol use, higher rates of delinquency, and greater autonomy from parental control (Kelly 1998). Students who worked more than 15 hours a week not only have relatively lower grades, retention and post-secondary completion rates, but they do less homework (Montmarquette, Viennot-Briot and Dagenais 2007). Those who worked 20 or more hours a week felt that they were not applying themselves fully; for example, they spent lesser amounts of time on assignments, studying and meeting with peers. In a survey of self-reports, as much as 38 per cent of teens who had a job during the year (averaging 19 hours per week), retrospectively felt that they would have done better in school (received 'mostly As' or 'As and Bs') had they not had a job, particularly those who worked 35 or more hours (Galinsky et al. 2000).

However, those who work at least 10 hours a week felt more compelled to manage their time well, especially those working in the 10–19 hour time range, although they also tended to report more stress. Indeed, students who worked 10 or fewer hours per week were those most likely to report minimal effort in classes and less studying time than the other groups (Stern and Briggs 2001). This is confirmed by longitudinal data that shows that four-year college students who worked 20 hours or less had a higher GPA than students who did not work, although the lowest GPAs were found in students who worked more than 20 hours per week (Kalenkoski and Pabilonia 2010). Other studies have found only small effects of an additional hour of study time on GPA, at least among college students in higher years (Lahmers and Zulauf 2000). Thus, there appear to be some advantages to time management, organization and efficiency when working a small number of hours per day or days per week.

A Theoretical Foundation: Production Possibilities and the Effects of Work while in School

The conventional economic model of labour supply predicts that an individual will seek employment if their going market wage rate per hour is expected to exceed the value of an hour of their 'leisure' or 'non work time'. Youth will thus choose to participate in the paid work force and desire more hours if their potential market wage rate opportunities are rising (a 'substitution effect'), their non-wage sources of income are depleting (an 'income effect') and/or their preferences for earnings *vis-à-vis* preferences for time are growing. However, virtually all theoretical and empirical analyses of labour supply behaviour treat the time allocation decision as a sequential one. It is presumed that those choosing to enrol in college do so to postpone entering the job market. Others may 'choose' to transition from school to work directly from high school. Higher education is portrayed as a human capital investment of both time and money in skills development, credentials or other benefits that is expected to yield higher net returns in income over one's lifetime.

Conventional models of household labour supply decisions typically identify no more than three categories of time use; work, leisure time and household production. Sometimes the household production time is broken down into housework time and parenting or care giving time. The latter use of time is to produce 'child quality'. However, when it comes to the time allocation decision making of students, even the conventionally deployed Becker (1985) model of households – allocating their time between paid work, household production (such as housework and caregiving) and leisure time – is under-equipped to directly account for the distinct uses of 'leisure' time. The Becker model does recognize the substitutability between uses of time, in terms of both hours and energy, and that time and energy spent in paid work may be a zero-sum with unpaid household production activities. Thus, for our purposes, the uses of time other than paid work can be further subdivided so that there will be an additional category of 'productive leisure'. This category refers to activities that enhance human capital development, such as attending classes and studying time in formal education or even career-relevant reading. Only rarely do such models consider the choice to pursue time investments in educational-type activities, such as an investigation of the demand for informal education (Fahr 2005). (Related uses of leisure time would be recuperative pursuits and activities that build social capital.)

From this foundation, we may formulate a *student's production function.* Let us assume that a student is trying to maximize production of two, alternative types of output – both a targeted level of income (Y) or goods and services to consume, and a targeted level of 'academic performance'. In a short run period of time, they are given the constraint that the only variable input at their disposal is time for labour. This may be devoted to either paid work or 'productive leisure' (such as class time and homework time). If we assume all resources are utilized, a production possibilities frontier exists (see Figure 7.2).

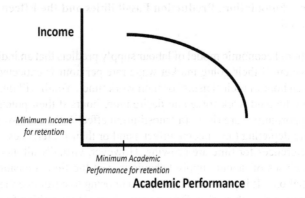

Income

Minimum Income
for retention

Minimum Academic
Performance for retention

Academic Performance

Figure 7.2   Working student's trade off between current income and higher academic performance

Realistically, each type of output has a minimum necessary (horizontal) level. There is a standard minimum level of Y at their (socially determined) subsistence level plus expenses uniquely associated with attending college, such as tuition, fees, books, transportation and perhaps housing expenses. There is also a minimum threshold level of academic performance indicators, such as grades and test performance, above a level that would result in either flunking out, or termination or dropping out (disengagement), before attaining their degree. This minimum standard outcome determines some minimum (presumably greater than zero) necessary time allotment into educational activities, including for class attendance and homework–research time. The student may begin with an endowment of both non-wage income (for example, parental transfers, subsidies, grants and loans, or savings/wealth). Thus, the minimum threshold point of Y needed rises with higher tuition rates and fees and falls with student subsidies. The maximum level of Y reflects the maximum possible time available for work, what remains of the 168 hours in a week (or 24 per day) after the minimum necessary productive leisure (plus recuperative leisure). Similarly, a student may possess an endowment of innate ability that allows them to reach a level of academic achievement without devoting any time in class or studying outside of class time. For most students, there is a minimum threshold point of studying time, to keep from flunking out or dropping out. The student's maximum level of academic performance is that which could be achieved by devoting all his or her discretionary time toward schooling related activities.

If academic performance is subject to positive but diminishing returns to studying time, then there are increasing costs that make the production possibilities concave in shape. Similarly, the potential sacrifice of knowledge and skills gained grows exponentially as work hours climb. (The inverted U is based on a cross section of students, not necessarily the experience of any particular student. For example, it is theoretically possible that, while working 2 hours per day may improve the efficiency per hour of study time, it is unlikely to increase the total volume of study time, *vis-à-vis* a given individual having no work hours at all.) The entire production possibilities frontier may be shifted outward over time with further income subsidies or grants, improvements in capital needed to produce better grades or productivity at work (for example, a portable computer, reduced commuting time or positive spillover effects from the job to student performance). The production possibilities also could be higher if the student's job had sufficient down time for engaging in studying, that is, a primary activity of work and secondary activity of studying. However, the output effects are likely to be less than additive with such 'multi-tasking' in the same block of time, and perhaps even less, as compared to performing the two tasks sequentially or separately (because overlapping activities are associated with higher stress; see Floro and Miles 2003). Picking the appropriate point along the production possibilities could depend on an individual's 'preferences' – the marginal rate of substitution of income for academic achievement. This model is a simplified version of those in which a student chooses to allocate time optimally among course enrolment, study, labour market employment and leisure time uses (Oettinger 2006) and models that incorporate the role of the price of schooling, parental resources and student's market wage rates (Lee and Orazem 2010). Academic performance subsequently is determined by the chosen course load and study time, as well as the student's personal characteristics. The theory leads to an empirical model in which school performance measures, such as college entry and GPA outcomes depend on course enrolment (credit) hours, employment hours, leisure expenditure and student characteristics.

We focus here on the direct association between work time and educational time – study time and class time. The analysis will control for observed personal and work characteristic factors that might affect a student's tendency to work, attend class and do homework. It aims to pinpoint when working longer hours may begin to impair students' time spent in their educational activities. Because the risk of lower student achievement potentially harms their future labour market outcomes, it is important to analyse not only whether, but the extent to which, additional hours worked in the paid labour market while in school tend to crowds out students' study time. More paid work unavoidably constrains time allocation elsewhere. Alternatively, it heightens the intensity of time use or time squeeze, multi-tasking and coordination challenges. Thus, paid work time, also may have indirect effects, via fatigue and stress, on both students' performance and the amount of time students devote to studying.

The American Time Use Survey and Descriptive Statistics

The ATUS asked participants to track the use of all blocks of time in the previous 24-hour period. It creates 17 'first tier' activities, and coded 452 total categories of detailed activities. The chief categories of concern here are paid work and education – class-time and studying time. The large sample in the annual ATUS of over 20,000 individuals contains extremely fine detail regarding the specific uses of time among the employed. It provides 17 broad categories of 'first tier' potential uses of time over the course of a day, breaking it down to specific uses of time. These data provide four new opportunities for research yielding new insights into the employment, pay and work schedules of enrolled college students. The key category in the ATUS (http://www.bls.gov/tus/current/education.htm) is:

Educational Activities

Educational activities include taking classes (including Internet and other distance-learning courses); doing research and homework; and taking care of administrative tasks, such as registering for classes or obtaining a school identity card. Activities are classified separately by whether the educational activity was for a degree or for personal interest. Educational activities do not include time spent for classes or training that respondents identified as part of their jobs. Time spent helping others with their education-related activities is classified in the 'caring for and helping' categories.

The focus here is on its two principal components, the amount of this time spent on: taking class for a degree (060101); and doing research/homework (0603), which reflects research/homework for class for degree (060301). From the 2006

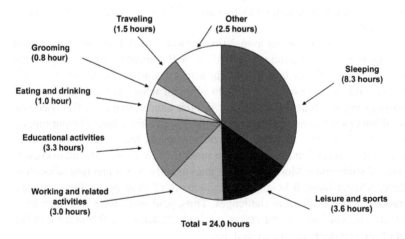

Figure 7.3   Time use on an average weekday for full-time university and college students

Note: Data includes individuals, aged 15 to 49, who were enrolled full-time at a university or college. Data includes non-holiday weekdays and are averages for 2004–2008.

Source: Bureau of Labor Statistics.

survey, about 9 per cent of the population engaged in educational activities on an average day. Those who attended class spent an average of 4.5 hours doing so, and those who did homework and research spent 2.4 hours in such activities. On an average day, persons ages 15–19 spent 3.3 hours engaged in educational activities (more than four times as long as individuals in any other age group). The average hours per weekday spent by high school students in educational activities were 6.3 hours if not employed and 5.6 hours if employed. Persons who did homework spent about the same amount of time doing it on weekdays (2.4 hours) and weekend days (2.5 hours). Figure 7.3 shows that among college students (aged 15–49), average hours of educational activity per day were 3.3 hours and work hours were 3.2.

In the four-year averages for the 2004–2008 ATUS samples, employed high school students spent about 42 fewer minutes per day engaged in educational activities than high school students who were not employed (see Figure 7.4).

Among those aged 15–49 in the 2003 ATUS, those who were enrolled in school worked about half the number of hours per day in the labour market as those who were not enrolled. This suggests that the typical school attendee does make a substantial commitment to paid work. Those who are employed part-time worked an average three hours on a given day and studied or attended school for an average hour and a quarter. Those who are employed full-time averaged about 6 hours of work per day and spend only a negligible amount of time in school or studying activities. The non-enrolled spent on average 2.4 hours a day more at work than the enrolled student. In the 2005 ATUS, employed high school students aged 15–19 worked about two hours on average on weekdays during the school year.

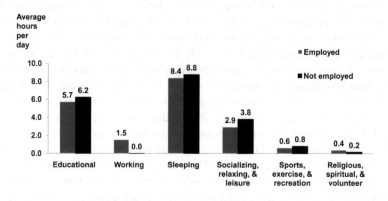

Figure 7.4   Average hours per weekday spent by high school students in various activities

Note: Data includes individuals, aged 15 to 49, who were enrolled in high school. Data includes non-holiday weekdays during the months of January–May and September–December and are annual averages for 2003–2006.

Source: Bureau of Labor Statistics.

Empirical tests and findings from the pooled 2003–2005 ATUS

The goal of this section is to estimate the empirical determinants of hours spent studying or in class by an enrolled student. The focus is on paid time at work as the key determinant. The empirical specification begins with a basic ordinary least square (OLS) regression model (which assumes the relationship is not entirely endogenous). The dependent variable is total hours spent per day in educational activities by a given individual (i). The regression model is specified as: $(EH)_i = (X; H; Z)$, where:

   EH = hours of educational activity (class time and studying time);
   X = demographic controls: gender, age, marital status, etc.;
   H = hours of work (raw number or ranges for actual hours); and
   Z = job characteristics, such as occupation and industry (wage rates excluded).

Specifically, the regression analyses are intended to observe if there appears to be a displacement of studying and class time with paid work among enrolled students who are employed, holding constant a variety of worker and job characteristics as control variables. If so, to what degree does the extent of such displacement depend on the number of hours of work per week? The key variable (PREMPHRS) in the ATUS recodes the *actual* hours responses into several ranges. Fortunately, information from respondents regarding hours are those at their current job in the concurrent month. (Other information from respondents is derived from the basic Current Population Survey (CPS), although observations are from jobs they were in 2–5 months prior to the ATUS interview date, when the subject rotated out of the monthly CPS process; see Polivka 2008.) This is useful for distinguishing the association of short, medium and long work hours with time spent in educational activities. The eight ranges are: 1–4; 5–14; 15–21; 22–29; 30–34; 35–39; 40; 41 or more. An alternate measure available, the '*usual* hours', divides the hours response into a much smaller number of ranges: 0–20; 21–34 … etc. This is far less useful because it groups those working 0 hours, thus not employed, with those who are employed for up to 20 hours. In addition, using 'actual' is preferable to 'usual' hours because the former includes, *overtime or extra hours,* which is over and above usual hours (PUHROT2), and, on the other side, time off taken (absences, sick time, holiday and so on). Thus, actual hours are more relevant than usual hours when it comes to impact on educational time. We have the luxury of observing first the effect associated with both the raw number of actual hours and the potential gradient by the range of hours, *vis-à-vis* working no hours. In addition, the sample universe includes anyone who is enrolled in school and is aged 16–24 (PESCHNER). Another variable (PESCHLVL), allows us to distinguish High School (HS) (Level 1) and COLLEGE (Level 2) students, for contrasting the two levels, using a dummy variable. This is in contrast to the current literature, which samples either on high school students or college students, but almost never both together. Furthermore, we distinguish between those enrolled full-time or part-time in school (PESCHFT), as a dummy variable. In addition, there are 11 'major' occupation and 14 'major' industry dummy variables, using NCAIS classification codes. Finally, there will be controls for whether a worker is paid as an hourly worker (PEERNHRY) and also, if they are a member of a labour union (PEERNLAB).

Key Statistical Findings

Table 7.1, columns 1 and 2, describe the variables and their names. Column 3 contains their raw regression coefficients and column 4, their standardized beta coefficient estimates. The latter show that the key variable of actual hours is negative and statistically significant, given its large t-values (displayed in column 5). This is not too surprising, given that the Pearson Correlation coefficient time spent taking classes for degree (T060101) and actual work hours per week (PEHRACT) is -.025 and significant at the .01 level in a two–tailed test. This shows that longer work hours are clearly associated with less time spent in educational activity. The usual interpretation challenges involved with standardized coefficients is somewhat compounded here by the fact that the dependent variable is hours spent per day and the independent variable is in units of hours per week. Nevertheless, the standardized coefficient suggests that, on average, every 10 hours of work per week is associated with 20 minutes fewer hours per day of educational activity such as studying. That is, students employed for 30 hours per week spend one hour less per day studying than students who are not employed, on average. The most salient finding is the negative association when broken out by range of work hours. Even working as few as 5–14 hours per week seems to crowd out time spent in class or studying. The size of this negative effect appears to be consistent across many ranges of work hours. The negative effect is not discernibly larger in the 35–39 hours range than in the 5–14 hours range. This is somewhat surprising since one might expect progressively greater negative effects, between 15 and 39 hours (relative to working no hours). However, when students are working 40 or more hours, indeed the negative effect doubles in size *vis-à-vis* working in the 15–39 hours range. While we should bear in mind that differences between students may reflect different levels of 'unobserved motivation' – for example, choosing more employment or heavier course loads (Oettinger 2006) – the results provide clear evidence that work time displaces study time in a linear fashion, up to full-time work-weeks, after which the effects become exponential.

The results of the control variable reveal the effect of demographics. Being married or having more children reduces the amount of time spent by students in educational activities. Age is strongly negatively associated with time for educational activities, as a 24 year old spends much less time on schooling in total than a 16 year old, not surprising since high school class time hours are longer; it may also reflect some bias because dropouts are excluded from the sample (as in Rothstein 2007). In contrast, better health and being a male increases educational

Table 7.1   OLS regression results, determinants of time spent studying or in class

Variable Definitions	Variable	Coefficient	Standardized Beta Coefficient	t-value
Independent variables:	Time spent on studying or taking classes for degree (n = 942) (T060101)			
	Range of hours worked:			
HRANGE1	1–4 hours	-7.26	-.005	-1.11
HRANGE2	5–14 hours	-10.26	-.015	-3.36
HRANGE3	15–21 hours	-8.09	-.015	-3.35
HARNGE4	22–29 hours	-7.46	-.013	-2.93
HRANGE5	30–34 hours	-6.64	-.015	-3.26
HRANGE6	35–39 hours	-7.02	-.013	-3.00
HRANGE7	40 hours	-5.70	-.026	-5.74
HRANGE8	Hours greater than 40	-5.83	-.022	-4.61
HRANGE9	No hours worked = 0 = *referent*			
Weekly Hours:*	Actual raw number worked	-.00703	-.032	-6.75
PTSTUD	= 1 enrolled as part-time student	-7.14	-.010	-2.17
LEVEL1	= 1 if high school student.	23.71	.090	20.02
LEVEL2**	= 1 if 4-year university student	4.59	.016	3.25
TEAGE	Respondent's age	-.541	-.195	-43.07
TRERNHLY	Hourly earnings	.00037	-.082	-13.88
SCHTRAIN	= 1 if not working because of school or training	9.16	-.003	-0.62
MALE	= 1 if sex is male	.435	.010	2.23
UNION	= 1 if a member of union		.005	1.16
OCC1***	Management, business, and financial occupations	-1.26	-.004	-0.77
Industry dummy variables****:				
R-squared			.051	

* The reported coefficients and t values were generated from an identical model that replaced the hours' ranges with the raw weekly hours. This model also included independent variables for one's self-reported health, which was positive and statistically significant t = 3.07, and being married, which was negative and statistically significant t value of -6.77.

** Referent group is student in a 2-year college.

*** Occupations statistically significantly reducing educational activity time.

****Referent industry chosen is armed forces. Controls included for agriculture, mining, construction, manufacturing, trade (wholesale and retail), transport/utilities, information services. Employment in the latter was highly significantly positively associated with educational time.

time. Being a union member had no measurable effect. However, being a high school student and being a full-time student had statistically significant positive effects on time spent on educational activities. This stands to reason since attendance in class is compulsory for high school but not college students. Finally, being employed in two particular non-agricultural industries – wholesale and retail trade, and especially information services – tends to be associated with more studying time, all else constant.

Implications for Student Employment Policies

Ultimately, policy intervention would be warranted if paid work time considerably impedes knowledge acquired, future earnings, or students' well-being. School performance among college students both suffer with greater work hours and job demands and strain, to the extent that work-school conflicts outweigh the possible work-school facilitation effects of having jobs (Butler 2007, Markel and Frone 1998). Moreover, strain is higher and satisfaction is lower, at least among college students who lack control over their jobs. Most college students appear to be at least somewhat aware and responsive to the risks. While those that are enrolled in college (between the ages of 16 and 24) are more likely than other workers to prefer more income and hours, when controlling for their given number of hours and type of job they are actually more likely to prefer reduced hours despite the loss of income (Golden and Gebreselassie 2007).

Deriving the implications for policies to promote academic achievement as well as enhance employment options will require more precise estimation of the effect of working hours, holding other influences constant, a task beyond the scope of this chapter. However, this exploratory research gets closer to identifying the tipping point where paid work hours begin to threaten or impair school performance.

The point at which work hours begin to place into peril the health and safety of young workers juggling school and work can be gleaned from other studies. Occupational health psychology research quite thoroughly documents the potential adverse consequences generally of working long or taxing hours – primarily via fatigue or stress – by heightening the risk of illness, disease, injury and work-life conflicts (Pocock 2001, Sparks, Faragher and Cooper 2001, Galinsky et al. 2005). Such adverse well-being effects occur for working high school students specifically, and similarly among college students, including dissatisfaction with leisure time (Weller et al. 2003, Lenaghan and Sengupta 2007). The combination of both high work hours and high recreational activity hours, for example, doubled the likelihood of sustaining a medically attended injury compared to those who worked few hours and had no recreational activity (Breslin et al. 2007).

The mental and physical health effects of youth labour depend not only on hours worked, but on the conditions of the work climate and the degree of compliance and enforcement of protective safety and health regulations (National Academy of Sciences 1998). The findings here suggest that working 14 (and perhaps even as few as five) hours of work per week is associated with spending somewhat less time studying or attending class than those without paid work hours. This should instruct and guide future thinking and policy proposals on college and career guidance, government financial aid, school-to-work programs, and youth employment regulations. For example, providing subsidies to students who both have jobs and use their own earned income toward tuition, fees and books might help induce a preference for less labour supply during the school year (if the income effect of this is dominant). Similarly, students' earnings could be made exempt from income tax (as was proposed recently in France). If the exemption were to apply to only the first 20 hours per week (or 1,000 per year outside of summer work), the effective wage rate increase would likely restrain students' desired hours of work.

Finally, the results also suggest that existing national (and most state) regulations, which apply only to those youths aged 14 and 15 years, could encourage students to spend more time in schooling. Current youth employment regulations stipulate that students' working hours must be no more than 3 hours on a school day, 18 hours in a school week, 8 hours on a non-school day, and 40 hours in a non-school week (see Rothstein 2001). Also, work may not begin before 7 am, nor end after 7 pm (except during summer). Similar limits could be considered regarding the hours worked for youth up to 18 years old if they are enrolled in high school or college. It has been proposed to extend to the US Department of Labor the authority to further limit the number of hours students can work per day and regulate the times when they start and stop working on school nights (Chaplin 1999, National Academy of Sciences 1998). Exceptions would be made for school-to-work programs and for students who must work out of economic necessity. The 'Youth Worker Protection Act' was introduced into the US House of Representatives in September 2003 (H.R. 3193). It included 'Working-Hour Restrictions for Minors', which would cover those aged 16–17. It would prohibit employers from scheduling work as follows: during school hours; before 7 am on any day; no later than 10 pm on a day before a school day or later than 11 pm on any other day. It would also prevent work that was: more than 4 hours on a school day; more than 8 hours on any other day; more than 20 hours during a week in which school is in session; more than 40 hours during any other week; and scheduled on more than six consecutive days. The Bill languished in Committee, was resubmitted in the 2005–2006 Congress (as H.R. 2870), but again it was never brought to a vote.

One alternative to direct regulation would be creating a wage premium for student work, analogous to a shift differential or overtime penalty. While this might have the desired enforcement effects of limiting employer hours demanded, since pay rates for working students tend to fall in the low range, this might also have the perverse effect of inducing longer desired hours of work among students, given their relatively higher rates of underemployment (see Golden and Gebreselassie 2007). An alternative, more individualized than collective approach, would be to provide those youth with both jobs and schooling responsibilities a legally protected 'right to refuse' hours per week beyond which this study and other similar studies find begin to seriously impinge on the input into students' school performance and/or mental and physical health. Students with part-time jobs, those entailing more than one day per week, might be considered more explicitly in the recent 'Right to Request' legislation pending (H.R. 1274) that would permit most employees to file a request for reduced or rescheduled work hours with their employers – modelled on rights recently granted in the United Kingdom and Australia. Such a right for students would support those youth who truly wish to prioritize time toward their educational activities.

The authors wish to acknowledge research assistance from Angelisa Cataldo, Eugene Shpolsky, Emma Harrigan, Katie Silveus, Ben Wolfert and Samantha Kelly.

References

Bailey, M. and Mallier, T. 1999. The summer vacation: Influences on the hours students work. *Applied Economics*, 31(1), 9–15.

Becker, G. 1985. Human capital, effort, and the sexual division of labor. *Journal of Labor Economics*, 3(1, Supp), S33–S58.

Breslin, F. C. Tompa, E., Zhao, R., Amick, B. C. III, Pole, J., Smith, P. and Hogg-Johnson, S. 2007. Work disability absence among young workers with respect to earnings losses in the following year. *Scandinavian Journal of Work and Environmental Health*, 33(3), 192–7.

Butler, A. B. 2007. Job characteristics and college performance and attitudes: A model of work-school conflict and facilitation. *Journal of Applied Psychology*, 92(2), 500–510.

Chaplin, D. and Hannaway, J. 1996. *High School Employment: Meaningful Connections for At-risk Youth*. Research Report. Washington DC: The Urban Institute.

Crawford, D. L., Johnson, A. W. and Summers, A. A. 1997. Schools and labor market outcomes. *Economics of Education Review*, 16(3), 255–69.

Curtis, S. and Shani, N. 2002. The effect of taking paid employment during term-time on students' academic studies. *Journal of Further and Higher Education*, 26(2), 129–38.

Dundes, L. and Marx, J. 2006–2007. Balancing work and academics in college: Why do students working 10 to 19 hours per week excel? *Journal of College Student Retention*, 8(1), 107–20.

Ehrenberg, R. G. and Sherman, D. R. 1987. Employment while in college, academic achievement and post-college outcomes: A summary of results. *Journal of Human Resources*, 22(1), 1–23.

Fahr, R. 2005. Loafing or learning? The demand for informal education. *European Economic Review*, 49(1), 75–98.

Floro, M. and Miles, M. 2003. Time use, work and overlapping activities: Evidence from Australia. *Cambridge Journal of Economics*, 27(6), 881–904.

Hamermesh, D., Frazis, H. and Stewart, J. 2005. Data watch: The American Time Use Survey. *Journal of Economic Perspectives*, 19(1), 221–32.

Galinsky, E., Kim, S., Bond, J. and Salmond, K. 2000. *Youth and Employment: Today's Students, Tomorrow's Work Force*. New York, NY: Families and Work Institute.

Galinsky, E., Bond, J., Kim, S., Backon, L., Brownfield, E. and Sakai, K. 2005. *Overwork in America: When the Way We Work Becomes Too Much*. New York, NY: Families and Work Institute.

Golden, L. and Gebrelselassie T. 2007. Which workers prefer to exchange income for a change in work hours in the US? *Monthly Labor Review*, 130(4), 18–37.

Häkkinen, I. 2006. Working while enrolled in a university: Does it pay? *Labour Economics*, 13(2), 167–89.

Hannah, R. 2002. An analysis of the linkages between high school allowance, high school market-place work, and academic success in higher education. *The High School Journal*, 85(3), 1–12.

Hannah, R. and Baum, C. 2001. An examination of college-bound high school students' labor market behaviour: Why some students work and why some do not. *Education*, 121(4), 787–94.

Hawkins, C., Smith, M., Hawkins II, R. and Grant, D. 2005. The relationships among hours employed, perceived work interference and grades as reported by undergraduate social work students. *Journal of Social Work Education*, 41(1), 13–28.

Heiselt, A. and Bergerson, A. 2007. Will work for a college education: An analysis of the role employment plays in the experiences of first-year college students. *Higher Education in Review*, 4, 83–106.

Kalenkoski, C. and Pabilonia, S. 2010. Parental transfers, student achievement, and the labor supply of college students. *Journal of Population Economics*, 23(2), 469–96.

Kelly, K. 1998. Working teenagers: Do after-school jobs hurt? *Harvard Education Letter Research Online*, July–August. Available at: http://www.edletter.org/past/issues/1998-ja/working.shtml. [accessed: 30 March 2011].

Krueger, A. 2007. Are we having more fun yet? Categorizing and evaluating changes in time allocation. *Brookings Papers in Economic Activity*, 38(2), 193–218.

Lacey, J. 2007. Grab bag: High school students' work and time use. *Occupational Outlook Quarterly* (Spring). Washington DC: US Bureau of Labor Statistics.

Lahmers, A. and Zulauf, C. 2000. Factors associated with academic time use and academic performance of college. *Journal of College Student Development*, 41(5), 544–56.

Lee, C. and Orazem, P. 2010. High school employment, school performance and college entry. *Economics of Education Review*, 29, 29–39.

Lenaghan, J. and Sengupta, K. 2007. Role conflict, role balance and affect: A model of well-being of the working student. *Journal of Behavioural and Applied Management*, 9(1), 88–99, 102–9.

Lerman, R. 2000. *Are Teens in Low-income and Welfare Families Working Too Much?* Policy Briefs, B–25 in Series, New Federalism: National Survey of America's Families. Washington, DC: Urban Institute.

Lillydahl, J. 1990. Academic achievement and part-time employment of high school students. *Journal of Economic Education*, 21(3), 307–16.

'Limit Children's Work Hours, Report Says'. 1999. *Public Health Reports*, 114(2), 105.

Manthei, R. and Gilmore, A. 2005. The effect of paid employment on university students' lives. *Education & Training*, 47(2/3), 202–16.

Markel, K. and Frone, M. 1998. Job characteristics, work-school conflict, and school outcomes among adolescents: Testing a structural model. *Journal of Applied Psychology*, 83(2), 277–87.

Marsh, H. and Kleitman, S. 2005. Consequences of employment during high school: Character building, subversion of academic goals, or a threshold? *American Educational Research Journal*, 42(2), 331–70.

McCoy, S. and Smyth, E. 2007. So much to do, so little time: Part-time employment among secondary students in Ireland. *Work, Employment and Society*, 21(2), 227–46.

Montmarquette, C., Viennot-Briot, N. and Dagenais, M. 2007. Dropout, school performance and working while in school. *Review of Economics and Statistics*, 89(4), 752–60.

Moreau, M. and Leathwood, C. 2006. Balancing paid work and studies: Working (-class) students in higher education. *Studies in Higher Education*, 31(1), 23–42.

Mortimer, J. T. and Johnson, M. K. 1998. Adolescent part-time work and educational achievement, in *Youth Experiences and Development: Social Influences and Educational Challenges*, edited by K. Borman and B. Schneider. New York, NY: National Society for the Study of Education, 183–206.

National Academy of Sciences 1999.

National Center for Education Statistics (NCES). 1998. *Postsecondary Financing Strategies: How Undergraduates Combine Work, Borrowing, and Attendance*. Statistical Analysis Report, February. Washington, DC: National Center for Education Statistics.

National Academy of Sciences. 1998. *Protecting Youth at Work: Health, Safety and Development of Working Children and Adolescents in the United States*. Committee on the Health and Safety Implications of Child Labor, National Research Council and Institute of Medicine. Washington, DC: National Academy of Sciences.

Nonis, S. and Hudson, G. 2006. Academic performance of college students: Influence of time spent studying and working. *Journal of Education for Business*, 81(3), 151–9.

OECD. 1996. *Employment Outlook*, July 1996. Paris: Organisation for Economic Cooperation and Development.

Oettinger, G. S. 1999. Does high school employment affect high school academic performance? *Industrial and Labor Relations Review*, 53(1), 136–51.

Oettinger, G. S. 2006. *Parents' Financial Support, Students' Time Use and Academic Performance in College*. University of Texas at Austin, February 20.

Orszag, J. M., Orszag, P. R. and. Whitmore, D. M. 2000. *Learning and Earning: Working in College*. Boston, MA: Upromise, Inc. Available at: http://www. brockport.edu/career01/upromise.htm [accessed: 31 March 2011].

Pocock, B. 2001. *The Effect of Long Hours on Family and Community Life: A Survey of Existing Literature*. A Report for the Queensland Department of Industrial Relations, August. Available at: http://www.actu.org.au/public/ campaigns/reasonable/pocock.html [accessed: 31 March 2011].

Polivka, A. 2008. Day, evening and night workers: A comparison of what they do in their nonwork hours and with whom they interact, in *How Do We Spend Our Time?: Evidence from the American Time Use Study*, edited by Jean Kimmel, Kalamazoo, MI: Upjohn Institute Press.

Porterfield, S. and Winkler, A. 2007. Teen time use and parental education: Evidence from the CPS, MTF and ATUS. *Monthly Labor Review*, 130(5), 37–55.

Post, D. and Pong, S. 2009. Student labour and academic proficiency in international perspective. *International Labour Review*, 148(1–2), 93–122.

Rau, W. and Durand, D. 2000. The academic ethic and college grades: Does work help students to 'make the grade'? *Sociology of Education*, 73(4), 19–38.

Rich, L. 1996. The long-run impact of teenage work experience: A reexamination. *Review of Black Political Economy*, 25(2), 11–36.

Riggert, S. C., Boyle, M., Petrosko, J. M., Ash, D. and Rude-Parkins, C. 2006. Student employment and higher education: Empiricism and contradiction. *Review of Educational Research*, 76(1), 63–92.

Roisman, G. 2002. Beyond main effects models of adolescent work intensity, family closeness and school disengagement: Mediational and conditional hypotheses. *Journal of Adolescent Research*, 17(4), 331–46.

Rothstein, D. S. 2001. Youth employment in the United States. *Monthly Labor Review*, 124(8), 6–19.

Rothstein, D. S. 2007. High school employment and youth's academic achievement. *Journal of Human Resources*, 42(1), 194–213.

Ruhm, C. 1997. Is high school employment consumption or investment? *Journal of Labor Economics*, 15(4), 735–76.

Singh, K. and Ozturk, M. 2000. Effect of part-time work on high school math and science course taking. *The Journal of Educational Research*, 94(2), 67–74.

Singh, K., Chang, M. and Dika, S. 2007. Effects of part-time work on school achievement during high school. *Journal of Educational Research*, 101(1), 12–23.

Sparks, K., Faragher. B. and Cooper, C. 2001. Well-being and occupational health in the 21st century workplace. *Journal of Occupational and Organizational Psychology*, 74(4), 489–509.

Staff, J. and Schulenberg, J. 2010. Millennials and the world of work: Experiences in paid work during adolescence. *Journal of Business Psychology,* 25(2), 247–55.

Steinberg, A. 1998. *Real Learning, Real Work.* New York and London: Routledge.

Steinberg, L. 1996. *Beyond the Classroom.* New York: Simon & Schuster.

Stern, D., Finkelstein, N., Stone, J. R. III, Latting, J. and Dornsife, C. 1995. *School to Work: Research on Programs in the US.* Washington and London: Taylor & Francis and Falmer Press.

Stern, D. and Briggs, D. 2001. Does paid employment help or hinder performance in secondary school? Insights from US high school students. *Journal of Education and Work*, 14(3), 355–72.

Stinebrickner, R. and Stinebrickner, T. 2004. Time-use and college outcomes. *Journal of Econometrics*, 121(1–2), 243–69.

'Students Who Work More Than 30 Hours Most Likely Dropouts'. 2003. *Child & Family Community Action*, 16 June.

'Study finds more undergraduates work while enrolled in college'. 2006. *Student Aid News*, 2(11), 8.

Svanum, S. and Bigatti, S. M. 2006. The influences of course effort and outside activities on grades in a college. *Journal of College Student Development*, 47(5), 564–76.

Tyler, J. 2003. Using state child labor laws to identify the effect of school-year work on high school achievement. *Journal of Labor Economics*, 21(2), 381–408.

US Bureau of Labor Statistics. 2004. *College Enrollment and Work Activity of 2003 High School Graduates*, 27 April.

US Bureau of Labor Statistics. 2005. *Work Activity of High School Students: Data from the National Longitudinal Survey of Youth 1997*, 05–732, 27 April.

US Department of Education. 2010. *The Condition of Education, 2010.* Indicator 45, College Student Employment, Institute of Education Sciences, National Center for Education Statistics.

Weller, N. Kelder, S., Cooper, S., Basen-Engquist, K. and Tortolero, S. 2003. School-year employment among high school students: Effects on academic, social and physical functioning. *Adolescence*, 38(151), 441–59.

Chapter 8

The Occupational Aspirations of Adolescents: Understanding the Developmental Context of Teenagers' Desires for Future Work Roles

Sampson Lee Blair

In the United States (US), as adolescents approach the end of their high school years, their thoughts begin to turn toward future goals and aspirations. For many, concern about careers and occupational paths becomes first and foremost in their lives, as thought has to be put into these choices quickly, so that decisions about college, vocational training or other alternative forms of preparation for an adult work role can be made. Researchers have long recognized the late adolescent years as being crucial to the development of aspirations concerning adult employment roles (Hitlin 2006), particularly as adolescents are undergoing so many other transitions, ranging from identity development to becoming more autonomous (for example, Adams, Montemayor and Gullota 1996, Feldman and Elliott 1990). Within this tumultuous stage of life, adolescents do not necessarily direct themselves toward a specific job but, rather, develop notions concerning the qualities of the job they eventually wish to have.

Occupational aspirations are a normal element of development within the late adolescent years. As teens approach the completion of their high school years, most begin to ponder their choices in regard to the future, and a great deal of time tends to be invested in contemplations about work and occupations. These aspirations essentially represent a means of orienting oneself towards a future goal (Schneider and Stevenson 1999), and may serve to both motivate and direct individuals towards the goals they seek (Reynolds et al. 2006). Frequently, these aspirations are rooted in the family, personal and social contexts of the individuals (Bowe, Bowe and Streeter 2000). For adolescents, the transitional period which occurs between high school completion and establishing oneself in a particular career can be a daunting task to face, yet the development of specific aspirations can help to provide substantive direction to their efforts, and help to allay fears and concerns along the way (Chaves et al. 2004). As the development of occupational aspirations proceeds during adolescence, these aspirations become very influential in the choice of careers and occupations (see Haller and Virkler 1993) in the long term, and also begin to influence the selection of educational paths to those careers and occupations (Rojewski and Hill 1998).

Occupational aspirations do not develop within a social vacuum; rather, a variety of factors serve as the social context in which adolescents formulate such notions. Of all contextual factors, it is, understandably, the family which represents the primary arena for the development of occupational aspirations. Parents, in particular, often convey their values and beliefs to their daughters and sons in tangible ways throughout the formative childhood and adolescent years, thereby leading to great similarities between the aspirations of the parents and their offspring (see Laramore 1984, Roberts and Bengston 1999, Young and Friesen 1992). Parents function as role models for their children's occupational aspirations in several direct and indirect ways: via their own careers and occupations, including their socio-economic status and educational attainment; through the provision of information about a range of occupational choices; and by facilitating children's career knowledge through their own peer networks (Eccles 1993, Jodl et al. 2001, Hill, Ramirez and Dumka 2003). This chapter explores the nature and determinants of adolescents' occupational aspirations, as well as the gender-based differences therein.

The Nature of Adolescent Work Aspirations

Throughout the childhood and adolescent years, individuals are constantly exposed to occupational roles models (for example, parents, neighbours) and will regularly be asked: 'What do you want to be when you grow up?' These formative experiences will eventually lead to the development of general beliefs about a particular occupation, and then, later, to more specific desires to obtain that occupation. These notions about what one can become are a crucial part of the development of possible selves. Possible selves constitute what an individual wants to become (for example, physician, architect, teacher), as well as what an individual wants to avoid becoming (for example, waitress, garbage collector, baggage handler). As individuals pass through the adolescent years, they increasingly attempt to develop more precise conceptualizations of their future occupational selves, through their experiences and social interactions with others (Kerpelman and Schvaneveldt 1999).

Researchers have often distinguished between occupational aspirations and occupational expectations (see Gottfredson 1996). Occupational aspirations are comprised of more general orientations toward a future job or career. Such orientations are often idealized, in the sense that adolescents envision a particular career as being the 'best' for themselves. Occupational expectations, on the other hand, are based, at least partially, upon actual experiences (such as part-time jobs during adolescence) and are regarded as a more realistic estimation of eventual jobs or careers. By the middle childhood years, children will typically have already gained an understanding of the relationship between work (paid labour) and money, and by the early adolescent years, they will have developed a firm understanding of the relationships between business owners, employees and customers (Berti and Bombi 1988). During the later teenage years, the aspirations of adolescents become increasingly crystallized, with a substantially increased degree of realism (Holland 1997). Eventually, the combination of role models, direct work experiences, peer influence and, in particular, family influences, lead adolescents to have a much greater congruence between occupational aspirations and their actual pursuit of a particular job or career (Reynolds et al. 2006). Many researchers have noted, however, that occupational and career aspirations are often quite different for female and male adolescents (see Weisgram, Bigler and Liben 2010).

Gender and Occupational Aspirations

Researchers (for example Kohn 1969) have long noted that the familial context provides a strong influence upon the development of adolescent aspirations, and can affect the attitudes, beliefs and values of children and adolescents concerning work and work roles. However, parents will, both directly and indirectly, influence the development of different types of aspirations in their daughters, as compared to their sons (Eccles 1994). This differential treatment and differential influence on the part of parents can occur in several distinct ways. Parsons and Bales (1955) argued that parents, by virtue of their status as mothers and fathers (which are normalized positions in society) are effectively influenced by those roles, as defined and maintained by the larger society. Essentially, parents, both in their behaviours and ideologies, become more traditional and conformist, and will seek to instill those same beliefs and behaviours in their children. Hence, any prevailing gender-typing of roles – in this case, those pertaining to occupations – will become part of the socialization experiences of children. Parents may attempt to create goals for their children, yet the adolescents themselves will also develop their own, independent notions of what they wish to do with their lives. This interplay and interaction between parents and children may eventually create a degree of shared views about what will be best for the adolescent (Young, Paseluikho and Valach 1997).

Ultimately, the gendered nature of societal roles, and particularly occupational roles, can affect the development of occupational aspirations by daughters and sons in a differential manner. Creamer and Laughlin (2005) have posited that the occupational views of females in late adolescence and early adulthood are often gender-typed (see also Li and Kerpelman 2007). Their research found that young women, compared to young men, consult significant others (parents in particular) more often, and are more readily influenced by the opinions of others. In terms of specific occupational aspirations, females, compared to males, have also been shown to place greater value on the altruistic qualities of work (Weisgram et al. 2010). Such findings suggest that there may be a gendered quality to particular job characteristics (see Eccles 1994), and that females and males may formulate aspirations which are more consistent with their own gender attitudes and ideologies. Males, for example, have been shown to prefer occupations which provide greater income and opportunities for power (Konrad et al. 2000), whereas females are more likely to prefer occupations wherein they can assist others and/or improve their skills and knowledge (Eccles 1994). Some researchers have suggested that, particularly in late adolescence, girls tend to espouse more prosocial values, as compared to boys (Beutel and Johnson 2004), suggesting that a divergence of the aspirations of females and males may take place during the mid to late adolescent years (Hitlin 2006). Among adolescents, such gender-based differences in occupational aspirations and career preferences have consistently been shown (see Rojewski and Hill 1998).

The Lifecourse Paradigm and Occupational Aspirations

Understanding how the development of occupational aspirations takes place obviously requires the recognition of the complex nature of socialization itself, as the values, beliefs, ideologies, and experiences of childhood and adolescence are extremely complex and interwoven with numerous social agents and contexts. A life-course paradigm has often been utilized as a means of explaining these complex processes (see Elder 1998). Within this perspective, the lives of parents and children are regarded as interwoven, as the developmental trajectory of each family member is linked inextricably with all others. Three particular elements within the life-course perspective are: 1. interdependent lives; 2. the timing of lives; and 3. human agency. Herein, the beliefs and attitudes concerning occupations are first conveyed and presented to children by parents, during the formative childhood years. Both as role models and as direct socialization agents, parents provide children within a 'foundation' of knowledge concerning the labour force in general, and specific occupations within it. Understandably, the knowledge, experiences and work characteristics of the parents come into play within this perspective (see Shu and Marini 2008). The life course paradigm is additionally useful in understanding the developmental processes which lead to aspirations, as it recognizes the larger social context. Both societal change (for example, economic recession which increases unemployment rates) and individual change (such as receiving a failing grade in calculus in the senior year of high school) can alter the occupational aspirations of adolescents.

In regard to the occupational aspirations of females and males, the life course paradigm also recognizes that differential treatment by parents, based on the sex of the child, is both entirely possible and likely to occur. The differential influence of parents upon daughters and sons, in regards to the development of aspirations, has been noted by many researchers (for example, Bankart, Bankart and Franklin 1988, Creamer and Laughlin 2005, Rainey and Borders 1997). Indeed, some researchers have suggested that the core ideologies associated with gendered occupational roles are tied directly to the gendered roles within the family itself (Ridgeway and Correll 2004). In order to better understand these possibilities, this study will now examine the relative effects of family and individual characteristics upon the occupational aspirations of adolescent females and males.

Data and Methods

Data for this study were derived from the 2008 wave of the Monitoring the Future survey (Monitoring the Future: A Continuing Study of American Youth). The sample comprised a nationally representative cohort of high school seniors, taken from approximately 130 public and private high schools throughout the US. Initiated in 1975, this cross-sectional survey attempts to gauge a combination of behaviours and attitudes of American adolescents. After removing cases containing missing data, the resulting sample consisted of 1,203 females and 1,043 males, all of whom were 17–19 years of age.

The measurements of occupational aspirations are taken from questions which asked the respondents how important particular characteristics would be to them in their employed work. The adolescents were given (on a scale comprised of 1 = not important, 2 = a little important, 3 = pretty important, and 4 = very important) 22 individual traits, and asked to respond how important each was to them. Based upon previous studies (see Herzog 1982; Johnson 2002, Marini et al. 1996), the responses were then used to create seven specific dimensions of work qualities: 1. extrinsic rewards; 2. intrinsic rewards; 3. altruistic rewards; 4. social rewards; 5. security; 6. influence; and 7. leisure. *Extrinsic rewards* resulted from questions asking if the respondent wanted a job: 1. where the chances for advancement and promotion are good; 2. which provides a chance to earn a good deal of money; 3. that most people look up to and respect; and 4. that has high status and prestige. *Intrinsic rewards* resulted from questions asking if the respondent wanted a job: 1. which is interesting to do; 2. which uses their skills and abilities and lets them do things they can do best; 3. where they can see the results of what they do; 4. where the skills they learn will not go out of date; 5. where they can learn new things and new skills; and 6. where they have the chance to be creative. *Altruistic rewards* resulted from questions asking if the respondent wanted a job: 1. that gives them the opportunity to be directly helpful to other; and 2. that is worthwhile to society. *Social rewards* resulted from questions asking if the respondent wanted a job: 1. that gives them a chance to make friends; and 2. that permits contact with a lot of people. *Security* resulted from questions asking if the respondent wanted a job: 1. that offers a reasonably predictable and secure future; and 2. which allows them to establish roots in a community and not have to move from place to place. *Influence* resulted from questions asking if the respondent wanted a job: 1. where they get a chance to participate in decision making; and 2. where most problems are quite difficult and challenging. Finally, *leisure* resulted from questions asking if the respondent wanted a job: 1. which leaves a lot time for other things in their life; 2. which leaves them mostly free of supervision by others; and 3. where they have more than two weeks of vacation; and 4. with an easy pace where they work slowly.

Respondents were also asked about their individual and household characteristics. In order to assess the desire to work, respondents were asked 'If you were to get enough money to live as comfortably as you'd like for the rest of your life, would you want to work?' (coded as 1 = work, 0 = not work). In regard to grade performance in high school, respondents were asked to describe their average grade so far (coded with a range of 1 = D through 9 = A). In addition, students were asked how likely it was going to be for them to graduate with a four-year college degree. Responses to this item ranged from 1 = definitely won't, 2 = probably won't, 3 = probably will, to 4 = definitely will. Since many high school seniors are actively working during their school year, students were asked if they were currently employed (coded as 1 = yes, 0 = no). Respondents were also asked if they could just work the number of hours they wanted to, how many hours per week they would prefer to work during the school year (coded as 1 = none, 2 = 5 or less, 3 = 6 to 10, 4 = 11 to 15, 5 = 16 to 20, 6 = 21 to 25, 7 = 26 to 30, 8 = 31 or more). In order to assess their usage of leisure time, respondents were asked, during a typical week, how many evenings they went out for fun and recreation. Among the household characteristics, respondents were asked if they lived in a two-parent home (coded as 1 = yes, 0 = no). Given that parents can be quite influential in the development of aspirations, both directly and indirectly, the level of parental educational attainment was also asked, with the higher of the parents being utilized (coded as 1 = grade school, 2 = some high school, 3 = high school degree, 4 = some college, 5 = college degree, 6 = graduate degree). The respondents were also asked whether their mother was employed for most of the time during their childhood years (coded as 1 = yes, 0 = no). In order to measure the relative effect of community size, a dummy measure for suburban residence (coded as 1 = lives in suburbs, 0 = lives other than in suburbs) was included. Finally, a pair of dummy measures were included to indicate the ethnicity of the respondents (either African-American or Latino).

Results

Table 8.1 presents the mean levels of occupational aspirations among adolescents, as shown for each sex. On the importance scale, which ranged from 1–4, it appears that both females and males place a high premium on the extrinsic rewards of employed work. Although the two sexes do not differ significantly in their desire to have extrinsic rewards from their jobs, it is worth noting that both consider this to be rather important. The intrinsic qualities of work, on the other hand, do yield a significant difference between the responses of females and males. In the relative comparison, female adolescents clearly place a much higher value on intrinsic job characteristics, as compared to male adolescents' preferences. Hence, qualities such as being able to use their skills, learn new things and be creative are all more highly sought after in work by female adolescents. Since these desires are quite likely to affect the selection of specific jobs as the adolescents later enter the paid labour force, such aspirations can have a very meaningful impact upon young adults' lives.

Table 8.1 **Mean levels of occupational aspirations among adolescents, by sex**

Desired job characteristics	Females		Males	
	Mean	SD	Mean	SD
Extrinsic Rewards	3.24	0.61	3.21	0.65
Intrinsic Rewards	3.45	0.43	3.31***	0.51
Altruistic Rewards	3.35	0.65	3.02***	0.77
Social Rewards	3.04	0.75	2.90***	0.81
Influence	2.66	0.69	2.71	0.72
Leisure	2.77	0.69	2.84**	0.71
Security	3.24	0.69	3.20	0.71

N = 1,203 females; 1,043 males

Note: Significance indicates difference between means, *** $p < .01$, ** $p < .05$, * $< .10$; Sample is limited to high school seniors, aged 17–19.

In a similar manner, female adolescents also placed a greater value upon the altruistic rewards of future jobs. Having job qualities such as being able to directly help others and perform work which is worthwhile to society are desired more highly by females as compared to males. Given the gender stereotypes of women being more compassionate and caring than men, this difference is not entirely surprising. However, it again suggests that gender plays a tangible role in the occupational aspirations of adolescents and young adults. Females were also shown to place a greater value upon the social rewards of paid labour (for example, having a chance to make friends), as compared to males.

In regard to being able to have influence in their respective future jobs, males and females do not differ significantly. In fact, it is worth noting that this particular characteristic was the least highly valued of the seven, perhaps suggesting that contemporary adolescents do not regard gaining influence or exercising influence in their future jobs to be important, as compared to other job characteristics. Interestingly, males placed a much greater value on the leisure component of work, as compared to females. Seemingly, this suggests that adolescent males are more likely to seek paid labour which provides them with an easier pace and which leaves them with more free time for other things. Finally, females and males place a high premium on job security, yet their respective responses do not differ significantly.

Table 8.2 presents the mean levels of individual and household characteristics, as presented for each sex. In terms of their desire to work for pay, females are shown to be much more likely to want to work, regardless of their current financial situation, as compared to males. Hence, it would seem that the work ethic, or at least the desire to work for pay, is stronger among adolescent females. Females reported substantially higher grade averages, as compared to males. This finding is congruent with the fact that females reported a much higher desire to complete a four-year college degree, as compared to males. These two differences between the sexes are consistent with the sex-based patterns of educational performance and attainment seen among contemporary youth in the US, wherein female students tend to perform slightly better in high school, and are more likely to continue on to college, as compared to males.

Table 8.2   Mean levels of individual and household characteristics among adolescents, by sex

Desired job characteristics	Females		Males	
	Mean	SD	Mean	SD
Desire to work	0.78	0.41	0.67***	0.47
Grade average	3.47	0.87	3.24***	0.95
Desire for college degree	3.47	0.87	3.24***	0.95
Currently employed	0.61	0.49	0.59	0.49
Earnings per week	4.86	3.44	5.10*	3.50
Preferred # of work hours	5.16	2.11	5.11	2.18
# Evenings goes out/week	3.26	1.29	3.61***	1.37
Two parents	0.63	0.48	0.68***	0.47
Parental education	4.31	1.25	4.38	1.19
Mother employed	0.67	0.47	0.66	0.47
Suburban home	0.20	0.40	0.24**	0.43
African-American	0.12	0.32	0.12	0.33
Latino	0.15	0.36	0.15	0.35

N = 1,203 females; 1,043 males

Note: Significance indicates difference between means, *** $p < .01$, ** $p < .05$, * $< .10$; Sample is limited to high school seniors, aged 17–19.

In regard to current employment, 61 per cent of females and 59 per cent of males have jobs during their senior year of high school. Overall, however, males report a slightly higher level of earnings, as compared to females. When the respondents were asked how many hours they would prefer to work per week during the school year, both males and female agree that between 16–20 hours would be best.

Females and males did differ, though, in regard to how many evenings each week they went out for fun, with males reporting that they do so much more frequently.

The household characteristics of the respondents were similar overall, yet there were several noteworthy distinctions. Males were slightly more likely to live in a two-parent home, as compared to females. The two sexes did not differ in regards to the levels of parental educational attainment, and both females and males reported that approximately two-thirds of their mothers were employed.

Table 8.3 presents the ordinary least square (OLS) regression models of adolescents' occupational aspirations, focusing on the extrinsic, intrinsic, altruistic and social rewards. In terms of extrinsic rewards, females' desire to work is significantly associated with lower concern for extrinsic rewards. Among males, by comparison, the desire to work does not yield a significant effect. This distinction may suggest that female adolescents are somewhat less concerned with the extrinsic rewards of future jobs. However, this possibility must be considered in conjunction with the other significant effects from the models. For example, a higher level of earnings was shown to significantly increase females' concern for extrinsic rewards, yet did not yield a significant effect in the same model for males. The more practical aspects of extrinsic rewards, such as making more money, may be evident in the effects shown for the frequency of going out for fun, where an increase in the number of evenings spent going out was associated with a greater concern for extrinsic rewards. Interestingly, males whose mothers were employed were significantly more concerned with extrinsic rewards in their future jobs, while the same effect was not significant in the female model. Overall, it appears that females' current work status (that is, having a current job), coupled with current earnings, preferred work hours and their desire to work, all result in a much more substantial influence upon their aspirations for extrinsic rewards, as compared to males.

In terms of intrinsic rewards, both males and females who desired to work, regardless of their financial standing, were shown to be significantly more concerned with their job's intrinsic characteristics. This suggests that, for both sexes, a greater desire for adult employment is equated with a greater desire to have work that is interesting, stimulating and provides the opportunity to be creative. Among males, however, a higher grade average in high school actually yields a negative association with intrinsic rewards. Simply, the better that males perform in school, the less interested they tend to be in intrinsic job characteristics. At the same time, though, males who desire to complete a college degree are shown to be more likely to value the intrinsic qualities of their future jobs. This is rather intriguing, as the desire to attain a college degree, among males, was also associated with a greater valuation of the extrinsic rewards of work. For both sexes, a higher preferred number of current work hours was linked with a greater valuation of the intrinsic rewards of work. Among females, having an employed mother was significantly linked (albeit meagrely) with a lower valuation of intrinsic work characteristics.

Table 8.3   **OLS regression models of occupational aspirations (extrinsic, intrinsic, altruistic, and social rewards) among adolescents, by sex**

Desired job characteristics	Extrinsic Rewards		Intrinsic Rewards		Altruistic Rewards		Social Rewards	
	Females	Males	Females	Males	Females	Males	Females	Males
Desire to work	-.08***	-.01	.10***	.22***	.15***	.20***	.03	.15***
	(-.11)	(-.01)	(.10)	(.24)	(.24)	(.33)	(.06)	(.26)
Grade average	-.04	-.01	-.03	-.09***	.03	-.05	-.01	-.03
	(-.01)	(-.00)	(-.01)	(-.02)	(.01)	(-.02)	(-.00)	(-.01)
Desire for college degree	.05	.13***	.04	.12***	.10***	.14***	.10***	.04
	(.03)	(.09)	(.02)	(.07)	(.07)	(.11)	(.08)	(.03)
Currently employed	-.08**	-.00	-.05	-.03	.00	-.01	-.00	.03
	(-.10)	(-.02)	(-.05)	(-.04)	(.01)	(-.01)	(-.00)	(.04)
Earnings per week	.08**	.08*	.06	.04	.04	.03	.06	.01
	(.02)	(.01)	(.01)	(.01)	(.01)	(.01)	(.01)	(.00)
Preferred # of work hours	.11***	.10***	.12***	.07**	.04	.04	.05	.05
	(.03)	(.03)	(.02)	(.02)	(.01)	(.02)	(.02)	(.02)
# Evenings goes out/week	.08**	.06*	.01	-.02	.00	-.01	.06**	.03
	(.02)	(.03)	(.00)	(-.01)	(.00)	(-.01)	(.04)	(.02)
Two parents	-.11***	-.02	.00	-.03	-.01	.02	.00	-.01
	(-.14)	(-.03)	(.00)	(-.03)	(-.01)	(.03)	(.00)	(-.02)
Parental education	-.04	-.06*	.00	-.03	-.00	-.02	.07**	.06*
	(-.02)	(-.03)	(.00)	(-.01)	(-.00)	(-.01)	(.04)	(.04)
Mother employed	.01	.06**	-.05*	.04	-.04	.03	.00	.05
	(.01)	(.09)	(-.05)	(.04)	(-.06)	(.05)	(.00)	(.08)
Suburban home	-.03	.02	.03	.01	-.00	-.04	-.02	.01
	(-.04)	(.03)	(.03)	(.01)	(-.01)	(-.08)	(-.04)	(.02)
African-American	.15***	.11***	.05	-.01	.04	.02	-.10***	-.03
	(.29)	(.22)	(.06)	(-.02)	(.08)	(.04)	(-.23)	(-.07)
Latino	.13***	.06**	.07**	.01	.02	.01	.02	.02
	(.22)	(.12)	(.08)	(.01)	(.04)	(.02)	(.04)	(.04)
R-Square	.10	.06	.04	.07	.04	.06	.04	.04
F	9.76***	5.00***	3.91***	6.06***	3.75***	5.07***	3.32***	3.02***

N = 1,203 females; 1,043 males

Note: *** p < .01, ** p < .05, * < .10; Unstandardized coefficients are shown in parentheses; Sample is limited to high school seniors, aged 17–19.

The third set of models examines the altruistic rewards of paid work. As with the extrinsic and intrinsic models, both females and males are shown to have a higher valuation of altruistic work characteristics when their desire to work is higher. Essentially, this implies that a greater desire to work is linked with a greater desire to be helpful to others or to do something which is worthwhile to society at large. For both sexes, a higher desire to complete a college degree is also positively associated with a higher valuation of the potential altruistic characteristics of future jobs. It is easy enough to envision that a greater desire to complete one's education, coupled with a greater desire to become employed, might also be associated with a desire to do something positive or pro-social with the 'fruits' of those efforts, and particularly so in the minds and hearts of adolescents.

In the models of the social characteristics of paid employment, males' desire for work is positively associated with a higher valuation of social rewards (for example, being able to make friends). Oddly, this same effect is not significant in the model for females. In contrast, females' desire for a college degree is shown to be positively associated with social occupational characteristics, yet the same effect is not significant in the model for males. As proposed previously, female and male adolescents may develop their preferences and aspirations for occupations in substantially different ways; in this case, the desire to work and the desire to obtain a college degree seemingly affect males and females quite differently. Females are also shown to place a higher valuation on the social qualities of their future employment when they spend more evenings out during the school year.

Table 8.4 presents the OLS regression models of occupational aspirations for adolescents, focusing specifically on influence, leisure and job security. As shown in the models for occupational influence (for example, being able to participate in decision making), both males and females who desired to work were significantly more likely to value influence in their future jobs. In addition, a greater desire for obtaining a college degree was also positively associated with aspirations for influence in the future jobs of both sexes. Interestingly, females who were currently employed were significantly less likely to want to have influence in their future jobs. This may, understandably, have something to do with the nature of their current jobs, as most adolescents tend to work in jobs where they have very little influence or control within the workplace. Among females, spending more evenings out (for fun) was positively associated with the desire for influence in their future jobs (this same effect was not significant in the model for males). In addition, females whose mothers were employed were significantly less likely to desire influence in their jobs (again, this effect was not significant among males). Although these data cannot capture much of the nuance and qualitative nature of the lives of adolescents, it nonetheless appears that females are more readily affected by the individual and household characteristics, as compared to males.

Table 8.4   OLS regression models of occupational aspirations (influence, leisure, and security) among adolescents, by sex

Desired job characteristics	Influence		Leisure		Security	
	Females	Males	Females	Males	Females	Males
Desire to work	.11***	.14***	-.17***	-.12***	-.02	.05
	(.18)	(.21)	(-.28)	(-.19)	(-.03)	(.08)
Grade average	.06*	.03	-.01	-.07**	-.02	-.01
	(.02)	(.01)	(-.00)	(-.03)	(-.01)	(-.00)
Desire for college degree	.05*	.09***	-.07**	-.01	.03	.10***
	(.04)	(.79)	(-.06)	(-.01)	(.02)	(.07)
Currently employed	-.09**	-.01	-.10**	.02	-.07*	-.04
	(-.13)	(-.02)	(-.15)	(.03)	(-.11)	(-.06)
Earnings per week	.05	.09**	.05	-.01	.09**	.03
	(.01)	(.02)	(.01)	(-.00)	(.02)	(.01)
Preferred # of work hours	.06*	.02	.01	.01	.11***	.09***
	(.02)	(.01)	(.00)	(.00)	(.04)	(.03)
# Evenings goes out/ week	.07**	-.02	.07**	.06*	.00	.00
	(.04)	(-.01)	(.04)	(.03)	(.00)	(.00)
Two parents	-.04	-.04	.00	-.02	-.01	.00
	(-.06)	(-.06)	(.01)	(-.02)	(-.01)	(.00)
Parental education	.03	.05	-.00	-.02	-.08**	-.02
	(.01)	(.03)	(-.00)	(-.02)	(-.04)	(-.01)
Mother employed	-.07**	.03	-.07**	.01	.01	.04
	(-.10)	(.05)	(-.10)	(.01)	(.01)	(.05)
Suburban home	.02	.05	.01	.01	-.07**	-.06*
	(.04)	(.08)	(.02)	(.02)	(-.12)	(-.10)
African-American	.04	.04	.05*	.03	.01	.02
	(.09)	(.08)	(.11)	(.07)	(.01)	(.04)
Latino	.09***	.02	.10***	.06*	.05*	.05
	(.16)	(.04)	(.20)	(.12)	(.10)	(.10)
R-Square	.04	.05	.06	.04	.05	.03
F	3.92***	4.00***	6.06***	2.99***	4.12***	2.26**

N = 1,203 females; 1,043 males

Note: *** p < .01, ** p < .05, * < .10; Unstandardized coefficients are shown in parentheses; Sample is limited to high school seniors, aged 17–19.

The data show that both females and males who desire to work express a much lower valuation for leisure. Seemingly, this may indicate a greater work ethic, such that adolescents who want to work have already begun to focus on work itself, and give less consideration to the leisure components of their forthcoming jobs and careers. Among females, both the desire for a college degree and being currently employed are negatively associated with the valuation of leisure. Oddly, these same effects are not significant among males. While the desire for a college degree is likely equated with the development of a work ethic, it is also quite likely that work experience itself leads adolescent females to have less of a desire for leisure. This contention may be supported somewhat by the association shown between females' frequency of going out (for fun) and their valuation of leisure in their future jobs, wherein a higher frequency of going out is positively linked with the valuation of leisure. The same association is shown in the model for males, although the strength of the association is somewhat weaker. Once more, it appears that substantially more variation is explained in the female models, as compared to those for males.

Finally, in terms of job security, males with a higher desire to complete a college degree are shown to have a greater desire for job security. Understandably, a higher preferred number of work hours has a significant positive association with the desire for job security; this is true for both males and females. Interestingly, although a higher level of current earnings is associated with a greater desire for job security among females, the same effect is not significant among males. Among females, the individual and household characteristics yield some rather intriguing results. For instance, employed females are actually shown to have lower levels of concern for job security, as are those females whose parents have higher levels of educational attainment. It is possible that either the sense of personal or family financial security (through having a job or having well-educated parents) may reduce females' desire for job security in the future. It is readily apparent, however, that the occupational aspirations of females and males are affected in very distinct ways by the combination of individual and household characteristics examined herein.

In order to better understand the more specific occupational aspirations of adolescents, Table 8.5 presents the percentage distribution of female and male adolescents' occupational goals. For the purposes of these selections, the respondents were presented with a list of 15 occupational choices, each of which provided a set of examples. Given that the respondents are all in their senior year of high school, many of them may not have yet solidified their occupational goals. These responses, however, do provide a better understanding of the occupational aspirations of adolescents, as well as the sex-based differences which may exist.

For both males and females, the most popular occupational aspirations centre around the professions. Among females, 42.64 per cent aspired to have a career in a profession which requires a college degree, but not a doctoral degree. Among males, 34.38 per cent also maintained such aspirations. Many adolescents reported even higher aspirations, as 23.26 per cent of females and 14.16 per cent of males stated that they wanted to eventually be in a profession which requires a doctorate degree. Hence, approximately half of all males aspire to be in a profession, while two-thirds of all females aspire to the same. This difference is rather striking, as it clearly indicates a strong tendency among females, more so than males, to pursue a professional career.

Table 8.5   Specific occupational aspirations of adolescents, by sex

Desired Future Job	Female	Male
Labourer (e.g., car washer, sanitary worker, farm labourer)	0.09	0.40
Service Worker (e.g., cook, waiter, barber, janitor, gas station attendant, practical nurse, beautician)	4.05	1.11
Operative or Semi-Skilled Worker (e.g., garage worker, taxicab, bus, or truck driver, assembly line worker, welder)	0.00	1.82
Retail (e.g., phone sales, department store clerk, drug store clerk)	0.53	0.30
Clerical (e.g., bank teller, bookkeeper, secretary, postal clerk or carrier, keyboard operator)	1.85	0.61
Protective Service (e.g., police officer, firefighter, detective)	2.47	6.67
Military Service	1.32	6.27
Skilled Worker (e.g., carpenter, electrician, brick layer, mechanic, machinist, tool and die maker, telephone installer)	0.97	8.59
Farm (e.g. farm owner, farm manager)	0.53	1.01
Small Business Owner (e.g., restaurant owner, shop owner)	7.84	7.48
Sales Representative (e.g., insurance agent, real estate broker, bond salesman)	1.06	2.63
Manager (e.g., officer manager, sales manager, school administrator, government official)	4.05	6.17
Professional – without doctoral degree (e.g., registered nurse, librarian, engineer, architect, social worker, accountant, actor, artist, musician, teacher, pilot, computer programmer, analyst)	42.64	34.38
Professional – with doctoral degree (e.g., lawyer, physician, dentist, scientist, college professor)	23.26	14.16
Full-Time Homemaker	1.23	0.78
Don't Know	8.11	7.68

$N = 1,203$ females; 1,043 males

Note: Sample is limited to high school seniors, aged 17–19.

Professional aspirations notwithstanding, several of the other occupational aspiration categories seem to support long-standing gender stereotypes concerning adolescents' preferences for future jobs. In regard to military careers, substantially more males than females (6.27 per cent versus 1.32 per cent, respectively) seek to serve in the military. As well, more males wanted to go into protective service occupations (for example, police officer), as compared to females (6.67 per cent versus 2.47 per cent, respectively). Substantially more males also wanted to pursue a skilled worker occupation (such a carpenter or mechanic) than did females (8.59 per cent versus 0.97 per cent, respectively). Female adolescents, on the other hand, were more likely to aspire to have a service worker job, as compared to males (4.05 per cent versus 1.11 per cent, respectively). Overall, the patterns of occupational aspirations suggest that there are still some sex-based patterns which follow traditional gender stereotypes in society. However, these patterns are evident among occupational preferences wherein only a small percentage of adolescents expressed a specific job preference. The overwhelming proportion of female adolescents who intend to pursue a professional career, particularly when considered in conjunction with the smaller proportion of male adolescents who intend likewise, suggests that there is a steady change forthcoming in regards to the gendered stratification of occupations in the US. With ever-increasing numbers of adolescent females pursuing a professional career, as compared to the numbers of male adolescents, it is likely that adult females will soon outnumber their male counterparts in professional careers. With the accompanying characteristics of higher incomes and higher occupational prestige, these changes may have far-reaching implications for gender issues in the larger society.

Conclusions and Discussion

As previously discussed, researchers have noted substantial differences in the occupational aspirations of adolescent and young adult females and males. In accordance with prevailing gender stereotypes, males have placed a much greater emphasis on the extrinsic rewards of work (namely income), along with the opportunity to obtain greater influence in their jobs, and more time to pursue their leisure interests. Likewise, females have been regarded as preferring the more intrinsic rewards of work, particularly the chance to improve their skills and education, along with having the chance to help others and to be able to socialize and make friends in the workplace. This study utilized a nationally representative sample of high school seniors in order to assess whether these differences exist, and to further analyse how such differences might arise from the combination of individual and family characteristics.

Given the results shown herein, there appears to be some support for the existing gender stereotypes concerning occupational aspirations. Although no significant difference was shown between females and males in regard to extrinsic rewards, there were several noteworthy distinctions. Female adolescents placed significantly more emphasis upon the intrinsic rewards of work, thereby suggesting that they desire more opportunities to improve themselves (for example, skills, education, abilities) through their jobs than do male adolescents. Females also placed a much greater value upon the altruistic rewards of paid labour. Since one of the prevailing stereotypes of femininity in American culture is that women tend to be more caring and nurturing, this difference is not entirely surprising. It does imply that female adolescents may actively seek careers and occupations wherein they can be of assistance to others, in whatever form those jobs allow. Females were shown to give greater emphasis to the social rewards of jobs. Here, there is some support for the stereotype that females are more communicative and tend to actively socialize with others more than males. Although no significant differences were shown in regard to the desire for influence or for job security, males are shown to have a greater desire for leisure in their jobs, as compared to females.

In the multivariate analyses, several very intriguing patterns were revealed. For both females and males, it appeared that the individual characteristics were much more influential than the household characteristics in regards to predicting variation in adolescent occupational aspirations. In particular, one of the predominant influences upon aspirations was the adolescents' reported desire to work. A stronger desire to work was equated with a greater desire for intrinsic rewards, altruistic rewards and influence on the job for both sexes. Likewise, a stronger desire to work was associated with a lower aspiration for leisure time for both sexes. Seemingly, the desire to work, or more simply, work ethic, readily affected the occupational aspirations for both sexes.

Surprisingly, although employment during the adolescent years is quite common, there appeared to be a deleterious effect of employment upon the aspirations of adolescent females. When teenage girls were employed, they appeared to have less desire for extrinsic rewards, influence in the workplace, leisure time and job security. Of course, some of this pattern may result from the nature of adolescent work itself; most adolescents tend to hold part-time jobs where the tasks are repetitive and menial, opportunities for advancement or promotion are few, and the job has little, if any, association with their future occupational goals. Simply, the negative qualities of adolescent jobs may lead teenage females to have lower occupational aspirations for their future careers. What makes this pattern particularly surprising is the complete lack of effect by employment upon the aspirations of teenage males. A more intensive examination of the relative impact of teen employment upon the development of aspirations is certainly warranted.

Overall, these findings suggest that the occupational aspirations of contemporary adolescents are readily influenced by the social context of their lives. Both individual and familial characteristics were shown to affect the development of aspirations, yet it would appear that the influence of family (both parent and household) characteristics may not be as substantial as in previous generations. Given that so many adolescents today access other sources for job information, most notably the massive amounts of information on the internet, it is not entirely surprising that the individual traits of teenagers have a greater effect upon their job aspirations. The clear differences between the aspirations of females and males, however, do suggest that there still exists a gendered divide between the perspectives of contemporary teenage girls and boys.

References

Adams, G., Montemayor, R. and Gullota, T. 1996. *Psychosocial Development During Adolescence: Progress in Developmental Contextualism*. Thousand Oaks, CA: Sage.

Bankart, B. Bankart, C. and Franklin, J. 1988. Adolescent values as predictors of self-reported achievement in young men. *Journal of Social Psychology*, 128(2), 249–57.

Berti, A. and Bombi, A. 1988. *The Child's Construction of Economics*. Cambridge, England: Cambridge University Press.

Beutel, A. and Johnson, M. 2004. Gender and prosocial values during adolescence: A research note. *Sociological Quarterly*, 45(2), 379–93.

Bowe, J., Bowe, M. and Streeter, S. 2000. *Gig: Americans Talk About Their Jobs*. New York, NY: Three Rivers Press.

Chaves, A., Diemer, M., Blustein, D., Gallagher, L., DeVoy, J., Casares, M. and Perry, J. 2004. Conceptions of work: The view from urban youth. *Journal of Counseling Psychology*, 51(3), 275–86.

Creamer, E. and Laughlin, A. 2005. Self-authorship and women's career decision making. *Journal of College Student Development*, 46(1), 13–27.

Eccles, J. 1993. School and family effects on the ontogeny of children's interests, self-perceptions, and activity choices, in *Developmental Perspectives on Motivation*, edited by R. Dienstbier and J. E. Jacobs. Lincoln, NE: University of Nebraska Press, 144–208.

Eccles, J. 1994. Understanding women's educational and occupational choices: Applying the Eccles et al. model of achievement-related choices. *Psychology of Women Quarterly*, 18(4), 585–609.

Elder, G. 1998. The life course and human behaviour, in *Handbook of Child Psychology, Volume 1: Theoretical Models of Human Development*, 5th edition, edited by W. Damon. New York, NY: Wiley and Sons, 939–91.

Feldman, S. and Elliott, G. 1990. Capturing the adolescent experience, in *At the Threshold: The Developing Adolescent*, edited by S. S. Feldman and G. R. Elliott. Cambridge, MA: Harvard University Press, 1–13.

Gottfredson, L. 1996. Gottfredson's theory of circumscription and compromise, in *Career Choice and Development*, 3rd edition, edited by D. Brown and L. Brooks. San Francisco, CA: Jossey-Bass, 179–232.

Haller, E. and Virkler, S. 1993. Another look at rural–nonrural differences in students' educational aspirations. *Journal of Research in Rural Education*, 9(3), 170–78.

Hill, N., Ramirez, C. and Dumka, L. 2003. Early adolescents' career aspirations: A qualitative study of perceived barriers and family support among low-income, ethnically diverse adolescents. *Journal of Family Issues*, 24(7), 934–59.

Hitlin, S. 2006. Parental influences on children's values and aspirations: Bridging two theories of social class and socialisation. *Sociological Perspectives*, 49(1), 25–46.

Holland, J. 1997. *Making Vocational Choices: A Theory of Vocational Personalities and Work Environments*. 3rd edition. Odessa, FL: Psychological Assessment Resources.

Jodl, K., Michael, A., Malanchuk, O., Eccles, J. and Sameroff, A. 2001. Parents' roles in shaping early adolescents' occupational aspirations. *Child Development*, 72(4), 1247–65.

Kerpelman, J. and Schvaneveldt, P. 1999. Young adults' anticipated identity commitments to career, marital, and parental roles: Comparisons of men and women with different role balance orientations. *Sex Roles*, 41(3–4), 189–217.

Kohn, M. 1969. *Class and Conformity: A Study in Values*. Homewood, IL: Dorsey Press.

Konrad, A., Ritchie, J., Lieb, P. and Corrigall, E. 2000. Sex differences and similarities in job attribute preferences: A meta-analysis. *Psychological Bulletin*, 126(4), 593–641.

Laramore, D. 1984. Parents' role in the education and career decision making process. *Journal of Career Education*, 10(4), 214–15.

Li, C. and Kerpelman, J. 2007. Parental influences on young women's certainty about their career aspirations. *Sex Roles*, 56(1–2), 105–15.

Marini, M., Fan, P.-L., Finley, E. and Beutel, A. 1996. Gender and job values. *Sociology of Education*, 69(1), 49–65.

Parsons, T. and Bales, R. 1955. *Family, Socialization, and Interaction*. Glencoe, IL: Free Press.

Rainey, L. and Borders, L. 1997. Influential factors in career orientation and career aspiration of early adolescent girls. *Journal of Counseling Psychology*, 44(2), 160–72.

Reynolds, J., Stewart, M., MacDonald, R. and Sischo, L. 2006. Have adolescents become too ambitious? High school seniors' educational and occupational plans, 1976 to 2000. *Social Problems*, 53(2), 186–206.

Ridgeway, C. and Correll, S. 2004. Unpacking the gender system: A theoretical perspective on gender beliefs and social relations. *Gender & Society*, 18(4), 510–31.

Roberts, R. and Bengston, V. 1999. The social psychology of values: Effects of individual development, social change, and family transmission over the life span, in *The Self and Society in Aging Processes*, edited by C. D. Ryff and V. W. Marshall. New York, NY: Springer Press, 453–82.

Rojewski, J. and Hill, R. 1998. Influence of gender and academic risk behaviour on career decision making and occupational choice in early adolescence. *Journal of Education for Students Placed at Risk*, 3(3), 265–87.

Schneider, B. and Stevenson, D. 1999. *The Ambitious Generation: America's Teenagers, Motivated but Directionless.* New Haven, CT: Yale University Press.

Shu, X. and Marini, M. 2008. Coming of age in changing times: Occupational aspirations of American youth, 1966–1980. *Research in Social Stratification and Mobility*, 26(1), 29–55.

Weisgram, E., Bigler, R. and Liben, L. 2010. Gender, values, and occupational interests among children, adolescents, and adults. *Child Development*, 81(3), 778–96.

Young, R. and Freisen, J. 1992. The intentions of parents in influencing the career development of their children. *Career Development Quarterly*, 40(3), 198–207.

Young, R., Paseluikho, M. and Valach, L. 1997. The role of emotion in the construction of career in parent-adolescent conversations. *Journal of Counseling and Development*, 76(1), 36–44.

Chapter 9

Youth and Precarious Employment in Europe

Luísa Oliveira, Helena Carvalho and Luísa Veloso

This chapter analyses the precariousness of youth employment in European Union (EU) countries. Youth employment has undergone harsh transformations in recent years. Although the younger generations have always been characterized by higher levels of unemployment, precarious employment and under-employment, the labour market has changed dramatically over the last two decades and it is now more difficult for young people to access work with the classic features of their parents' employment. There are various analytical articulations of this phenomenon, but we will focus on just three of these. First, the changes observed in the state's role, considering the different welfare state models in the European countries, namely the heterogeneous systems of transition into the labour market. Second, the changes taking place in the economic sector, for example the rise of the financial sector, the growth of unqualified jobs in the third sector and the decline of some industrial activities in a number of countries. Third, and taking the global scenario into account, how all these transformations affect the representations of young people's role in society and their social recognition processes. It is therefore vital to analyse the precariousness of youth employment in order to: discuss the configurations of the labour market and the effects current changes will have in the future; reflect on the conceptions of employment, work and stability, in short, the socially desired model of employment; consider the state's role in the management of conditions for transition to the labour market and the shaping of public policies in this domain.

The analysis is made from a structural stance and strives to assess whether precarious employment among young people is linked to the special characteristics in their life cycle, particularly to the transition between school and the labour market or if, on the contrary, they are affected by this phenomenon in the same way as other workers regardless of age.

A discussion of precarious employment inevitably involves an analysis of the state's role in EU countries and some of the changes taking place in the economy. A number of authors, namely Esping-Andersen (1990) and Ferrera (1996), have distinguished between different social protection systems, mainly due to the distinct roles played by the state, market and family. Generally, the models can be addressed by focusing either on the role of the state, or on the importance of individual action in a more liberalized market. These trends have visible consequences on employment models and public policies, as employment relationships are part of welfare arrangements (Bosch, Lehndorff and Rubery 2009: 1). Hence, rather than defining one single European social model, we must define various models. The growth of precariousness in youth employment in the EU raises the question of whether public policies must prevail or even be strengthened so as to support youth, on a temporary basis as they enter the labour market.

The changes in the capitalist model also influence labour market dynamics, namely, with the rise of the service sector and of the activities related with Information and Communications Technologies (ICT) and the 'dominant trend towards a more liberal economic model' (Bosch et al. 2009: 31), coexisting with a 'continuing commitment to state-based social protection' (Bosch et al. 2009: 31). The ICT sector, among others, is of utmost importance due to its employment capacity, but includes a considerable amount of low skilled and precarious jobs (for example, call centre work), frequently occupied by highly educated young people.

This chapter aims to examine the transformations taking place in the EU, notably the rise in precarious employment, to discuss the differences between the European countries and propose some possible explanations.

The analysis will show that precarious employment is found in all EU countries. Countries with the biggest increases are also those in which the younger generation is most affected, particularly Spain, Germany, Portugal, Sweden and France. In Denmark and the United Kingdom (UK), the temporary employment rate is declining. However, not all countries understand temporary and precarious employment as one and the same thing and this variation depends also on the role played by the state. For instance, in countries like Denmark and the UK, youth combine work and school and/or receive state support in the first months of their working life. On the other hand, temporary employment in Portugal and Poland is linked to the difficulty in finding full-time work. Hence, temporary employment leads to a discussion of the various employment models in different countries. Finally, we will highlight the distinct reasons for temporary employment in the various countries.

The chapter is structured in five sections. In section two we present the theoretical background of the study, focusing on the precarious employment concept. The following section specifies this concept for youth. Section four discusses the methodology and section five presents the analysis. The chapter ends with the discussion of the results and conclusions.

Precarious Employment: Theoretical Background

International comparisons of precarious employment are complicated in part by the fact that the terms used in each country for the same or similar phenomena vary. This is because labour markets are organized and regulated differently across EU countries.

The term 'flexibility' is used in much of the current literature in English to refer to the various kinds of transformations taking place in the world of work and employment (see, for instance, Rimmer and Zappala 1988). The *standard* employment model is used as the benchmark for these definitions (Barbier and Nadel 2000). This model is described as a full-time job; regulated by a legal contract guaranteeing lifelong employment (mobility takes place at the employee's will); entitlement to social protection during unemployment, illness, and old-age, and a professional career based on seniority (Castel 2003, 2009, Auer and Gazier 2006, Gazier 2005).

This *classical employment* model was in force during the post-war period of expansion in most developed European countries. The notion of precarious employment contrasts with this *classical employment model*, and refers to jobs regulated by a short term contract, with no professional career, low salaries and no guarantee of a professional future.

However, there are exceptions to this classical employment model, especially in countries with a more liberal position towards dismissals such as the UK and Nordic countries, namely Denmark which is well-known for its flexicurity model (Madsen 2002, 2004). These countries have strong social protection systems and dynamic economies sustaining employment mobility. As a result, precarious employment does not involve the same insecurity, fear and risk (Beck 1992).

The problem with the notion of flexibility is that it covers situations ranging from job insecurity, uncertain careers, worsening working conditions to downgraded access to standard social protection (external mobility). The same term is also used to refer to multi-skilling in the workplace, flexibility in employment conditions (internal flexibility), and the freedom to dismiss in countries where labour markets are not so liberalized (Oliveira and Carvalho 2009, 2010). The *Employment Protection Regulation* indicator presented in an Organisation for Economic Co-operative Development (OECD) report in 2004 enables us to measure the level of protection provided by a country's labour legislation, using the following parameters: the difficulty of dismissing an employee with an open contract, the limitations on temporary contracting and the difficulty in making collective dismissals. Using these indicators (Oliveira and Carvalho 2009, 2010), the authors of this chapter concluded that there are fewer temporary contracts in countries where the law is not an obstacle to dismissals, for example in Denmark where the liberalization of dismissals goes back over 100 years. In other words, the facilitation of the dismissal process means there is less need for temporary contracts.

It is within this framework that the emphasis on the issue of precarious employment varies across Europe. Precarious employment is at the centre of labour issues in some countries, for example Spain, France, Italy and Portugal, and gives rise to theoretical debates on liberalizing labour market regulation (Boyer 1981, 1986, Barbier 2004). However, the term precarious employment has no relevance in the public debate in other countries like Germany, Denmark or Anglo-Saxon countries (such as England, Ireland, Scotland and Wales) (Düll 2003). Atypical employment is a more commonly used term; it refers to part-time work, including the so called German specific '*mini-jobs*' (with monthly gross earnings of up to 400 euros), temporary agency work and fixed term contracts. The discussion on precariousness in Germany seems more focused on low wages (Weinkopf 2009), the lack of a living wage or opportunities to get better jobs. Weinkopf (2006: 1) argues that low-wage work has been rising in Germany since the mid-1990s, and rose to 22.2 per cent of all employees in 2006. In Denmark, the liberalization of dismissal means, theoretically at least, that firms do not need to use short term contracts to sidestep the dismissal problem. As Bredgaard and Larsen (2005) state, the ordinary workforce can be considered 'temporary workers' due to high job mobility and high job turnover rates. However, different types of employment are found in Denmark, some of which can be classified as precarious employment, for example, independent contracting, job-sharing, secondary jobs, seasonal jobs, undeclared work, family work, etc. and the so-called growing number of 'flex-jobs', that is jobs with a permanent wage-subsidy (Kalleberg 2000: 343–44). Although the scenario is similar in England, precarious jobs are labelled 'bad jobs' as opposed to the classical employment mode (Nicole-Drancourt and Roulleau-Berger 2001).

The European Commission recently recognized the risk of a polarization of labour markets as secure contractual arrangements under 'standard' contracts co-exist with 'precarious situations' in 'non-standard/atypical' forms of employment. Furthermore, there is a growing gap in the employment conditions (wages, career opportunities, level of qualification, etc.) between those looking for work, those in non-standard work – sometimes with precarious contractual situations (the so-called 'outsiders') – and those in permanent, full-time jobs (the 'insiders') (European Commission 2006).

In this chapter we analyse the precarious employment of youth using the Eurostat indicator of *temporary employment,* which 'includes work under a fixed-term contract, *vis-à-vis* permanent work where there is no end-date. A job may be considered temporary employment (and its holder a temporary employee) if both employer and employee agree that there are objective rules defining when it ends (usually established in a work contract of limited duration). These rules may specify a date, the end of a task, or the return of another employee who has been temporarily replaced' (Eurostat n.d.). The concept of precariousness is multidimensional and not restricted to temporary employment. However, indicators other than which kind of contract can or cannot be considered precarious must be included in the discussion, namely career opportunities, qualification level and even subjective precariousness, measured for instance by the fear of losing the job. Our analysis here is limited to the Eurostat data which is a key indicator for scrutinizing precariousness, allows some cross analysis with other indicators (like the education level) and includes a wide range of European countries.

Precarious Youth Employment

Precarious youth employment is analysed in the context of the transition from school to the labour market. During this period, which varies in length, the job offers and conditions available to young people are worse and temporary work is more frequent.

In these circumstances, having a precarious as opposed to a 'standard' job could be considered a natural part of entering the labour market. Thus the theoretical debate on precarious employment affecting young people is part of the *professional transition* concept. This concept emerged as a corollary to a theoretical debate that began in the 1980s (Vincens 1981) as an alternative to that of professional insertion, and it highlights the multidimensional and lasting nature that characterizes the process of entering active working life. Rose (1992) proposes the *professional transition* notion as a socially structured process that is the result of interaction between firms, the state and other agents.

In this case, firms play a determinant role as they create employment, define the recruitment criteria and choose whether to establish precarious employment contracts or not. The state also plays an important role through its public policies in support of the insertion process into the labour market. Following Rose on this matter, Boyer (1986) talks of the state's regulation of wage mobility.

The structural transformations that have taken place in the labour markets in recent decades and their growing liberalization within the context of the EU (Oliveira and Carvalho 2009) raise questions about the notion that precarious employment is specific to this period of entering active working life, and to the younger generation. Indeed, lifelong training linked to external employment mobility is the basic principle in the recruitment and human resource management policies adopted by companies for the organization of labour markets following Europe's latest employment policy guidelines (Auer and Gazier 2006). Therefore, intermittent periods of work, unemployment and training – the so-called transactional markets (Gazier 2005) – will occur throughout professional life regardless of age. The expansion of precarious employment becomes a fundamental instrument for the management of workers' mobility (Paugam 2000).

On the other hand, studies show marked generational gaps between the young and the older groups in the labour market in which youth are at a disadvantage (Contini 2010, Bory 2009, OECD 2010). It is therefore meaningful to study the matter in terms of professional transition, or even to use the expression *youth labour markets* as markets with their own structural specificities. It is argued that youth are even more 'discriminated' than other generations as one would expect their employment conditions to improve due to the potential impact of the decline in the birth rate on the labour market, the general increase in education levels *vis-à-vis* previous generations, and the lower salaries for newcomers to the labour market.

Young people should be taken as a group and an analysis made of their precarious conditions on entering the labour market as they are more vulnerable and tend to accept precarious work more readily (Baron, Dugué and Nivolle 2005).

This is the framework in which we question whether precarious employment affects youth most or if, on the contrary, it is the same for all workers regardless of age.

Methodology

We examined statistical information on temporary employment derived from data in the Eurostat Labour Force Survey (LFS); more specifically, the detailed annual and quarterly survey results. We follow the EUROSTAT methodology and define this group as 15–24 years old; the period of life that most significantly marks the transition to the labour market. Eurostat uses the UNESCO (1997) International Standard Classification of Education (ISCED) to define the following education levels: ISCED 0–2, which includes pre-primary education, primary education – first stage of basic education (the start of compulsory education) and lower secondary education – second stage of basic education; ISCED 3–4, integrating the upper secondary education and the post-secondary non tertiary education; and ISCED 5–6, corresponding to the first and second stages of tertiary education.

The data analysed relates to the following indicators:

1. the EU15 rate of youth in temporary employment (15–24) in 1985, 1995, 2005, 2008;
2. the EU15 rate of temporary employment by age: 15–24; 25–39 and 40–64 in 2005 and 2008;
3. the EU27 rate of youth in temporary employment by the following educational levels in 2008: ISCED 0–2; ISCED 3–4; and ISCED 5–6; and
4. the EU27 rate of youth in temporary employment by the main reasons given for this status (2008).

A structural analysis was made based on the temporary employment rate which articulated an intra- and inter-country comparison. We gauge the extent to which this phenomenon is transversal to all generations, or, alternatively, has a generational effect that hits youth most by analysing: 1. the temporary employment rate per age group; and 2. the temporary employment rate in three distinct generations. The structural analysis was complemented by the segmentation of temporary youth employment per qualification level.

The EU 27 countries were mapped according to the association between the reasons youth give for having a temporary job and their qualification levels by means of a multivariate analysis: *Principal Components Analysis for Categorical Data* (CatPCA). There are two advantages to using such a non-linear analysis: 1. the optimal scaling to which the data are submitted allows them to be projected in the same space variables and objects (countries); and 2. the use of CatPCA was essential when managing non-response as we were unable to avoid eliminating 10 of 24 countries. Estonia, Lithuania and Malta were excluded from the multivariate analysis due to a lack of information on the indicators related to the reasons youth were in temporary work.

Results

Evolution of Precarious Employment in Europe and the Generational Impact

An analysis of precarious employment in the EU reveals that the phenomenon is common to every country although its relative weight in the employed population varies. In the countries where precarious employment has increased most, the rise is common to every age group, but the younger generation is affected most (Figures 9.1, 9.2, 9.3). This trend towards precarious employment is structural in most countries; it contrasts with others in which the phenomenon is quite limited and has been stable for the past 20 years. In fact, the general trend is contradicted in some countries as the number of fixed-term contracts is not only very low but declining; Denmark and the UK are the paradigmatic examples of this. Moreover, Denmark, Belgium, and the UK have the lowest rates of precarious employment. It is worth noting that although the pattern of the evolution in Ireland was the same as in Denmark and the UK, this trend inverted in all age groups between 2005 and 2008; this was most evident in the youngest group where the rate of precarious employment doubled from 11.6 per cent to 22.0 per cent. Whereas many countries registered a fall in the precarious employment rate, it continued to rise in others.

In terms of the generational effect, the youngest age group (15–24 years) is by far the most affected by precarious employment in all 15 European Union countries, most notably in Spain, Germany, Portugal, Sweden and France where the figure exceeds 50 per cent (Figure 9.1). These differences remain and in some cases worsen in 2008. Although Spain has the highest rate (59.4 per cent) of precarious employment, the downward trend registered in 2005 is also confirmed among youth. Ireland is worthy of note because the rate of precarious youth employment doubled in this short three-year period, as mentioned above. The worsening structural trend continues in Portugal where it increased 8.6 per cent between 2005 and 2008. The situation deteriorated in some countries but there was a positive evolution in others.

As stated previously, these data must be carefully interpreted as many of the 15–24 age group may still be at school or in professional insertion processes which, as we know, can take time. However, the disparity between youth and the other age groups, and above all the evolution of this indicator across three distinct young generations (born in the 1970s, 80s and 90s) shows the phenomenon is clearly worsening from one generation to the next (Figure 9.4).

170 *Young People and Work*

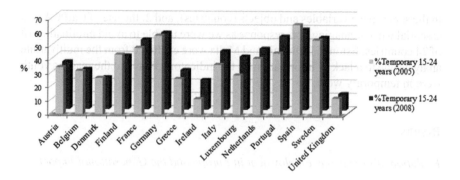

Figure 9.1   Temporary employment 15–24 years – 2005 and 2008

Source: Eurostat 2005 and 2008.

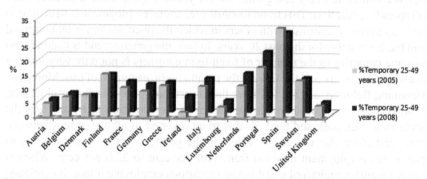

Figure 9.2   Temporary employment 25–49 years – 2005 and 2008

Source: Eurostat 2005 and 2008.

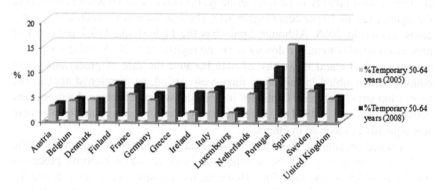

Figure 9.3   Temporary employment 50–64 years – 2005 and 2008

Source: Eurostat 2005 and 2008.

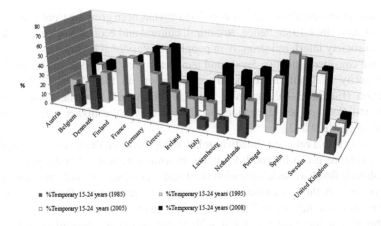

■ %Temporary 15-24 years (1985)   ▫ %Temporary 15-24 years (1995)
□ %Temporary 15-24 years (2005)   ■ %Temporary 15-24 years (2008)

Figure 9.4   Temporary employment 15–24 years, per country – 1985 and 2008

Source: Eurostat 1985, 1995, 2005 and 2008.

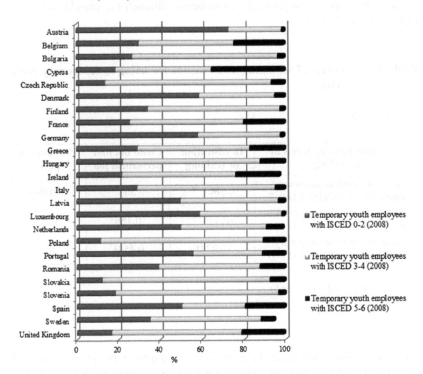

Figure 9.5   Educational structure for youth in temporary employment in the EU, by country – 2008

Source: Eurostat 2008.

Adult precarious employment (for ages 25 to 49) has been growing from generation to generation since 1985; hence, structural, cultural and economic changes taking place in society interfered strongly in people's professional trajectories.

If we consider education levels and temporary work relationship (Figure 9.5), the majority of youth in temporary employment in the EU have secondary education (ISCED 3–4). However, Germany, Denmark, Austria, Luxembourg, Spain and Portugal are exceptions to this as they have higher rates of basic education (ISCED 0–2).

There is also a relevant statistical relationship between the levels of schooling and the reasons given by youth for being in temporary work. For the youth who have already finished basic education (first and second stages) and who now have a temporary job, there is a moderate and positive correlation ($r = 0.580$, $p = 0.005$) with the fact that they *are still studying or in training*.

This is not the case for youth with upper secondary education and post-secondary education where we find a negative correlation between being in temporary employment and *education or in training* ($r = -0.434$, $p = 0.032$). This group seems to be in temporary employment because they *could not find a permanent job* or *are in professional training*, although the correlations are not significant (Table 9.1).

Table 9.1   Levels of schooling and reasons for being in temporary work – 2008

(Pearson correlation)

Part-time rates by levels of schooling	In education or training	Could not find permanent job	Probationary period
Rate of youth in temporary employment with ISCED 0–2	0.580***	-0.383**	-0.046
Rate of youth in temporary employment with ISCED 3–4	-0.434**	0.186	0.153
Rate of youth in temporary employment with ISCED 5–6	-0.338*	0.453*	-0.219

* $p<0.10$ ** $p<0.05$ *** $p<0.01$

Source: Eurostat 2008.

The reason given for being in precarious employment by youth with higher education (ISCED 5–6) is that they cannot find a permanent job ($r = 0.453$, $p = 0.011$).

As can be seen in Figure 9.6, temporary employment is a constraint in most countries as young people *could not find a permanent job*. This is the situation in countries like Belgium, Spain, Poland, Portugal, Slovakia, Greece, Czech Republic, Romania and Cyprus where rates are over 60 per cent. In a few countries such as Germany and Austria, youth have an option because they are in education/ training systems or doing a work placement. In countries where temporary work is 'voluntary', youth enter the labour market much earlier than their counterparts and conciliate student life with a job (Nielsen, Guerreiro and Brannen 2002, Couppié and Mansuy 2001); as youth are still studying, the levels of education are lower in the age group analysed, in unemployment, employment and working activity rates. This is intrinsically linked to a culture that promotes autonomy from an early age with the support of public youth policies such as a monthly support allowance, the availability of accommodation at reasonable rents, free education, etc. This autonomy means youth need to supplement their income by doing temporary or part-time work. Indeed, it is mainly in Nordic countries (Denmark, Finland, the Netherlands and Sweden) the UK and the Netherlands that part-time figures tend to accompany the activity rates. It is also in these countries and in Ireland that the reason given by most youth (between 75 per cent and 85 per cent) for having a part-time job is that they are still at school or in training.

These social practices are so intrinsic to the culture of these countries that young people who remain dependent on their families until later are even socially stigmatized (Caroleo and Pastore 2003). The Danish government was forced to take measures in 1996 to curb the increasingly early start to working life by forbidding under 12 year olds to work (Veloso, Gonçalves and Parente 1997).

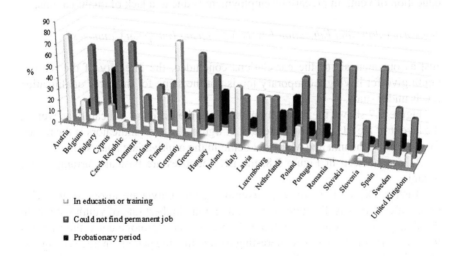

⊔ In education or training

▤ Could not find permanent job

■ Probationary period

Figure 9.6   Reasons for having a temporary job, by country – 2008

Source: Eurostat 2008.

The cases of Portugal and Spain, on the other hand, are quite different. Youth enter the labour market after finishing their studies; the two countries have a very low part-time employment rate, and about 33 per cent and 40 per cent respectively state that they have a part-time job because they cannot find full-time employment. When we add some data on education levels, we find that in Portugal, only 8 per cent of youth have basic schooling (up to Year 9) compared with 18.6 per cent in Spain; this contrasts sharply with Denmark (63 per cent), Holland (81.5 per cent), Sweden (63 per cent) and Finland (54 per cent).

In southern European countries, school life and working life are much more distinct and are likely to be organized into first the student cycle and then the cycle that begins when entering the labour market. In this kind of culture, society expects youth to take a standard length of time to complete a given study cycle, and those who deviate from this model are stigmatized (in almost complete contradiction to what happens in Denmark). This *modus vivendi* places pressure on youth and the school, and the extent to which this influences the relationship these youngsters have with school and its contribution to the non-achievement rate, particularly the early dropout rate, has yet to be assessed. The early school leaving rates in Portugal and Spain are among the highest in the EU (35.4 per cent and 32 per cent respectively, in 2008), exceeded only by Malta. However, Portugal has made great progress in the last decade, for in 1998 the early school leavers were 46.6 per cent for youth aged between 18 and 24 in 1998.

This does partly explain the low levels of education of youth entering the labour market and who have already left school. It also explains that, contrary to what one would expect, we cannot make the generalization that the low level of education of youth in precarious employment is due to a lack of qualifications.

Temporary Jobs and Education Levels: Clustering European Countries

Just as our analysis of the correlations concluded, the intensity of the reasons youth give for having a temporary job is not the same for the three qualification levels under study.

Figure 9.7 shows the associations between the different indicators as well as the layout of the EU countries (the lack of figures for most indicators is the reason for Estonia, Lithuania and Malta not being in the multivariate analysis).

As can be seen in Figure 9.8, the EU countries are basically arranged in a triangle.

Austria, Denmark, Germany, Luxembourg and Latvia are in one vertex. This group of countries is distinguished for having the highest rate of youth with up to the ninth year of schooling (ISCED 0–2) in temporary employment as they are still *in education or training*. It is interesting to note that the pattern characterizing this group is also associated with lower rates of: 1. youth in temporary employment with higher education (ISCED 5–6); and 2. youth in this situation because they *could not find a permanent job*.

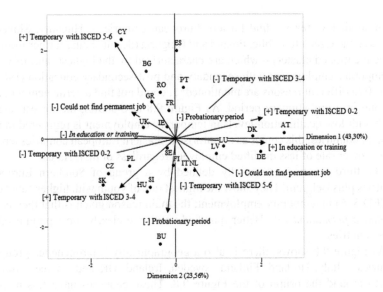

Figure 9.7   Education levels and reasons for temporary youth work in EU – 2008

Source: Eurostat 2008.

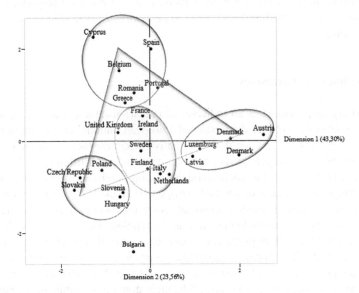

Figure 9.8   Education levels and reasons for temporary youth work: mapping EU countries – 2008

Source: Eurostat 2008.

In another vertex we find Eastern European countries – Hungary, Slovenia, Slovakia, the Czech Republic, Poland and Bulgaria (despite being farther from the above mentioned cluster) – which are characterized by the highest rates of youth in temporary employment with secondary and post-secondary education (ISCED 3–4). Two different reasons are mentioned: 1. could not find a permanent job; and 2. being in a probationary period. As Figure 9.8 also shows, the lowest rate of youth with low qualification levels in temporary employment is registered in this group of countries; this comes as no surprise as Eastern European countries tend to have a lower rate of less qualified employees regardless of their status.

The third vertex is essentially defined by a group of Southern European countries plus Belgium. They show the highest rate of youth with higher education (ISCED 5–6) in temporary employment; the main reason given is that they *could not find a permanent job*. Better qualified youth are clearly most prejudiced in these countries.

As Figure 9.8 shows, there is also a geographically heterogeneous group of countries – Italy, Holland, Finland, Sweden, Ireland, UK and France – mostly located around the origin of the Figure 9.8. These countries have less marked profiles. There is a combination of youth with ISCED 3–4 (secondary and post-secondary education) in temporary employment around the second quartile and rates of ISCED 0–2 between the first and second quartiles. The reasons youth give are also more diverse. Although *could not find a permanent job* is the predominant explanation, *being in education or training* is also a common response in some countries (France and Italy) and *being in probationary period* in the case of the Netherlands.

Discussion and conclusions

Temporary employment as an indicator of precariousness in European countries comes within the broader discussion of European national employment models (Bosch et al. 2009: 1). Although the normative discourse focuses on the European social model, the analysis provides evidence of national differences. Hence, the literature on the European social models (Esping-Andersen 1990, 2000, Ferrera 1996) proposes a discussion on the heterogeneity in the EU countries with regard to the state intervention models for social protection. However, our analysis shows that a number of countries do not 'fit' into the typology proposed, probably due to the fact that 'national employment models each have their own cycle'. National employment models represent 'historical commitments that are successful for a particular period, but then have to be renewed' (Bosch et al. 2009: 11). Employment (and employment protection) is one of the main domains of public intervention (or lack of it), and nowadays precarious employment is a key issue. Our conclusion is structured around four dimensions of the research on this subject.

First, the concept of temporary employment as precarious employment. Eurostat presents data on temporary employment for all countries, but the role played by the state in each country can change the meaning of the term. In countries like Denmark, Finland, the Netherlands, Sweden, the UK and Ireland youth combine work and school or have public support when they first start their working life. On one hand, the liberal model in the UK and Ireland, means a lack of state support for youth when accessing the labour market; in contrast, the others generally have a social-democrat model where it is usual to conciliate work and education. Hence, the least and the strongest intervention of the state, respectively, have different impacts on the configurations of temporary employment. On the other hand, in countries like Spain, Portugal, Poland, Sweden and, to a certain extent also France, Italy, Finland, Netherlands and Luxembourg, temporary employment is related to the difficulty of finding full-time work. Spain and Portugal are Southern/ Mediterranean countries where the part-time employment rate is very low, there is a clear distinction between work and school and temporary employment is synonymous with a lack of alternatives. The same does not apply to the other countries. Poland is nearer a liberal model (closer to Spain, as we will discuss later), characterized by very expensive social protection, high levels of inequality and poverty and a low level of demographic growth (Pedroso 2008). We also identified situations in this set of countries traditionally characterized by strong state intervention and part-time work. It can be assumed that some changes are taking place where greater debate is required about the employment models and the welfare state regimes. Let us take two examples to illustrate the importance of an analytical reflection on this subject. Following problems with long-term sustainability in the early 1990s, the Swedish model recovered in the mid-2000s and has maintained its social protection system (Anxo and Niklasson 2009), but youth associate temporary employment with the difficulty of finding a full-time job. Although still strongly based on a social-democratic model, Sweden shares some features with the southern European countries. Spain, which has the highest level of unemployment in Europe, has moved towards a more liberal model and yet 'the most important challenge today is how to develop a more sustainable (in economic, social and environmental terms) and a more equitable employment model for the future' (Banyuls et al. 2009: 247). In 1997, the Spanish Government passed a labour reform in 1997 aimed at reducing the severance pay gap between permanent and temporary contracts. Despite a slight decrease in temporary work from 33 per cent to 31 per cent in Spain between 1998 and 2007 (Bentolila et al. 2010: 5), it remains very high.

In this context, precarious employment defined as temporary employment is a key indicator, not only to discuss the concept of precariousness in itself when analysing the different national employment models. This is our second line of discussion. The multivariate analysis leads to a number of conclusions which raise questions about the future of the European employment models. First, one can state the persistence of the Continental model joining Denmark, traditionally social-democratic. It reveals lower social protection and a 'flexicurity' orientation. Therefore, the application of active measures of employment may be a way of reducing youth dependence on the state, but it can also mean a bigger gap between the 'insiders' (in the labour market) and the 'outsiders' (out of the labour market) (Ferrera, Hemerijk and Rhodes 2000). Second, the Eastern European countries generally have the highest rates of youth in temporary employment with secondary and post-secondary education and also the lowest rate of youth in temporary employment and with low qualifications levels. These countries share high levels of education and are still dealing with a past strongly linked to extensive state intervention and significant levels of inequality. Third, we must emphasize the grouping of the southern European countries and Belgium, defined as a continental model. Here we have contradictory trends with stronger intervention of the state at the employment and educational levels (Portugal) on one hand, and a more liberalized labour market on the other (also Portugal and, for example, Spain and Belgium). An important indicator for these contradictory trends is that these countries have the highest rate of youth with higher education who are in temporary employment because they could not find a full-time job. Youth with more educational qualifications are clearly most penalized in these countries.

Thirdly, the analysis shows that despite some distinctions, precarious employment is common to all EU countries. Although its relative weight in the employed population varies, the younger generation is the most affected in the countries with the biggest increase in precarious employment, notably in Spain, Germany, Portugal, Sweden and France. The general trend is contradicted only in Denmark and the UK, where the rate of temporary employment is declining. As stated before, these are countries with a flexible labour market and in which temporary employment is not necessarily due to having no alternative to a full-time job; it is also an option of conciliating work and education. On the other hand, the rate of precarious youth employment between 2005 and 2008 in Ireland, another liberal model, doubled due to the economic recession.

Fourth, we highlight the different conceptions of youth, their ways of life and the relationships between work and learning activities in the various countries. As the analysis shows, the reasons for having temporary employment differ from country to country, giving us clues as to structural features of the education and employment systems. This project warrants further research in light of changes in the labour market and immobility/mobility features and associated constraints and opportunities. The discussion should also be continued on the model of the European Welfare State and the differences between countries, focusing on the European employment models.

References

Anxo, D. and Niklasson, H. 2009. The Swedish model: Revival after the turbulent 1990s?, in *European Employment Models in Flux: A Comparison of Institutional Change in Nine European Countries*, edited by G. Bosch, S. Lehndorff and J. Rubery. London: Palgrave Macmillan, 81–104.

Auer P. and Gazier, B. 2006. *L'introuvable Sécurité de l'Emploi*. Paris: Flammarion.

Banyuls, J., Miguélez, F., Recio, A., Cano, E. and Lorente, R. 2009. The transformation of the employment system in Spain: Towards a Mediterranean neoliberalism?, in *European Employment Models in Flux: A Comparison of Institutional Change in Nine European Countries*, edited by G. Bosch, S. Lehndorff and J. Rubery. London: Palgrave Macmillan, 247–69.

Barbier, J-C. 2004. *A Comparative Analysis of 'Employment Precariousness' in Europe*. Paper presented to the Seminar Learning from Employment and Welfare Policies in Europe, Paris: ESRC – CEE.

Barbier J. C. and Nadel, H. 2000. *La flexibilité du travail et de l'emploi*. Paris: Flammarion.

Baron, C., Dugué, E. and Nivolle, P. (eds) 2005. *La Place des Jeunes dans la Cité. De l'Ecole à Emploi?* Tome I. Paris: Harmattan.

Beck, U. 1992. *Risk Society. Towards a New Modernity*. London: Sage.

Bentolila, Samuel, Cahuc, Pierre, Dolado, Juan J. and Le Barbanchon, Thomas. 2010. *Unemployment and Temporary Jobs in the Crisis: Comparing France and Spain*. Documento de Trabajo 2010–07. Available at: http://www.fedea.es/pub/Papers/2010/dt2010-07.pdf [accessed: 3 January 2011].

Bory, S. 2009. Trajectoires réversibles: Le cas des jeunes adultes italiens. *Informations Sociales*, 6(156), 132–41.

Bosch, G., Lehndorff, S. and Rubery, J. 2009. European employment models in flux: Pressures for change and prospects for survival and revitalisation, in *European Employment Models in Flux: A Comparison of Institutional Change in Nine European Countries*, edited by G. Bosch, S. Lehndorff and J. Rubery. London: Palgrave Macmillan, 1–56.

Boyer, R. 1981. Les transformations du rapport salarial dans la crise: Une interprétation de ses aspects sociaux et économiques. *Critiques de l'Économie Politique*, 15/16, 185–228.

Boyer, R. (coord.) 1986. *La Flexibilité du Travail en Europe*. Paris: La Découverte.

Bredgaard, T. and F. Larsen (eds) 2005. *Employment Policy from Different Angles*. Copenhagen: DJØF Publishing.

Caroleo, F. E. and Pastore F. 2003. Youth participation in the labour market in Germany, Spain and Sweden, in *Youth Unemployment and Social Exclusion in Europe*, edited by T. Hammer. London: T. Hammer, 115–41.

Castel, R. 2003. L'Insecurité Social. Qu'est ce qu'être protégé? Paris: Seuil.

Castel, R. 2009. *La Montée des incertitudes. Travail, Protections, statut de l'individu*. Paris: Seuil.

Contini, B. 2010. *Youth Employment in Europe: Institutions and Social Capital Explain better than Mainstream Economics*. Working Paper, Laboratorio R. Revelli.

Coupiée, T. and Mansuy, M. 2001. *La Place dês Debútants sur les Marches du Travail Européens*, Paris: BREF/ CEREQ, 164.

Düll, N. 2003. *Defining and Assessing Precarious Employment in Europe: A Review of Main Studies and Surveys*. Munich: Economix.

Esping-Andersen, G. 1990. *The Three Worlds of Welfare Capitalism*. Oxford: Polity Press.

Esping-Andersen, G. 2000. *A Welfare State for the 21st Century*. Report to the Portuguese Presidency of the European Union. Lisbon: EU.

European Commission 2006. *Modernising Labour Law to Meet the Challenges of the 21st Century*, Green Paper, Brussels, 22 November 2006, available at: http://europa.eu/legislation_summaries/employment_and_social_policy/growth_and_jobs/c10312_en.htm. [accessed: 12 November 2010].

Eurostat. Labour Force Survey (LFS) series – *Detailed Annual Survey Results (1985, 1995, 2005)*. Available at: http://epp.eurostat.ec.europa.eu [accessed: 11 January 2010].

Eurostat. Labour Force Survey e LFS series – *Detailed Quarterly Survey Results (2008)*. Available at: http://epp.eurostat.ec.europa.eu [accessed: 11 January 2010].

Eurostat. n.d. *Glossary: Temporary Employment*. Available at: http://epp.eurostat.ec.europa.eu/statistics_explained/index.php/Glossary:Temporary_employment [accessed: 11 January 2010].

Ferrera, M. 1996. The 'Southern Model' of welfare state in Social Europe. *Journal of European Social Policy*, 6(1), 17–37.

Ferrera, M., Hemerijk, A. and Rhodes, M. 2000. *O futuro da Europa Social: Repensar o Trabalho e a Protecção na Nova Economia*. Oeiras: Celta Editora.

Gazier, B. 2005. *Vers un Nouveau Modèle Social*. Paris: Flammarion.

Kalleberg, A. 2000. In search of flexibility: Changing employment relations in industrial societies, in *Scandinavia in the World and the World in Scandinavia: Nordic Working Life Conference 1999,* edited by M. Gjelsvik and K. Hansen. Copenhagen: Nordisk Ministerråd, 19–36.

Madsen, P. 2002. *The Danish Model of 'Flexicurity' – A Paradise with Some Snakes*. Paper presented at the European Foundation for the Improvement of Living and Working Conditions, Brussels.

Madsen, P. 2004. The Danish model of flexicurity: Experiences and lessons. *Transfer: European Review of Labour and Research*, 10(2), 187–207.

Nicole-Drancourt, C. and Roulleau-Berger, L. 2001. *Les Jeunes et le Travail 1950–2000*. Paris: PUF.

Nielsen, A., Guerreiro, D. and Brannen, J. 2002. 'Most choices involve money': Different pathways to adulthood, in *Young Europeans, Work and Family. Futures in Transition*, edited by J. Brannen, S. Lewis, A. Nilsen, and J. Smithson. London: Routledge/ European Sociological Association Studies in European Societies, 162–84.

OECD. 2004. Employment protection regulation and labour market performance. *Employment Outlook*. PARIS: OECD, 61–125. Available at http://www.oecd.org/dataoecd/8/4/34846856.pdf [accessed: 13 November 2009].

Oliveira, L. and Carvalho, H. 2009. Towards the liberalisation of labour markets in Europe. *Portuguese Journal of Social Science*, 8(2), 147–64.

Oliveira, L. and Carvalho, H. 2010. Inequalities between generations: Youth and temporary employment in European Union, in *Desigualdades Sociais*, edited by R. M. do Carmo. Lisboa: Mundos Sociais, 191–98.

Paugam, S. 2000. *Le Salarié de la Précarité*. Paris: PUF.

Pedroso, P. 2008. *Modelos de Activação dos Desempregados: os Desafios Estruturais e as Condicionantes Conjunturais*. Lisboa: GEP/Ministério do Trabalho e Solidariedade Social.

Rimmer, M. and Zappala, J. 1988. Labour market flexibility and the second tier. *Australian Bulletin of Labour*, 14(4): 564–91.

Rose, J. 1992. Transition professionnelle et recomposition des status salariaux, in *Mutations Industrielles et Reconversions des Salariés*, edited by M. C. Villeval. Paris: L'Harmattan, 255–300.

Veloso, L., Gonçalves, C. and Parente, C. 1997. *Formação e Emprego Juvenil em Portugal, França e Dinamarca. Um Estudo nas Áreas da Metalurgia e Mecânica e do Têxtil e Vestuário*. Porto: Fundação da Juventude/Comissão das Comunidades Europeias.

Vincens, J. 1981. *Problématique Générale de l'Insertion dans la Vie Active*, Colloque sur l'Insertion Professionnelle à la Sortie des Etudes Postsecondaires. Louvain: Université Catholique de Louvain.

Weinkopf, C. 2006. *Germany: Precarious Employment and the Rise of Mini-jobs*. Working paper. Available at: http://www.genderwork.ca/cpdworkingpapers/weinkopf.pdf. [accessed: 24 January 2010].

Weinkopf, C. 2009. Job quality in call centres in Germany. *International Labour Review*, 148(4), 395–411.

PART III
The Other Actors

Chapter 10

Regulating Youth Work: Lessons from Australia and the United Kingdom

Andrew Stewart and Natalie van der Waarden

The question of how to regulate the work performed by young people has attracted relatively little attention in some developed countries. This chapter explains Australian and British regulatory approaches to child employment, sampling two countries that might be considered to have few child labour problems. The chapter will comment on the appropriateness of a modern statement of rights for young workers in the context of discussion around various sources of regulation. Some of the failings of present frameworks are highlighted, and a set of goals and principles (based on those set out in Stewart 2008) are put forward to guide the design of child employment regulation for developed economies. It is assumed that young workers will continue to play a role in contemporary labour markets, and that they require safeguards to assist them in benefiting from their first work experiences.

In Australia, one explanation for the lack of research attention lies in the distinctive and highly complex approach adopted to labour regulation. For the bulk of the twentieth century, where other countries looked to a mixture of voluntary collective bargaining and legislated standards to moderate the operation of the labour market, Australia took a different path. Despite a strong tradition of trade unionism, it primarily relied on state-established tribunals to fix minimum wages and working conditions on an industry and occupational basis. The tribunals did this through a network of awards – legally binding instruments applicable to most forms of non-managerial employment, and created through compulsory processes of conciliation and arbitration (Creighton and Stewart 2010). For both younger and older employees, including those working as apprentices, the tribunals and awards offered a strong, flexible and dynamic set of protections against the exercise of managerial prerogative and the vagaries of market forces. Conversely, that system had little to say about the informal (and especially unpaid) work performed by young people for the likes of family businesses, neighbours or community organizations. At most, legislation sought to ensure that paid work did not interfere with compulsory schooling. However, as this chapter will explain, there has been a move away from the award system in recent years, in favour of a regulatory approach that gives primacy to workplace-level bargaining. There has also been a greater role for the direct statutory regulation of employment conditions – including for the specific benefit of younger workers.

In Britain, an interesting comparator by reason of its close relationship to Australia both historically and culturally, regulation of young people's work has evolved over a longer period. Originally reactive to social concerns about the health and safety of young workers and the increasing value of education, early nineteenth century legislation limited the use of British children as a source of labour. The minimum age for admission to employment and maximum hours of work in particular industries were formal constraints on employers that reflected public outrage over exploitative practices. Beyond this, however, regulation of the working conditions for those of minimum age was not sustained as a regulatory concern. Just as in Australia, primary attention in the twentieth century was on the prioritization of schooling. More recent regional influences have, however, progressed British regulation in relation to improving the welfare of their working children.

The Australian Framework: Origins

As already indicated, regulation of the work performed by young Australian workers was not a focus of the compulsory arbitration systems that operated for most of the twentieth century. But there have been at least two important recent changes. One has been a shift in the general focus of Australian labour regulation, with a greater emphasis on enterprise-level negotiations to fix wages and conditions (Creighton and Stewart 2010, Nolan 1998). Awards have survived, but as a 'safety net' for collective or individual bargaining. For a brief but important period in 2006–2007, the conservative Government's controversial Work Choices reforms gave employers the freedom to negotiate (or in reality impose) contracts that removed key award entitlements. Under the current Labor Government's Fair Work legislation (2009) the protective operation of the award system has been restored, although it is now complemented by a set of legislative standards more familiar in scope and operation to those in other countries (Forsyth and Stewart 2009). But the Work Choices episode focused attention on the vulnerability of certain groups in the labour market, including young workers (Fair Employment Advocate 2008).

Even before this happened, there had already been moves to strengthen protections for young workers. These occurred against the background of a changing pattern of engagement in paid work. Young Australians are now more likely to stay at school for longer, but combine their studies with part-time (and generally temporary) employment (Abhayaratna et al. 2008, Commission for Children and Young People and Child Guardian 2004). Their experiences of such work are generally positive. They 'value highly the opportunity to develop new skills, exercise more responsibility and self-reliance, earn money and make a contribution' (New South Wales Commission for Children and Young People 2005). At the same time, it has been recognized that:

In work situations children inherently face greater risks than adults because of their vulnerability, their level of physical, emotional and cognitive development, and their inexperience in dealing with a range of life situations ... Where children do experience work problems or are exposed to unnecessary risk of physical or emotional harm, children often find it hard to voice their concerns in an appropriate or effective way ... Young people are also less likely to benefit from an organized form of voice within the workplace, such as a trade union, or simply [do] not have the knowledge of the ways and means by which they can voice concerns and gain support to resolve workplace problems. (Industrial Relations Victoria 2001)

Concerns such as this have led to a range of legislative initiatives. Australia has a federal system, under which responsibility for labour regulation has historically been shared between the Commonwealth of Australia, and its six states and two territories. For most purposes, at least in the private sector, working conditions are now generally regulated by the federal *Fair Work Act 2009*. But under s 27 of that Act, the states and territories retain the power to pass laws on child labour, as well as on other important subjects such as occupational health and safety. It is they who, albeit in an often piecemeal and inconsistent fashion, have primarily sought to address the special needs of young workers.

Legislation dealing with child employment in Australia originally developed in a colonial environment with chronic labour shortages. It arose during a period of rapid industrialization when children made up a relatively large portion of the population (ABS 2006). Early statutes regarding the young focused on taking parentless children off the street and into care, and encouraging the performance of supervised and suitable work (see for example Victoria's *Neglected and Criminal Children's Act 1864*). Limits on hours of work and minimum ages for specific types of employment were the subject of factories legislation (such as Victoria's *Supervision of Workrooms and Factories Act 1873*). Both varieties of local legislation involved timely recognition that child work was of social concern and something to be regulated.

In the first part of the twentieth century the employment of Australian children was frowned upon by religious and community groups who considered it had negative implications for a child's physical and educational development (Tierney 1963). Concepts of childhood were becoming clearer, with regulation of child employment aimed at protecting children from a denial of their childhood (Kociumbas 1997), a life stage during which the individual could play and socialize without hazard to their health or well being. The issue of child exploitation was recognized as employers maximized the use of this cheap and pliable labour resource (Bowden and Penrose 2006). The primary aim of legislation was therefore to exclude children from the labour market in an effort to minimize this opportunity. Compulsory education legislation, first introduced in the late nineteenth century (see for example Victoria's *Education Act 1890*), indirectly curtailed the ability of children to work by ensuring they could only work part-time, later adding clear prohibitions on employment within school hours (such as the Victorian *Education Act 1915*).

By contrast, the award system that emerged in the twentieth century readily accommodated the employment of young workers. A few instruments imposed special protections, some of which remain under the modern award system that has recently taken effect. For example, the *Hospitality Industry (General) Award 2010* restricts shift lengths to 10 hours for employees under 18 years of age. The same instrument provides that apprentices must not be required to do overtime or shift work, unless they consent.

On the other hand, the award system has sanctioned differential and less favourable payment of young workers – allowed by an exemption in the federal *Age Discrimination Act 2004*. Minimum wages for such workers are commonly set at a percentage of the adult wage rate that starts at the age of 20 or 21. For example, in the *Hospitality Industry (General) Award 2010*, the rate for 16 year olds is 50 per cent of the relevant adult wage; 17 year olds, 60 per cent; and so on up to the full rate at 20 years of age. The last major consideration of the practice of setting different rates on the basis of age occurred in 1999, when the Australian Industrial Relations Commission conducted a review of the feasibility of replacing junior rates with non-discriminatory alternatives. It found that none of those alternatives were feasible in practical terms and concluded that well designed junior rate classifications, framed to reduce the capacity for exploitation, could justifiably be used to create or protect employment opportunities for young people (Australian Industrial Relations Commission 1999). This is a position still strongly supported by employer groups. The issue remains a controversial one, however, and seems likely to attract attention when the current federal workplace agency, Fair Work Australia, conducts a review of junior rates of pay.

Aside from specifically permitting awards to include junior wage rates, the main federal labour statute, the *Fair Work Act 2009*, has little to say about young workers. There is a requirement for parental consent to be obtained for flexible work arrangements affecting workers under 18, but that is about all. The same is true of other labour legislation covering matters such as leave entitlements, discrimination, occupational health and safety, and even training. An exception is Queensland's *Children and Young Workers Code of Practice 2006* which identifies particular workplace hazards and provides guidance to manage those risks. It seems to be assumed that general processes and protections offered by labour legislation are intrinsically suitable for young workers.

Child Employment Law in Australia: The Current Position

A number of Australian state and territories have moved to deal more directly and specifically with the issue of child employment. This has not happened everywhere. In South Australia (SA) and Tasmania (Tas), for example, there are few laws dealing with child employment, beyond those restricting employment during school hours for those of compulsory school age (see *Education Act 1972* (SA) ss 78, 81A; *Education Act 1994* (Tas) s 82). Although there is a specific power under s 98A of the *Fair Work Act 1994* (SA) to regulate child employment by award, it has not been exercised. The South Australian government has, however, proposed legislation that would provide more comprehensive protections for young workers (see Child Employment Bill 2011 (SA)).

By contrast, New South Wales, Victoria and Queensland already have much more detailed laws on child employment, though with significant variations. For example, while both New South Wales and Victoria have a rule that children under the age of 15, and in some instances 16, cannot be employed without an official permit or authorization, they define employment rather differently. The New South Wales law applies only to paid work, and the permit requirement currently applies where the employment involves taking part in an entertainment, exhibition or recorded performance, or door-to-door selling (*Children and Young Persons (Care and Protection) Act 1998* (NSW) s 223). In Victoria, by contrast, a permit is required as a general rule for any type of participation in, or assistance of, a business, trade or occupation carried on for profit, whether the child is paid for their work or not (*Child Employment Act 2003* (Vic) s 4). The main exemptions from the permit requirement also differ significantly. Victoria has a general exemption for work in family businesses, while New South Wales exempts short-hours employment for those over the age of 10, subject to certain conditions being met (*Children and Young Persons (Care and Protection) (Child Employment) Regulation 2010* (NSW) regs 5, 7(1)(a) and Sch 1; *Child Employment Act 2003* (Vic) s 9(3)).

Queensland adopts a different approach, with no permit system (Mourell and Allan 2005). Like Victoria, its legislation applies to both paid and unpaid work. A general requirement is for parental consent to be given in respect of school-aged and young children (*Child Employment Act 2006* (Qld) s 10). All three states have outright prohibitions on employment in certain occupations or circumstances, controls on the number of hours that children may work, and special rules for work in the entertainment industry, but again, the details differ (Stewart 2008). Western Australia, the Australian Capital Territory and the Northern Territory also impose certain limitations on child employment, though again to varying degrees (see *Children and Community Services Act 2004* (WA) Pt 7; *Children and Young People Act 2008* (ACT) Ch. 21; *Care and Protection of Children Act 2007* (NT) Ch 3 Pt 3.2).

In addition to these measures, in 2006 New South Wales and Queensland introduced measures that were specifically intended to protect workers under 18 from the effect of the federal government's Work Choices reforms. The *Industrial Relations (Child Employment) Act (NSW)* and the *Child Employment Act 2006 (Qld)* allowed such workers to bring an unfair dismissal claim under state law, even if they would have no claim under the federal system because of the small business exemption then operating (Chapman 2009). It was also provided that a young worker could not be employed below state award conditions, even for private sector employers to whom state awards would not in other respects apply.

These laws took advantage of the child labour exception mentioned earlier, which allows state laws on that subject to apply to employers otherwise subject to federal labour regulation. However, it is far from clear how many New South Wales and Queensland employers were ever aware of their responsibilities under the measures. They posed significant compliance challenges by reason of the overlap with the federal regime (Stewart 2008). Given the subsequent changes made to that regime by the Fair Work laws, the need for specific protection has arguably now disappeared – with employment conditions and unfair dismissal protections restored. In addition, the *Fair Work Regulations 2009* limit the scope of state child labour legislation by clarifying federal legislative coverage of some aspects of child employment, largely those relating to hours of work, pay and leave.

    The numerous sources of law relevant to determining an Australian child's experience of work might be blamed on the repertoire of labour market regulation, including the inherent diversification in Australia's federal system, employers' freedom to choose regulatory mechanisms, and the multifaceted aspects of regulating for children (Gahan and Brosnan 2006). In theory, it would be open to the federal government to introduce national laws on child employment. It could do so by calling upon the Commonwealth's power under s 51(xxix) of the *Australian Constitution* to make laws with respect to 'external affairs', enabling the enactment of international labour standards on child labour. Or it could further utilize its 'corporations' power under s 51(xx), and specifically protect child employees working for corporations as an extension of the Fair Work legislation. But there has been no sign of the federal government seriously considering making national law, it appearing content to leave the matter to the states and territories. Nevertheless, the Workplace Relations Ministers Council has recently agreed to investigate the possibility of greater harmonization of child labour laws (Workplace Relations Ministers Council 2009: 3). It remains to be seen whether anything will come of this initiative.

Child Employment Law in Britain: Origins

It was the issue of child employment that occasioned the first industrial legislation in modern British history. The legislation concerned conditions of employment for children, in particular pauper apprentices, and later became a model for other European industrializing economies (Hepple 1986). Not only was child employment legislation the origin for regulating basic conditions of employment, it was also an example of nationalizing local poor law, early welfare based regulation. Local magistrates' efforts to limit the working hours of children and penalize mistreating employers within their jurisdictions were adopted as national principles (Hutchins and Harrison 1911). A series of enactments, now known as the Factories Acts, began in 1802 (see for example the *Health and Morals of Apprentices Act 1802*, and the *Cotton Mills and Factories Act 1819*). They imposed financial punishment on employers who engaged young children and worked them for long and overnight hours in hazardous occupations. For example, the *Factory Act 1833* prohibited children of less than nine working in textile mills and limited hours of work for those up to 11 years to 9 hours per day and 48 per week, with no hours of work between 8:30pm and 5:30am for anyone under 18. Education legislation used half time systems to require some schooling, eventually leading to compulsory education being introduced for those over 10 years of age in 1918, and extending to age 14 (Nardinelli 1990). School hours were short enough to allow for many work engagements to continue.

Such legislation was introduced against a background of exploitative child labour practices that caused poor health and education consequences for children (Pinchbeck and Hewitt 1969, Rose 1991, Thompson 1963). For protracted hours and sometimes in squalid conditions, children worked as coal miners, textile factory hands, in sawmills, up chimneys, making bricks, and on the street selling newspapers (Humphries 2010). Female children might also work in the home, sewing hats and dresses, and similarly for extended hours (Tuttle 1999). Modern notions of childhood, involving a period of play and unfettered development, were unknown for working class children.

The protective legislation progressively introduced in the nineteenth century was fuelled by British society's increasing acceptance of a reformed family ideal, where women and children were situated as dependants of the male breadwinner, their best interests served by keeping them safely inside the home (Kent 1999). At the same time, society developed a preference for statutory regulation, with the recognition that child employment was an issue of public welfare and not only an issue of familial or private concern. Removal of children from the workplace created a childhood, a time of leisure and education (Cunningham 2005). Physical safety was increasingly a priority, with medical knowledge suggesting working children were most vulnerable to developmental health detriments (Horrell and Humphries 1999).

A decreased use of child labour in the twentieth century has been correlated with societal reform, restrictive legislation and technological advancement, replacing the need for child workers (Zelizer 1985). Late twentieth century statistics revealed a drop in the percentage of children entering the workforce on a full-time basis, with children making up a smaller percentage of a workforce that included more and more adult females (Cregan 2001, Richards 1974). Part-time employment of children, accompanied by full-time education, became a socially acceptable outcome, in the context of compulsory schooling laws and a steady demand for youth labour.

Child Employment Law in Britain: Current Approaches

Regulation of child employment in Britain currently relies on dedicated legislation, statutory instruments and delegated law detached from general employment legislation. There is limited specific coverage of child employment in the *Employment Rights Act 1996* (in the form of rights to time off for some study and training), and the *National Minimum Wage Act 1998* (a minimum wage is set for 16 and 17 year olds). These statutes broadly cover all British employees, including apprentices. Law that relates explicitly to child employees is split into two, based on the age of the child. Child employees of 15 and over who are above the compulsory schooling age, set for the year they turn 16, are categorized as young workers, a distinct group of employees. Their maximum hours of work, breaks and leave entitlements are protected by the *Working Time Regulations 1998*, a progressive statutory instrument that has come about as a result of two regional directives to be discussed later in the chapter. The Regulations oblige employers to offer regular health and capacity assessments for night work, more frequent and lengthier rest breaks during work, and longer between shift and weekend rest breaks.

For children aged below the earliest school leaving age, the *Children and Young Persons Act 1933*, originally enacted to consolidate the law on neglected children, has been amended to deal specifically with employment. (The *Children and Young Persons Act 1937* is Scotland's equivalent legislation.) Most recently, the *Children (Protection at Work) Regulations 1998* and *2000*, made to implement the regional directives referred to above, provided new minimum age, hours of work and type of work distinctions to modify previous standards. The Act remains the major piece of national legislation restricting employment of school-aged children. In this regard, coverage is not of young persons, when distinguished from younger children, as the Act's name might suggest. The legislation also contains provisions that create offences involving ill treatment of children, and pays particular attention to children working in entertainment and performance, and overseas. Additional regulations apply to performances (*Children (Performance) Regulations 1968*). Apart from these areas of extra protection, the Act places three main restrictions on children's employment, in terms of age, type and time. A child must be at least 14 years to be employed, with an exception for light work, which can be engaged in from the age of 13 where local byelaws allow it. Light work is the only work that can be lawfully undertaken by 13, 14 and 15 year olds, and 16 year olds who are still required to attend school. This is work which is not harmful, in the broadest sense. Limits on hours worked are based on daily and weekly maxima, and also on whether the work is performed during school terms or on holidays. Before and after school work is limited, and during school hours work is prohibited altogether. Sunday work is also restricted. On any day, morning work before seven and night time work after seven is banned.

These restrictions are supplemented by local authority byelaws. The currency of byelaws, and their consistency with national legislation, can be an issue where child employment is not a priority for the scarce resources of a locality (Department of Children, Schools and Families 2009). Various byelaws specify examples of light work which children aged 13 and over can perform, typically including cleaning, shelf stacking, waitressing, car washing, stable duties, office work and sales. Byelaws may list locations where light work may be performed, such as shops, hairdressing salons, offices, cafés, restaurants and hotels (e.g. Portsmouth City Council 2010). They also list prohibited employment. In addition, local authorities are armed with the task of operating permit and licence systems for street trading, entertainment, performance and overseas work by children.

All children, both young and adolescent, benefit from the specific duties placed on employers in the *Management of Health and Safety at Work Regulations 1999*. While the parent legislation, the *Health and Safety at Work Act 1974*, imposes general duties on employers and other participants in the workplace, these regulations require risk assessment before employment of a child, and special protection from risks that arise as the consequence of a lack of experience, absence of awareness of risks and immaturity. Prohibitions on employers are a part of the regulations. For example, employers are not to employ young persons to do work which is beyond their physical or psychological capacity. For children still of compulsory schooling age, parents are to be informed about risks and safety precautions taken. Other legislation also affects the employment of children. The *Employment of Women, Young Persons and Children Act 1920* still places a full prohibition on children working in industrial undertakings such as mines, factories and workshops. Similarly, licensing, shipping, betting and gambling, and agricultural regulations all restrict the work engaged in by children (see for example the *Licensing Act 2003*, *Merchant Shipping Act 1995*, *Gambling Act 2005*, and *Prevention of Accidents to Children in Agricultural Regulations 1998*).

This fragmented approach has been criticized both for its complexity (McKechnie, Anderson and Hobbs 2007, Papworth 2010), and its tendency to disguise child employment issues (McKechuie, Hobbs and Anderson 2009, Whitney 1999). Where byelaws are recognized as applicable, it appears they are not consistently implemented, with requirements for permits and licences ignored (McKechnie and Hobbs 1999) and applicable fines not imposed (Hobbs, McKechnie and Anderson 2007, McKechnie et al. 2007). Misperceptions that British children only perform acceptable light work have developed (McKechnie et al. 2007). Community confusion about the law in this area spurred a government task force to make recommendations for reform of child employment regulation in 2004 (Better Regulation Task Force). The Task Force concluded simply and predictably that regulation needed to be consolidated into a national legislative scheme. This has not been pursued to date. At a regional level, Britain's regulation of child work is probably representative of the complication that results from a mix of traditional prohibitive statutes, indirect regulation and contemporary facilitative instruments.

The Role of International and Regional Law

International and regional law have had various influences on the development of policy on child employment in developed countries like Britain and Australia (Bond 1995, Creighton 2001, Cullen 2007). Both levels of regulation have approached child employment from a protective and, more recently, a human rights basis. Firstly, conventions and recommendations of the International Labour Organisation (ILO) set international standards which guide national and state legislatures. For example, the Worst Forms of Child Labour Convention No. 182 clearly prohibits forced labour, sale and trafficking of children, and other illicit and dangerous uses of children's labour. Most of these activities are not a concern in Australia and Britain, although trafficking of migrant children for prostitution and other sexually exploitative work is an exception (ECPAT UK 2010). Nevertheless, the standards have been ratified (by Britain in 2000 and by Australia in 2006) and legislated (such as the *Coroners and Justice Act 2009* (UK) s 71, *Sexual Offences Act 2003* (UK) ss 57–59, and *Justice Legislation (Sexual Offences and Bail) Act 2004* (Vic)). ILO standards on minimum ages for employment have been adopted by Britain, complying generally with the international prescription for employment not to start before completion of schooling or attainment of the age of 15 years. The core minimum age convention, ILO Convention No. 138 on Minimum Age for Admission to Employment, was ratified in 2000. While Australia has not yet ratified that convention, it has been recently considered (Creighton 2001). Such standards take a traditional protective view on child labour, limiting the involvement of children in work or banning it altogether if the work is unsuitable.

Other international law creates rights for children: rights to protection from exploitation, to education, to health care, to privacy and more. Such rights reflect modern attitudes that encompass and expressly contemplate the child's right to participate in paid work. The United Nations Convention on the Rights of the Child is an example. It details the right of the child to be protected from economic exploitation and from performing any work that is likely to be hazardous or to interfere with the child's education, or to be harmful to the child's health or physical, mental, spiritual, moral or social development. British society's approval of rights to protection from economic exploitation can be seen in the setting of minimum wages for those above compulsory school age, aged 16 and 17, and apprentices in the *Minimum Wage Act 1998*. Australian award wage entitlements for trainees, apprentices and 16 and 17 year olds serve an equivalent protective purpose. Other rights are recognizable in health and safety laws, accommodating children in the workplace by imposing additional responsibilities on employers of young people. The British *Management of Health and Safety at Work Regulations 1999* is one example, and Queensland's *2006 Code of Practice* is another.

Regional law arising from European Union and Council of Europe instruments also reflects rights-based attitudes toward the regulation of child employment. The European Social Charter, a Council of Europe treaty, provides an extensive range of protections to children in employment. It offers protection in terms of minimum age for employment with light work exceptions, limits on working hours, and fair wages for young people and apprentices. Other protections include paid training, minimum leave accrual, medical monitoring for children engaged in specific work, and special protections from physical and moral danger. The acceptance of children as workers with equal, if not privileged, rights, is implicit in such law. Many of these protections have become part of British national law. Most recently, parliament has been influenced by the European Committee of Social Rights (2005) recommending introduction of a minimum wage for children over the compulsory school leaving age. The British Low Pay Commission (2004) also recommended a minimum wage for young workers.

The European Community's Young Workers Directive 94/33/EC and Working Time Directive 93/104/EC are separate sources of rights which recognize the place of children in the European workforce. The first directive seeks to ensure children have working conditions that suit their age, limiting, amongst other things, young people's working hours on a daily and weekly basis, providing for rest breaks, and prohibiting night work, allowing only for temporary exceptions. It distinguishes between light work and other work, enabling children to work in a wide variety of workplaces, and also imposes on employers a duty to provide for the health and safety of their young employees. As a result, employers must accommodate special rostering, division of work tasks, risk assessment and medical supervision requirements. The second directive, while covering working time for all European employees, addresses young workers' needs as a particular issue in relation to night work and rest breaks. These directives have had an obvious influence on British regulation, in the form of amendments to legislation and the issue of regulations, as already mentioned.

Clearly, the ILO Conventions, and European Directives have played a significant role in highlighting the importance of regulating child labour. Unfortunately, some of the rights and protections that flow from international and regional law advantage only those children who work as employees, despite their stated intention in relation to those who perform other forms of work. This is because national statutory protections often hinge on the existence of an employment relationship, albeit widely defined to include unpaid work. Where the law is linked to wider concepts of health and safety, discrimination and criminal behaviour, working children who are not employed may benefit, but internationally or regionally derived principles about minimum age, limits on hours, types of work and other protections tend to apply only to child employees.

Crafting Better Child Employment Laws

Despite a continuing concern about child worker exploitation (ECPAT UK 2010, UNICEF 2005), there has been a significant change in attitudes about the employment of children in developed countries like Australia and the UK. Rather than adopting a prohibitive view, often based on historic abuse, industrialized countries have increasingly taken a positive approach to the beneficial use of child workers in the mainstream workforce (e.g. Leonard 1999, New South Wales Commission for Children and Young People 2005). Indeed, young workers are preferred to older workers by employers in a number of sectors, and parents often applaud the participation of their children, recognizing it as part of career development. Children themselves see their participation as a step toward maturity and independence. A society wide commitment to wholesale restrictions on child work has dissipated and been replaced by an attitude of facilitation. Rights to participate in employment are now thought to be a significant element of a child's public life (Leonard 2004), with regulation emerging as a suitable vehicle for assertion of that right (White 1994, Morrow 1999).

As we have shown, both Australia and Britain have, in this context, recognized the need for special regulation to protect the interests of children when they perform work. The approach adopted has, however, been fragmented and haphazard, especially in Australia. There are effectively no national standards in Australia, except in restricting the performance of work during school hours. There are also problems of integration and consistency. Some Australian businesses are required to comply with both federal and state labour laws when employing someone under the age of 18. It is questionable how widely such a requirement is understood or complied with, especially in small business. The same can be said of the mix of national and local regulation in Britain.

We advocate an approach to the regulation of child employment that has four main premises:

- a *national focus*, to be achieved in Australia either by the passage of a federal law on child employment, or through harmonization of state and territory laws;
- the adoption of *clear and simple* rules and processes;
- a need for those rules and processes to be *consistent* with general labour laws, in particular by dealing only with those matters that cannot or should not be left to those general laws; and
- the adoption of various strategies for informing those concerned of their entitlements and obligations, and for overcoming the problems that many young workers encounter in asserting their rights.

What ties each of these principles together is a common objective, to promote a better *understanding* in the community of what is required when engaging a child to perform work, and, in turn, achieve a better level of *compliance* with those requirements. Laws are more likely to be observed when they apply on a uniform basis, where they can be readily understood, where they do not unnecessarily duplicate or overlap with other legal regimes, and where they are backed by appropriate informational and enforcement strategies (Argy and Johnson 2003).

It is also important that child employment laws are realistic, in terms of what can practicably be achieved. Any prohibitions need to accord with community values and expectations, not defy them. Required procedures need to be workable and not impose undue costs or delays, especially where small business is concerned. This is not to propose a minimalist approach to regulation, or one that gives up on seeking to impose decent working conditions for children. Again, it is a question of promoting the broadest possible compliance. The more targeted and efficient a law, the more likely it is to be observed.

The benefits to children obviously lie in achieving greater levels of practical protection at work. But there are also potential benefits for the many businesses that employ children. A simpler, streamlined and uniform set of rules and processes should reduce compliance costs. It should also produce a more level playing field, to the extent that it becomes harder for a business to achieve a competitive edge by underpaying or otherwise exploiting young workers.

Having a sound national platform for child employment law would be an obvious improvement to existing legal frameworks in both Australia and Britain. The benefits of localized laws in this area are hard to identify. In Britain in particular, national principles apply in relation to children's education and training, and should apply in relation to their employment without district variations. On the presumption that many children will have little or no consciousness of their rights at work, any legislative framework should start with an employer's responsibility to give basic information to the child about the status of their work relationship, wage rates, hours of work, training entitlements, dismissal protections and safety precautions. Governments should also continuously provide or fund advisory services that are specifically directed to the needs of young workers.

To ensure a desired application of the law, employment should be broadly defined (as it currently is under some Australian laws) to include all forms of work performed for a business or organization, whether paid or unpaid, and whether pursuant to an employment contract or not. This is not to suggest that all forms of work should necessarily be regulated in the same way. Certain types of work arguably warrant 'light touch' regulation, compared to more formal arrangements. This includes babysitting arrangements, work in family enterprises, and also voluntary work for sporting clubs, community organizations, schools, churches and the like. But even in those cases it may still be appropriate to set some limits, or to specify obligations in relation to appropriate supervision.

Minimum age restrictions need to be consistently applicable, with higher age requirements for dangerous work. Hours of work prohibitions should be generally determined by schooling and training parameters. Days of the week and night hour prohibitions are not expressly needed if these parameters are set out clearly. The prescription of maximum daily hours of work could add to this. Age, type and work time restrictions can meet international and regional requirements in these settings.

Child permits, parental consent, licenses to employ and other bureaucratic requirements should not be necessary if safety legislation imposes appropriate duties on employers and other workplace participants, and if industry codes of practice are developed to specifically consider young workers. Inspectorates should have a targeted role in educating and enforcing occupational health and safety requirements in relation to children. Penalties on employers of children below the minimum age, in contravention of prohibitions on hours, or other breach, should be sizeable, to reflect the importance of child employment protections. Penalties on children and their parents serve little purpose if employers have reasonable age-checking responsibilities and are in control of the work they expect a child to perform.

A reorganization of child employment laws to facilitate the suitable and protected participation of children in our workforces is an imperative that promises not only to give children a positive start to their working lives, but also to clarify and consolidate specific employer responsibilities for business certainty. A study of the current Australian and British regulatory frameworks for child work has revealed multiple sources of prohibition and restriction. The two countries, although operating unique labour regulatory regimes, appear to share a lack of focus on the rights of their working children. This chapter recommends that a new emphasis be placed on the protection of a most valuable resource – the workforce of the future – via clear and consistent regulation that facilitates participation while obliging employers to take extra care of their youngest workers.

References

Abhayaratna J., Andrews, L., Nuch, H. and Podbury, T. 2008. *Part Time Employment: The Australian experience*. Staff Working Paper, Productivity Commission. Melbourne: Productivity Commission.

Argy, S. and Johnson. M. 2003. *Mechanisms for Improving the Quality of Regulations: Australia in an International Context*. Staff Research Paper, Productivity Commission. Melbourne: Productivity Commission.

Australian Bureau of Statistics (ABS). 2006. *Australian Historical Population Statistics*. Catalogue No. 3105.0.65.001. Canberra: ABS. [Online]. Available at: http://www.abs.gov.au/AUSSTATS [accessed: 10 September 2010].

Australian Industrial Relations Commission. 1999. *Junior Rates Inquiry – Report of the Full Bench inquiring under Section 120B of the Workplace Relations Act 1996*. AIRC, Q9610, 4 June.

Better Regulation Task Force. 2004. *The Regulation of Child Employment*. [Online]. Available at: http://www.bis.gov.uk/policies/better-regulation [accessed: 27 July 2010].

Bond, A. 1995. European developments: The young persons directive. *Industrial Law Journal*, 24(4), 377–82.

Bowden, B. and Penrose, B. 2006. The origins of child labour in Australia, 1880–1907: A health and safety perspective. *Journal of Occupational Health and Safety Australia and New Zealand*, 22(2), 127–35.

Chapman, A. 2009. The decline and restoration of unfair dismissal rights, in *Fair Work: The New Workplace Laws and the Work Choices Legacy*, edited by A. Forsyth and A. Stewart. Sydney: Federation Press, 207–28.

Commission for Children and Young People and Child Guardian. 2004. *Queensland Review of Child Labour*. Brisbane: Queensland Government.

Cregan, C. 2001. What's happened to the labour market for early school-leavers in Britain? *Industrial Relations Journal*, 32(3), 126–35.

Creighton, W. B. 2001. Australian law and practice relating to child labour and ILO Convention No. 138, in *Children on the Agenda: The Rights of Australia's Children*, edited by M. Jones and L. A. Basser Marks. Sydney: Prospect Media, 199–221.

Creighton, B. and Stewart, A. 2010. *Labour Law. 5th Edition*. Sydney: Federation Press.

Cullen, H. 2007. *The Role of International Law in the Elimination of Child Labor*. Leiden: Martinus Nijoff Publishers.

Cunningham, H. 2005. *Children and Childhood in Western Society since 1500*. Harlow: Pearson and Longman.

Department of Children, Schools and Families. 2009. *Child employment byelaws: Light agricultural and horticultural work*. [Online]. Available at: http://www.dcsf.gov.uk/everychildmatters/publications/documents/lettertodcssabout-childemploymentbyelaws/ [accessed: 18 August 2010].

ECPAT UK. 2010. *Ending Child Prostitution, Pornography and Trafficking. Working Against Child Trafficking*. [Online]. Available at: http://www.ecpat.org.uk/child_trafficking.html [accessed: 29 September 2010].

European Committee of Social Rights. 2005. *Conclusions XVII–2 (United Kingdom), Articles 7, 8, 11, 14, 17 and 18 of the Charter*. [Online] Available at: http://www.coe.int/t/dghl/monitoring/socialcharter/conclusions/conclusionsindex_EN.asp [accessed: 29 September 2010].

Fair Employment Advocate. 2008. *Vulnerable Workers: Young People*. Fair employment discussion paper 3. Perth: Fair Employment Advocate.

Forsyth, A. and Stewart, A. (eds) 2009. *Fair Work: the New Workplace Laws and the Work Choices Legacy*. Sydney: Federation Press.

Gahan, P. and Brosnan, P. 2006. The repertoires of labour market regulation, in *Labour Law and Labour Market Regulation*, edited by C. Arup et al. Sydney: Federation Press, 127–46.

Hepple, B. A. 1986. Introduction, in *The Making of Labour Law in Europe, a Comparative Study of Nine Countries up to 1945*, edited by B. A. Hepple. London: Mansell.

Hobbs, S., McKechnie, J. and Anderson, S. 2007. Making child employment in Britain more visible. *Critical Social Policy*, 27(3), 415–25.

Horrell, S. and Humphries, J. 1999. Child labour and British industrialization, in *A Thing of the Past? Child Labour in the Nineteenth and Twentieth Centuries*, edited by M. Lavalette. Liverpool: Liverpool University Press, 76–99.

Humphries, J. 2010. *Childhood and Child Labour in the British Industrial Revolution*. Cambridge: Cambridge University Press.

Hutchins, B. l. and Harrison, A. 1911. *A History of Factory Legislation*. London: King.

Industrial Relations Victoria. 2001. *Children at work? The protection of children engaged in work activities: policy challenges and choices for Victoria, issues paper.* Melbourne: Department of State and Regional Development.

Kent, S. K. 1999. *Gender and Power in Britain, 1640–1990.* London: Routledge.

Kociumbas, J. 1997. *Australian Childhood, a History.* Sydney: Allen and Unwin.

Leonard, M. 1999. Child work in the UK, 1970–1998, in *A Thing of the Past? Child Labour in the Nineteenth and Twentieth Centuries*, edited by M. Lavalette. Liverpool: Liverpool University Press, 177–91.

Leonard, M. 2004. Children's views on children's right to work, reflections from Belfast. *Childhood*, 11(1), 45–61.

Low Pay Commission. 2004. *The National Minimum Wage: Protecting Young Workers.* [Online]. Available at: http://www.lowpay.gov.uk/lowpay/rep_a_p_index.shtml [accessed: 29 September 2010].

McKechnie, J. and Hobbs, S. 1999. Child labour: A view from the north. *Childhood*, 6(1), 89–100.

McKechnie, J., Anderson, S. and Hobbs, S. 2007. *Cumbria's Working Youngsters, Making the Legislation Work.* [Online]. Available at: http://www.nspcc.org.uk/Inform/research/findings/cumbriasworkingyoungsterspdf_wdf51979.pdf [accessed: 27 September 2010].

McKechnie, J., Hobbs, S., Anderson, S., Howieson, C. and Semple, S. 2007. Child employment: Policy and practice in Scotland. *Youth and Policy*, 96, 51–63.

McKechnie, J., Hobbs, S. and Anderson, S. 2009. Can child employment legislation work? *Youth and Policy*, 101, 43–53.

Morrow, V. 1999. We are people too: Children's and young people's perspectives on children's rights and decision-making in England. *International Journal of Children's Rights*, 7(2), 149–70.

Mourell, M. and Allan, C. 2005. The statutory regulation of child labour in Queensland, in *Reworking Work: Proceedings of the 19th Conference of the Association of Industrial Relations Academics of Australia and New Zealand*, edited by M. Baird, R. Cooper and M. Westcott. Sydney: AIRAANZ, 395–404.

Nardinelli, C. 1990. *Child Labour and the Industrial Revolution.* Bloomington: Indiana University Press.

New South Wales Commission for Children and Young People. 2005. *Children at work.* Sydney: NSW Commission for Children and Young People.

Nolan, D., ed. 1998. *The Australasian Labour Law Reforms: Australia and New Zealand at the End of the Twentieth Century.* Sydney: Federation Press.

Papworth, J. 2010. Does your child work? Make sure they aren't falling foul of the law. *The Guardian.* September 18 [Online]. Available at: http://www.guardian.co.uk/money/2010/sep/18/child-work-legal-restrictions [accessed: 20 September 2010].

Pinchbeck, I. and Hewitt, M. 1969. *Children in English Society*, London: Routledge.

Portsmouth City Council. 2010. *Bye-laws Child Employment*. [Online]. Available at: http://www.portsmouth.gov.uk/business/1009.html [accessed: 28 September 2010].

Richards, E. 1974. Women in the British economy since about 1700: An interpretation. *History*, 59(197), 337–57.

Rose, L. 1991. *The Erosion of Childhood.* London: Routledge.

Stewart, A. 2008. *Making the Working World Work Better for Kids*. Sydney: NSW Commission for Children and Young People.

Thompson, E. P. 1963. *The Making of the English Working Class*. London: Penguin.

Tierney, L. 1963. *Children Who Need Help*. Melbourne: Melbourne University Press.

Tuttle, C. 1999. *Hard at Work in Factories and Mines: The Economics of Child Labor During the British Industrial Revolution. Boulder: Westview Press.*

UNICEF. 2005. Child Labour Today. New York/Geneva: UNICEF.

White, B. 1994. Children, work and 'child labour': Changing responses to the employment of children. *Development and Change*, 25, 849–78.

Whitney, B. 1999. Unenforced or unenforceable? A view from the professions, in *A thing of the past? Child labour in Britain in the Nineteenth and Twentieth Centuries*, edited by M. Lavalette. Liverpool: Liverpool University Press, 231–47.

Workplace Relations Ministers Council. 2009. *Communiqué from Australian, State, Territory and New Zealand Workplace Relations Ministers Council. September 25.* [Online]. Available at: http://www.deewr.gov.au/WorkplaceRelations/WRMC/Pages/Communiques.aspx [accessed: 30 September 2010].

Zelizer, V. 1985. *Pricing the Priceless Child: The Changing Social Value of Children*. New York: Basic Books.

Chapter 11

Employers' Management of Part-time Student Labour

Erica Smith and Wendy Patton

The majority of young full-time school, vocational education and university students internationally work part-time while they are studying. Their ability to earn enough to support themselves, or to augment support they receive from their families, depends on the availability of jobs. Considering the importance of such work to young people's ability to continue in education, and also the vital role that such work plays in the service industries, relatively little scholarly attention has been paid to why companies employ young students and how they manage them.

The Longitudinal Surveys of Australia Youth data, and other studies such as Smith and Green (2001), show that at least two-thirds of school students of working age have formal part-time jobs. Young university students are even more likely to work (McInnis, James and Hartley 2000). While this phenomenon was commonplace in the United States (US) throughout the second half of the twentieth century (Greenberger and Steinberg 1986), it has only recently become widespread in Australia. Students' jobs have not generally been seen as important except as a preparation for 'real' working life (that is, that which commences once full-time study ceases). One likely reason for such undervaluation is that student jobs are part-time and usually in the service industries, where jobs tend to be undervalued and often depicted as low skilled (Korczynski 2005).

Student working is likely to continue as a mass phenomenon, partly because students need jobs. Recent Australian Government policy changes in relation to participation in tertiary education will result in greater numbers of tertiary students and, possibly, to reduced funding per student. In addition, students need to work while studying to show that they have employment experience and employment-related skills (Holmes 2008). At the same time, industry needs student workers (Curtis and Lucas 2001). The shift in the balance of industries within the Australian and other economies from primary and secondary to tertiary industries means an increasing need for people available during non-standard working hours and for short shifts.

This chapter reports on findings from a national study in Australia that examined student working careers and two major employers' use of youth labour. By student working careers we mean the careers that young students have in their part-time jobs during the period when they are at school and, for those who do not go straight into full-time work on leaving school, in immediate post-school education such as university, Technical and Further Education (TAFE) colleges and other education providers. This is the first major Australian study of student working to include a detailed examination of the employer viewpoint.

The chapter focuses on three major issues:

- Why employers choose to employ student labour;
- What strategies they use to manage this young, sometimes transient, workforce that is available only for limited hours;
- What strategies they use to retain the young part-time workers during their educational career and into full-time employment with the company.

The findings relating to these issues are presented and then analysed within a framework regarding alignment between employer and employee interests (Boxall 1998). This framework enables an analysis of results from the perspectives of both employers and student workers.

Background

The part-time jobs that young people do are sometimes depicted as being menial and their employers as exploitative (Tannock 2001). Other researchers present a less negative view, focusing on the recounted experiences of the student workers (Bailey and Bernhardt 1997, Allan, Bamber and Timo 2005). A relatively small proportion of literature examines how organizations actually manage young people (for example, Hsiao, Baum and Teng 2009) and might seek to recruit their managerial workforce from their part-time student workers (Canny 2002). This background section examines some of this literature using the three main foci of the chapter.

Why Employers Choose to Employ Student Labour

The industries in which school students most often find part-time work are in retail, fast food and cafés. In fact, one study reported that almost two-thirds of employed school students work in these industries (Smith and Green 2001). Full-time university students are able to work in a wider range of industries than school students because, being older, they can perform jobs that involve serving alcohol and they can work later at night. The retail and hospitality industries, in which the majority of young people work, form the largest sector of Australia's economy, contributing almost 15 per cent to Gross Domestic Product (GDP) (Service Skills Australia 2010a, 2010b). The retail industry in particular faces a number of unique challenges, including low profits when compared with other industry areas (Maglen, Hopkins and Burke 2001); hence the industry's need to minimize labour costs by the use of student worker labour. Employers, however, cite a number of other reasons why they like to employ young student workers, including their willingness to learn and their higher 'calibre' compared with young school leavers (Canny 1999: 296, Cregan 1997). Factors such as the mouldability, enthusiasm and energy of youth, their availability at non-standard times, and their capacity to perform the many jobs in retail that do not require experience have also been cited by employers as influencing their decision to employ young workers (Smith 2004). More altruistic reasons for employing youth have also been given by employers such as the desire to contribute to the stock of skills in the workforce and to young people's development (Smith 2004).

Employers' Strategies to Manage the Student Workforce

Work organization provides major challenges in typical student working industries, which are primarily based on a pattern of short shifts and non-standard working times (Hsiao et al. 2009). While this provides the flexibility required in those industries, it means that filling rosters becomes a major challenge for managers, particularly at times when many student workers request time off for examinations (Hsiao et al. 2009). Because of the fast moving, customer-focused nature of the workplaces, shifts cannot be left unfilled. Thus, student workers may often be asked to work extra shifts at short notice. This potentially leads to conflict between students and managers, particularly as the power imbalance between school student workers and their employers can be wide. The New South Wales, (NSW) Commission for Children and Young People (2005) has identified that many student workers feel unable to negotiate terms and conditions as equals.

Management staff in retail and fast food companies are sometimes characterized in the industrial relations literature as being uncaring and under-educated (Tannock 2001). Supervisors in 'teenage workplaces' themselves tend to be young (NSW Commission for Children and Young People 2005); school students may be first-line shift supervisors and full-time managers may be barely out of their teens. While this may make the workplaces attractive to young people, some young managers may not have sufficient skills to manage appropriately in all situations (Smith and Comyn 2003). The larger employers of student labour are well aware of this, training their managers appropriately and developing comprehensive human resource management policies (Smith and Comyn 2003: 96). However, students working at particular worksites and in some small businesses may experience poor management, underpayment of wages and withholding of conditions (NSW Commission for Children and Young People 2005).

Even in workplaces with good policies and procedures, there are certain sectoral characteristics that create risk. Working in food service always carries safety risks, associated with lifting, heavy machinery and hot fat (NSW Commission for Children and Young People 2005, Mayhew 2006), and the fast moving nature of many student workplaces makes work pressured and could result in a temptation to cut corners. It also creates a relatively high risk of being verbally abused by customers (NSW Commission for Children and Young People 2005). Most student workplaces operate with extended hours, meaning that students may work late at night, with fatigue naturally creating increased risk of injury. It has been argued that these factors lead to different safety risks from those experienced by very young workers half a century ago, where many young workers worked in apprenticeship arrangements with regular working hours and close supervision (Mayhew 2006).

Trade unions are often seen as unresponsive to the needs of student workers (Tannock 2001). The retail trade is better organized by trade unions than the fast food industry (Tannock 2001), especially among the larger companies. However, as union density among 16–24 year olds in Australia is generally very low (Bailey et al. 2010), few student workers are likely to have access to union assistance.

Training is a vital part of employing young and inexperienced labour. The retail trade in Australia has been an enthusiastic adopter of qualifications-based training for all workers, including student workers, with reforms in Australian training policy in the 1990s leading to increased provision of work-based training (Smith and Keating 2003). Career progression is offered by qualifications which span Certificate I to Advanced Diploma level, and some companies (for example, the supermarket chain Coles) link to qualifications offered through partner universities. While skill or labour shortages have not been identified as serious in the retail trade to date in Australia (although they have in the US, as Hughes (1999) points out) the Retail Industry Working Group (2003) identified middle management as an area where skills shortages were increasingly being felt in large companies. In this context, retention and development of student workers is vital.

Employers' Strategies Regarding Retention of Student Labour

Young people are more job mobile than older workers. During the year ending 2004, for example, 17.4 per cent of teenage workers and 22 per cent of those aged 20–24 changed their employer, compared with 7 per cent of people aged 45–54 (ABS 2004). This 'milling and churning' has been noted internationally as a feature of youth labour markets (Athanasou 2001). The picture is not uniform; while many young workers leave within a few weeks of commencing work, many remain in their jobs for several years (Curtis and Lucas 2001, Smith and Green 2005). The challenge of retaining part-time workers who are also students is significant, with employers said to tolerate high labour turnover and high disaffection among their workers because of the standardization of work (Lucas and Ralston 1996).

Much literature on the work-related aspects of student worker jobs (as opposed to the effects of those jobs on other aspects of young people's lives) comes from the disciplines of industrial relations and sociology. The literature contains assumptions, often implicit and at times explicit, that student jobs are a 'stop gap' (Oppenheimer and Kalmijn 1995); that students generally dislike their work; that they would not consider such work in the long term; and that those who do remain in their student worker occupation after ceasing to be students have failed in some way (Tannock 2001). The industries in which student workers are employed tend to be regarded more generally as low skilled and second rate and it is sometimes assumed that few people would want long-term careers in such work (Leidner 1993).

The current research study set out to explore some of the issues raised in the above discussion, with a particular focus on employer strategy. This chapter utilizes a framework propounded by Boxall (1998) regarding alignment between business and employee interests, in order to examine the ways in which employer strategy responds to the needs of student workers by developing managerial and human resource processes which are favourable to both parties. Boxall's key argument is that the stability of a workforce depends on the level of mutuality between the interests of the company and its workers. Where the alignment is weak, companies are likely to have what Boxall (1998: 272) describes as 'chronic HR problems'; where it is strong, the company is likely to be able to reach high productivity levels.

Research Method

The study, funded by the Australian Research Council (ARC), examined the part-time working careers of full-time students in the 15–24 age group. What this working career means to youth now and as a precursor to the rest of their working lives were explored. The fieldwork took place in three Australian states: New South Wales, Victoria and Queensland. Data collection included longitudinal surveys of school students during the final three years of schooling, focus groups and interviews with university students through their first three years of university study, and in-depth case studies involving managers and student workers at head office and branch level in two companies. The data for this chapter are drawn from interviews with managers and workers which formed part of the longitudinal company case studies. These each involved three annual visits, at national and branch levels, from 2006–2008. Annual visits were undertaken because the focus of the project was on the development of student working careers. The companies were two of the project's industry partners, namely an Australian discount retail company, 'Discount Co.', and a multi-national fast food chain, 'Burgers Inc.' Discount Co. was rapidly expanding at the time of the research, with 140 shops in 2008 in the south-eastern states. Burgers Inc. had 745 outlets in Australia, many franchised, each employing around 60 staff. Interviews took place annually with the national human resources (HR) manager, and at Burgers Inc, with two regional managers in Year 1 (there was no regional structure in Discount Co.). Within each of the six stores the manager, assistant manager and two or more student workers were interviewed.

In some cases, turnover of staff meant that different people were interviewed in successive visits. In others, the original interviewees had taken on new roles (for example, having moved from student-work to full-time work); these were interviewed in their new roles. Almost all of the interviews took place during the site visits, generally in staff rooms but occasionally in the customer area. In a few instances, telephone interviews were undertaken to access people who had not been at work on the day of the visit. Tables 11.1 and 11.2 show the nature and number of participants in Years 1, 2 and 3 for each company.

Table 11.1   Respondents interviewed each year (Total Burgers Inc. = 54)

Level	Position	Year 1	Year 2	Year 3
National	National people resources manager	1	1	1
Regional	VP and regional manager (Southern Region)	1	-	-
	People resources manager (Southern Region)	1	-	-
Site 1 Metro New South Wales	Restaurant manager	1	1	1
	Assistant manager	1	2	1
	Student workers	5	3	2
Site 2 Metro New South Wales	Restaurant manager	1	-	1
	Assistant manager	1	1	1
	Student workers	8	5	2
Site 3 Regional New South Wales	Restaurant manager	1	-	-
	Assistant manager	-	1	1
	Student workers	4	3	2

Table 11.2   Respondents interviewed each year (Total Discount Co. = 42)

Level	Position	Year 1	Year 2	Year 3
National	National human resources manager	1	1	1
Site 1 Suburban Victoria	Store manager	1	1	
	Assistant manager	1	-	
	Student workers	4	4	2
Site 2 Regional New South Wales	Store manager	1	1	1
	Assistant manager	1	1	1
	Student workers	2	2	2
Site 3 Metro Queensland	Store manager	1	1	
	Assistant manager	1	1	1
	Student workers	3	3	3

Some of the student workers were still at school and the others were at university or TAFE colleges. Some moved from school to university during the life of the project. Burgers Inc.'s student workers were all employed on a casual basis, except when they were offered traineeships, as is explained below. At Discount Co. the company had moved by the time of the third visit to offering casual workers permanent part-time positions.

Interview protocols for each type of respondent were prepared, for managers focusing on the ways in which they managed student workers, and for the student workers on their student–working careers, their learning from work, and the relationship between their jobs and their other activities. Interviews/focus groups lasted between 15 and 40 minutes and were taped with permission and transcribed. The resulting data were analysed for a range of themes, with the data for this chapter being drawn from those themes relating to management of student workers. The interviews with senior company managers focused on how they managed their student workforces. The researchers also read induction materials and manuals.

The limitations of the research reported in this chapter are twofold. Firstly, the researchers were directed to particular sites and it is possible that these were selected to represent good practice, although there was nothing to indicate that this was the case. Sites were in fact provided by the companies to suit the researchers' own locations. Secondly, it could be argued that because the companies were industry partners in the research project, interviewees' responses may have been influenced by a wish to present the company in a favourable light; the confidentiality of the process under the study's ethical requirements minimized this as much as practicable.

Findings and Discussion

Reasons for Recruiting Student Labour

The use of student labour involved both demand- and supply-side issues; that is, issues to do with the type of labour needed and to do with the nature of students. In both companies, and particularly in Burgers Inc., there was a very clear understanding that their branch operations depended entirely upon student labour. Perhaps surprisingly, neither company flagged its HR records to show student status, but Burgers Inc. estimated that 80 per cent of its workers were students. Discount Co.'s reliance on student workers was lower, although no figures were provided. There were two major reasons for reliance on students as workers. The first was flexibility and availability, and the second was cost. In both companies, most of the branches ran on a skeleton staff of a few adults, with a manager and perhaps an assistant manager or one or two other senior workers. Young workers under the age of 21 were cheaper than older workers, but there was no indication that there was a preference for younger students over older students because they cost less, rather that different jobs required different levels of maturity and so

210 Young People and Work

younger workers were appropriate for only some jobs, and older students for others. It should be noted, however, that one Burgers Inc. manager thought that individual differences among student workers were more important than chronological age:

> There is a cost involved because the majority of the retail awards, there are junior rates and so a 14 year old is cheaper than a 21 year old. However we recognize the fact that we're going to have to retain them longer so the only thing I think of in terms of cost is retaining them and utilising them better, keeping them in the business for longer so retaining them for longer and just utilizing those skills and the investment you've made in the training. (Regional HR Manager, Burgers Inc.)

University students were available during the week and later at night and school students after school and at weekends. All were employed at times that suited their age and their preferences:

> Our Responsible Student Policy means that nobody under the age of 17 works past eleven o'clock on a school night, so Sunday through to Thursday, whereas with uni students that wouldn't apply; they decide what they want – their working commitments can be in relation to their studies. (National HR Manager, Burgers Inc.)

University students tended to be, as one manager put it, 'hungry for hours' because they needed their pay to live, while school students' hours tended to be limited by their parents' views about what working hours were appropriate. University students, including overseas students, also filled positions in Burgers Inc. city stores where travelling times to work were longer. Schedules were changed every semester at Discount Co. to take account of the university students' lecture timetables. Burgers Inc. staff were mostly employed on a casual basis and schedules varied quite considerably; although some student workers reported receiving approximately the same number of hours every week, others reported variations.

A mix of very young and older students was considered desirable by managers for quality reasons. At Burgers Inc., older students were needed for safety reasons because the company policy was that stores that were open all night or until the early hours needed to employ people aged over 18 who were more likely to be able to cope with difficult situations. Recruitment of university students who had not previously worked for the company was quite common for these reasons. The relative 'expense' of such students did not appear to be an issue. Discount Co. did not have late opening hours, but had reviewed its use of student labour and found that stores that relied predominantly on student labour on certain days of the week had developed a different culture from those that had a more even distribution of student labour and adults. The company decided to re-align the procedures across stores so that each store employed a mix on each day of the week.

Burgers Inc. reported that over the previous five years people had become more specific about the hours they wanted to work, and branch managers were prepared to work with their preferences. The Regional HR Manager said, 'If someone can give you a Monday, Wednesday and Friday for three to five hours and they meet the interview criteria, [they are recruited]; that's how we've changed our focus'.

This section has summarized the reasons why employers preferred to utilize students for the majority of their shop-floor jobs and the ways in which employment processes reflected the mutual needs of worker and company. The findings are in line with much other literature, although the emphasis on well-being reflected in Burgers Inc.'s policy on late-night working does not accord with Mayhew's (2006) more pessimistic view of safety risks to young workers. These findings demonstrate the effectiveness of employers' attempting to construct an alignment between their needs and those of their student worker workforce (Boxall 1998).

Management Processes

Since their workforces were primarily students, companies indicated that they needed to ensure that their line managers in the branches understood young people well. Senior managers reported that branch managers needed to be very aware of the needs and likes of teenagers and those managers who were able to relate best to this age group seemed to have the most success in attracting and retaining young workers. For example, of the two city centre stores of Burgers Inc., one had a branch manager who was clearly regarded by the young workers as being 'cool' while the other, although caring and conscientious, did not have the same 'hipness'; student workers reported that the first store found it much easier to attract staff.

Most managers and supervisory staff interviewed had been student workers themselves and thus, as might be expected, they were able to understand the needs and aspirations of these young workers. Managers sometimes mentioned a lack of maturity among younger workers. For instance, a Burgers Inc. store manager said:

> The older people have a bit more, more common sense. Right? Which I'm not saying that the younger people don't have common sense, but obviously the older people, you know, they're more mature, they think like ... an adult pretty much, they will know what the customers would need and things like that.

A Discount Co. manager referred to occasional conflict between supervisors and young workers, but stressed that it was not a major issue:

> Kids are rebellious, or not rebellious, but like, they've got to test the boundaries sometimes ... Like taking longer lunch breaks and things, like, we only allow 15 minutes for a normal break and sometimes they'll be like 20, 25; [they test] how long they can go before you come and ask them.

Some managers were highly informal in their relationships with their workers while others maintained a greater distance. A student worker in one Burgers Inc. store said:

> When [my friend] asks about my managers I'm like, 'they're cool'... Like when they're serious they're serious but they are part of a joking community and they like to make fun of you; you just pick on each other and it's like in a fun way ... it's just funny.

Such an atmosphere might suit some student workers, but others might feel uncomfortable. It was clear, though, from student worker interviews, that there was generally respect by the managers for their young workforce. Managers appeared to deal well with issues such as errors. At Discount Co. one student worker said, 'If we don't do it very well, [the manager] just comes and explains what's wrong and stuff. He doesn't yell at you or anything'. In general, then, there appeared to be good relationships between the managers and workers.

In line with the fact that work was only one among many priorities in young students' lives, in the views of most interviewees, managers were flexible and allowed them time off when they needed it, for example for exams or holidays. At a policy level, the two organizations expected their store managers to respect student workers' out-of-work activities. National HR managers reported that absenteeism was low if this was done well. There was a system at Burgers Inc. for staff to report any issues through PAL (Personal Action Letter) forms which were available in every staff room. Staff could send personal or anonymous notes through this postage-paid letter system that went directly to the Regional HR Manager. However, the company's senior managers said that there were few industrial relations issues that led to formal complaints or actions.

A perennial problem, though, reported by senior managers and some branch managers, was that some managers asked young staff to do too many hours. One senior manager commented, of managers in some branches:

> ... they [these particular branch managers] haven't sourced enough employees and they are focusing on the employees they've got and asking more and more for them to do additional shifts. That's the employee relations calls I'll get – when someone doesn't have enough staff at the restaurant and the existing staff are having to do [extra] shifts, they eat into our promise of flexibility and you know they've got an exam the next day and someone's called them in to do a night shift. (Regional HR Manager, Burgers Inc.)

Both companies had very structured, competency-based, training programs. At Burgers Inc., for example, employees are taught specific Burgers Inc. procedures for every stage of food preparation and service. Managers reported that systems were designed so that the very youngest employees (who might be only 13 or 14 years of age) could cope with what they had to learn. As they became older their duties are expanded to include more complex and responsible work. These comments were confirmed by interviews with the student workers.

The same principles informed the development of supervisory responsibilities. The principle of progressive responsibility applied to the more senior jobs available to student workers:

> It's quite amazing because my husband owns a small business and I sometimes see people come to work in his business who have never really had part-time jobs. I see people in their twenties who can't delegate a simple task. I've got 15 or 16 year olds in [Burgers Inc.] who are fantastic leaders because they've been able to build upon those skills as they've gone along. (Regional Training Manager, Burgers Inc.)

In both companies, additional training was available that led to promotional positions even while still at school, such as in this case:

> I just moved up to be a supervisor … and stuff like that. So that was like a month ago. And yeah, I couldn't (previously) see myself managing, like running shifts. (Discount Co. student worker)

Burgers Inc. had both company-owned branches and franchised branches. The national HR manager reported that the company put a great deal of resources into developing its franchisees and helping the franchisees to develop their staff. There were what were described as 'robust' systems in place to ensure that franchisees carried out appropriate training. Audits of franchises were reported to focus very heavily on training systems.

Many workplaces are structured around the expectation that people work full-time. While part-time employment is now substantial, increasing from 10 per cent of the labour force in 1966 to 29 per cent in 2007 (Abhayarantna et al. 2008), part-time workers are, overall, still in the minority and their needs can be neglected. In the workplaces studied, however, part-time labour was the norm. Therefore, communication processes were specifically aimed at involving those who worked limited numbers of hours and with varying shift patterns. For example, in both companies, any new procedures and products were explained by signage at the appropriate workstations, as well as in the staff rooms, which meant that all workers were aware of changes.

As most managers (in the case of Burgers Inc., all managers) had been student workers themselves, they were sympathetic to students' needs for flexible hours. One Discount Co. manager said:

> I can relate to them quite well; I think I understand what they're talking about when they're saying, you know, with homework and managing their time and how many hours their parents want them to work as well cos that always comes

into it, so I can relate to all that because that was exactly what I went through
as well.

In general it appeared that the students found employers very flexible; time off
was given when it was asked for, often to an extent that surprised the interviewers.
For example, one student worker at Burgers Inc. said that at his branch it was
acceptable to phone in within hours of a shift and say that he had another
commitment. Participants in a Burgers Inc. focus group valued this flexibility,
saying that it was possible both to ask for time off for any reason, and to ask for
extra hours if they were saving money. At Discount Co. an assistant manager said:

> One of the girls asked to go back [home], she can't work Christmas Eve cos
> she's got to go back to her family and I understand that she's got to travel – and
> you know the girl that's from Melbourne will have to do the same thing because
> her family's there; she's got no one else here, so you take that into consideration.

One of the companies had experimented with strategies regarding permanent
workforce status. By year three of the study, Discount Co. had placed its longer-
term casual student workers in permanent part-time jobs. However, managers
and students alike indicated that this had created difficulties because managers
needed to organize rosters around students' designated total weekly hours and this
sometimes led to students receiving shifts that were not necessarily at preferred
times. The very fact that the company was flexible with time off requests meant
that it was difficult to promise other students fixed rosters. In other words, the
combination of complex rostering systems, extended opening hours and flexibility
to accommodate students' outside-work commitments cannot accord with attempts
to regularize individuals' working hours.

Safety and wellbeing are concerns in relation to student workers, particularly
young teenagers. Burgers Inc. not only had clear policies in place to prevent
school students working late at night, as mentioned earlier, but also recommended
a maximum of two shifts a week for school students. Late hours were not an
issue at Discount Co. because it had limited evening opening. Written training
materials, procedural manuals and visual training aids assisted workers' integration
into workplaces and alerted them to issues such as bullying and safety risk. They
were written in language that would have been easily understandable to workers
in their mid-teens. Burgers Inc. crew rooms all contained many posters and notices
about safety, as did those at Discount Co., albeit to a lesser extent. The interviews
did not reveal any instances of serious safety incidents. Risks could, however, be
inferred through gendered division of labour as reported by the student workers. At
Discount Co., the students said that boys tended to work with stock and disposing
of rubbish, work that was described by one female student worker as being 'very
heavy'. At Burgers Inc., boys tended to work in the kitchen where there were more
serious safety risks. However, there was some mention of work generally being

tiring and creating minor aches and pains, particularly after long shifts. A female student worker at Discount Co. said:

> Sometimes it gets really tiring ... shifts like Thursday night are all right, but when you are working behind the register it's like every time you go to sit down and do another job it's like, you have to get back up straight away and you are standing for a long period of time, so it's just painful.

While the fast food workers evidently found their jobs sufficiently attractive to keep them there, it could be that safety and working environment issues discouraged other student workers from working in fast food. For example one student at Discount Co. said:

> I've got friends that work at like, [Burgers Inc.], and they don't really like it that much. You're constantly on your feet, getting the food and stuff like that, it gets hot in there.

This section has indicated that the companies developed their management and training processes with a young, part-time workforce in mind. Flexibility of rostering allowed for outside-work commitments, but inevitably had the effect of removing the availability of regular and certain shifts. The emphasis on training and the opportunities for progression to more complex work contradicts the conclusion of Mayhew and Quinlan (2002: 264) that there is an absence of opportunities for promotion for young fast food workers. Rather it is evident in these data that employers continue to align policies and practices with student worker needs (Boxall, 1998) emphasizing their understanding of the value of this alignment.

Retention and Recruitment into Management

The companies employed various strategies to retain their student workers over several years and to encourage them to develop management careers within the organization. Burgers Inc. had more strategic policies regarding the latter point than did Discount Co. As both companies were national, it was possible to retain their student workers even if they moved house; workers could be easily transferred. The transition from school to university often meant young people moved away from their family home. Informal arrangements for transferring to a job at the new location were made between managers at the different sites. Managers expressed a strong preference for students who had already worked for the company, commenting that their induction period was much shorter and that they could be confident that the student worker would enjoy the work and would stay in the job.

Although some student workers remained with the organizations for some time, their 'loyalty' sometimes more closely resembled inertia than an active commitment. Some students reported that on leaving school they thought they should move into a more 'adult' type of part-time job, but nevertheless stayed in their former jobs because they were comfortable and easy, and they had earned enough 'capital' at work to be able to ask for changes of shift and other concessions when they needed them. One Discount Co. student worker said:

> I thought I'd leave at uni but I didn't think, like I thought once I finished Year 12 I'd go find another job ... while at uni but like I dunno, I think I just grew ... and it's just too hard with uni. Like [I can only work] certain hours and I just know that I'll get shifts here and so it's a bit too hard to find anywhere else.

This finding underlines the importance of employers' flexibility with their student workers; if they did not allow time off or shift changes they would not retain staff. As well as flexibility of working, Burgers Inc. had extra 'perks' for its workers including social club activities and reward schemes. These were appreciated by some student workers, although others were not interested in them.

During the period of the study, when national unemployment rates remained below 5 per cent, the tight labour market coupled with job mobility caused problems for many employers. In many geographical areas, the case study organizations were competing for scarce part-time youth labour. For this reason, Burgers Inc. instituted part-time positions for university students that involved some assistant branch manager responsibilities. However, by the third year of the project, the national HR manager said that this policy was being wound back as it had proved difficult for the young managers to adopt a managerial position while their limited working hours precluded them from some of the activities of a manager, such as budgeting. However, students continued to fill frontline supervisory positions.

Both companies looked to their student workers to fill future branch management and senior management positions, but differed in their approach. All managers – local, state and national – interviewed at Burgers Inc. had previously been student workers. Indeed, one of the senior managers mentioned the difficulty she faced in telling her parents she had decided to leave university and work full-time for Burgers Inc.:

> It really took me a long while to come to the realization that actually I really enjoyed what I was doing at Burgers Inc. and I could have a career and I wanted to have a career. I remember calling my parents overseas saying I know you've just paid my university fees again but I don't want to do this and this [Burgers Inc.] is what I want to do.

In 2009, this interviewee was appointed Australian Managing Director of Burgers Inc., indicating that her decision had been appropriate. While Discount Co. also looked to its student workers for future management, branch managers reported that the company did not have specific strategies for doing so; for example, they were not asked specifically to identify talent. The primary focus in stores was on efficient management of the individual store and there was less focus on the needs of the company as a whole. Branch managers at Discount Co. were recruited externally as well as internally.

Few of the university students, however, said that they wanted to work long-term for Burgers Inc. or Discount Co. There seemed to be a status issue with typical student worker companies. As a regional training manager with Burgers Inc. put it:

> ... [There is] a perception thing that it's not as aspirational as we would like it to be having a career at Burgers Inc. A lot of times if you're out and about, and I travel a lot on planes talking to people, they say 'Where do you work?' and I say 'Burgers Inc.' and then you get into the whole conversation. I find as a business person they like to talk about it because they obviously understand the structure behind it. But if you're talking to people who aren't actually involved in business in any way and it's not just their [special] interest, it's very hard because Burgers Inc. is such a big brand and it's so clear in what [sic] people's minds what Burgers Inc. is for most [people] – it's hamburgers and fries. Those people wouldn't give a second thought to the fact that well it's a workforce of 50,000, it requires a HR department, and it's a huge marketing machine and so on.

Therefore part of a Burgers Inc. branch manager's role was to encourage retention of good student workers and to educate them about opportunities within the company. Interviews indicated that often student workers believed that the only jobs in the companies were those that they saw in branches. One Burgers Inc. student interviewee, for example, who wanted to study accountancy at university and then work overseas, was not aware that she could have done so with the company.

In both companies, the route to management generally began with traineeships in retail. Traineeships resemble apprenticeships but are shorter, and involve the attainment of nationally-recognized qualifications while working (Smith et al. 2009). They involve formal training overseen by a training provider, and companies are allowed, as with apprentices, to discount wages during the training period, although neither of these companies in fact did so. Good workers were offered part-time traineeships at both Discount Co. and Burgers Inc. as a track to managerial careers; they were used selectively and strategically. In a typical Burgers Inc. branch less than one-fifth of the workers were trainees and, similarly, at a typical Discount Co. store, only two or three people would be undertaking traineeships, with the traineeship being seen as a recognition of good performance and thus as a motivational tool: 'We really do select the best of the best and reward them [with a traineeship], because then they become permanent part-time employees' (National HR Manager, Discount Co.). In both companies, successful completion of a Certificate II in retail led to enrolment in further qualifications, the level of which was determined by job roles or potential job roles.

   This section has shown than Burgers Inc. in particular was focused on retaining workers long-term into managerial roles (Canny 2002) and that both companies utilized traineeships (Smith and Keating 2003) as a means of developing staff that seemed to wish to progress in the company. However, the awareness of promotion prospects among student workers appeared to be patchy. The framework of alignment between employer and employee interests (Boxall 1998) is again evident in these strategies where employers appreciate the value of retention of well trained student workers who can develop into managerial positions.

Conclusion

The research provides insight into why companies utilize student labour, how they manage the labour to take account of its particular nature (such as the need for flexible hours and limited working experience) and how companies try to retain student workers while they are students and beyond. It needs to be remembered that the findings from this research study are not necessarily generalizable to other companies. However, the companies were approached for the study because they presented many features of typical student workplaces, and Burgers Inc. in particular could be described as 'paradigmatic' (Flyvberg 2003).

   The tightness of the Australian labour market at the time of the research was an important contextual factor. It was clear in discussion with the national HR managers that this factor dominated their thinking. Companies knew they needed to exhibit flexibility and offer interesting work in order to retain people. Should the labour market move in employers' favour, it is possible that companies might become less accommodating towards their student workforce. While this point cannot be tested, however, our feeling is that companies would be unlikely to change their policies to any great extent; the need for workforce stability and the desire to recruit future senior managers (Canny 2002) would still exist even if companies were able to 'pick and choose' amongst more applicants.

   Both the companies sold low-cost products and therefore needed to keep their labour costs down. In terms of competitive strategy they were 'defenders' (Miles and Snow 1984), focusing on efficiency and operating in a stable environment. However, it would be a mistake to consider that the only reason they employed students was because of the low cost of young people's labour. The research clearly indicated the complexity of the decision-making processes of companies and students alike. The companies needed to recruit young people who could adequately do the job, who would stay with them for reasonable periods of time and some of whom at least would be willing to consider long-term careers in the organizations. The students needed jobs that paid a reasonable wage, were enjoyable, provided flexible working hours but also security and, if possible, provided for transfer between sites.

   There was little evidence, in the interviews with student workers at the company case sites (or indeed with interviewees in other parts of the larger project) to support the views of Tannock (2001) or Oppenheimer and Kalmijn (1995) about the unpleasantness of student worker jobs. The interviews made it evident, however, that the deep understanding on the part of senior managers of young people's needs was not always matched by branch managers, who were often young people as well, and faced daily operational realities. Senior managers attempted to put systems in place to train branch managers and supervisors appropriately and to protect young workers through company policies such as working-hours rules.

In sum, Boxall's (1998) model of alignment between business and employee interests is a useful way of looking at the relationship between these organizations and their student workforce. The coincidence of the needs of student workers with those of their employers (insofar that companies offer appropriate flexibility, opportunities for short-term advancement and an enjoyable social atmosphere) provides the conditions for high levels of productivity and efficiency. However, the companies appeared to have less success in presenting themselves as the sites for long-term careers. Boxall differentiates, in his model (1998: 272), between the short-term and the long-term business context, pointing out that companies need to create an alignment between their own and workers' interests that secures workers who can become strategic leaders. It could be that the companies in this study needed additional strategies to attract more, and higher calibre, student workers for the long-term, but that there might be inherent difficulties in reconciling the image of a flexible, fun, sociable workplace attractive to student workers, with perceptions of a company with high-level, long-term career prospects. This would be a fruitful area for further research.

References

Abhayarantna, J., Andrews, L., Nuch, H. and Podbury, T. 2008. *Part-time Employment: The Australian Experience.* Productivity Commission Working Paper. Melbourne: Productivity Commission.

Allan, C., Bamber, G. and Timo, N. 2005. McJobs, student attitudes to work and employment relations in the fast food industry. *Journal of Hospitality and Tourism Management*, 12(1), 1–11.

Athanasou, J. 2001. Young people in transition: Factors influencing the educational-vocational pathways of Australian school-leavers. *Education and Training*, 43(3) 132–8.

Australian Bureau of Statistics (ABS). 2004. *Labour Mobility*, cat 6209.0. Canberra: ABS.

Bailey, J., Price, R., Esders, L. and McDonald, P. 2010. Daggy shirts, daggy slogans? Marketing unions to young people. *Journal of Industrial Relations*, 52(1), 43–60.

Bailey, T. and Bernhardt, A. 1997. In search of the high road in a low wage industry, *Politics and Society*, 25(2), 179–201.

Boxall, P. 1998. Achieving competitive advantage through human resource strategy: Towards a theory of industry dynamics. *Human Resource Management Review*, 8(3), 265–88.

Canny, A. 2002. Flexible labour? The growth of student employment in the UK. *Journal of Education and Work*, 15(3), 277–301.

Cregan, C. 1997. *What's Happened to the Labour Market for School Leavers in Britain?* Melbourne University Department of Management and Industrial Relations, Working Paper 108. Melbourne: Melbourne University.

Curtis, S. and Lucas, R. 2001. A coincidence of needs? Employers and full-time students. *Employee Relations*, 23(1), 38–44.

Flyvberg, B. 2006. Five misunderstandings about case-study research. *Qualitative Inquiry*, 12(2), 219–45.

Greenberger, E., and Steinberg, L. D. 1986. *When Teenagers Work: The Psychological and Social Costs of Teenage Employment.* New York: Basic Books.

Holmes, V. 2008. Working to live: Why university students balance full-time study and employment. *Education & Training*, 50(4), 305–14.

Hsiao, S.-H., Baum, T. and Teng, C.-C. 2009. *Employing Student Workers in the Hotel Industry on a Part-time Basis.* International Council on Hotel, Restaurant and Institutional Education Conference, Amherst, Mass., 29 July–1 August. Available at http://scholarworks.umass.edu/org, [accessed: 14 February 2011].

Hughes, K. 1999. *Supermarket Employment: Good Jobs at Good Wages?* Institute on Education and the Economy Working Paper No. 11. Available at http://www.tc.columbia.edu/iee/PAPERS/workpap11.pdf [accessed: 14 February 2011].

Korczynski, M. 2005. Skills in service work: An overview. *Human Resource Management Journal*, 15(2), 3–14.

Leidner, R. 1993. *Fast Food, Fast Talk: Service Work and the Routinization of Everyday Life.* Berkeley, CA: University of California Press.

Lucas, R., and Ralston, L. 1996. Part-time student labour: Strategic choice or pragmatic response? *International Journal of Contemporary Hospitality Management*, 8(2), 21–4.

Maglen, L., Hopkins, S., and Burke, G. 2001. *Training for Productivity.* Adelaide: National Centre for Vocational Education Research.

Mayhew, C. 2006. OHS hazards and risks for young workers. *Journal of Occupational Health and Safety*, 22(2), 91–7.

Mayhew, C. and Quinlan, M. 2002. Fordism in the fast food industry: Pervasive management control and occupational health and safety risks for young temporary workers. *Sociology of Health and Illness*, 24(3), 261–84.

McInnis, C., James, R. and Hartley, R. 2000. *Trends in the First Year Experience in Australian Universities.* Canberra: Department of Education, Training and Youth Affairs.

Miles, R. and Snow, C. 1984. Designing strategic human resources systems. *Organizational Dynamics*, 13(1), 36–53.

NSW Commission for Children and Young People 2005. *Children at Work*. Surry Hills: NSW Commission for Children and Young People.

Oppenheimer, V. and Kalmijn, M. 1995. Life-cycle jobs. *Research in Social Stratification and Mobility*, 14, 1–38.

Retail Industry Working Group. 2003. *National Industry Skills Initiative: Retail Industry Report*. Canberra: Commonwealth of Australia.

Service Skills Australia. 2010a. *Floristry, Retail and Wholesale Services: Environmental Scan* 2010. Sydney: Service Skills Australia.

Service Skills Australia. 2010b. *Tourism, Hospitality and Events: Environmental Scan 2010*. Sydney: Service Skills Australia.

Smith, E. 2004. Teenage employability: Views of employers. *Youth Studies Australia*, 23(4), 47–53.

Smith, E. and Comyn, P. 2003. *The Development of Employability Skills in Novice Workers through Employment*. Adelaide: National Centre for Vocational Education Research.

Smith, E., Comyn, P., Brennan Kemmis, R. and Smith, A. 2009. *High Quality Traineeships: Identifying What Works*. Adelaide: National Centre for Vocational Education Research.

Smith, E. and Green, A. 2001. *School Students' Learning from their Paid and Unpaid Work*. Adelaide: National Centre for Vocational Education Research.

Smith, E. and Green, A. 2005. *How Workplace Experiences While at School Affect School Leavers' Pathways*. Adelaide: National Centre for Vocational Education Research.

Smith, E. and Keating, J. 2003. *From Training Reform to Training Packages*. Tuggerah Lakes: Social Science Press.

Tannock, S. 2001. *Youth at Work: The Unionized Fast-food and Grocery Workplace*. Philadelphia, PA: Temple University Press.

Chapter 12

Social Inclusion for Young People in the Nordic Countries: Similar but Not Identical

Jonas Olofsson and Eskil Wadensjö

Twin goals in all Nordic countries – Denmark, Finland, Iceland, Norway and Sweden – are to create equitable conditions in work and education for youth and young adults, regardless of background conditions such as class, gender and ethnicity. The development of welfare state institutions in Nordic countries during the twentieth century is linked to this goal. The countries however have different views on how these goals should be reached. Their fairness strategies vary. Further, while the Nordic countries are considered to have well-developed public policies that foster social inclusion, none of the countries have been able to achieve equality for young people in work and education.

The purpose of this chapter is to examine how these different strategies affect youth transition patterns. Labour market regulation differs between the countries, affecting demand for qualifications and the conditions under which young people enter the labour markets. Systems of vocational education also differ; in Finland and Sweden the labour market is less related to education for different trades than in the other Nordic countries. These and other differences in institutional settings are worth a closer study, given that the differences between the Nordic countries concerning other aspects of societal life are small. These differences are also interesting in view of comparative research on welfare states and labour markets (see Esping-Andersen 1990, Hall and Soskice 2001, Kangas and Palme 2005), which shows that even countries with similar characteristics in some respects – for example strong unions and large public sectors – may show important differences in other respects which makes comparisons too simplistic. Fruitful comparisons have to be supported by detailed knowledge of institutional preconditions in every single country. At the same time, our findings tell us that even rather minor differences in institutional settings between countries can have substantial effects on youth establishment patterns.

We begin this chapter by examining the labour market conditions for youth before turning to the countries' education systems, and then to labour market regulation and labour market policy. The chapter then examines the central research question: are the employment conditions for youth in terms of work and employment in the five Nordic countries equitable and, if not, what factors account for differences in outcomes?

Employment and Unemployment

How has youth unemployment developed in the Nordic countries and what are the patterns of youth employment? Has unemployment followed the same unfavourable trends as in many other industrialized nations? Figure 12.1 provides an overview.

Unemployment varies greatly between the Nordic countries, as Figure 12.1 shows. Unemployment among youth and young adults (under age 25) has been very high in Finland but has dropped. In Sweden, youth unemployment has been increasing since the late-1990s and has in recent years exceeded the EU15 average. On the other hand, Denmark, Iceland and Norway have considerably lower youth unemployment than EU15.

Relative unemployment levels – youth versus older workers – are presented in Figure 12.2, which shows that within EU15 youth unemployment is more than twice as high as unemployment among middle-aged and older workers (aged 25–64). In recent years, Denmark has been the only Nordic country with relative youth unemployment lower than the EU15 average. In Norway and Iceland, relative youth unemployment is considerably higher than the EU15 average, and in Sweden it is about four times higher.

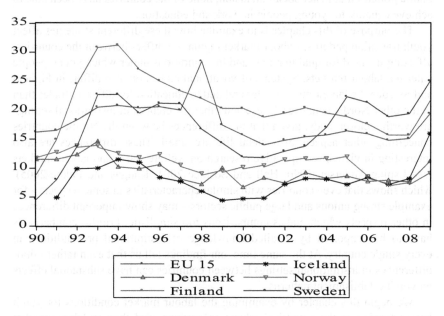

Figure 12.1   Open unemployment in age groups under 25 years of age within the Nordic countries and EU15, 1990–2009

Sources: OECD.n.d. Data on unemployment in Iceland do not cover the entire period. EU15 includes Austria, Belgium, Denmark, Finland, France, Germany, Greece, Ireland, Italy, Luxembourg, the Netherlands, Portugal, Spain, Sweden and the United Kingdom.

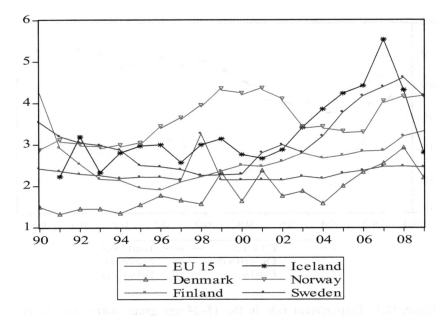

Figure 12.2   Relative youth unemployment (the proportion of unemployed in the labour force aged between 15 and 24)/(the proportion of unemployed in the labour force aged between 25 and 64), 1990–2009

Source: OECD.

The youth employment rate also varies considerably between the Nordic countries. Figure 12.3 shows that young people have a higher employment rate in Denmark, Iceland and Norway than in Finland and Sweden. The levels in Finland and Sweden are close to the EU15 average. One reason for differences between countries is that the percentage of students in the 15–25 age group varies, being higher in Finland than in the other countries, although the differences are not very large. In 2008 the proportion of students in the 15–24 age group was 70.5 per cent in Finland compared to 65.0 in Sweden, 66.5 per cent in Denmark, 65.4 per cent in Iceland and 65.3 per cent in Norway – all much higher than the EU15 figure of 60.5 per cent (Eurostat n.d.). The differences are however largely a statistical artefact. In Denmark and Norway, as in other countries where large cohorts of youth undergo apprenticeship training, the employment rate is higher because apprentices are counted as employed. In countries where school-based vocational training programs dominate, as in Sweden and Finland, students are not counted as employed or members of the labour force and the employment rate is therefore lower and the unemployment rate higher. This should be borne in mind when comparing youth employment across the Nordic countries.

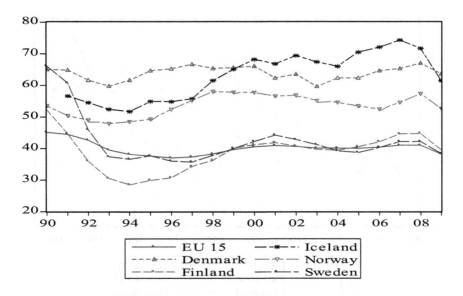

Figure 12.3   Employment rate in the 15–24 age group within the Nordic countries and EU15, 1990–2009

Source: OECD n.d.

Regulation of the Labour Market

The regulation of labour markets in the Nordic countries has an impact on youth employment and unemployment. A distinctive feature of Nordic countries' employment relations is that collective agreements between the social partners and legislation play a major role. In comparative research on labour market regimes, following the usual division between co-ordinated and liberal market economies, the Nordic countries are often used as examples of regulated and co-ordinated regimes (Hall and Soskice 2001). Large comprehensive trade unions in these countries assume broad socio-economic responsibility and do not oppose new technology; a culture based on the collective bargaining system promotes collaboration and counteracts conflict; and a relatively limited wage spread and long-term employment relations facilitate investment in specific occupational competence. The dominant view among researchers dealing with labour market conditions in the Nordic countries is that regulation can increase efficiency (see Agell 1999, Ahlberg, Bruun and Malmberg 2006), although there are dissenting views about this (Skedinger 2005). In short, high unemployment in general and high youth unemployment in particular has been linked to general conditions of supply and demand and changing qualification requirements, rather than labour market regulations (ILO 2000).

Union Density and Collective Bargaining

While employment relations in the Nordic countries have broad similarities, there are a number of differences. Union density is about 70 per cent in Denmark, Finland, Iceland and Sweden, much higher than the EU15 average of 35 per cent (ETUI, n.d.). Norway is an exception, with just over 50 per cent union density. An explanation for this lower level is that unemployment insurance is compulsory in Norway but linked to the trade unions, and voluntary in Denmark, Finland and Sweden. This means that the unemployment insurance system in Norway does not automatically result in higher rates of union membership. Further, it is important to note that in all countries collective bargaining coverage exceeds union density, since agreements apply to non-unionized workers. The prevalence of collective agreements is lowest in Norway where they cover about 70 per cent of the labour force (Dølvik and Eldring 2006).

Relative Wages

An important issue is how labour market systems influence the lowest wages in the labour market, and whether this in turn affects youth employment and unemployment. We will use the concepts of starting wage, lowest wage and minimum wage. The starting wage can affect young people's ability to compete for vacant positions. Table 12.1 shows the lowest wage relative to the average wage in the Nordic countries, except Iceland. This ratio is sometimes called the minimum wage bite.

Table 12.1   Lowest wage as a percentage of the average wage

Denmark	0.54
Finland	0.52
Norway	0.64
Sweden	0.51

Source: Neumark & Wascher (2004).

The Nordic levels are not particularly high compared to other European countries. The corresponding figures for France and Germany are 0.62 and 0.58, respectively. On the other hand, the lowest wage levels in the Nordic countries are considerably higher than in liberal market economies such as the United Kingdom (UK) and the United States (US), where the minimum wage bite is 0.42 and 0.36, respectively. The data on minimum wages presented here have been questioned by Skedinger (2005) who has examined the lowest wages in different sectors in Sweden. His results suggest that the average Swedish minimum wage is considerably higher than shown in international comparisons, such as that presented in Table 12.1.

What effect does the minimum wage have on the prospects for young people entering the labour market? In theory, high entry wages can have a variety of effects. High relative wages can induce young people to drop out of studies and look for work, and therefore lead to increased youth employment. On the other hand, high entry wages can lead to prolonged studies and lower labour supply in the short run by making young people less attractive for employers. The question of whether raising the minimum wage reduces or increases employment has been much debated in labour economics research, especially in the US (Manning 2003). High entry wages should – if there indeed is a negative employment effect – primarily affect persons with the lowest education, namely those in the least skilled jobs. A high minimum wage could lead to more limited job opportunities for such individuals. Data in Table 12.2 do not support this hypothesis. In countries with low wage spread, the employment rate is fairly high, especially among those with the lowest education. This suggests that factors other than relative wages are important in creating employment.

Table 12.2   Employment rate in the 25 to 64 age group by education level in 2008

	Compulsory school	Upper secondary school	College/ university
Denmark	67	80	89
Finland	69	77	83
Iceland	83	89	87
Norway	67	82	94
Sweden	83	83	87
United Kingdom	52	82	86
USA	57	73	80
EU19	60	75	83
OECD	62	75	82

Source: OECD, *Education at a Glance 2010*. Table A6.1b (web only). EU19 consists of EU15 plus Poland, Slovakia, Czech Republic and Hungary.

Unemployment Benefits

Nordic countries usually offer generous unemployment benefits (OECD, n.d.), especially for workers with low income. But it needs to be emphasized that a high proportion of unemployed youth is not qualified for unemployment benefits because of insurance rules demanding longer periods of labour market attachment before access to benefits. The alternative for youth – especially for younger cohorts – is often social assistance.

In sum, there is no evidence that highly regulated labour markets, including strong trade unions, high collective bargaining coverage and relatively generous welfare benefits, necessarily lead to higher unemployment. While a study by Bassanini and Duval (2006) indicates a weak negative association between the degree of unionization and youth unemployment in Organisation for Economic Co-operation and Development (OECD) countries, it also shows that cooperative structures in the labour market, defined in terms of collective agreement coverage, reduce unemployment among both younger and older workers.

In order to analyse the labour market entry conditions for youth, we must also examine how education is organized, and variations in student dropout rates, amongst the Nordic countries.

Educational Participation

The Nordic countries are characterized by high education participation rates. Table 12.3 shows that the Nordic countries on average have more students than the EU19 and OECD countries.

Table 12.3   Proportion of students aged 15–19 and 20–29. Full-time and part-time students at all education levels in 2008

	15–19 years	20–29 years
Denmark	84	37
Finland	87	43
Iceland	84	35
Norway	87	29
Sweden	86	33
EU19	82	25
OECD	85	25

Source: OECD, *Education at a Glance 2010*. Table C1.1. EU19 consists of EU15 plus Poland, Slovakia, Czech Republic and Hungary.

Consistent with participation rates, average tertiary education levels are high in Denmark, Finland, Norway and Sweden, as shown in Table 12.4, but low in Iceland. Gender differences are largest in Iceland, where many women lack an upper secondary school education because of earlier low participation in education. In 1980 the proportion of Icelandic women progressing to upper secondary studies was only 60 per cent; while it is over 90 per cent today, earlier low participation rates affect current education levels. Adult education is also far less developed in Iceland than in the other Nordic countries (Ministry of Education, Science and Culture 2002).

Table 12.4   Percentage of women and men aged 25–64 with upper secondary education or tertiary education as the highest level in 2008

	Upper secondary education		Tertiary education	
	Women	Men	Women	Men
Denmark	41	47	35	29
Finland	41	47	41	31
Iceland	29	30	34	28
Norway	38	44	40	32
Sweden	45	48	37	28
EU19	45	48	26	25
OECD	42	45	29	28

Source: OECD, *Education at a Glance 2010*. Table A1.1b and A1.1c (web only). EU19 consists of EU15 plus Poland, Slovakia, Czech Republic and Hungary.

The proportion of students who complete an upper secondary or post-secondary education is high in all the Nordic countries compared to the average in EU15 and OECD countries. However, as Table 12.5 shows, the dropout rate among those aged 18–24 years varies a great deal between the Nordic countries. More women than men complete secondary education in all countries. In Denmark, Norway and Sweden, the dropout rate has risen both among women and men. In Iceland the dropout rate has declined markedly among women and slightly among men. In Finland it has declined slightly among both women and men. Amongst EU15 countries the average dropout rate declined considerably between 1995 and 2009. How can we explain the differences in dropout rates between the Nordic countries? A closer look at individual countries in Table 12.5 shows that Iceland is the deviant. The proportion of young people who embark on an upper secondary school education has increased strongly in recent years but many males, in particular, fail to complete their studies. One explanation may be that the demand for labour has been very high in Iceland, at least until the financial crisis of the past few years, leading to lower incentives to complete education. The differential dropout rates are also influenced by differing upper age limits for participation in upper secondary studies. Sweden has an upper limit for starting upper secondary school studies at age 20, Denmark has no upper age limit and in Norway those with an incomplete education are entitled to seek admission to upper secondary school. The financial help for young adults completing their upper secondary education is also much more generous in Denmark and Norway than in Sweden. Low financial help is certainly a factor that makes it harder to motivate young adults with poor results from previous schooling to complete their upper secondary education in Sweden. Two final factors that contribute to explain the negative trend in dropout rates in Denmark, Norway and Sweden, compared to Finland and Iceland, are the rising participation in upper secondary school from the beginning of the 1990s (especially in Norway), and the growing number of foreign born pupils. The growth in the number of immigrants has been especially high in Denmark, Norway and Sweden, whereas in Finland and Iceland youth immigration is low (Olofsson and Panican 2008).

Table 12.5   Percentage of 18–24 year-olds who dropped out of upper secondary education in 1995 and 2009

	Women		Men	
	1995	2009	1995	2009
Denmark	6.9	7.7	5.2	13.2
Finland	10.8*	9.0	11.4*	10.7
Iceland	32.7*	17.5	28.1*	25.2
Norway	11.1**	13.4	10.6**	21.8
Sweden	6.0**	9.5	9.0**	11.9
EU15	23.5	13.7	29.0	18.1
EU27	-	12.5	-	16.3

Note: * 1999 data; ** 1996 data.

Source: Eurostat, Early school leavers (http://epp.eurostat.ec.europe.eu).

All Nordic countries have problems with high dropout rates. This is of concern because, as in other countries, young people without completed secondary education face huge difficulties in entering the labour market. At the policy level, all countries recognize this as a social problem of utmost importance. The Nordic countries have developed very different approaches for tackling risks of social exclusion among young people.

Vocational Education and Training

In Finland, Norway and Sweden, education is integrated; that is, academic and vocational programs are gathered into a single institution. In the other two Nordic countries, preparatory academic studies and pre-vocational training occur in separate schools. The organization of vocational training also differs between countries. Sweden has had very little apprenticeship training, but this will change shortly when apprenticeship programs will be introduced in upper secondary schools. In Denmark, Iceland and Norway, on the other hand, most vocational training includes elements of apprenticeship training. Apprenticeship contracts are regulated via collective agreements and apprentices receive wages during their training. Apprenticeship training also occurs in Finland where it is regulated through special agreements that govern employment conditions and wages.

There are also important differences in how the countries deal with the dropout problem within the upper secondary school system. Denmark and Norway have designed ambitious measures connected to a follow-up system for school dropouts. This system is also combined with generous support for young adults who have not completed an upper secondary education. The primary goal of the youth guarantee in these countries is secondary education for every youth. These measures overcome the usual division between labour market policy and education policy. This is an aspect of utmost importance and we will return to it in the next section. We cannot find anything like this in the other Nordic countries.

All these differences are important when we want to explain differences in patterns of youth establishment and social inclusion in the Nordic countries. The organization of vocational and training systems affects social conditions for youth. A more flexible and multifaceted set of vocational streams at upper secondary level make it possible for more students – even those with little interest in schooling – to take part in the educational system. This is especially so if they are offered rather generous income support while studying. If the vocational educations are shaped in close cooperation with the parties of working life and in accordance with the demands of regulated trades, it is also more likely that the students and apprentices will get jobs shortly after completing their education. An employer can be more certain about new job applicants' working capabilities if they have gone through apprenticeship periods aiming at regulated trades, than if the applicants have experienced school based and preparatory vocational educations. These conditions may contribute to explain relatively low rates of unemployment and high rates of employment among youth in Denmark and Norway compared to both Finland and Sweden. These discrepancies are, as we will now see, strengthened by the differences in youth labour market policy measures.

Labour Market Policy Measures

The scope and orientation of labour market policy measures for unemployed youth differ between the Nordic countries. Activation policy has often been pointed out as a key plank of Danish policy making in recent years, gaining currency also in other countries (Johansson 2006, Andersen and Pedersen 2006). Its basic premise is that the long-term unemployed and long-term welfare dependent should be activated rather than offered passive assistance. Both unemployment insurance benefits and social assistance should be made conditional. This policy is similar to what is called *workfare* in the Anglo-Saxon countries. Activation policy has characterized youth measures in all the countries discussed, but the details vary between countries. In Denmark, education is given priority; in Norway the youth guarantee is orientated towards work placement and shorter vocational training;

and in Finland measures are also varied, including both employment and training. In Sweden job coaching and short periods of job placements are the main ingredients. It is instructive therefore to explore the similarities and differences between youth policy in the Nordic countries. In this section we will investigate the differences in labour market policies and discuss how these differences affect the conditions for youth, especially those from less privileged socio-economic backgrounds.

Denmark

Denmark has focused on the use of training and educational measures to counteract youth unemployment and prevent social marginalization among the young. This strategy has resulted in establishment of production schools as well as other shorter and flexible initial vocational training variants. This in turn has reduced the significance of traditional labour market policy measures such as employment subsidies and public works (Walther et al. 2002). Coordination has been a keyword in Danish policy. One expression of this has been the development of job and training centres at the local level. These centres include various services ranging from labour exchanges and social services to schools, with the aim of giving individuals better opportunities to obtain coordinated assistance relevant to their needs.

The system has evolved gradually over two decades. The first so-called youth guarantee was introduced in 1990. Its purpose was to guarantee unemployed youth rapid activation measures, primarily in the form of training. Initially targeted to youth aged 18–19 years without entitlement to unemployment benefits, the system was gradually expanded to include young adults under the age of 30. In 1995 a requirement was introduced that stipulated that those under age 25 who had been unemployed for six months had to accept training or have their social assistance reduced. A more radical step came in 2005 with the decision that youth and young adults would receive no assistance at all if they refused to undergo training. The parents of youths who dropped out of school would also face reduced assistance (Andersen and Pedersen 2006). While requirements have become stricter, Danish compensation systems remain very generous by international standards. Social assistance is 60 per cent of the unemployment benefits to single individuals and 80 per cent to those who cohabit. Unemployment insurance provisions are also generous. The maximum compensation period is four years.

The Danish arrangements are a form of 'flexicurity'; that is, an attempt to increase mobility and facilitate matching in the labour market through a combination of generous compensation systems and the absence of job security legislation (Egger and Sengenberger 2003). Andersen and Pedersen refer to it as 'workfare-light' (2006, 14). Activation for youth has all revolved around training in Denmark. In recent years researchers have invented a new concept in an attempt to distinguish the main features of a constructive future policy mix: *mobication* (Andersen 2009), a combination of *mobility* and *education*. Underpinning the concept is the notion that investment in education and job competencies is the main road to mobility and job security.

Finland

In Finland, training measures have also had a very high priority. Unemployed youth are often referred to standard training programs, as in Denmark. But the training focus is not as dominant as in Denmark. Youth measures also include more traditional labour market policy approaches. As in Denmark, activation has been a keyword in the framework of youth measures. This has meant a drive for increased flexibility and individual adaptation of measures as well as coordination between social services, social insurance systems and the labour exchange. Special service centres for unemployed youth have been established. It is possible to use funding from unemployment insurance to create employment opportunities for the long-term unemployed, e.g. through hiring grants.

The activation policy is based on a form of youth guarantee. A job is to be offered within three months of the start of unemployment. The Finnish youth guarantee is also linked to a training guarantee. The service centres are free to arrange training or work placement, all depending on the individual's background and needs. The process is based on an individualized action plan. Those who do not participate actively in the activities offered can be refused assistance.

Employment grants are an important feature of Finnish labour market policy. There are two types of grants: one for private companies and one for the public sector (Eurostat 2004). These measures are primarily directed at long-term unemployed youth who risk becoming permanently excluded from the labour market.

Norway

In Norway, labour market policy measures for youth and young adults are organized within the framework of a youth guarantee. A special guarantee to activate unemployed youth under age 20 was formulated in the late-1970s. In the mid-1990s the system expanded to include long-term unemployed aged 20–24 years. In accordance with the principles of activation policy, sanctions in the form of reduced or denied assistance are used when an unemployed person refuses to participate in assigned activities. The youth guarantee is a part of the package usually referred to as Reform 94 (Hardoy et al. 2006). Under that reform, everyone has the right to a three-year upper secondary school education.

Those unemployed for four months or longer are called to the labour exchange for an interview in order to design an individual action plan. Failure to adhere to the plan leads to the person losing the right to social assistance. The guarantee comprises a number of activities such as work placement, participation in job clubs, labour market training and standard school-based training. There is a supply of shorter vocational streams connected to the apprentice system for those who have not completed a secondary school education. The aim of these streams – even if the education contains less school based subjects – is that the participant gains a licence connected to a recognized trade.

Sweden

Sweden also has a youth guarantee aimed at providing youth and young adults under 25 with some form of activity after no more than 100 days of unemployment. There is a municipal follow-up responsibility for tracking down youth under 20 years of age who are not studying. Under a 1998 amendment of the Social Services Act, social assistance to unemployed youth can be made conditional on taking part in different activities.

In Sweden the coordination of measures has been a major problem. The division of responsibility between secondary schools, social services and the labour exchange has been unclear. Labour market policy measures in the framework of the youth guarantee have been financed by the national Labour Market Administration but organized by the municipalities. There has been tension between the socio-political aim of the program at the municipal level and the labour market policy intentions at the government level. A new job guarantee replaced the old youth guarantee in 2008. The Labour Market Administration was given the full responsibility. Individual coaching and active job search are priorities within the new job guarantee.

The follow-up responsibility has primarily meant that municipalities have had to keep informed about employment among youth under age 20. A review of the follow-up responsibility carried out some time ago shows major deficiencies, including a lack of information on about 30,000 youth under age 20 who are outside the education system (National Agency for Education 2006).

In contrast to the other Nordic countries, training measures have been of minor importance in Sweden, and have not been designed to accommodate unemployed youth under the age of 25. Sweden also differs in terms of the sharp demarcation between education and job training within labour market policy and the standard education system. The fundamental concept has been that training provided with labour market policy funding should eliminate temporary bottlenecks and short-term competence shortages in the labour market.

Comparison of Labour Market Policies

The youth labour market strategies of the Nordic countries can be demarcated from each other in terms of *flexibility* and *breadth*. Sweden stands out as the country that to the highest extent separate measures within employment policy and education policy, especially compared to Denmark and Norway. One explanation may be that labour market authorities in Sweden want to keep the costs of youth-specific strategies low. Educational measures are very expensive compared to job coaching and job placement. A complementary explanation may be that Sweden lacks the systems of recognized trades and corresponding trade licences that are characteristic of countries with strong apprentice systems. It is therefore not easy to assess educational measures against labour demand. It also makes it difficult to equip the young unemployed who have little education with job capabilities that are demanded by the employers. This, in turn, has clear implications for the possibility to reach policy goals connected to fairness and social inclusion.

Strategies for Fair and Effective School-to-work Transitions

How do we judge the overall fairness and equity of the Nordic countries' arrangements with respect to young people and work? The dual concepts of fairness and effectiveness often surface in political contexts. The issue in education and labour market policy has been that measures should compensate for differences in conditions related to gender, class and ethnicity. The overall goal is to promote social inclusion. In the Nordic countries there has traditionally been a strong focus on concepts like fairness and social equality, partly reflecting the strong position of unions and social democratic political parties since the early twentieth century. Naturally these concepts also influence the understandings of what measures should be used to integrate less privileged groups of youth into the labour market.

There are European Union (EU) imperatives that influence national policies in these areas. Within the Lisbon process (an action and development plan for the economy of the EU between 2000 and 2010), the EU defined clear and measurable goals for countries to reduce perceived fairness deficiencies relating to the proportion of youth who fail to complete an upper secondary school education, become unemployed, etc. There are 29 fairness indicators for education systems in EU member countries. Several of these indicators are linked to the Program for International Student Assessment (PISA) studies performed regularly by the OECD. PISA studies measure the outcome effectiveness of education systems in different countries. The aim of these indicators is to create measures of fairness.

It is against this background that it is interesting to compare the labour market situation for young people in the different Nordic countries. Table 12.6 provides some comparative data. The differences between Denmark and Norway on the one hand, and Finland and Sweden on the other hand, can partly be explained by differences in economic conditions. But institutional conditions may also play an important role. As earlier discussed, it is likely that the education measures offered at different levels and with different orientations, both within and outside the standard education system, have facilitated efforts to reduce unemployment and inactivity in Norway and especially Denmark.

Table 12.6   Percentage unemployed and inactive by age in 2007

Country	20–24 years	25–29 years
Denmark	8.2	8.9
Finland	13.3	13.3
Norway	8.7	10.4
Sweden	13.1	10.6

Source: OECD, Education at a Glance 2009.

Denmark and Sweden are, as we have seen in earlier sections, the outliers among the Nordic countries in terms of upper secondary school education systems and the design of supplementary measures for youth who are unemployed and have difficulty coping with standard training programs. Sweden's fairness strategy aims to make conditions equitable for all youth by having the same curriculum as far as possible for everyone. One important aim has until recently been to make it possible to achieve admission to post-secondary studies. By contrast, Denmark has opted for several alternative education pathways at different levels. The Swedish strategy has resulted in a larger proportion having difficulty completing an upper secondary school education, more long-term unemployed and increased dependence on social assistance. In Denmark the alternative education measures have allowed a larger proportion of youth and young adults to avoid unemployment and inactivity. The level of dependence on long-term unemployment benefits and long-term social assistance is low. However, does the Danish strategy come with a higher cost in the long run for those trained as apprentices? The policy may contribute to segmentation, reduced mobility and greater social gaps. It has also sometimes been claimed that traditional forms of initial vocational training have lost their relevance in the modern technology and knowledge intensive economy. If this is true, it would speak in favour of the Swedish strategy even if it has a social price in the short run.

From a social distribution perspective it could be claimed that vocational training offers youth from less privileged home environments better opportunities of obtaining work and increasing income (see Estevez-Abe, Wersen and Soskice 2001 and Ashton and Green 1996). As we have indicated, the Danish experience suggests that this probably is the case. Students in vocationally orientated training programs more often come from low-income families without experience of higher education than students in programs preparing for further studies. Apprenticeships and other complementary training measures for youth and young adults seem to have effects that are desirable and contribute to social redistribution.

Summary and Conclusion

Our aim in this chapter has been to analyse differences between the Nordic countries in the field of education and labour market policy against the background of variations in institutional conditions. In which way does initial vocational training differ between the countries? What efforts are made for young people who have problems at school and resultant difficulties in getting jobs? Even though the Nordic countries show similarities in terms of socio-economic and social conditions, there is much that separates them. Welfare policy ambitions may be similar, but when we examine the conditions for youth in establishing themselves in the labour market and earning a living, we find significant variations. Youth face considerably less favourable labour market conditions in Finland and Sweden than in the other Nordic countries. The measures aiming at facilitating social inclusion among youth also vary considerably.

Upper secondary school education shows clear differences between the countries. Finland and Sweden offer mainly school based and preparatory vocational training programs. The other countries offer apprenticeship training linked to a regulated system of trade licenses. Apprenticeship training offers no guarantee of low dropout. The dropout problem in Danish apprenticeship training is large compared to Finland, despite Finland having a school based and academically more demanding vocational training system. One factor that mitigates problems in Denmark, Finland and Norway, compared to Sweden, is the availability of multifaceted training options at various levels. These three countries also have no upper age limit for upper secondary studies. More extensive efforts are made to prepare students for upper secondary school studies, partly through an optional supplementary year, while follow-up of those who drop out of school is also more extensive and action orientated. Sweden allocates fairly modest resources for special youth labour market policy programs. This is reflected not only in higher youth unemployment, but also in a higher level of inactivity among young adults. While Denmark, for example, activates unemployed and poorly educated individuals through various education programs, long-term unemployment and social assistance dependence is more common among youth in Sweden. We also found that Sweden, in contrast to the other Nordic countries, differs by a more rigid demarcation between the standard education system and labour market policy measures. In Sweden, standard education is in principle not permitted within the framework of labour market policy.

The different institutional settings seem to have different effects on social inclusion patterns for youth. The clearest differences can again be seen between Denmark and Sweden. Vocational training and labour market policy in Denmark is based on coordination, individual adaptation and generous funding conditions. Educational measures and labour market policy in Sweden are characterized by a division of responsibility between the school, labour exchange and social services, strict demarcations between standard education and youth labour market policy measures, and an emphasis on general or academically orientated upper secondary school education.

The question remains, finally, whether anything can be said about the effectiveness of these different strategies. We wish to formulate a few suggestions. The experience from the Nordic countries suggests that measures for unemployed and inactive youth would benefit from closer coordination between different actors: the school, labour exchange, social services and labour market organizations. There are also strong arguments for the proposition that initial vocational training in various forms and at different levels should be offered in the framework of the upper secondary school and that regulated apprenticeship training offer favourable conditions for entering the labour market. There is also a strong case for more generous opportunities for vocational education for young adults (over the age of 20). In general, the demarcations between standard education and labour market policy should be re-examined.

References

Agell, J. 1999. On the benefits from rigid labour markets. Norms, market failures, and social insurance. *Economic Journal*, 109(453), F143–F164.

Ahlberg, K., Bruun, N. and Malmberg, J. 2006. Employment protection, mobility and economic growth, in *Routes to a more open labour market,* edited by J. Olofsson and M. Zavisic. Stockholm: The National Institute for Working Life Yearbook, 159–67.

Andersen, J. and Pedersen, J. 2006. *Continuity and Change in Danish Active Labour Market Policy: 1990–2005,* Welfare State Change Conference, St. Restrup, Denmark, 13–15 January. Available at: http://www.socsci.auc.dk/welfare/conference-2006/papers/Paper-Goul-Jacob.pdf/ [accessed: 11 April 2011].

Andersen, S. 2009. *Responses to Growing Unemployment and Mismatch between Skills and Job Openings in EU Member States.* Available at: http://faos.ku.dk/pdf/artikler/videnskabelige_artikler/2009/tackling_job-losses_-_varieties_of_european_responses.pdf/ [accessed: 11 February 2011].

Ashton, D. and Green, F. 1996. *Education, Training and the Global Economy.* Cheltenham: Edward Elgar.

Bassanini, A. and Duval, R. 2006. *Employment Patterns in OECD Countries: Reassessing the Role of Policies and Institutions.* OECD Economics Department Working Papers No. 486, Paris: OECD.

Dølvik, J, and Eldring, L. 2006. *The Nordic Labour Market Two Years after the EU Enlargement. Mobility, Effects and Challenges,* Copenhagen: Nordic Council of Ministers.

Education at a Glance 2008. OECD indicators. Paris: OECD.

Education at a Glance 2009. OECD indicators. Paris: OECD.

Education at a Glance 2010. OECD indicators. Paris: OECD.

Equity of the European Education Systems. A Set of Indicators. European Group of Research on Equity of the Education Systems. 2005, A Project supported by the European Commission Directorate General of Education and Culture. Available at: http://www.okm.gov.hu/download.php?ctag = download&docID = 296. [accessed: 11 April 2011].

Esping-Andersen, G. 1990. *The Three Worlds of Welfare Capitalism.* Cambridge: Polity Press.

Estevez-Abe, M., Iversen, T. and Soskice, D. 2001. Social protection and the formation of skills: A reinterpretation of the welfare state, in *Varieties of Capitalism. The Institutional Foundation of Comparative Advantage,* edited by P. Hall and D. Soskice. Oxford: Oxford University Press, 145–83.

ETUI. n.d. Union Coverage Rates, Available at: http://www.worker-participation. eu/National-Industrial-Relations/Across-Europe/Trade-Unions2 [accessed: 11 March 2011].

Eurostat 2004. *Labour Market Policy Statistics. Qualitative reports. Finland.* Available at: http://circa.europa.eu/Public/irc/dsis/labour/library?l = / publications/qualitative_descriptions/qualitative_2004/qualitative_fi-2004/_ EN_1.0_&a = d [accessed: 11 February 2011].

Hall, P. and Soskice, D. (eds) 2001. *Varieties of Capitalism. The Institutional Foundation of Comparative Advantage.* Oxford: Oxford University Press

Hardoy, I., Røed, K., Torp, H. and Zhang, T. 2006. *Ungdomsgarantien for 20–24-åringer: Har den Satt Spor?* Oslo: Institute for Social Research.

International Labour Organization (ILO) 2000. *Employing Youth: Promoting employment-intensive growth.* Geneva: ILO.

Johansson, H. 2006. *Svensk Aktiveringspolitik och Aktiveringsgarantin i Nordisk Belysning.* Report to ESS (Expertgruppen för Samhällsekonomiska Studier). Stockholm: Fritzes.

Kangas, O. and Palme, J. (eds) 2005. *Social Policy and Economic Development in the Nordic Countries.* Basingstoke: Palgrave MacMillan.

Manning, A. 2003. *Monopsony in Motion. Imperfect Competition in Labor Markets.* Princeton: Princeton University Press.

Ministry of Education, Science and Culture. 2002. *The Education System in Iceland.* Monograph 6, Reykjavík: Ministry of Education, Science and Culture.

National Agency for Education (Skolverket) 2006. Information om icke skolpliktiga ungdomar – det kommunala uppföljningsansvaret. Available at: http://www.skolverket.se [accessed: 1 February 2011].

Neumark, D. and Wascher, W. 2004. Minimum wages, labor market institutions, and youth unemployment: A cross-national analysis. *Industrial & Labor Relations Review,* 57(2), 223–48.

Organisation for Economic Co-operation and Development (OECD). n.d. Benefits and Wages: OECD Indicators. Available at: www.oecd.org/els/social/ workincentives, [accessed: 14 March 2011].

Olofsson, J. and Panican, A. (eds) 2008. *Ungdomars väg Från Skola till Arbetsliv. Nordiska Erfarenheter.* Köpenhamn: Nordic Council of Ministers.

Skedinger, P. 2005. *Hur Höga är Ingångslönerna?* IFAU (Institutet för arbetsmarknadspolitisk utvärdering), Uppsala: IFAU.

Walther, A., Hejl, G., Jensen, T. and Hayes, A. 2002. *Youth Transitions, Youth Policy and Participation.* Research Project YOYO. Working Paper 1–2002, Tübingen, Germany: IRIS (Institut für regionale Innovation und Sozialforschung).

Chapter 13

University Student Employment in Germany and Australia and its Impact on Attitudes toward Union Membership

Damian Oliver

Trade unions across the developed world face a crisis of membership, especially among the young. If unions are to recover their strength, they need to dramatically alter their membership profile to include more young workers. To meet this objective, trade unions in a number of countries have begun targeting university students as potential members. The study conducted for this chapter explores the factors that influence university students' attitudes towards union membership. Specifically, it examines two questions: First, do experiences of union membership during student employment affect students' intention to join a trade union following graduation? Second, does the duration, intensity and quality of student employment affect university students' intention to join a trade union following graduation? The focus is on university students because across the developed world combining part-time employment with university study is now commonplace. Further, university students are a growing component of the youth workforce.

The chapter compares the intentions of German and Australian university students. Germany and Australia are logical choices for the comparative focus of the study. Both countries have a similarly high standard of living and most university students in each are employed, comprising a significant portion of the labour market. Historically, the two countries have also given an institutional role to unions in determining wages and conditions. As detailed later in the chapter, union membership has declined in both countries to around one in five workers. The case study environments also differ on two important dimensions. Outside the professions and some licensed trades, entry into most occupations in Australia does not rely on possessing particular qualifications (Richardson and Tan 2007). Consequently, university students are able fill a wider range of roles and are often sought after by employers in many service industries for their perceived ability and flexibility (Lucas and Ralston 1996). The German labour market by contrast exhibits a much tighter connection between qualifications and occupations (Bosch 2010). Senior jobs in the retail and hospitality industries that may be filled by university students in Australia are more likely to be reserved for workers who have completed relevant vocational training. German and Australian university students therefore typically work in a different spread of industries. The second difference is the distribution of union membership. The German trade union movement remains heavily concentrated in blue collar industries (Ebbinghaus 2000) whereas Australian unions represent a greater proportion of service sector and professional workers (ABS 2010). Unions therefore have greater visibility and perceived relevance for students in Australia than in Germany, in relation to their current situation as student workers and their future roles in the graduate labour market.

Both the German and Australian components of the study conducted for this chapter demonstrated that the quality of student employment affects whether students intend to later join a union, but whether they work, or how much they work, has no impact on intentions. University students in low quality jobs (defined here as being demanding as well as lacking the opportunity to exercise and develop skill and independent judgment) are less likely to want to join a union. Of much greater consequence though for unions looking to recruit young student workers is direct exposure to union membership during the student phase. Here, Australian unions have an advantage over their German counterparts because of the structural differences between their labour markets and distribution of union membership.

University Students – A Growing Part of the Youth Labour Market

Access to tertiary education has continued to expand in developed countries. In 1995, the average enrolment rate of 20–29 years olds for Organisation for Economic Co-operation Development (OECD) countries was 18.41 per cent. By 2008, this had increased to 24.89 per cent. The participation rates in Australia and Germany are higher than the OECD average but have nonetheless increased over the same period. Between 1995 and 2008, the enrolment rates of 20–29 years olds in Germany increased from 20.29 per cent to 28.38 per cent. In Australia, the proportion rose from 23.14 per cent in 1995 to 33.00 per cent in 2008 (OECD 2010a: Table C1.2).

The proportion of university students combining study with paid employment is also increasing in many countries. Australia, second only to the Netherlands at 75 per cent (Euro Student 2008), has one of the highest rates of university student employment in the world. In 2006, 70.6 per cent of Australian full-time undergraduate students worked an average of 15 hours per week during semester (James et al. 2007). In 2006, 63 per cent of German undergraduate students worked an average of 11 hours per week during semester (Isserstedt et al. 2007: 316). These levels of student employment in Australia and Germany are comparable to many other OECD countries. In the United States (US), various studies have put the rate of term-time employment as 55–80 per cent (Miller 1997; King 1998); in England and Wales, 47 per cent (Callender and Wilkinson 2003) and in Canada, just under half the tertiary student population engage in paid work (Marshall 2010).

Trade Union Membership and University Student Workers

Germany and Australia share a history of high trade union membership and strong institutional support for the involvement of trade unions in wage-setting (Visser 2006). In the case of Germany, this was through industry-wide collective bargaining and co-determination in many areas, including the regulation of vocational training and apprenticeships (Keller and Kirsch 2011). In Australia, trade union involvement was secured through the award system and a series of accords with government. One of the criticisms of this approach of trade unionism is that it left unions remote from their membership (Peetz 1998). When the institutional supports began to erode around 30 years ago, both German and Australian trade unions experienced a precipitous decline in membership. Between the early-1980s and 2003, union density decreased in Germany from 34.9 per cent in 1980 to 22.6 per cent and in Australia from 49.5 per cent in 1982 to 22.9 per cent (Visser 2006: 45). Although total union density in both countries is currently between one in five and one in four workers respectively, the distribution of union members in Germany and Australia differs markedly. German union membership remains concentrated in mining, manufacturing and utilities, with much lower densities recorded in the commercial and services sector. By comparison, as Table 13.1 shows, Australian union membership is more evenly distributed throughout the workforce.

Table 13.1   Trade union density by industry, Germany and Australia, 1997

Year	Germany (per cent)	Australia (per cent)
Total	30.4	30.3
Primary[a]	18.2	7.1
Industry[b]	59.5	38.7
Building	17.6	33.5
Commerce[c]	9.6	18.6
Transport & Communication	74.0	51.3
Finance	14.5	35.5
Services[e]	19.9	31.1
Government	44.1	43.5
Education	34.2	49.3

Notes: 1997 is the latest year for which industry-level membership data in Germany are available. The density calculations for Germany are overstated because the union membership figures include non-active members (students and retirees). The corresponding industry categories for the Australian data are: (a) Agriculture, forestry and fishing; (b) Mining, Manufacturing, Utilities; (c) Wholesale trade, Retail trade, Accommodation, cafés and restaurants; (d) Transport and storage, Communication services; (e) Property and business services, government administration and defence, education, health and community services, cultural and recreation services, personal and other services.

Source: Ebbinghaus 2000, OECD 2010b, ABS 1998.

Mirroring trends in other countries, the decline in union membership in Germany was especially marked among the young. Fewer young German workers today join trade unions in comparison to earlier cohorts, which has accelerated the overall decline in trade union membership (Schnabel and Wagner 2008). Between 1998 and 2006 the membership density among young workers (those aged less than 30 years) in West Germany fell from 10 per cent to 8 per cent, and in East Germany, it decreased more dramatically over the same period from 15 per cent to 5 per cent (Statistisches Bundesamt 2008: 395). Among this decreasing base, young union members are also less active. According to the German Youth Institute, the proportion of young members who were active in their union has decreased from 65 per cent in 1992 to 54 per cent in 2003 in East Germany and 50 per cent in West Germany (Gaiser, Gille and de Rijke 2006). At the same time, German youth continue to express relatively positive attitudes towards unions and collective action. In a 2003 survey by the German Youth Institute, 38 per cent of young people in West Germany and 37 per cent of young people in East Germany expressed a high level of trust in trade unions (Gaiser et al. 2006). Indeed, German youth placed greater trust in trade unions than in the government, the church and political parties.

Similarly, Australian studies have consistently found that a low level of union membership among young workers coexists with high levels of support for trade unions. Data from the Australia at Work study (van Wanrooy et al. 2007: 89) showed that although union density among workers aged 16–24 was only 12.0 per cent, a further 13.2 per cent of young workers would join a union if asked. Teicher et al. (2007) identified an even larger representation gap (the difference between current union density and the proportion who say they would join given the opportunity) among young Australian workers. According to data from the Australian Worker Representation and Participation Survey, only 10.6 per cent of those aged less than 25 years belonged to a union but the total potential union density for young workers is 46.2 per cent (Teicher et al. 2007: 130).

The gap between sentiment and membership among young workers is not peculiar to Germany and Australia; rather it has been observed in the United Kingdom (UK), Canada, the US (Bryson et al. 2005), and New Zealand (Haynes, Vowles and Boxall 2005). Bryson et al. (2005: 166) found that even though the union density of younger workers in Canada, the US and Britain is less than half that of older workers, this can mostly be explained by young workers being less likely to work in unionized workplaces. Waddington and Kerr (2002) found no evidence that falling levels of union membership among young British workers can be attributed to any generational shift in attitudes. Instead, they identify workplace size, rates of labour turnover and the direct effects of employer resistance as the principal factors behind the decline in union membership (Waddington and Kerr 2002: 314). Haynes et al. (2005: 110) similarly found that differences in attitudes to unions between young and older workers in New Zealand are 'slight or non-existent'. Rather, a major reason why young New Zealand workers are less likely to belong to a union is that they are more likely than older colleagues to be in a workplace with low union presence (Haynes et al. 2005: 111). Evidence to the contrary – that young workers are less supportive of trade unions than in the past – is much harder to find. Allvin and Sverke (2000) claimed that younger Swedish workers were adopting more instrumental attitudes toward trade unions and were less ideologically motivated to join unions. However, their study had a number of limitations; principally, that the sample was limited to blue-collar workers who were already union members and that it did not examine young workers as a distinct group.

Considering attitudes toward union membership during the student employment phase is crucial because student employment typically occurs during a critical period for union membership patterns. Visser (2002: 416) observed that 'people join the union within the first few years following their entry into the labour market, or they do not'. Even though student employment may be a transitional phase occurring prior to full-time graduate employment, early exposures to trade union activity still matter. Booth, Budd and Munday (2010) found that nearly half (43.8 per cent) of US workers experiencing union membership for the first time were still studying at the time of their exposure. Wholesale and retail trade was one of the most common industries for first exposure to union membership, along with professional and related services and manufacturing. Oliver (2010) reported that Australian graduates who had had a positive experience of trade union membership during their student phase were eight times more likely than other graduates to have joined a union 12 months after finishing their studies. Similarly demonstrating the importance of examining university students' attitudes towards union membership was a study by Lowe and Rastin (2002) which revealed Canadian university graduates who had previously belonged to a union had a greater willingness to join a union than those who had never been union members. Hence:

Hypothesis 1: *Current or former union members will be more likely to want to join a union after graduation.*

A further reason to suspect that student employment might constitute a critical window of opportunity for stimulating preferences for union membership is the conditions of typical student jobs. Low job quality is associated with a stronger preference for union membership among adult workers (Barling, Fullagar and Kelloway 1992). Contrary to strereotypes, student jobs vary markedly in terms of job quality (Mortimer 2003: 215). While some work in low skilled, low paid jobs, university students may be valued workers and are frequently extended opportunities for skill development and autonomy beyond typical entry-level jobs in retail or hospitality (Lucas and Ralston 1996). Dekker, Greenberg and Barling (1998) investigated union attitudes among a sample of high school and first-year university students. They found that, contrary to their hypotheses, job quality (which was defined in their study as skill variety, task significance and feedback) was not associated with union attitudes. However, Lowe and Rastin (2000), who used panel data to examine Canadian university graduates, found converse results.

They demonstrated that graduates whose student jobs allowed greater decision-making expressed less willingness to join a union. The study reported in this chapter adopts a similar approach, focusing on two dimensions of job quality: job demands and skill discretion. It hypothesizes that:

Hypothesis 2: *Student job demands will be positively related to willingness to join a union after graduation.*

Hypothesis 3: *Student job skill discretion will be negatively related to willingness to join a union after graduation.*

The increasing duration and intensity of student employment could also have a bearing on union attitudes. Lowe and Rastin (2000) found that respondents who had worked more years in part-time employment expressed greater willingness to join a union. A longer period in part-time employment could diminish the sense that student employment is just a transitional phase and result in work experiences having a more durable impact on attitudes. No existing studies of student workers appear to have examined the impact of working hours on willingness to join a union. However, working hours have been reported to be a predictor of union membership status among the general working population, with workers who work more hours being more likely to belong to a union (Deery and DeCieri 1991). Students working more hours may also be more likely to be positive toward trade union membership:

Hypothesis 4: *The proportion of time spent working since commencing university studies will be positively related to willingness to join a union after graduation.*

Hypothesis 5: *The number of hours worked in student employment will be positively related to willingness to join a union after graduation.*

In testing for the effect of duration of employment, working hours, job demands and the opportunity to exercise skill and discretion on trade union membership, the analysis controls for other factors known to influence workers' attitudes toward union membership. These include age and socio-economic background (Charlwood 2002), whether parents were trade union members (Kelloway and Newton 1996, Blanden and Machin 2003) as well as discipline of study (Pesek, Raehsler and Balough 2006, Oliver 2009a).

Method

The Australian Study

The initial study was based on data from the Student Employment and Graduate Attitudes Survey, a panel study of Australian university students. The survey was designed to capture information about university students' experiences in the labour market, their attitudes toward work, employment and trade unions, and their expectations of what work would be like after they finished studying and moved into the graduate labour market. During 2003–2004, 1,200 university students nearing the end of their studies drawn from two universities in the same capital city participated in the study. Classes were approached based on a stratified sample and questionnaires were completed in class or returned later. In total, 2,000 questionnaires were distributed, giving a response rate of 60 per cent. The sample is broadly representative of the age and area of study profile of Australian university students. More information on the study can be found in Oliver (2006).

The German Study

A German replication of the initial study was undertaken in 2008–2009. The questionnaire was based on a translation of the Australian University Students and Work questionnaire 2003 (Oliver 2006). Survey responses were collected from students currently enrolled at five universities in Germany. The universities were a mix of older and newer universities, with four located in the former West Germany and one located in the former East Germany. At two universities, 402 students were asked to participate in the study and 387 completed questionnaires were received. At three other universities, 331 students were emailed a description of the study and invited to complete a questionnaire online, with 157 full responses received. In total, 544 usable surveys were returned. In comparison to the population of all university students (Isserstedt et al. 2007: 67), economics and business students are heavily over-represented, and engineering, IT and science students under-represented. Medicine students, comprising 4 per cent of all enrolments, were not included in the sample. For further details, see Oliver (2009b).

Data Items

The data items are summarized in Table 13.2 (categorical variables) and Table 13.3 (continuous variables). Beginning with the background characteristics, age and area of study are measured as categorical variables. Respondents were grouped into those aged 18–22, 23–24, and those aged 25 and over. The following area of study categories was used: business and law; arts, social science and creative arts; and science, engineering and information technology (IT).

Table 13.2   Categorical background and employment variables

Variable	Germany (per cent)	Australia (per cent)
Age****		
18–22	27.5	49.7
23–24	39.7	26.8
25+	32.8	23.5
Area of study****		
Business or Law	55.5	31.3
Arts, Social Science or Creative Arts	21.0	36.9
Science, Engineering or IT	23.6	31.8
Current employment status****		
Working	59.6	72.9
Not working	40.4	27.1
Industry****		
Education	27.5	5.0
Retail or wholesale trade	12.8	29.6
Hospitality	9.6	17.7
Manufacturing	6.4	3.7
Social Industries	4.1	9.9
Banking and finance	4.6	1.2
Public administration	3.5	2.1
Trades	2.3	4.5
Transport	2.0	1.4
Other industries	27.2	24.9
Union membership****		
Current union member	3.7	11.6
Former union member	4.0	17.8
Never a union member	92.3	70.6
Socio-economic background **		
Low/Middle-low	34.7	32.4
Middle	34.7	30.2
High/Middle-high	30.6	37.4
Parental union membership***		
At least one parent was a union member	26.5	33.8
Neither parent was a union member	73.5	66.2
N	544	1200

Note: Chi-square test results: * < 0.1 level of significance ** <0.05 level of significance *** < 0.01 level of significance **** < .0001 level of significance

Table 13.3   Means and standard deviations for continuous predictor variables and dependent variable

Variable	Germany		Australia	
	M	**Sd**	**M**	**Sd**
Proportion of time spent working while at university***	0.551	0.418	0.709	0.371
No of hours worked per week****	12.2	7.8	18.2	10.6
Job demands	19.8	4.1	19.5	5.0
Skill use and discretion	18.4	4.7	18.4	4.9
Preference for union membership as graduate ****	0.151	0.359	0.315	0.465

Note: t- test results: * < 0.1 level of significance ** <0.05 level of significance *** < 0.01 level of significance **** < .0001 level of significance

In the Australian study, socio-economic status (SES) was operationalized as an index combining parents' highest level of education and parents' occupation. This measure was taken from a previous study of Australian university student employment (Long and Hayden 2000). SES was categorized according to three levels, each comprising approximately a third of respondents: low to medium-low; medium; and medium-high to high. In the German study, SES was operationalized as a combination of parents' highest level of school education and highest post-school training or qualification and was subsequently categorized as low, medium and high. This measure takes account of the very strong connections between level of education and occupation and was used in a previous study of German university students and their employment patterns (Nienhüser 2001).

German and Australian respondents were asked if either parent had belonged to a trade union while they were at school. A quarter of German respondents (26.5 per cent) and a third of Australian respondents (33.8 per cent) reported that at least one of their parents had been a union member. Most students in the Australian (72.9 per cent) and German samples (59.6 per cent) were working. In comparison to the German participants, Australian survey participants had been in paid employment for a longer period of time since commencing at university (70.9 per cent vs 55.1 per cent) and worked more hours per week than German respondents (18.2 hours vs 12.2 hours).

There were also clear differences in the industries in which the Australian and German respondents worked. More than a quarter of German respondents were working at the university or were involved in tutoring or translation. This is quite common in Germany, where university students (especially those in the final years of their study, as was mostly the case in this sample) are frequently employed as *Studentische Hilfskräfte* (student assistants) (Nienhüser 2001). In the Australian sample, nearly half of the respondents worked in retail or wholesale trade or in hospitality.

Current trade union membership was much more common in the Australian sample than in the German sample, as was former union membership. Three times as many Australian respondents were union members (11.6 per cent) as German respondents (3.7 per cent). In addition, many more participants in the Australian sample had previously been a member of a union. Seven in ten Australian respondents (70.6 per cent) had never been a member of a trade union, compared with more than nine in ten German respondents (92.3 per cent). This is relatively consistent with the union density statistics presented in Table 13.1. German union density is concentrated in the manufacturing and energy industries, in which few students work. Even though union density in the Australian retail and hospitality industries is below the Australian average, it is still higher than in Germany.

Also included in the analysis were two job quality variables. The first variable measured job demands, using the six item Karasek (1979) scale. This achieved acceptable reliability in both samples (Cronbach's alpha = 0.80 (Australia), 0.79 (Germany). Possible values range from 6–30. A higher score indicates higher job demands. Skill use and discretion was measured using a combined six-item scale based on Karasek (1979). Possible values again range from 6–30. A higher score indicates greater skill use and discretion. The skill use and discretion scale also achieved acceptable reliability in the Australian sample (Cronbach's alpha = 0.80) but was less reliable in the German sample (0.67). Despite the differences in the industries that employed the German and Australian students and the number of hours worked, there were no significant differences in the job demands or skill discretion scores between the two countries.

The dependent variable of interest is preference for union membership after graduation. It is measured using a binary score based on the responses to the question: 'In the job that I expect to have 12 months after I graduate, I will want to belong to a union'. Respondents answering agree or strongly agree were coded 1, all other responses (neither agree nor disagree, disagree, strongly disagree, don't know) were coded zero. Approximately one in seven German respondents (15.1 per cent) and one in three Australian respondents (35.9 per cent) agreed or strongly agreed that they would want to join a union. Overall, respondents in the German sample were significantly less likely than respondents in the Australian sample to report that they would want to join a union after graduation.

Results

Preference for union membership after graduation was modelled using logistic regression. Two models are presented in Table 13.4. The first model includes the demographic control variables (age, parental union membership and socio-economic background) and the proportion of time spent working since starting university. By modelling the proportion of time spent working separately, we can include in the analysis students who are not currently working. There was no effect for the proportion of time spent working in the German sample. In the

Australian sample, the proportion of time spent working while at university did diminish respondents' preference for union membership after graduation, but the size of the effect is small. A ten percentage point increase in the proportion of time spent working since starting university study reduced the probability of wanting to join a union after graduation by around 1.5 percentage points.

Table 13.4   Regression of expectation of joining a union after graduation – job duration

	Germany		Australia	
	Exp(B)	**.**	**Exp(B)**	
Constant	0.136	****	0.338	****
Age 22–24	0.722		1.060	
Age 25+	0.829		0.645	**
Arts, Social Science or Creative Arts	1.728	*	2.095	****
Science, Engineering or IT	1.141		1.253	
Socio-economic status 2	0.794		0.819	
Socioeconomic status 3	0.931		0.840	
Parent union member	2.940	****	2.624	****
Current union member	7.404	****	2.175	****
Former union member	1.804		0.980	
Proportion of time spent working while at university	0.733		0.660	**
-2 Log likelihood	369.0		1326.9	
N	484		1149	

Sig levels: * < 0.1; ** < 0.05; *** < 0.01; **** < 0.001

In the German sample, there was no significant effect for age (at the 0.1 level) whereas in the Australian sample respondents aged 25 and older were around 1.5 times less likely than respondents aged 18–22 (the reference category) to want to join a union after graduation. This is the inverse of the odds ratio (0.654). In both the German and Australian samples, arts, social sciences and creative arts students were more likely than business and law students (the reference category) to want to join a union after graduation though the effect was stronger in the Australian sample (2.1 times more likely) than in the German sample (1.7 times more likely). The strongest predictors were the union membership status of the respondents and their parents. German and Australian respondents were more likely to want to join a union after graduation if either of their parents had belonged to a union than if neither of their parents had belonged to a union. The effect was marginally stronger among German respondents (2.9 times more likely) than among Australia respondents (2.6 times more likely). Respondents who were current union members were 7.4 times more likely in the German sample and 2.2 times more likely in the Australian sample, to want to join a union after graduation than respondents who had never been a union member. Socio-economic background did not predict the likelihood of wanting to join a union after graduation in either the Australian or German sample.

In the second model, working hours, job demands and skill use and discretion were added to the demographic control variables and the proportion of time spent working since starting university. Adding these variables noticeably changed the effect of the control variables on the preference for union membership in two ways. First, there was no longer any significant age effect in either the German or Australian sample. Second, being an arts student in the German sample no longer significantly increased the likelihood of wanting to join a union after graduation. Controlling for working hours, job demands and skill use and discretion increased the impact in the German sample of having a parent who is a union member from 2.9 times to 4.2 times. In the German sample, current union members were found to be 26.2 times more likely than those who have never belonged to a union to want to be a union member after graduation. When working hours, job demands

Table 13.5 Regression of expectation of joining a union after graduation – job intensity and job quality

	Germany		Australia	
	Exp(B)		**Exp(B)**	
Constant	0.191	*	0.234	**
Age 22–24	1.393		1.224	
Age 25+	1.524		0.676	
Arts, Social Science or Creative Arts	1.981		2.348	****
Science, Engineering or IT	1.391		1.191	
Socio-economic status 2	0.369	*	0.865	
Socioeconomic status 3	0.666		0.790	
Parent union member	4.241	***	2.899	****
Current union member	26.150	****	2.010	***
Former union member	9.410	***	0.946	
Proportion of time spent working	0.251	*	0.676	
Working hours	0.961		0.991	
Skill discretion	0.902	**	0.966	*
Job demands	1.101	*	1.052	**
-2 Log likelihood	133.7		889.159	
N	232		807	

Sig levels: * < 0.1; ** < 0.05; *** < 0.01; **** < 0.001

and skill discretion were added, former union members in the German sample were 9.4 times more likely than those who have never been members to want to join a union after graduation. German respondents from middle socio-economic backgrounds were 2.7 times less likely than those from low socio-economic backgrounds to want to join a union after graduation. In the larger Australian sample, the changes to the effect of the control variables were more modest.

Both job demands and skill use significantly predicted the likelihood of wanting to join a union after graduation among German and Australian respondents, but the effect size was small. A one unit increase in the job demands score (indicating greater job demands) increased the likelihood of wanting to join a union by 1.1 times in the German sample and 1.05 times in the Australian sample. A one unit increase in the skill use and discretion score (indicating greater skill use and discretion) reduced the likelihood of wanting to join a union after graduation by 1.1 times in the German sample and 1.04 times in the Australian sample. Working hours did not significantly change the likelihood of wanting to join a union after graduation in either sample (refer Table 13.5).

Discussion

Consistent with other studies looking at preferences for union membership (Bryson et al. 2005, van Wanrooy et al. 2007, Haynes et al. 2005, Waddington and Kerr 2002), the results show that young students (those aged under 25) are not more antagonistic toward trade union membership than their older colleagues. Indeed, the results from the first model suggest that, if there is any difference, it is that Australian students aged 25 and over are less favourable toward union membership than Australian students aged 18–21.

The results demonstrate that student employment affects the attitudes of German and Australian university students toward trade unions, albeit modestly. The number of working hours did not have any impact in either the German or the Australian sample. The proportion of time spent working since commencing at university had a small impact in the German sample and no impact in the Australian sample. Job demands and skill discretion were significant predictors of preference for union membership among Australian and German respondents, but the magnitude of the effect of job demands and skill discretion is similarly small in both samples. High job demands and low skill use and discretion in typical student jobs result in a lower expectation of future union membership, while students with less hectic and more fulfilling jobs are less likely to see a role for unions in their future working life. While the effect of job demands and skill discretion is small, it may have some effect at the margins. Students with particularly high-quality student jobs would be appreciably less likely to want to join a union after graduation than those with typical, lower-quality student jobs. Likewise, students with particularly low-quality student jobs may be more likely to want to join a union subsequently, even after they move into graduate employment.

The influence of student employment is small when compared with direct and indirect exposure to union membership. The children of union members, from both the Australian and German samples, are at least 2.5 times more likely than the children of non-members to say they expect to join a union once they finish their studies. This is a finding consistent with Blanden and Machin (2003) and Oliver (2010); in both studies parental union membership predicted actual union membership among young workers, not just a preference for union membership. Based on their strong preferences, the only barriers to becoming a union member for students with these characteristics may be their strong propensity to work in a non-unionized workplace (Haynes et al. 2005), employer resistance, or limitations with union organizing (Waddington and Kerr 2002: 313). Hence, there may be scope within union strategy to identify potential young union members by targeting union members who are parents of student workers.

Also strong were the effects of current union membership. In Germany, the number of respondents who were current union members was less than one in 20, but they form a very enthusiastic core. These respondents were 18 times more likely than those who had never belonged to a union to express a willingness to join a union after graduation. In the Australian sample, the effect of current union membership on future preferences was not as strong, but the proportion of current union members within the sample was three times larger. In the German sample, former members were also more likely than those who had never been a union member to say they would join a union after graduation. It may be that many of these respondents also comprise a 'core' of union supporters (Cregan 1999: 101) but for structural reasons are not current union members. For example, they may be not currently employed or they may be working in non-union workplaces. In Australia, former union members were less likely to want to join a union after graduation than non-members, although the effect was small and non-significant. This is potentially discouraging for Australian unions but the small size of the effect suggests that initial experiences of union membership have not created a cohort of disenchanted non-members (see also Oliver 2010: 513) and many may be more open to union membership at some later point.

The effect of discipline of study – another potential source of socialization – was also consistent across the two countries studied. In Australia, students studying arts and social science courses are much more likely than students studying business, science or engineering courses, to express support for joining a union after graduation. Arts, social science and creative arts students from the German sample were also more likely to want to join a union after graduation, as evident in the first model presented. This particular result was not significant for the second model, but the size of the effect remained similar. The possible sources of this are not explored in this study but the literature suggests two possible explanations. First, the curriculum of certain courses may prompt students to view unions in an unfavourable or favourable way. This may be in a general sense, for example, in that arts and humanities courses promote more left-wing ideologies (Pesek, Raeshler and Balough 2006) or more specific, such as business courses teaching that unions are a source of inflation (Shuster and Buckley 1981). Second, the discipline of study differences may reflect differences in what respondents know about their intended labour market after graduation. It may be that arts, social sciences and creative arts students know that they are more likely to work in the public sector or in occupations such as teaching, which are heavily unionized. Conversely, business, law, science engineering and information technology graduates are more likely to work in professional roles in industries that have low levels of unionization. Oliver (2010) suggests it is likely to be a combination of both. When looking at the union membership patterns of university graduates, there remained discipline of study effects, even after controlling for industry of graduate employment.

In relation to trade union membership during student employment, the differences between the German and the Australian samples are stark. German student employment does not systematically expose a sizable proportion of student workers to trade unions in the same way that Australian student employment does. Although a quarter of the German sample worked in education, where the union density was higher than overall union density, union membership in the main union *Gewersckshaft Erziehung und Wissenschaft* (Union for Education and Science) is primarily concentrated among full-time tenured teachers and professors (Ebbinghaus 2000: 299). Otherwise the next most popular industries for student employment – retail and wholesale trade and hospitality – are poorly organized. Only the 8.4 per cent of German respondents working in manufacturing or transport (see Table 13.1), are more likely to be union members than not.

The data in this study suggest that Australian student workers are much more likely to be exposed to union membership. The Australian retail union, the Shop, Distributive and Allied Employees' Association (SDA), is the largest union in Australia (SDA 2011a) and retains some presence in the retail sector particularly in the large supermarkets and department stores (SDA 2011b). Union density in the retail trade industry is currently 13.6 per cent, having declined from 21.3 per cent in 1998 (ABS 2010). Many Australian students spend some period working in these industries, starting in high school (Smith and Wilson 2002). Thus, although students working in the retail industry might not actually become union members, they have the opportunity to work in a unionized workplace and work under a union-negotiated collective agreement (Oliver 2011). In contrast, the retail sector is not as strongly unionized in Germany (around 10 per cent in 1998) and union density is particularly low in smaller outlets, where most of the employment is situated (Dribbusch 2005). The few student workers in the German sample who did have experience of trade union membership were generally older and had experience working in traditionally unionized industries, such as manufacturing or the public sector. It is also possible that they completed a traineeship or apprenticeship, although this was not covered in the survey.

This has direct consequences for how trade unions (and by extension, other organizations) might choose to engage with university students and graduates. The results from the Australian study demonstrate that discipline of study, even at the three broad groupings used here, has a much stronger effect on the formation of attitudes than experiences in student employment. Students studying degrees in the arts and social sciences disciplines were much more positive toward trade union membership than students studying business, science and engineering degrees. Australian and German unions looking to increase their appeal among student workers and recent graduates could focus on the discipline and career aspects and focus less on students in jobs outside of their field of study (Oliver 2009a).

For this reason, rather than pursue an approach focusing on the student job, unions in Germany might be better advised to develop alternative strategies. In Germany, practicums are used to gain practical experience working in a chosen field of study. Practicums are well embedded in Germany and are perceived by German universities, students and potential graduate employers as the best yardstick by which to assess a graduate's work readiness and are consequently given great weight by graduate employers and accordingly, students (Krawietz, Müßig-Trapp and Willige 2006: 3). Anecdotal evidence suggests that students attach more importance to finding and completing practicums than maintaining an ordinary student job, even though practicums are often poorly paid or unpaid and are almost always of a limited duration (usually up to three months). Reaching out to students undertaking practicums is one practical means by which the union movement in Germany is attempting to increase its influence (DGB-Jugend 2009). Such a strategy would concede that unionizing students in their student jobs is a secondary issue, but at the same time, lessens the need for inter-union collaboration which can be costly and create political tension (Oliver 2009a). In Australia, practicums are common requirements of professional degrees such as medicine, nursing, engineering, education and social work, but are not usually compulsory parts of generalist degrees in arts, business and science.

Conclusion

The results of this study suggest that the growing importance of student employment is having an impact on what Australian and German university students think about trade union membership. Australian students are employed for a larger proportion of the time they spend at university and work more hours than the German respondents, but these employment patterns have little or no impact on attitudes toward unions. That is, while both German and Australian respondents reported they were more likely to want to join a union after graduation if they currently worked in a job that was demanding or that offered fewer opportunities for skill use and discretion, the size of this effect was trivial. A significant influence on students' attitudes toward union membership however, was whether they were a current or former union member. Students in the German sample were much less likely than Australian respondents to be working in industries with above-average union densities and hence, were nearly four times less likely to have ever directly experienced union membership.

The results presented in this chapter suggest that trade unions in Australia and Germany looking to engage a new generation of young workers need to pursue creative and different strategies. In Australia, three factors offer unions cause for optimism. First, university student workers are clustered in the retail and hospitality industries, which make them easier to target, notwithstanding the low levels of union membership in these industries. Second, there are strong and growing professional unions, which can capitalize on the very positive attitudes towards unions expressed by students in some disciplines. Third, family influences continue to play out, suggesting an alternative route to identifying potential union members. In Germany, university students are much less likely than Australian students to experience trade union membership before finishing their studies. Discipline effects are also weaker among German university students. This leaves the practicum-centred strategies and exploiting family connections as the best approaches for German unions.

References

Australian Bureau of Statistics (ABS). 1998. *Weekly Earnings of Employees – August 1997*. Catalogue No. 6310.0, Canberra: ABS.

Australian Bureau of Statistics (ABS). 2010. *Employee Earnings, Benefits and Trade Union Membership – August 2009*, Catalogue No. 6310, Canberra: ABS.

Allvin, M. and Sverke, M. 2000. Do new generations imply the end of solidarity? Swedish unionism in the era of individualization. *Economic and Industrial Democracy*, 21(1), 71–95.

Barling, J., Fullagar, C. and Kelloway, E. 1992. *The Union and its Members*. New York: Oxford University Press.

Blanden, J. and Machin, S. 2003. Cross-generation correlations of union status for young people in Britain. *British Journal of Industrial Relations*, 41(3), 391–415.

Booth, J., Budd, J. and Munday, K. 2010. First-timers and late-bloomers: Youth-adult unionisation differences in a cohort of the U.S. Labor force. *Industrial and Labor Relations Review*, 64(1), 53–73.

Bosch, G. 2010. The revitalisation of the dual system in Germany, in *Vocational Training: International Perspectives*, edited by G. Bosch and J. Charest. New York: Routledge, 136–61.

Bryson, A. 2006. *Union free-riding in Britain and New Zealand*. [Online: Centre for Economic Performance Discussion Paper No. 713]. Available at http://cep.lse.ac.uk/pubs/download/dp0713.pdf [accessed: 4 March 2011].

Bryson, A., Gomez, R., Gunderson, M. and Meltz, N. 2005. Youth-adult differences in the demand for unionization: Are American, British and Canadian workers all that different? *Journal of Labor Research*, 26(1), 155–67.

Callender, C. and Wilkinson, D. 2003. *2002/03 Student Income and Expenditure Survey: Students' Income, Expenditure and Debt in 2002/03 and Changes since 1998/99.* Research Report RR487, London: Department for Education and Skills.

Charlwood, A. 2002. Why do non-union employees want to organise? Evidence from Britain. *British Journal of Industrial Relations,* 40(3), 463–91.

Cregan, C. 1999. *Young People in the Workplace: Job, Union and Mobility Patterns.* London: Mansell.

Deery, S. and Di Cieri, H. 1991. Determinants of trade union membership in Australia. *British Journal of Industrial Relations,* 29(1), 59–73.

Dekker, I., Greenberg, L. and Barling, J. 1998. Predicting union attitudes in student part-time workers. *Canadian Journal of Behavioural Science,* 30(1), 49–55.

DGB-Jugend (German Trade Union Federation Youth Organisation) 2009. *Praktika* [Online]. Available at http://www.dgb-jugend.de/studium/praktika [accessed 15 July 2009].

Dribbusch, H. 2005. *Trade Union Organising in Private Sector Services.* Düsseldorf: Wirtschafts- und Socialwissenschaftliches Institut.

Ebbinghaus, B. 2000. Germany, in *Trade Unions in Europe since 1945,* edited by B. Ebbinghaus and J. Visser. London: MacMillan, 279–338.

Euro Student 2008. *Social and Economic Conditions of Student Life in Europe 2008.* [Online]. Available at: http://www.eurostudent.eu/results/download_files/documents/Synopsis_of_Indicators_EIII.pdf [accessed: 3 March 2011].

Gaiser, W., Gille, M. and de Rijke, J. 2006. Beteiligung von jugendlichen in organisationen und der stellenwert von kirchen und gewerkschaften, in *Jugend und Politik,* edited by U. von Alemann, M. Morlok and T. Godewert. Baden-Baden: Nomos, 23–41.

Haynes, P., Vowles, J. and Boxall, P. 2005. Explaining the younger–older worker union density gap: Evidence from New Zealand. *British Journal of Industrial Relations,* 43(1), 93–116.

Isserstedt, W., Middendorff, E., Fabian, G. and Wolter, A. 2007. *Die Wirtschaftliche und Soziale Lage der Studierenden in der Bundesrepublik Deutschland 2006.* [Online: Bundeministerium für Bildung und Forschung]. Available at http://www.bmbf.de/pub/wsldsl_2009_kurzfassung.pdf [accessed: 3 March 2011].

James, R., Bexley, E., Devlin, M. and Marginson, S. 2007. *Final Report of a National Survey of Students in Public Universities.* [Online: Centre for the Study of Higher Education, University of Melbourne]. Available at: http://www.universitiesaustralia.edu.au/resources/135/Final%20AUSF%20report.pdf [accessed: 3 March 2011].

Karasek, R. 1979. Job demands, job decision latitude and mental strain: Implications for job redesign. *Administrative Science Quarterly,* 24(3), 285–309.

Keller, B. and Kirsch, A. 2011. Employment relations in Germany, in *International and Comparative Employment Relations: Globalisation and Change,* edited by G. Bamber, R. Lansbury and N. Wailes. 5th edition. Sydney: Allen & Unwin, 196–223.

Kelloway, E. and Newton, T. 1996. Preemployment predictors of union attitudes: The effects of parental union and work experiences. *Canadian Journal of Behavioural Science*, 28(2), 113–20.

King, J. 1998. Too many students are holding jobs for too many hours. *Chronicle of Higher Education*, 1 May, A72.

Krawietz, M., Müßig-Trapp, P. and Willige, J. 2006. *Praktika im Studium, HISBUS Blitzbefragung – Kurzbericht Nr. 13*. [Online: Hochschul-Informations-System] Available at https://hisbus.his.de/hisbus/docs/Praktika_im_Studium_09.06. pdf [accessed: 3 March 2011].

Long, M. and Hayden, M. 2000. *Student Income and Debt*. [Online: Australian Vice-Chancellor's Committee] Available at http://www.universitiesaustralia. edu.au/resources/138/2000%20Paying%20Their%20Way %20survey%20 report.pdf/ [accessed: 3 March 2011].

Lowe, G. and Rastin, S. 2000. Organizing the next generation: Influences on young workers' willingness to join unions in Canada. *British Journal of Industrial Relations*, 38(2), 203–22.

Lucas, R. and Ralston, L. 1996. Part-time student labour: Strategic choice or pragmatic response? *International Journal of Contemporary Hospitality Management*, 8(2), 21–4.

Marshall, K. 2010. Employment patterns of postsecondary students. *Perspectives* [Online: Statistics Canada], Summer, 5–17, Available at http://www.statcan. gc.ca/pub/75-001-x/2010109/pdf/11341-eng.pdf [accessed: 12 January 2011].

McDonald, P., Bailey, J., Pini, B., and Oliver, D. 2007. Compounding vulnerability? young workers and the impact of the Work Choices Act. *Australian Bulletin of Labour*, 33(1), 60–88.

Miller, B. 1997. Waiters, painters and Big Mac makers. *American Demographics*. February, 26.

Mortimer, J. T. 2003 *Working and Growing Up in America*. Cambridge MA: Harvard University Press.

Nienhüser, W. 2001. *Studentische Erwerbstätigkeit und Probleme im Studium – Eine empirische Analyse geschlechtspezifischer Unterschiede [University student employment and problems with study – an empirical analysis of sex-specific differences]*. Essen: Universität Essen.

Organisation for Economic Co-operation and Development (OECD). 2010a. *Education at a Glance 2010: OECD Indicators*. [Online]. Available at http:// dx.doi.org/10.1787/888932310415. [accessed: 12 January 2011].

Organisation for Economic Co-operation and Development (OECD). 2010b. *STAN database for structural analysis*. [Online] http://stats.oecd.org/Index. aspx?DataSetCode = STAN08BIS [accessed 12 January 2011].

Oliver, D. 2006. *Undergraduate Student Employment and its Effect on Graduates' Attitudes Toward Work, Employment and Trade Unions*. PhD Dissertation, Brisbane: Griffith University.

Oliver, D. 2009a. University student employment and experiences of union membership. *Labour & Industry*, 19(3), 97–136.

Oliver, D. 2009b. *Attitudes of University Students Toward Work, Employment, and Trade Unions: A Comparison between Germany and Australia*, report prepared for Hans Böckler Stiftung, Essen: University of Duisburg-Essen.

Oliver, D. 2010. Union membership among young graduate workers in Australia: Using the experience good model to explain the role of student employment. *Industrial Relations Journal*, 41(5), 505–19.

Oliver, D. (2011). University student employment and expectations of the graduate labour market. *Journal of Industrial Relations*, 53(1), 123–31.

Peetz, D. 1998. *Unions in a Contrary World*. Melbourne: Cambridge University Press.

Pesek, J., Raehsler, R. and Balough, R. 2006. Future professionals and managers: Their attitudes toward unions, organizational beliefs and work ethic. *Journal of Applied Social Psychology*, 36(6), 1569–94.

Richardson, S. and Tan, Y. 2007. *Forecasting Future Demands: What We Can and Cannot Know*. Adelaide: National Centre for Vocational Education Research.

Schnabel, C. and Wagner, J. 2008. The aging of the unions in West Germany, 1980–2006. *Jahrbücher für Nationalökonomie und Statistik*, 225(5/6), 497–511.

Shop, Distribute and Allied Employees Association (SDA). 2011a. *About Us* [Online]. Available at http://www.sda.org.au/about.php?p = about_us, [accessed: 14 January 2011].

Shop, Distribute and Allied Employees Association (SDA). 2011b. *Awards*. [Online]. Available at http://www.sda.org.au/about.php?p = awards. [accessed: 14 January 2011].

Shuster, M. and Buckley, J. 1981. The impact of management education on student attitudes toward labor unions. *The Mid-Atlantic Journal of Business*, 20(1), 9–20.

Smith, E. and Wilson, L. 2002. The new child labour? The part-time student workforce in Australia. *Australian Bulletin of Labour*, 28(2), 120–37.

Statistisches Bundesamt 2008. *Datenreport 2008 – Der Sozialbericht für Deutschland*. Wiesbaden: Statistisches Bundesamt.

Teicher, J., Holland, P., Pyman, A., Haynes, P. and Boxall, P. (2007) Australian workers: Finding their voice?, in *What Workers Say: Employee Voice in the Anglo-American Workplace*, edited by R. Freeman, P. Boxall and P. Haynes. Ithaca: Cornell University Press, 125–44.

Van Wanrooy, B., Oxenbridge, S., Buchanan, J., and Jakubauskus, M. 2007. *Australia at Work: The Benchmark Report*. Sydney: Workplace Research Centre.

Visser, J. 2002. Why fewer workers join unions in Europe: A social custom explanation of membership trends. *British Journal of Industrial Relations*, 40(3), 403–30.

Visser, J. 2006. Union membership statistics in 24 countries. *Monthly Labor Review*, 129(1), 38–49.

Waddington, J. and Kerr, A. 2002. Unions fit for young workers? *Industrial Relations Journal*, 33(4), 298–315.

Chapter 14

Declining Youth Membership: The Views of Union Officials

Linda Esders, Janis Bailey and Paula McDonald

Across the industrialized west there has been a sharp decline in union membership (Frege and Kelly 2003, Peetz 2002). Even more alarming are the lower unionization rates of young people and the steeper decline in these rates compared to older workers (Serrano and Waddington 2000). At the same time increasing numbers of young people still at school are participating in the labour market. There have been a number of explorations internationally of young people's union membership, but most either track membership decline over time, comparing adult and youth union density (Blanden and Machin 2003, Bryson et al. 2005, Haynes, Vowles and Boxall 2005, Canny 2002, OECD 2006), explore the general experience of young people in the labour market (for example, Mizen, Bolton and Pole 1999) or examine young people's view of unions (for example, Bulbeck 2008). This chapter however takes a different approach, exploring union officials' constructions of 'the problem' of low union density amongst youth. While the data in this study was obtained from Australia, the Australian context has strong similarities with those in other industrialized economies, not least because globalization has meant the spread of neo-liberal industrial relations (IR) policies and structures. Assuming that unions have choices open to them as to how they recruit and retain young people, it is important to analyse officials' construction of 'the problem', as this affects union strategizing and action.

The Australian context of youth labour is that around half of secondary school children are working at any one time, and around three quarters of school students will have been employed for some time before completing school (Smith and Wilson 2002, ABS 2008). However, young people's union membership is very low and rapidly declining; in 2009, only 10 per cent of employees in the age range 15–24 years were members of a union, compared with 30 per cent in 1990 (see Figure 14.1) (ABS 2010). Given that young people are the movement's future members, this indicates something of a developing crisis for unions. It is also a problem for young people themselves, and for society more generally. The escalating participation of youth in part-time jobs combined with low rates of youth union membership is occurring as reductions in job security have eroded various aspects of occupational health and safety, remuneration and redress for unfair employer conduct (Standing 2002). This is particularly so in the case of young people, who are often unaware of rights such as procedural fairness in dismissal and the options they can take if they are unfairly dismissed (Allegretto and Chase 2005). More generally, young people have less capacity to bargain with employers than older workers (Denniss 2005). Young people thus have heightened vulnerability in the labour market, and even more need of protection than other workers. In addition, if young members are retained by unions, they become ongoing members. Thus young workers are in many senses the future of the labour movement.

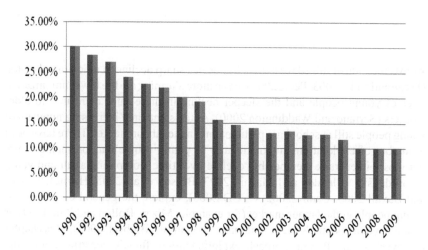

Figure 14.1   Union membership density for youth 15–24 years of age (ABS, 2009)

In this chapter, we firstly summarize the extant literature which addresses youth union membership issues and the various theoretical explanations for declining levels. In the empirical section of the chapter we address, in the Australian context, the way in which different actors within the union movement construct the problem of declining youth union membership and the challenge of recruiting young workers, via an analysis of interviews conducted with union organizers and other union officials.

Reasons for Union Membership Decline amongst Youth

The steep decline in youth membership rates in Australia has been variously ascribed to labour market, legislative and/or socio-cultural/political factors. Profound shifts in labour market composition have undoubtedly contributed to the decrease in youth membership. Employment has fallen in traditional strongholds of union membership such as the manufacturing and transport industries and the public sector (Bray, Waring and Cooper 2009) while the growth of the service sector and information technology (Peetz 1998), which do not have a strong union presence, has compounded the problem. To explain why these areas are 'non union', Pyman et al. (2009) studied unmet demand for union membership in Australia and found that the potential for recruitment is greatest amongst low-income workers, those who have been in the workforce for less than five years and those in 'routinized' occupations. Youth then, are clearly a prime target for union recruitment, with high levels of casual, part-time and low-paid employment, which often has poor working conditions (including low standards of occupational health and safety), high levels of workplace bullying and harassment, and low job quality (Allan, Bamber and Oliver 2006, Brosnan and Loudoun 2006, McDonald et al. 2007).

Paradoxically, however, the increasing likelihood of non-standard forms of employment amongst youth has increased unions' recruitment task, as casual (temporary) workforces are notoriously difficult to organize (Campbell 1996). The dimensions of the problem are illustrated by the fact that in 1983, three quarters of young employees were engaged in full-time employment, many of them in industries with strong union presence, but a mere one third in 2005 (ABS 2005), increasingly in service industry jobs with low union presence. The causes of the rise in non-standard work are manifold: higher education participation rates, fewer opportunities to take up 'career' positions in apprenticeships, employers' increasing use of 'flexible labour' strategies (Wooden 1998) and the nature of Australian's IR system, which has entrenched 'casual' employment (that is, by the hour employment with no security, although with a 'casual loading' to compensate for lost holiday and other benefits). Using shift-share analysis, Peetz (1990) estimated that up to 50 per cent of the decline in union membership can be attributed to these labour market changes and changes to occupational trends. Clearly young people still at school are restricted to part-time, casual jobs, which becomes a key component of their vulnerability.

The union membership crisis can also be explained in terms of legislation and/or government policy. Up until the mid-1990s, IR legislation legitimized unions as representative bodies that collectively bargained for their members (Harbridge, Fraser and Walsh 2006). In a paradigm break with the past, the *Workplace Relations Act* of 1996 and the *Workplace Relations Amendment (Work Choices) Act* of 2006 reversed this position. These pieces of legislation endorsed an individualistic approach to workplace negotiations. They introduced statutory individual agreements to Australia for the first time at a national level, and reduced protections for the low-paid by diminishing the power of third parties, such as unions and industrial tribunals, thereby allowing employer interests to predominate (Bray et al. 2009: 268). This 'de-legitimizing' of unions came about as a result of a linked series of changes, including the abolition of union preference clauses and unions' rights to access workplaces, restrictions on industrial action, and changes to freedom of association laws that emphasized the right *not* to associate – that is, not join a union – rather than the right to do so (Barton, Snell and Fairbrother

2008). While these changes affected all workers, they had a particularly strong impact on young workers who are more likely to work in non- or weakly organized workplaces.

Socio-political factors have also played a part in youth union membership decline. Specifically, a change in the Australian political paradigm produced a marked shift to the Right, typical of broader, global shifts to neoliberal economic philosophies. Even the movement's traditionally supportive ('left' leaning) political ally, the Australian Labor Party, has increasingly adopted neo-conservative, free-market ideologies (Crosby 2006). A feature of this new socio-political environment has been the move towards 'self-reliant individualism' centred around the notion of 'individual choice' (Johnson 2007: 196) that has had a particular impact on working life. Influential government discourses have disrupted and refashioned long-held narratives about a 'fair go all round' which was one of the cornerstones of Australia's IR system (Dyrenfurth 2007, Johnson 2007, Bailey, Townsend and Luck 2009). While general sympathy towards unions has increased over the past 20 years (Murray and Peetz 2010), the shift in government discourse coupled with legislative changes influenced public perceptions of unions' role affecting joining behaviour (Barnes 2006), including that of young people.

The reasons for declining youth union membership described above are largely beyond the direct control of the union movement. Arguably, however, the union movement failed to recognize and/or was ill-equipped to deal with the threats posed by changes to the employment, social, political and IR landscapes.

The impact of declining youth membership of unions is not just upon immediate aggregate numbers (and density) and therefore union resources, but has long term and possibly terminal implications for the movement. For example, research in the United States (US) by Budd (2009) shows that of those workers who are members of unions after the age of 40, 50 per cent were members by the age of 23, and 85 per cent were members by the age of 30, suggesting that there is a 'recruitment window' for new workforce recruits which unions need to exploit. If a young person has not joined a union in the first few years of employment, they are unlikely ever to become a member (Visser 2000). Further, Bryson et al. (2005) argue that if one's first work experiences are in a non-unionized workplace, and the experience meets a basic level of satisfaction, this increases the chances of remaining non-union. For all these reasons, therefore, it is timely to explore how union officials construct the problem of low youth membership. Some years ago, Pocock (1998: 19) argued that Australian unions were suffering from 'institutional sclerosis' and that the characteristics and features that served unions well in the past had not been modified to adjust to the neoliberal landscape. Failure to recognize and respond to the youth union membership problem may be one of the signs of 'institutional sclerosis'. Before we move to our data from union officials, however, we explore several theoretical approaches that other researchers have used in studies of young people's union membership.

Theoretical Perspectives Used to Explore the Decline in Young People's Union Density

Two approaches, social identity theory, and economic explanations (in particular, the notion of unionism as an 'experience good'), emphasize factors external to unions as central to youth union membership decline. In contrast, mobilization theory by emphasizing union agency attempts to explore issues *within* unions' control. These perspectives are canvassed below.

Social Identity Theory and Individualism

Approaching the youth union membership dilemma from a psychosocial perspective, some researchers have used social identity theory to question whether young people's reluctance to identify with 'collectivist' social groups such as unions is at the core of the decline in youth membership levels. Social identity theory is in part concerned with how and why individuals identify with and become involved with social groups and social movements. Allvin and Sverke (2000) examined youth union membership in Sweden where membership has been historically high, around 70 per cent (Fulton 2009). They concluded that although Sweden is a nation that has integrated union values into its socio-cultural, political and institutional realms more thoroughly than most other nations, young Swedes exhibit stronger 'instrumental' reasons for seeking union membership than older workers and do not have a firm ideological position about the benefits of collectivism. Similarly, Bulbeck (2008) found that many Australian high school students do not think they need unions and express negative views about them. In contrast, a study of young British employees by Waddington and Kerr (2002) found that only 14 per cent of young people cited ideological opposition to unions as the reason for not joining, and a wish to 'go it alone' with regards to workplace protection was not a common theme in their findings. Respondents often indicated, however, that they confronted structural barriers to joining unions, such as employers who did not allow or recognize unions and perceptions that joining a union might damage their careers (Waddington and Kerr 2002). Supporting these findings, Haynes et al. (2005) reported that young people have a more favourable view of unions than their older colleagues and support 'collective' notions of resolving workplace issues. Similar findings were cited by Bearfield (2003) who showed that 51 per cent of Australian youth (aged 18–24 years) would rather be in a union than not.

On balance, therefore, while a small number of studies suggest that young people are more individualistic than older people, some of this research is limited in focus (for instance, Allvin and Sverke's (2000) research only canvassed blue collar workers). Evidence suggests that while young people may be ignorant of unions (McDonald et al. 2010), they are not strongly ideologically opposed to them. Further, the 'generational cliches' that often colour popular perceptions are not supported by credible research, and ignore factors that relate to age *per se*. For instance, discussion of young workers and their attitudes to unions often fails to take into consideration that, typically, political attitudes do not stabilize until the mid-20s (Krosnick and Alwin 1989) and that attitudes to unions have been shown to change during workers' first few years in the workforce; that is, exposure to part-time, casual and other non-standard work arrangements increase young people's propensity to join unions (Lowe and Rastin 2000). Other explanations are found of the youth union membership dilemma, including explanations drawn from the fields of economics and marketing.

Unionism as an 'Experience Good'

Using the consumer theory of supply and demand, researchers have proposed that the 'cost' of union membership is high for young people because of 'supply constraints'; that is, young people have to go out of their way to contact unions in order to purchase membership because unions find it hard to reach them (Bryson et al. 2005, see also Bryson and Gomez 2005). This is because of the characteristics of the 'youth' workplace referred to earlier, including casualization, a propensity to work in low-waged occupations that are not well unionized, and frequent evening and weekend work. According to this view, supply and demand inefficiencies – a mismatch between demand and access to membership opportunities – are the major impediments to youth recruitment (Bryson et al. 2005).

To counter this mismatch between 'supply and demand', IR researchers have borrowed the notion of the 'experience good' – used in consumer theory to define a product or service that is difficult to assess for value and quality prior to purchasing, but one that the consumer understands more fully upon consumption (Haynes et al. 2005). Researchers using consumer theory as an analytical lens argue that lack of experience of and exposure to unions reduces young people's uptake of union membership. Bailey et al. (2010) further argue that unions need to understand fully their 'marketing' task with respect to young workers, including how they can provide low-cost 'sampling' experiences that nevertheless avoid the 'free rider' problem; that is, non-unionist workers who benefit from union action but do not join.

Mobilization Theory and 'Union Renewal'

The psychosocial and economic theories canvassed above place the weight of explanation on factors external to unions (although they offer some useful insights to unions regarding how they could more effectively recruit young people). In contrast, the sociological literature on mobilization and union renewal emphasizes union agency. Mobilization theory has as its central tenet the importance of *action* on the part of unions and workers, based on individual perceptions of injustice which in turn lead to member participation and mobilization (Kelly 1998, Johnson and Jarley 2004, Tilly 1978). The theory offers a dynamic view of unions and their interactions with their members, suggesting that union agency can achieve successful recruitment outcomes and increase member engagement, thereby overcoming 'institutional sclerosis'. A concept closely related to mobilization is 'union renewal' which refers variously to new organizing success, revitalization in terms of new strategies, more membership engagement and/or increased union density (Fiorito 2004, Heery 2003, Hickey, Kuruvilla and Lakhani 2010). One sign of union renewal would be an increase in youth union density. Many factors play a role in renewal, including union leadership and, arguably, conscious union strategies to appeal to 'identity groups' such as young workers. Mobilizing young people is difficult – but not necessarily impossible – for the reasons referred to previously: that is, the casual part-time nature of most youth jobs hinders the generation of a common injustice frame which is the precursor to mobilization (see Bailey et al. 2010). But how do unions themselves frame the problem of youth union membership?

Methods

The study therefore addressed the following research question: How do union officials construct the problem of declining youth union membership? The primary data were gathered by means of semi-structured interviews with senior elected officials in union peak bodies nationally and in various states, and less senior officials – mainly organizers – of individual unions in one state. To capture a range of views from different locations within the movement, six senior officials from the Australian Council of Trade Unions (ACTU), the national peak body, and state peak bodies were interviewed, and two 'youth recruitment officers'. These interviewees were located in five of Australia's eight states and territories. In addition, fourteen officials from ten individual unions in one state were also interviewed, consisting of an assistant general secretary and 13 organizers. A convenience sampling strategy influenced the selection of the organizers, necessitated by the pragmatic issue of accessibility. However, a purposeful strategy was employed to the extent that the sample was varied according to characteristics theoretically likely to affect the range of possible responses, including type of union (white, blue and pink collar), and gender and age of organizers. The 13 unions included those in manufacturing, metal work, labouring, mining, education, clerical, retail, professional, media, communication, childcare and hospitality.

National and state peak body senior officials were selected on the basis of their 'leadership' roles within the movement and their capacity to take an overarching view of recruitment at the broader state and national level. Such officials are central to union decision making in strategic, state and national, arenas and play a major part in determining the political strategy that the movement adopts to achieve its aims (Griffin and Moors 2004). Two youth workers attached to one state council's pilot youth recruitment program and the organizers were included in the sample because they have a primary role in recruiting new members.

The interviews were conducted over a 12 month period starting approximately 18 months after the November 2007 Australian federal election. This election was a significant one for the union movement in Australia, as the preceding two years had seen the introduction of the so-called 'Work Choices' legislation, which was then countered by the ACTU's 'Your Rights at Work' (YR@W) campaign. The campaign played a significant role in delivering government to the Australian Labor Party after 13 years in opposition (Muir and Peetz 2010). This campaign is viewed by most political commentators as highly successful in both affecting the election outcome and in lifting the profile of unions (Muir 2008). The campaign's success had a significant effect on the psyches of union officials, organizers and members, arguably heightening their awareness of the need to take union issues to the broader public (Muir 2008) and giving unions a taste of (political) success after more than a decade under a difficult legislative and political regime.

The interview questions explored the ways in which union officials attributed youth membership decline, and the youth-targeted strategies officials had organized, witnessed or were aware of. The focus in this chapter is on the first issue; the strategies unions used have been analysed elsewhere (Bailey et al. 2010).

Results and Discussion

Across the board, respondents acknowledged the general failure of the movement to respond to the youth recruitment crisis, but at times also spoke about tactics their unions used to recruit and organize youth. Interviewees emphasized a range of influences external to the union movement that were beyond its control. They were however less successful in articulating a broad vision or set of strategies for the movement as a whole with respect to responding to these external influences, particularly recruiting and organizing young workers.

Exogenous Reasons for Membership Decline

Of the exogenous factors cited to explain declining youth membership, reference was made most frequently to the individualistic nature of youth and their high levels of self belief and 'independence'. One organizer noted in particular the tendency for tertiary educated youth to have the view that unions are 'great' but that they believe 'I can do it for myself' (female organizer, 20–30s, white collar union). Respondents deplored what they saw as young people's self-interested attitudes as well as their apparent apathy and low interest in supposedly important issues. One organizer noted that many young people's response to being asked to join the union is, 'What's in it for me?' or 'What are you going to give me?', saying that when he advises them of the benefits and conditions of union membership, they reply that they already receive the same benefits without having to pay for membership (male organizer, 30–40s, blue collar union).

Respondents also consistently asserted that young people lacked knowledge of what unions were and how they functioned, and that they had limited understanding of the important gains that the union movement has made for the wages and conditions of working people more broadly. They argued that because young people were not involved when the 'fight' for conditions and wages occurred they do not appreciate that benefits such as superannuation, public holiday pay and long service leave were hard fought 'battles'. One organizer commented that it is 'because we are in good times' that youth think that 'the stuff, the conditions and the pay have always been there and always will be' (male lead organizer, 40–50s, blue collar union). Respondents also noted that, in contrast to earlier generations where young people were in contact with at least 'one family member who was a member of a union', 'union culture' was no longer passed on through families (male senior officer, 50–60s, state peak body). This historical-familial shift was considered crucial in youth's lack of awareness of the role and functions of trade unions.

A theme consistently raised by senior officers was that globalization had had an impact upon labour markets by altering the composition of the workforce and increasing the casualization of employment. The introduction of labour hire companies and group training organisations was linked to less secure working conditions, particularly for young apprentices, and this was viewed as a significant hindrance to the movement's ability to access and recruit young workers. One organizer in the manufacturing sector felt that 'the casualization of the workforce through labour hire and group training' caused 'a dip in union membership'. He added, 'It wasn't that the unions lost those people, it was just that they couldn't access those people' (male organizer, 30–40, blue collar union).

Similarly, many respondents discussed the propensity of young people to walk away from a workplace issue or problem rather than staying and 'fighting' to fix the problem. This purported tendency to resign and seek alternative employment, rather than persist in solving a workplace problem, was premised on the nature of the youth job market, which allowed young people to find alternative employment relatively easily. The propensity for youth to 'pack up shop and move jobs' was viewed as a disturbing trend that underscores the challenges that youth recruitment poses for organizers.

In addition to youth's alleged intrinsic characteristics, respondents also attributed youth union membership decline to fundamental changes to legislation and IR policy, which were viewed as contributing to a more 'hostile' environment for unions. A number of interviewees discussed the idea that the 'tradition of union membership' that existed in Australia via 'collective workplaces' had disappeared due to legislative changes that altered the 'closed shop' IR environment that had prevailed until the 1990s. Until this time 'union preference' and 'closed shop' provisions were included in many state and federal awards. These policies in effect artificially inflated membership because many people became union members by virtue of the fact that their employment occurred in a 'no union ticket – no job' industry. Once these provisions were removed from state and federal jurisdictions and it became illegal to discriminate against employees on the basis of their lack of union membership (Wooden 1998), union membership declined further, eroding the 'member for life' phenomenon (male executive member, 20s–30s, state peak body).

There was much emphasis on the effects of neoliberal IR legislation. One senior officer, for example, suggested that, during the decade of conservative rule in his state (prior to Work Choices at the national level), 'weapons, agreements and all the de-unionization laws' that were introduced contributed significantly to the demise of union membership (senior officer, 50–60s, state peak body). Respondents – many of whom are drawn to working within the field because of their commitment to the 'cause' – consistently referred to the effects of Work Choices in creating an 'anti-union' climate.

Senior officers' perspectives at times differed from those of organizers. For senior officers, it was 'big picture' changes to IR that affected young people's joining behaviour, such as labour market changes including the declining manufacturing base in Australia and the casual, transient nature of youth employment. These senior officers are involved in union matters at a policy level that affect all or most of the union movement and hence are more likely to be able to reflect on broader issues pertinent to youth recruitment. Conversely, most organizers are busy at the 'coalface' of their organization and are involved in the minutiae of day-to-day operations, including the recruitment and servicing of members. Further contextualizing these findings was that organizers usually had a shorter history in the movement than more senior officers and may only have worked in the movement for a few years; older officials while equally critical of Work Choices also referred to neoliberal changes under Australian Labor Party governments of the 1980s and early 1990s.

Some of the broad themes in the responses regarding exogenous reasons for youth membership decline are consistent with previous research. Officials are only too aware of shifts in the youth labour market and the growth of casual, 'student' jobs which have had a marked impact on youth membership (Peetz 1990, Sappey et al. 2006, Payne 1989). Respondents noted with concern the increase of the 'never-membership' phenomenon (Bryson et al. 2005) and were concerned about its longer-term implications. Officials were also very well aware of the unfavourable political and legislative environment that was a feature of Work Choices but also had continuities with the past, in that even the Australian Labor Party, in power from 1983 to 1996, and again from 2007, has adopted neoliberal policies (Lavelle 2010).

Reflecting on this data in the context of social identity theory and the extant research on young people's views of unions would suggest that union officials may be misconstruing the 'problem' of excessive individualism amongst young people. Indeed, the balance of research on young people and unions canvassed earlier indicates there is no need for unions to adopt extreme pessimism regarding young people's resistance to unions. While ignorance about the function and history of unions is widespread (and indeed was revealed by another component of this study which asked young people about their experience of work; McDonald et al. 2010), the balance of research suggests that young people have at least as favourable a view of the role of unions as older people. Organizers' attribution of high levels of 'individualism' to young people may propagate a self-defeating message to unions regarding young people's willingness to unionize. That is, assuming lack of knowledge about unions is one issue, but assuming that young people have individualistic beliefs and attitudes may be counterproductive, given the complexity of the development of young people's political and social attitudes. The emphasis on the evils of Work Choices is understandable, given the recent memory of the legislation and the vigour of the union campaign. However, union narratives that emphasize past history and difficult governments might serve to deflect attention to strategies that could be implemented from within the union movement. We turn to these themes in the following section.

Endogenous Reasons for Youth Membership Decline

Around half the respondents referred to factors contributing to youth membership decline that were potentially within the control of the union movement itself. Respondents offered optimistic responses about what the union movement could and should do to improve recruitment as well as retrospective, evaluative responses that focused upon the failures of unions to stem the flow of youth recruitment losses. These themes included union 'attitudes' towards youth, their lack of focus on the problem of recruitment itself, the need to connect with the values of youth, and issues of resourcing.

Typical of responses reflecting a need for an attitude shift was a response by a young organizer who viewed unions as being 'stuck in the past' and which had failed to adjust to a new environment. His view was that a problem existed because 'you have a lot of unions that operate like they are still in the 1960s' and that unions are 'stuck in the glory-day times'. He stated that the union movement needed to understand the impact of declining membership on their 'bottom line' and that they needed to 'wake up to themselves and the realities that youth recruitment is a cost point' (male youth organizer, 20–30s, state peak body).

Some respondents suggested the union movement lacked focus when it came to addressing the issue of youth recruitment and that it had demonstrated a lethargic response to the circumstances in which they have found themselves over the last 30 years. One senior officer noted that he was 'not sure if people see it as a crisis' (male senior officer, 50–60s, state peak body). Another interviewee indicated a sense of 'hopelessness' when he responded that 'no-one really knows what to do' (male executive member, 20–30s, state peak body). In another commentary on the issue a young organizer said that in order to overcome the youth recruitment problem 'unions need to utilize this opportunity to be a little self-reflective about the issue' (female youth organizer, 20–30s, state peak body).

In addition to the need for unions to be cognisant of the challenges of recruiting youth and to respond effectively to the needs of young workers, respondents frequently suggested that many leaders within the union movement leave the 'youth problem' to dedicated and passionate activists who are left unsupported. Their view was that the problem is individualized, and one that was approached as simply needing to be 'organized better', rather than directing resources appropriately or giving attention to specific policies. One organizer described her frustration thus:

> I applied to the [state's peak body] for funding to get a young [unionists'] movement started. We used to have one but it all fell apart because they didn't really have any young people and it wasn't anyone's priority. But it has to be driven by someone and you don't get any support. So it's not working well. (Female organizer, 20–30s, white collar union)

In contrast to these more pessimistic views for youth membership decline, a few respondents optimistically spoke of the 'natural' fit between youth values and those of unions. One respondent asserted that 'young people understand the core values of unions' and that those values of 'fairness and treating people well' are those that youth hold dear (male executive member, 20–30s, state peak body). They suggested this parallel afforded unions an opportunity to connect with young people's interests on social justice issues and to link this with recruitment strategies. Another organizer felt that many of the young people he spoke to were very 'receptive to the message' and that when he talked to youth they were often 'very keen to join' (male organizer, 20–30s, blue collar union). Of the respondents who did articulate this position most were young people themselves, suggesting they may have had a desire to attribute union values to their generation because of their own identification. However, one senior officer also asserted the need for unions to alter their message from one centred upon the successes of the past to one that is linked to current issues that resonate with contemporary youth. She stated:

> It's got to be more than join and listen to these old fogeys talk about the glory days or working conditions. It's got to be some organic link with the things that they care about. The broadly based social and economic issues that are important to them. Because the value fit is absolutely strong with young people. (Female senior officer, 50–60s, peak body)

Also reflecting a greater need to respond in youth-friendly ways, union officials often criticized the visual image that unions project on their websites and in written material, and the lack of technological sophistication in union strategy generally (Bailey et al. 2010: 53).

Some respondents noted that in order for unions to attract youth they needed to appoint young organizers to whom young potential recruits can relate. One young organizer suggested that using 'like-with-like' organizers – those with characteristics that are mirrored in their potential recruits – was an important recruitment strategy that should be adopted more frequently. She stated, 'You need someone who speaks their language and identifies and knows all the buttons to be pushed' (female organizer, 20–30s, white collar union). This reflects a central principle of organizing, that is, 'like-best-recruits-like' (Waddington and Kerr

2009: 28; Heery et al. 2000). This purported need to specifically target youth by appointing youthful organizers and via advertising was noted by one respondent who reflected upon her thoughts during the YR@W campaign:

> I thought, why isn't there a TV ad targeted at 14 and 15 year olds who are starting work? Why aren't we educating young people? I thought of that when we were doing the YR@W ads. We were putting all this money into this, but why [weren't] we educating [them]? (Female organizer, 30–40s, white collar union)

In the YR@W campaign, unions failed to make the connection between a highly successful political campaign and the need for recruitment, a fact which most interviewees acknowledged. Whilst the intent of the YR@W campaign was to highlight to a general public (largely) uninformed about IR issues (Muir 2008), the failure to use this vehicle to recruit youth was mentioned by a number of interviewees who believed the campaign should have developed an industrial dimension by promoting union membership, not merely a change in voting behaviour.

Many interviewees referred to the lack of resources to develop and implement recruitment strategies that are directed specifically to youth. One state peak body senior officer stated that he would 'like to appoint a youth coordinator if [he] had the resources' (male senior officer, 50–60s, state peak body). Another respondent suggested that the issue for most unions is a lack of adequate resources and that 'unions' first responsibility is to the people who are current members' (male senior officer, 50–60s, state peak body). This officer felt that this was particularly a problem for unions who are 'coordinating across a range of industries and hundreds of employers', and who are 'just keeping [their] heads above water to maintain services and EBs [enterprise bargaining agreements], [as that] sucks up most of [their] resources'. General organizing and servicing resources were also a problem, to ensure that unions were 'on the ground' when a young employee experiences a work-related problem such as underpayment of wages, unfair shifts or workplace bullying. As one official put it, a positive experience of union intervention has a powerful demonstration effect of the strength of the 'collective' and 'rusts them [young people] on' to the union movement (female organizer, 30–40s, professional union).

These views expressed by organizers are consistent with economic explanations for young people's low membership; that is, unions use a range of strategies to address the 'experience good' problem of unionism identified by scholars such as Bryson et al. (2005), Bryson and Gomez (2005) and Haynes et al. (2005). For example, retail unions in Australia, in which half the membership are under age 25, offer textbook vouchers and scholarships to partially offset the cost of membership. Professional unions – such as those covering teachers and occupations such as engineering and pharmacy – offer university students free or low-cost union membership in their last year of study with a limited suite of services focused on those of most value to students but relatively inexpensive for unions to provide (Bailey et al. 2010). However, such strategies are patchy across the movement, and unions' 'follow up' strategies once students have moved into full-time employment are variable. Hence, unions have further challenges in devising creative 'sampling' strategies for young people which do not over-encourage the 'free rider' phenomenon.

Applying the lens of mobilization theory to the data suggests that while unions are aware of their servicing role and address it as diligently as resources allow, they are less aware of their role in organizing and mobilizing young people. For instance, the story of the Young Unionists' Movement (YUM), which was discussed by a number of young unionists during the interviews, was one of discouragement and failure to get support or funding for initiatives such as Facebook and MySpace pages, networking amongst themselves, or young-worker specific projects. In some Australian states however, there have been more successful initiatives (see UnionsACT 2009), as there have been with the union Unite in New Zealand. Mobilization theory suggests that such initiatives should be supported, as they arise from the felt needs of an identity group which is best placed to develop its own injustice frames (Kelly 1998) that can be subsequently taken up by the wider movement.

Related to this point, unions could not point to particular labour movement successes or campaigns on issues of interest to young people. For instance, there have been no particularly visible campaigns to improve youth wages. Low wages are an entrenched feature of the Australian wage system (for instance, 15 year olds in many industries receive less than 50 per cent of an adult rate). Incrementally, unions attempt to push down the age at which the 'adult' wage is paid (which in some industries is 19, 20 or even 21), but this is done via enterprise bargaining which is largely invisible to the average young union member. While it is difficult to generate activism amongst a casual, part-time workforce, union movements in other countries (such as 'Unite' in New Zealand) are seeking to generate highly visible union 'success stories' which directly involve young workers, and support website activism such as that promoted by 'GetUp' which draws young people in. Supporting and resourcing groups such as YUM and pursuing and publicizing – in a systematic, strategic way – campaigns of particular salience for young people, would represent a process of 'frame extension' whereby a mature trade union movement redefines legitimate worker interests more inclusively (Snow et al. 1986). Hence there is space for unions to generate hopeful activism amongst young workers through a focus on relevant, youth-specific issues.

Conclusions

The need to maintain and indeed increase membership is fundamentally important to union viability and survival. Whilst recent Australian membership data shows a very slight increase (ABS 2010), density is at low levels not seen for over a century, indicating a need for a recruitment 're-think'. Past research into declining youth membership levels has generally adopted an 'autopsy' approach, analysing the factors that have contributed to the decline. But it is only by understanding insiders' perspectives, in this case union officials, and in particular their construction of the 'problem', that strategies can be developed that allow unions to exert agency to address the problem. Future research could focus on a broader cross-section of unions, seek data from young union activists who are not full-time officials, and take a comparative approach between countries to examine the strategies of those movements that are relatively more successful at recruiting and retaining young workers. Where policies and interesting strategies exist, they are unevenly distributed and not consistently pursued over time. The views of officials canvassed in this research makes it clear that unions urgently need to engage with youth in a new social, cultural and economic environment, and to avoid making pessimistic assumptions about the 'individualism' of young people which permits unions to 'opt out' of the problem. Unions need to act decisively in order to make the recruitment and retention of young workers a central plank of union renewal.

References

Allan, C., Bamber, G. and Oliver, D. 2006. Student experiences at work and attitudes to unionism: a study of retailing and fast food, in *21st Century Work: High Road or Low Road. Proceedings of the 20th Conference of the Association of Industrial Relations Academics of Australia and New Zealand*, edited by B. Pocock, C. Provis and E. Willis. Adelaide: University of South Australia, 29–38.

Allegretto, A. and Chase, T. 2005. *Inquiry into Workplace Relations Amendment 'Work Choices' Bill 2005*. Submission to Senate Employment, Workplace Relations and Education References Committee. Brisbane: Young Workers Advisory Service.

Allvin, M. and Sverke, M. 2000. Do new generations imply the end of solidarity? Swedish unionism in the era of individualization. *Economic and Industrial Democracy*, 21(1), 71–95.

Australian Bureau of Statistics (ABS). 2005. *Australian Social Trends 2005*, Catalogue No. 4120.0. Canberra: ABS.

Australian Bureau of Statistics (ABS). 2008. *Year Book*. Catalogue No. 1301.0. Canberra: ABS.

Australian Bureau of Statistics (ABS). 2010. *2009 Survey of Employee Earnings, Benefits and Trade Union Membership*. Catalogue No. 6310.0. Canberra: ABS.

Bailey, J. Townsend, K. and Luck, E. 2009. WorkChoices, ImageChoices and the marketing of new industrial relations legislation. *Work, Employment and Society*, 23(2), 285–304.

Bailey, J., Price, R., Esders, L. and McDonald, P. 2010. Daggy shirts, daggy slogans? Marketing unions to young people. *Journal of Industrial Relations*, 52(1), 43–60.

Barnes, A. 2006. Trade unionism in 2005. *Journal of Industrial Relations*, 48(3), 369–83.

Barton, R., Snell, D. and Fairbrother, P. 2008. The state of unions and union research in Australia, in *Workers, Corporations and Community: Facing Choices for a Sustainable Future. Proceedings of the 22nd Conference of the Association of Industrial Relations Academics of Australia and New Zealand*, no editors' details. Melbourne, 6–8 February 2008: n.p. Available at http://www.airaanz.org/ [accessed: 12 January 2011].

Bearfield, S. 2003. Australian employees' attitudes towards unions, ACIRRT Working Paper 82. Sydney: Australian Centre for Industrial Relations Research and Training.

Blanden, J. and Machin, S. 2003. Cross-generation correlations of union status for young people in Britain. *British Journal of Industrial Relations*, 41(3), 391–415.

Bray, M., Waring, P. and Cooper, R. 2009. *Employment Relations: Theory and Practice*. North Ryde, NSW: McGraw Hill.

Brosnan, P. and Loudoun, R. 2006. Labour market experiences of teenage Australian workers in the 21st century, in *21st Century Work: High Road or Low Road: Proceedings of the 20th Conference of the Association of Industrial Relations Academics of Australia and New Zealand*, edited by B. Pocock, C. Provis and E. Willis. Adelaide: University of South Australia, 93–102. Available at http://www.airaanz.org/ [accessed: 12 January 2011].

Bryson, A. and Gomez, R. 2005. Why have workers stopped joining unions? The rise of never membership. *British Journal of Industrial Relations*, 43(1), 67–92.

Bryson, A., Gomez, R., Gunderson, M. and Meltz, N. 2005. Youth-adult differences in the demand for unionization: Are American, British and Canadian workers all that different? *Journal of Labor Research*, 26(1), 155–67.

Budd, J. 2009. *When do workers first experience unionisation?: Implications for Voice and Representation in a New World of Work*. Paper to the 15th World Congress of the International Industrial Relations Association, Sydney, Australia, 24–27 August 2009.

Bulbeck, C. 2008. Only 'victim' workers need unions? Perceptions of trade unions amongst young Australians. *Labour & Industry*, 19(1/2), 49–64.

Campbell, I. 1996. Casual employment, labour regulation and Australian trade unions. *Journal of Industrial Relations*, 38(4), 571–99.

Canny, A. 2002. Flexible labor: The growth of student employment in the UK. *Journal of Education and Work*, 15(3), 277–301.

Crosby, M. 2006. *Power at Work: Rebuilding the Australian Union Movement*. Sydney: Federation Press.

Denniss, R. 2005. Young people's attitudes to workplace bargaining. *Journal of Australian Political Economy*, 56, 145–55.

Dyrenfurth, N. 2007. John Howard's hegemony of values: The politics of 'mateship' in the Howard decade. *Australian Journal of Political Science*, 42(2), 211–30.

Fiorito, J. 2004. Union renewal and the organizing model in the United Kingdom. *Labor Studies Journal*, 29(2), 21–53.

Frege, C. and Kelly, J. 2003. Union revitalization strategies in comparative perspective. *European Journal of Industrial Relations*, 9(1), 7–24.

Fulton, L. 2009. *Workplace Representation*. European Trade Union Institute (ETUI). Available at: http://www.worker-participation.eu/National-Industrial-Relations/Across-Europe/Workplace-Representation2 [accessed: 12 January 2011].

Griffin, G. and Moors, R. 2004. The fall and rise of organising in a blue-collar union. *Journal of Industrial Relations*, 46(1), 39–52.

Harbridge, R., Fraser, B. and Walsh, P. 2006. Industrial relations in Australia and New Zealand: The path from conciliation and arbitration, in *Global Industrial Relations*, edited by M. Morley, P. Gunnigle and D. Collins. London: Routledge, 124–45.

Haynes, P., Vowles, J. and Boxall, P. 2005. Explaining the younger-older union density gap: Evidence from New Zealand. *British Journal of Industrial Relations*, 43(1), 93–116.

Heery, E. 2003. Trade unions and industrial relations, in *Understanding Work and Employment*, edited by P. Ackers and A. Wilkinson, New York: Oxford University Press, 278–304.

Heery, E., Simms, M., Simpson, D., Delbridge, R. and Salmon, J. 2000. Organizing unionism comes to the UK. *Employee Relations*, 22(1), 38–57.

Hickey, R., Kuruvilla, S. and Lakhani. T. 2010. No panacea for success: Member activism, organizing and union renewal. *British Journal of Industrial Relations*, 48(1), 53–83.

Johnson, C. 2007. John Howard's 'values' and Australian identity. *Australian Journal of Political Science*, 42(2), 195–209.

Johnson, N. B. and Jarley, P. 2004. Justice and union participation: An extension of mobilization theory. *British Journal of Industrial Relations*, 42(3), 543–62.

Kelly, J. 1998. *Rethinking Industrial Relations: Mobilization, Collectivism and Long Waves*. London: Routledge.

Krosnick, J. and Alwin, D. 1989. Ageing and susceptibility to attitude change. *Journal of Personality and Social Psychology*, 57(3), 416–25.

Langer, B. 2005. Consuming anomie: Children and global commercial culture. *Childhood* 12(2), 259–271.

Lavelle, A. 2010. The ties that unwind? Social democratic parties and unions in Australia and Britain. *Labour History*, 98 (May), 55–75.

Lowe, G. and Rastin, S. 2000. Organizing the next generation: Influences on young workers' willingness to join unions in Canada. *British Journal of Industrial Relations*, 38(2), 203–22.

McDonald, P., Bailey, J., Oliver, D. and Pini, B. 2007. Compounding vulnerability? Young workers' employment concerns and the anticipated impact of the Work Choices Act. *Australian Bulletin of Labour*, 33(1), 60–88.

McDonald, P., Bailey, J., Pini, B. and Price, R. 2010. *Social Citizenship and Employment for Secondary School Students*. Report to Partner Organisations. Available at: http://eprints.qut.edu.au/32249/2/YOUTH_REPORT_TO_INDUSTRY_PARTNER_e_Print_version.pdf.

Mizen, P., Bolton A. and Pole C. 1999. School age workers: The paid employment of children in Britain. *Work, Employment and Society*, 13(3), 423–38.

Muir, K. 2008. *Worth Fighting For: Inside the 'Your Rights at Work' Campaign*. Sydney: University of New South Wales Press.

Muir, K. and Peetz, D. 2010. Not dead yet: The Australian union movement and the defeat of a government. *Social Movement Studies*, 9(2), 215–28.

Murray, G. and Peetz, D. 2010. Ideology down under and the shifting sands of individualism, in *Labour and Employment in a Globalising World: Autonomy, Collectives and Political Dilemmas*, edited by C. Azais. Brussels: PEI Peter Lang.

OECD 2006. *Education at a Glance 2006: OECD Indicators*, OECD Publishing. doi: 10.1787/eag-2006-en.

Payne, J. 1989. Trade union membership and activism among young people in Great Britain. *British Journal of Industrial Relations*, 27(1), 112–32.

Peetz, D. 1990. Declining union density. *Journal of Industrial Relations*, 32(2), 197–223.

Peetz, D. 1998. *Unions in a Contrary World: The Future of the Australian Trade Union Movement*. Melbourne: Cambridge University Press.

Peetz, D. 2002. Sympathy for the devil?: Australian unionism and public opinion. *Australian Journal of Political Science*, 37(1), 57–80.

Pocock, B. 1998. Institutional sclerosis: Prospects for trade union transformation. *Labour & Industry*, 9(1), 17–36.

Pyman, A., Teicher, J., Cooper, B. and Holland, P. 2009. Unmet demand for union membership in Australia. *Journal of Industrial Relations*, 51(1), 5–24.

Sappey, R., Burgess, J., Lyons, M. and Buultjens, J. 2006. *Industrial Relations in Australia: Work and Workplaces*. Frenchs Forest, NSW: Pearson.

Serrano, P. A. and Waddington, J. 2000. *Young People: The Labour Market and Trade Unions*. Report prepared for the Youth Committee of the European Trade Union Conference, May 2000, Brussels.

Smith, E. and Wilson, L. 2002. The new child labor? The part-time student workforce. *Australian Bulletin of Labor*, 28(2), 118–34.

Snow, D., Rochford, F., Wordern, S. and Benford, R. 1986. Frame alignment processes, micromobilization and movement participation. *American Sociological Review*, 51(4): 464–81.

Standing, G. 2002. *Beyond Paternalism: Basic Security as Equality*. New York: Verso.

Tilly, C. 1978. *From Mobilization to Revolution*. New York: McGraw-Hill.

UnionsACT. 2009. *National Young Unionists and Workers Conference, October 2009*. Available at: at http://unionsact.org.au. [accessed: 17 April 2011].

Visser, J. 2000. Why fewer workers join unions in Europe: A social custom explanation of membership trends. *British Journal of Industrial Relations*, 40(3), 403–30.

Waddington, J. and Kerr, A. 2002. Unions fit for young workers? *Industrial Relations Journal*, 33(4), 298–315.

Waddington, J. and Kerr, A. 2009. Transforming a trade union? An assessment of the introduction of an organising initiative. *British Journal of Industrial Relations*, 47(1), 27–54.

Wooden, M. 1998. The labour market for young Australians, in *Australia's Youth: Reality and Risk. A National Perspective on Developments that have Affected 15–10 Year Olds during the 1990s*, edited by Dusseldorp Skills Forum. Sydney: Dusseldorp Skills Forum, 31–50.

Index

For Product Safety Concerns and Information please contact our
EU representative GPSR@taylorandfrancis.com / Taylor & Francis
Verlag GmbH, Kaufingerstraße 24, 80331 München, Germany